THE TRAGEDY OF
POLITICAL THEORY

J. PETER EUBEN

✦✦✦✦✦✦✦✦✦✦✦✦✦✦✦✦✦✦✦✦✦✦✦✦✦✦✦✦✦

The Tragedy of Political Theory

✦✦✦✦✦✦✦

The Road Not Taken

PRINCETON UNIVERSITY PRESS
PRINCETON, NEW JERSEY

Library of Congress Cataloging-in-Publication Data
Euben, J. Peter.
The Tragedy of Political Theory / J. Peter Euben.
p.   cm.
ISBN 0-691-07831-9.—ISBN 0-691-02314-X (pbk.)
1. Greek drama (Tragedy)—History and criticism.
2. Political plays, Greek—History and criticism. 3. Greece—
Politics and government. 4. Politics and literature—Greece.
5. Political science—Greece. I. Title.
PA3136.E93   1990
882'.0109—dc20   89-27573

Publication of this book has been aided by the
Whitney Darrow Fund of Princeton University Press

This book has been composed in Linotron Sabon

Princeton University Press books are printed on
acid-free paper, and meet the guidelines for permanence
and durability of the Committee on Production Guidelines for
Book Longevity of the Council on Library Resources

Printed in the United States of America by
Princeton University Press,
Princeton, New Jersey

10 9 8 7 6 5 4 3 2 1
(Pbk.) 10 9 8 7 6 5 4 3 2 1

For Olga, Donna, and Roxanne

CONTENTS

Preface   ix

PART I – INTRODUCTION

Chapter 1 Conventions and Misgivings   3

Chapter 2 The Road Not Taken   32

PART II – GREEK TRAGEDY AND
POLITICAL THEORY

Chapter 3 Justice and the *Oresteia*   67

Chapter 4 Identity and the *Oedipus Tyrannos*   96

Chapter 5 Membership and "Dismembership" in the *Bacchae*   130

PART III – POLITICAL THEORY
AND TRAGEDY

Chapter 6 The Corcyrean Revolution: Corruption,
Dismemberment, and Political Theory in Thucydides'
History   167

Chapter 7 Plato's *Apology of Socrates*: Political Identity and
Political Philosophy   202

Chapter 8 Plato's *Republic*: The Justice of Tragedy   235

PART IV – CONCLUSION

Chapter 9 The Road Home: Pynchon's *The Crying of Lot 49*   281

Index   309

PREFACE

WHEN I was a sophomore at Swarthmore, I took "Greek Literature in Translation" with Martin Ostwald. I enjoyed the course immensely and was moved though also embarrassed by his occasionally beginning class with readings from the original Greek which none of us, of course, could understand. My interest showed, and perhaps because of it my visit to his office to discuss a paper topic turned into a discussion of my pursuing classics. I was no doubt flattered, probably polite, and certainly thought the idea mad. There was a world out there and I would be damned if I was going to waste my time on "books" written twenty-five hundred years ago in some language that sounded, well, Greek to me.

With the public debate over Great Books and the publications of I. F. Stone's *The Trial of Socrates*[1] and Allan Bloom's *The Closing of the American Mind*,[2] the world and the Greeks have come together. For whatever reason, issues central to our identity as a nation—the place of education in a democratic polity, the relationship between high and popular culture or elite learning and common experience, the question of moral relativism and the status of knowledge, the conflict between transcendence and "secular humanism"—are being debated in terms of Socrates' death and Plato's *Republic*. Because Stone and Bloom are largely responsible for this astonishing development it is worth looking at their representations of Socrates and Plato as a clue to why the latter have become significant characters in our cultural narrative.

Stone is contemptuous toward Socrates the philosopher. Because Socrates takes refuge in cloud cuckooland and stratospheric nonsense, he is impractical and so, at best, unaware of how his views helped establish an atmosphere favorable to right-wing demagogues. More likely he is aware of but unconcerned about how his antidemocratic arguments and disregard for democratic practices directly contributed to the oligarchic coup by his friend Critias. When Athens needed courageous public actions from its great moral teacher, it got politically suspect moral pieties and a preoccupation with perfecting the soul.

Stone's indictment is that of a political man with a contemporary political agenda, part of which is salvaging the reputation of Athenian democracy against contemporary critics of democracy who may find in the Athe-

---

[1] I. F. Stone, *The Trial of Socrates* (Boston: Little Brown, 1988).

[2] Allan Bloom, *The Closing of the American Mind* (New York: Simon and Schuster, 1987).

nians' condemnation of Socrates a justification for their own condemnation of democratic activism. He does not justify what Athens did, but rather thinks, as I do, that the city was being untrue to itself when it convicted Socrates. But Stone does want to explain the politics of the time to show just how provoked the Athenians were and how Socrates' actions and inactions were understood by his compatriots.

Surely Stone has a point. The claim that it is better to suffer injustice then commit it, a claim that Socrates says distinguishes him from almost all others,[3] may be an admirable guide for personal relations but seems suspect as a politics. Similarly, concentration on philosophical purity may lead to political evasions. Stone has also done us a real service by reminding us of the political stakes and context of the trial. (The responses his book has provoked also suggest the political stakes in the present debate over it.)[4] By taking Socrates out of the academy and putting him back into the streets, Stone has saved him from the academicians and, without intending it, revived the questions of where and by whom "philosophy" should be done, and why. But theses virtues, while considerable, cannot compensate for what is, in the end, Stone's dogmatic literal-mindedness. One cannot read the *Republic* or *Gorgias* as if it were the Pentagon Papers. If one does, one is likely to beg precisely the questions about practicality, politics, and democracy that Socrates was trying to raise and address. The irony of Stone's silencing Socrates is that his book began as a project in the study of free speech.

Far more astonishing than the relative success of Stone's book is the extraordinary popularity, or at least extraordinary sales, of Allan Bloom's. More astonishing still is the prospect that Plato's *Republic*, which is Bloom's Bible, and the contemplation of Socrates' death, which is our most urgent "task," will inspire the institute of public policy Bloom is establishing with William Bennett. The ironies here are wondrous: that Bloom shows how his book cannot be popular in a democratic society; that he warns philosophers to resist the blandishments of relevance, worldliness, fame, and political partisanship; that he insists that one cannot be political and philosophical since philosophers who try to change the world are inevitably changed by it; that he is helping to "realize" (his version of) the *Republic*, though he does not think Plato intended to do so.

Whatever one's ultimate judgment on the tone and argument of the book, or the uses to which it has been put by its defenders, Bloom too has performed an important service by turning Socrates against the political and intellectual fashions now prevalent in many elite universities. To the

[3] *Crito*, 49d.
[4] As Donald Kagan's review in *Commentary* 85 (March 1988): 72, makes clear.

degree that the book is aimed at an academic audience, it has accomplished what might be called a Socratic task: provoking people to think about their deepest commitments and unacknowledged choices, to be critical about their vocations and their professions. But if, as Saul Bellow assures us in the Foreword, Bloom "is not addressing himself primarily to professors,"[5] then the book becomes something quite different. Rather than making people think, it contributes to thoughtlessness; instead of enhancing the commitment to reason, it reinforces contempt for reason and fact; rather than exemplifying the theoretical life, it becomes part of a right-wing political agenda; instead of providing alternatives to what we have, it fits into a national mood made up of equal parts nostalgia and revenge. The nostalgia is for the 1950s, projected now as a simpler time when people had values, parents did not divorce and thus their offspring remained susceptible to the lure of great minds and works, universities benefited from benign neglect, and the best and brightest (or most privileged) were drawn to the theoretical life. The revenge is directed at what disturbed this tranquil scene—the 1960s with its loss of Vietnam and "Cornell." In *this* book Bloom is less Socrates than an intellectual Rambo, reversing defeat and avenging humiliation. Here he is less provoking than pronouncing.

In either reading Bloom begs the same questions Stone does but for the opposite reasons. At least that is so when he transforms Socrates' tensions and probing into oppositions certain and permanent enough upon which to build an educational if not political edifice.

Where Bloom insists, on Socrates' authority, that there can be no third way between philosophy and politics, I argue, also on Socrates' authority, that there might be, or that, at the very least, their absolute separation corrupts rather than insures the integrity of each. Where Bloom regards Socrates' death as conclusive proof for his argument about the philosophical life and the nature of the university, I see the circumstances of Socrates' death—his surprise at the closeness of the initial vote given his provocations and his surprising claim that if given more time he could have convinced the jury of his innocence—as complicating that proof and so the view of philosophy and education founded on it.[6]

In part my disagreement with Bloom hinges on my argument that political philosophy (as Socrates seems to understand it in the *Apology*, *Crito*, and *Republic*) emerges from a democratic political tradition significantly shaped by tragedy and that tragedy presented to a popular audience the need for distance from one's own, which Bloom regards as the

---

[5] *The American Mind*, p. 12.

[6] I do not offer my arguments as conclusive proofs of what "Socrates" is or says but to add dimension to what seems to me a one-dimensional view of "who" he is.

unique perspective, special insight, and singular function of "the" philosopher. Let me offer Aeschylus's *Persae* as an example.

The *Persae* celebrates the Athenian-led Hellenic victory over Persia at Salamis. A messenger to the Persian court repeats the mighty shout that reached their ears just prior to the battle.

> O Sons of Hellas, go now and
> Bring freedom to your native land,
> to your children and your wives,
> to the shrines of your ancestral gods,
> the tombs of your fathers: now the struggle is
> for all we have.
>
> (402–5)

The struggle is for "one's own." Yet the play takes place not in Athens (where it is being watched) but in the Persian capital of Susa. For the Athenians to see their victory through the eyes of a once powerful, still noble, but now defeated enemy meant that the theatrical occasion united loss and gain in a single moment, bringing to the victors in their exultation a wisdom borne of suffering and loss. This sense of common mortality mitigated the patriotism that the audience no doubt also felt. Such dual vision provided at least a momentary disengagement from (but also a further articulation of) the web of relations and narratives that constituted the Athenians as a people. One could call this extension of sensibility and sympathy a philosophical moment, or better, given the ties to place that continue to frame it, a politically philosophical moment. It is this moment, repeated each year in the dramatic festivals at Athens, that is rearticulated in Socratic political philosophy and present in the attempt by American universities both to honor our national traditions and to recognize the parochialism of what is honored. That the moment in the *Persae* accords honor to a non-Western people should remind us of what the nineteenth-century German rereading of Greek cultural authority tried so hard to make us forget—that the Greeks understood how much of value in their culture was derived from Afro-Asiatic sources.[7]

The idea that there is some third way is suggested not only by "Socrates" but by Aristotle as well. That is part of the reason he insists that, although contemplation may be the highest activity, we cannot *be* contemplative beings, and by his complementary effort to define practical wisdom as a way of mediating Plato's (supposedly) stark contrast between philosophy and politics. Michael Walzer echoes Aristotle and Socrates of the *Apology* when he writes that there is "no such realm of ab-

---

[7] See Martin Bernal's extraordinary *Black Athena: The Afroasiatic Roots of Classical Civilization*, vol. 1 (New Brunswick, N. J.: Rutgers University Press, 1987).

solute intellectuality, at least not one inhabited by human beings." We can pretend that the academy is such a place, but this pretense is unlikely to encourage political modesty. Philosophers "in touch with eternity are all too likely to seize the present moment" in their ignorance "that knowledge of truth is always incomplete and the passion for truth is always impure." Truth itself may be universal and immutable but every "practical embodiment of it in philosophical doctrine or poetic vision is partial and ideological, a parochial mix of insight and myopia."[8]

IN 1961 I went to graduate school at Berkeley as much by accident as by design, mostly to study China rather than political theory. Two things changed my mind; I wasn't very good at studying China (let alone Chinese), and I took two classes in political theory—one with John Schaar, the other with Sheldon Wolin. As I remember, I took Schaar's class because it was recommended and because it met early in the morning, which left me free to be with my daughter in the afternoon while my wife did whatever invertebrate embryologists did in the bowels of the Life Sciences Building. Schaar's extolling of Puritan virtues (which to my relief he does not follow) seemed as wacky as Ostwald's reading of Greek. Given such oddness I was tempted to leave the academy for the real world, except that, as a budding theorist, I wasn't sure where it was. But I stayed and Schaar joined me at Santa Cruz. He is still defending the Puritans and I still think he is a bid odd. But he is also a treasured colleague who has reminded me of my insufficiencies in moments of self-congratulation and of what matters about our work in times of confusion. The richness of his mind is matched by the generosity of his friendship. Not the least pleasure of his friendship are the friends of his who have become mine, particularly Hanna Pitkin. I know no one who combines, as she does, such an elegant mind, wide learning, common sense, and an endless capacity for punning.

I took Sheldon Wolin's lecture course because it was required. But to my amazement (and no doubt to his) I did well in it and, more important, greatly enjoyed it, perhaps seduced by his lecture on "The Judicious Hooker." He was then, and remains now, an unexcelled teacher, able to help students do what they choose to do while leading them to recognize the implications of their choices. An he has, in his life and writings, articulated the tensions present in "political theory," demonstrating what it means to be intellectually serious and politically engaged. That our interests, style, and conclusions are somewhat different is a testament to his teaching and friendship. If there is a "Berkeley School" of political theory,

[8] Michael Walzer, *The Company of Critics: Social Criticism and Political Commitment in the Twentieth Century* (New York: Basic Books, 1988), pp. 40–41.

it comes less from doctrine than from the sense of vocation he helped define and continues to exemplify.

Such a conception comes too from the events at Berkeley in the mid-1960s. For Bloom the sixties means Cornell, blacks with guns, administrative capitulation and faculty cowardice, the destruction of the university, and the triumph of democratic excess. I do not doubt that some equated democracy with "doing your own thing," that others convinced themselves that democratic processes insured democratic outcomes, and that still others (myself included) gave way too easily to student pressures when they ought to have been independent if sympathetic critics. Bloom is right to complain about self-righteousness and the susceptibility to apocalyptic solutions.

But Cornell was not the sixties[9] (and even there I can imagine a different principled response to events than the one Bloom embraces). For some of us at Berkeley, the community of scholars was being debased not by students but by an administration that defined the university as "a mechanism held together by administrative rules and powered by money"[10] and faculty members who created an increasingly fragmented and specialized curriculum and who were more preoccupied with methodological purity, research strategies, and career trajectories than with teaching.[11] As we saw it, the university was already politicized, some of its faculty compromised by often unacknowledged ties to government and industry, its services offered to certain of the state's constituencies at the expense of others. Finally, where Bloom sees the sixties as an era of democratic excess in a society uncritically and thoroughly democratic, we saw "pluralists" or "democratic revisionists" as antidemocrats who had coopted democratic rhetoric and underminded democratic aspirations.

For Bloom, Bennett, and Bellow (called "The Killer Bees" by some Stanford faculty),[12] the sixties meant know-nothingness, philistinism, and the abandonment of "Great Books." But for some of us at Berkeley, it led to those books as a way of understanding events around us. If nothing else, Plato and Aristotle, Hobbes, and Rousseau, Arendt and Oakeshott

[9] Bloom "confesses" (*The American Mind*, p. 338) that he was "momentarily and partially" sympathetic to the initial protests at Berkeley.

[10] Clark Kerr, *The Uses of the University* (Cambridge, Mass.: Harvard University Press, 1972), p. 20.

[11] Ibid., p. 43: "A professor's life has become, it is said, 'a rat race of business and activity, managing contract and projects, guiding teams and assistants, bossing crews of technicians, making numerous trips, sitting on committees for government agencies, and engaging in other distractions necessary to keep the whole frenetic business from collapse' " (Kerr is quoting Merle A. Tuve).

[12] For a general discussion of the Great Books controversy at Stanford, see Mary Louise Pratt, "Humanities for the Future: Reflections on the Western Culture Debate at Stanford" (Unpublished manuscript, Stanford, September 1988).

taught us the danger of theory losing its critical distance or seeking too much distance. And for several of us these texts offered a vantage point outside the confluence of liberalism and Marxism that seemed to define modernity.

ALTHOUGH I began reading classical political theory at Berkeley I did not study it seriously until I got to Santa Cruz where Wolin as well as Schaar joined me. Over a drink at the Red Room in the Santa Cruz Hotel (surely the only institution in the world with three chairs of political theory), it was decided by a two to one vote (me dissenting) that I teach classical political theory since I knew too little of it. (Think what that principle generalized would mean for academic life.) As I did, I began a "return to the Greeks," unknowingly emulating countless others.

Santa Cruz made this return possible. Without generous monetary support from the Faculty Research Committee (and a fellowship from the National Endowment for the Humanities), this book would not exist. Without Santa Cruz's educational philosophy encouraging interdisciplinary study I would not have had valued colleagues in classics and the history of consciousness as well as in politics. Gary Miles, Mary Kay Gamel, and Laura Slatkin resisted pulling the plug on their phones when pestered about Greek historiography, performance conditions of tragedy, declining aorists, or Achilles. For years Laura has been an astute and sympathetic critic of my work. She has also introduced me to people and literatures invaluable to a novice in classical studies. It was because of her that I could impose on Helene Foley and met Arlene Saxonhouse. Although Arlene and I sometimes disagree in our interpretations of texts (such as the *Republic*), we have found ourselves working on the same themes, concentrating on the same passages, and unexpectedly coming to parallel conclusions, all of which can only be explained by our both having attended Forest Hills High School in New York City.

Without my "histcon" colleagues and graduate students I would be narrower and more ignorant than I already am. They have done their best to contain my polis envy and Hellenic romanticism and have shown me how a literary canon becomes a form of power in which nonwhite male or female authors appear as special interests to be measured against "The Great Books of Western Culture." They have also reminded me of what it means for a multicultural society to have a Eurocentric paradigm of culture (and a truncated view of Europe and culture at that), and the dangers of monumentalizing texts and authors. I have not always understood the full force of their criticism, or agreed with them when I did. But without them there would be no self-critical voice within this work.

No one has taught me more about these matters than Ann and Warren Lane. For twenty years they have been patient and loving friends, responding to my whining with the gentle ridicule it deserves and holding my reactionary impulses in check. It is at their urging (badgering is a better word) that I have read more widely than I wished, and tried to resist the insularity that accompanies academic security.

My undergraduate students at Santa Cruz have taught me as much as I have taught them, though I have no intention of sharing my salary with them. They have been both skeptical and appreciative, insisting that I justify what and how I teach yet willing to parenthesize their suspicion of initially alien ideas and texts. They have trusted me with their thoughts and concerns and usually put up with my provocations, teasing, and snide references to hottubs, peacock feathers, tofu, sprouts, and Californese. I have taught better-educated students (some of whom have read Plato twice in elite private schools), but Santa Cruz students have, at their best, a unique wonder and excitement over texts that challenge them to move outside themselves and see their world afresh. They are quite special.

Anyone publishing a book on texts that have engaged some of the greatest intellects in history is demonstrating inordinate hubris. If I have anything provocative or insightful to say about these texts, it comes as much from what I learned casually and unexpectedly outside the classroom and books as from inside them. It is Aeschylus after all who suggests that we only learn from experience that touches the heart. So I have learned about heroism from my sister Julie's calmness in the face of death from cancer at forty-three when she had so much and so many to live for; about otherness and marginality from the lives of my gay friends; and why women need to "Take Back the Night" from the look of absolute fear on the face of my friend, Kitty, who did not hear me say her name or immediately recognize me when I stopped to offer her a ride home one night.

Most of all I have been a student (not always a good one) of my wife and daughters. They have taught me to listen when I only wanted to speak, to see the world from another's point of view when I was complacent about my own, and to understand that in the family as in the polity a shared life must respect the distinctiveness of its members. For these and many other reasons this book is dedicated to them.

Of course they are not responsible for any errors of commission or ommission. My four-year-old nephew, Benjamin, has taken on that task in exchange for a dinner of shrimp fried rice.

I WOULD like to thank the *American Political Science Review* for permission to reprint a revised version of "Justice and the Oresteia." Chris Rocco deserves thanks, not only for the index, but for the care he took for the manuscript as a whole and the ideas in it.

PART I
INTRODUCTION

We are all prisoners of a rigid conception of what is important and what is not. We anxiously follow what we suppose to be important while what we suppose to be unimportant wages guerrilla warfare behind our backs, transforming the world without our knowledge and eventually mounting a surprise attack on us.

—Milan Kundera

ONE

Conventions and Misgivings

IN ITS CHOICE and treatment of texts and in its respect for Athenian democracy, this book is somewhat conventional. Usually such conventionality coincides with an indifference to the distinctiveness of the modern (or postmodern) self and discourse, to recent developments in literary theory, and to the undemocratic aspects of Athenian society. For those concerned with such issues, the continued privileging of classical texts, the disregard of the vast transformations of social scale during the last three hundred years, and the silence about the subordinate status of women, slavery, and class warfare in "democratic" Athens virtually guarantees that the privileged texts will be misunderstood or misappropriated and that a vision of political community and political theory will be perpetuated that has more to do with fantasy than reality. If we are to live in this world rather than some other, we need ideals, methods, theories, and practices appropriate to it rather than some world that is certainly passed and probably never was.

Skepticism about the contemporary significance of classical texts does not necessarily deny the relevance of classical political theory to the polis or other post-classical but premodern political societies. Nor does it necessarily deny the democratic polis's moral superiority relative to other less democratic contemporary regimes or denigrate the beauty of Greek poetry, the originality of Greek philosophy, and the pleasure of reading Plato and Aristotle. But such skepticism does insist that the admirable features of the polis were distinctive to it as a historical form and rejects the idea that Greek poetry, philosophy, or political theory is adequate (or even relevant) for understanding, let alone living in, the modern nation-state. Although it may be true that no man or woman who is ignorant of classical texts can call themselves educated, it is certainly true that if those texts form the core of that education, such men and women will be illiterate.

This plausible view is held by most social scientists and some political theorists for whom "the" world begins with Locke or Marx. But there are other theorists who share *some* of these views because they want to redress (or undress) the romanticized celebration of Athens and the uncritical veneration of Plato and Aristotle. For them social history is a way of debunking the myth of Athenian participatory democracy and of putting the two great classical theorists "in their place" (in both senses of that phrase).[1]

While the study of classical texts may be losing its place among social scientists and political theorists, it retains its hold among literary theorists and philosophers, whether structuralist, hermeneutical, or poststructuralist. Some of the most "radical" literary theorists remain deeply engaged with "texts" such as the *Phaedrus*, *Symposium*, and *Poetics* if only by way of critique and with the sophists by way of alliance. For such thinkers this book is conventional not in its choice of "authors" but in its treatment of them. They would, no doubt, find my selective reliance on Vernant, Vidal-Naquet, Goldhill, Segal, and Zeitlin, as well as my analysis of Foucault and occasional references to Derrida, as domesticating radical interpretative strategies for conventional ends.[2]

In this first chapter I want to look at these criticisms with the help of an essay by Stephen Holmes that appeared in the *American Political Science Review* in 1979, a more recent book by Michael Ignatieff entitled *The Needs of Strangers*, and a selective survey of the work of Michel Foucault. I choose Holmes and Ignatieff because—despite their different sensibilities, subjects, and intended audiences—they both regard continued deference to the classical polis (especially its participatory ideals) and to classical political theory as anachronistic[3] and nostalgic. For them my choice of texts simply perpetuates myths that must be overthrown. I choose Foucault because his critique of humanism challenges not so much my choice of texts as the themes I address and the way I address them.

I choose him for two less obvious reasons. One has to do with certain affinities between Foucault and Greek tragedy, affinities that provide a contemporary introduction to my argument about tragedy and theory. The principal object of this book is to consider Greek tragedy insofar as it provides a preface for understanding classical political theory and to suggest that the tragedians and these theorists provide in turn a ground for contemporary theorizing. Once more Foucault is useful. I do not think contemporary political theory can ignore Foucault's critique of theorizing, most dramatically symbolized by the transformation of *theōria, thea-*

---

[1] It also means criticizing contemporary theorists who do not.

[2] Paul Bové objects to critiques of Foucault such as those by Charles Taylor, Michael Walzer, and Nancy Fraser because they treat Foucault's writing as if it "were merely a failed attempt at transparently presenting positions; something merely unfortunately obscure" (in his foreword, "The Foucault Phenomenon: The Problematics of Style," to *Foucault*, by Gilles Deleuze, trans. and ed. Sean Hand, [Minneapolis: University of Minnesota Press, 1988]). Bové is right to warn against writing Foucault into discourses he was criticizing. But there is a danger in insisting that Foucault can be criticized only by those who share his fundamental assumptions about modernity, politics, method, and theory.

[3] I have dealt with the charge of anachronism in my introduction to *Greek Tragedy and Political Theory* (Berkeley and Los Angeles: University of California Press, 1986), pp. 4–6.

tron and its cognates (seeing, beholding, gazing, viewing, spectating, and sight) into "le régard" (the gaze), a technique of power-knowledge whereby administrative elites manage their institutional populations. Despite this transformation, aspects of Foucault's critique of theorizing are anticipated in Greek tragedy and in the classical theorists he criticizes. Where they are not, Foucault may be right in his criticisms or the disparity may indicate why and how "we" need to move beyond as well as with genealogy.

My aim in this chapter is mostly preparatory. I want to situate my argument and approach within a contemporary debate in order to defuse (but not refute) the disparagement of classical politics and theory, thereby creating a space for the themes presented in chapter 2 and elaborated in chapters 3 through 9. At the very least, I want to indicate that my "traditionalism" is chosen rather than inadvertent and to ask whether the antitraditional emphasis on "decentered" play and genealogy are sufficient for the living of a political life. I am not sure critics are attentive enough to the practical implications of what it means for "us" to believe that we are the creators of our own purposes, values, and natures, and whether they are as appreciative of the mythopoetic Nietzsche as the deconstructive Nietzsche.

The whole issue of conventionality and tradition, of academic insiders and outsiders, becomes complicated when a thinker like Foucault becomes an academic industry and a "sign" of being at the forefront and on the cutting edge. Determining what is and is not the cutting edge, radical, new, anti-traditional, and nonconventional becomes itself radically uncertain if Tocqueville is right that it is an American tradition to be anti-traditional.[4] If he *is* right, then being radical in the sense of embracing what is new and antitraditional may be as American as apple pie. This paradox is, of course, too neat and too self-serving: the academy is notoriously persistent in assuming that the world divides itself into academic disciplines and is largely unrepentant in its deference to canonical texts. But the paradox does at least confuse any easy opposition between conventional and whatever it is conventions are opposed to.

STEPHEN HOLMES is perturbed by, even contemptuous of, the persistent influence of principles derived from classical political theory on con-

---

[4] See *Democracy in America*, vol. 2, pt. 2, chap. 1. The uniform method Americans unknowingly accept dictates that they "escape from imposed systems . . . accept existing facts as no more than a useful sketch [and] seek by themselves and in themselves for the only reason for things." Given such a culture it is not clear what Foucault becomes in America with its very different legal tradition, with a shorter history of and less accommodating stance toward state bureaucratization, with a less dominating educational hierarchy, and without either an established religion or a Marxist tradition of critique.

temporary political theorists. Despite the massive transformations in the underlying structure of European society, most notably the presence of social differentiation and the distinction between state and society, many of us—whether conservative, neo-Marxist, or liberal—remain in thrall to an image of the polis and to classical thinkers who are peripheral at best and positively pernicious when taken seriously as political or theoretical exemplars. "The principles of Greek politics become flagrant and despotic archaisms when transported, even with the best of intentions, into the institutional context of modern society." Given this, we need to demythologize the old *res publica* conception of politics lest it serve, as Constant warned, to overlegitimate a technically efficient bureaucratic agency with police power and to consecrate the tyranny of the political.

The two premises of Greek political thinking that draw Holmes's ire are the supposition that "the state can be 'humanized' as a dialogue, family or emotional communion with a 'true' and therefore unifying purpose" and the proposition that "individuals, being thoroughly 'political animals,' can fully realize themselves in political participation." More specifically, he wants to debunk Aristotle's "notorious" claims that the polis is prior to the individual, that human beings are born for citizenship in a city-state, that ethics and politics coincide, and that "political science" studies everything of human value. Whatever plausibility these ideas may have had in and for the polis, they necessarily lead to "personal and governmental deformations when revived in highly differentiated and rapidly changing modern societies." Thus it is "irrational and patently absurd" to claim that politics now can "solve all our problems and make us feel free and in touch with ourselves." It is pointless to juxtapose an ancient regime and a modern one and "solemnly ask which is better." Because ancient regimes and modern systems of government present solutions to very different problems, such evaluative comparisons are, to say the least, "notably unilluminating."[5]

Holmes's object then is to break the spell and the influence of classical politics and political theory, to redirect our gaze and our reading from Athens and Sparta, Plato and Aristotle, Strauss and Arendt to contemporary modern societies and to Weber, Durkheim, and Simmel. His effort to change who we read and why we read them is political as well as theoretical, his means rhetorical as well as rational.

One of the striking aspects of the essay is its self-conscious escalation of language and the heightened drama such an escalation creates. To take the "obsolete," "out of step," "worn out," "notorious" premises and

[5] Stephen Taylor Holmes, "Aristippus in and out of Athens," *American Political Science Review* 73 (March 1979): 113–28. See also the "Comment" by James H. Nichols, Jr., and Holmes's "Reply" in the same issue, pp. 129–33 and 134–38 respectively. The quotations are from pp. 113, 114, and 120.

principles of Greek political thinking seriously is "irrational," "patently absurd," "ludicrous," "bizarre," "wildly implausible," "flagrantly archaic," and totalitarian. Like Locke, Holmes would turn the paternal king into a lion-wolf, devouring the young it supposedly nourishes. He would force us out of our reverence and reveries to confront the problems of modernity rather than allowing us to turn away from them on the authority of writers and images drawn from a premodern culture.

Much could be said about Holmes's general argument and the view of politics and theory advocated, presupposed, or implied by it. One might take issue with the literal reading of texts,[6] with the ungenerous reading of Arendt,[7] with his exaggeration of claims then dismissed as absurd,[8] or his confident assertions (usually prefaced by "in fact") such as that the private public distinction is "too crude to help us understand ourselves."[9] One might wonder about what Holmes thinks of Tocqueville's belief that taking politics away from Americans would be taking away half their lives and about his admittedly selective reading of Weber and Durkheim. In their work (as in Marx's), one can find arguments and sensibilities that undercut the moral force of arguments Holmes makes on their behalf and with their authority. For instance, Weber's discussion of rationalization and bureaucracy suggests (as do some of Marx's writings on capitalism's destruction of all previous forms of community) a fundamental homogenization of society that is both a product and foundation for the social differentiation Holmes thinks definitive of modernity. It may be that differentiation vitiates differences and that, "absurd" as it sounds, Athens may have been a more diverse society than the modern capitalist state. And if "modernity" is hegemonic (which arguments like Holmes's may help bring about), then it may not be absurd or reductivist to regard it as a whole prior to (or at least importantly determinative of) the parts. Certainly there are anthropologists, philosophers, and literary theorists who believe that "culture" precedes individual life and action, that it constitutes the terms in which we make ourselves and conceive the world, such

[6] For instance, with the idea that Plato favored a closed, collectivist, regimented state.

[7] Arendt herself has insisted that one cannot use the past to argue for or against the present and was suspicious of Greek political philosophy which she regarded as perverting prephilosophical political life. For a defense of Strauss, see Nichols's response to Holmes.

[8] Such as that the Greeks believed that politics could solve all of humanity's fundamental problems. That is not my reading of, e.g., the great choral ode to man in the *Antigone*, or of the *Republic* or the *Politics*.

[9] One could say a number of things about this: (1) that the tragedians and even Aristotle agreed; (2) that it depends on what about ourselves we want to understand; (3) that much interesting work by feminists revolves around this distinction even if, in the end, they want to dissolve its hierarchizing implications; and (4) that, as Habermas has suggested, the modern welfare state has rendered the distinction between state and society obsolete.

that the political self is a cultural construct, subject to discursive practices.[10]

Nor is it absurd to wonder whether we can thrive or should adapt to
the (presumed self-evident) "realities" of modernity if we look at what
seems to be its cost—a cost that a reading of Weber, Durkheim, and Simmel informed by a reading of Plato and Aristotle, as well as Strauss and
Arendt—can help disclose. It is at least worth asking whether the modern
state does not sustain what modernization was thought to transcend: religious cults, drug abuse, alcoholism, child abuse, wife beating, teenage
suicide, and communicative mush. Thomas Pynchon captures these costs
brilliantly in his image of wrecked cars and wrecked lives, the endless
trade-ins of "motorized metal extensions of themselves, of their families
and what their whole lives must be like . . . frame cockeyed, rusty underneath, fender repainted in a shade just off enough to depress the value . . .
inside smelling helplessly of children, supermarket booze, two sometimes
three generations of smokers, or only of dust—and when the cars were
swept out you had to look at the actual residue of these lives, and there
was no way of telling what things had been truly refused . . . and what
had simply (perhaps tragically) been lost. . . ." In this parade of bloodless
killing, "each owner, each shadow filed in only to exchange a dented,
malfunctioning version of himself for another, just a futureless automotive projection of somebody else's life."[11]

We might also want to complicate the opposition between liberty and
community fundamental to Holmes's view that the attempt to revive ancient liberty in a modern context "inevitably" produces the triumph of
totalitarianism and the obliteration of liberty. In what sense and to what
degree is the very idea of an "individual" and private liberty an "ideological" construct propagated at times and in part for self-consciously pursued, if incompletely realized, political ends? One thinks here of Karl Polanyi's discussion of the "free market"[12] or J. S. Mills' justification of
despotism (in *On Liberty*) to create the conditions for liberty and liberals.
What are we to make of the argument, expressed in different terms by

[10] This can easily be exaggerated. Holmes has a point in insisting on the "vast differences
between the ways in which a constitutionalist pluralist regime and a totalitarian regime
characterize or influence their respective societies." He goes on to argue that individual
liberty depends upon "the *successful functioning* of society, on the capacity of various nonpolitical institutions to create those possibilities of 'communication chances' which are the
preconditions for freedom or meaningful choice" (Holmes, "Reply," p. 135). This begs the
question of how liberal society creates liberals (i.e., those who are mature, rational, indus-
trious, etc.).

[11] *The Crying of Lot 49* (New York: Bantam Books, 1967), pp. 4–5.

[12] See his "Our Obsolete Market Mentality," in *Primitive Archaic and Modern Econo-
mies: Essays of Karl Polanyi*, ed. George Dalton (Garden City, N.Y.: Doubleday, 1968), pp.
59–77, and his *The Great Transformation* (Boston: Beacon Press, 1957).

Rousseau, Tocqueville, and Arendt, that individualism fostered by modernity does not make us free individuals but "social men," like Eichmann; that there are forms of community and membership that enhance liberty and others that do not. All suggest that men and women preoccupied with private liberty and interest lose both.

Even if Holmes is right to characterize totalitarianism as "an attempt at the coercive politicization of diverse arteries of social interaction" such as unions, the press, and the police, it is "wildly implausible" (to use Holmesian language) to suppose that Aristotle—with his emphasis on plurality of political contributions, his warning about too much precision in the study of politics and about an overemphasis on order in the living of it, his emphasis on *praxis* (against *poiēsis*) and *phronēsis* (against *technē* and *sophia*), and his insistence that while the polis is the highest association, contemplation is the highest activity—could justify totalitarianism any more than Constant justifies anarchy.[13]

Except perhaps if one equates the state, government, and politics as Holmes does, on the first page of his essay. Then the moral primacy Aristotle claims for politics would accrue to the state even though Aristotle's very conception of political activity can be taken as denying that the state is a political entity at all.[14] Aristotle's silence about empire, his failure to consider it as a possible regime (as he does tyranny), is sometimes taken as a sign of his lack of perceptiveness and of the bankruptcy of political theory tied to the polis. But it may be that his silence is due to the fact that he did not regard empire as a *political* regime at all. If politics is a moral activity in which men (we would add women) realize what is distinctively human about them, and if such activity requires the direct participation of citizens in the administration of justice, then the institutional structures of totalitarian regimes are antipolitical. If the polis is the highest, most comprehensive and self-sufficient "association" (to use Barker's tepid translation of *koinōnian*) such that political activity is intrinsically rather than instrumentally valuable, then people become politically and morally educated only by living a public life. It follows that representation makes no sense. When politics is a partnership in virtue, how could I designate someone to be virtuous for me? No one can act in my name for me, not because he or she will misrepresent my interests, but because such designation is a resignation of my "humanity." Unlike alliances, aggregations, commercial collaborations, or contractual agreements that guarantee rights or stipulate principles of mutual forbearance, political activity changes the character of the people engaged in it. "If," as Aris-

---

[13] To show how Aristotle can lead to totalitarianism by finding a fascist author able to excerpt passages for propaganda purposes is an extremely shaky enterprise given Holmes's sense that Nichols misunderstands *him*.

[14] That claim has its problems but sustaining the totalitarian state is not one of them.

totle writes in the *Politics* "the spirit of their participation and the nature of their interaction are the same after they have come together as they were before they left their separate spheres, their community would not be a polis" (1280a22–b32).

Moreover, it can be argued on Aristotelian (and Arendtian) grounds that a claim for the moral primacy of politics is not like claiming superiority for some other activity because it is in the political realm that what counts as morally superior is subject to public debate and scrutiny. "To say we are political animals," Hanna Pitkin writes in the spirit of Arendt but only after some sharp criticism of her, "is to say we have the power to take charge of the forces which shape and limit us and that our full development as human beings depends on our exercising this power. Only citizenship enables us jointly to take charge of and take responsibility for the social forces that otherwise dominate our lives and limit our opinions, even though we produce them."[15]

Penultimately, even if such arguments are unpersuasive, do we not need to ask why some people "choose" to be political and others do not? What would I have to know or have experienced to accept a decision not to be political as being an informed and free decision, especially if political participation is itself a primary form of political education? Is there a sense in which renouncing political participation is like selling yourself into slavery?

Finally, we need to explain why it is that the thinkers Holmes would displace retain such a hold in such seemingly altered circumstances and among such otherwise self-conscious critical beings. No doubt the sheer weight of academic tradition and having the status of a "classic" helps. But could it be that, by pushing us to think of a distinctively human scale as a precondition for politics, writers like Aristotle and Arendt enable us to understand part of the contemporary world Holmes's authors do not; that they help us recognize possibilities present within modernity below or outside the technical rationality that marks the administrative state?[16] It seems to me that Aristotle and Arendt help explain and have even helped inspire the new politics of protests,[17] a politics that both argues

[15] Hanna Fenichel Pitkin, "Justice: On Relating Private and Public," *Political Theory* 19, no. 3 (August 1981): 327–52.

[16] "Today, however, the resurgence of regionalism, the claims (and the need) for decentralization at all levels, the renewed strength of religious movements, the emergence of separatist nationalism, the emphasis on localism, all bear witness in their diversity and vigor to the surviving or resurrected heterogeneity of cultural codes underneath the universalistic rationalism of the dominant culture" (Megali Sarfatti Larson, "The Production of Expertise and the Constitution of Expert Power," in *The Authority of Experts*, ed. Thomas L. Haskell [Bloomington: University of Indiana Press, 1984], p. 47). I do not mean to suggest that I find this general efflorescence unproblematic.

[17] For the significance of Aristotle and Arendt for contemporary thinkers and actors, see

for and demonstrates principles of self-governance and offers a new praxis based on opposition cultures and spheres organized around the demands of autonomous social movements that take the elimination of domination as their starting point.[18] I am thinking of those groups and writers who emphasize the decentralization of the state and economy, who are concerned with environmental and feminist issues, the right to unalienated labor, ethical pluralism, and human rights in opposition to the usual focus on the distribution of material goods by the welfare state. Many of these writers have emerged from direct action groups—nuclear protesters, neighborhood associations, women's health collectives, the sanctuary movement, or have sought to understand the significance of such groups, as with Jonathan Schell's discussion of Polish Solidarity in his introduction to Adam Michnik's prison writings. That introduction could not have been written without Arendt, which suggests that though Weber's definition of the modern state may be more "realistic" than Arendt's romantic image of the polis, the state is not the same as politics and her discussion of the latter may be as essential as his of the former.[19]

While Stephen Holmes has written an article for the central journal in the profession, Michael Ignatieff has written a personal book whose literary power makes it professionally marginal. Holmes relies on social scientists like Weber, Durkheim, and Simmel to make Constant's argument against ancient political theory, and modern theorists like Arendt and Strauss; Ignatieff's "authors" include Shakespeare and Augustine, Bosch and Hume, Adam Smith and Rousseau.[20] Whereas Holmes is intent on protecting liberty against the potentially totalitarian claims of political solidarity, membership, and citizenship, Ignatieff wants to reinstate those sentiments and resuscitate that language while being attentive to those modern developments that have made older incarnations irrelevant. For Aristippus, as Holmes sympathetically summarizes and quotes him, polit-

---

Jose Miguez Bonino, *Toward a Christian Political Ethics* (Philadelphia: Fortress Press, 1983), pp. 9–19; Martha A. Ackelsberg, "Women's Collaborative Activities and City Life: Politics and Policy" in ed. J. A. Flammang, *Political Women* (Beverly Hills, Calif.: Sage Publications, 1984), pp. 242–90, and her " 'Sisters' or 'Comrades'? The Politics of Friends and Families," in *Families, Politics and Public Policy*, ed. Irene Diamond (New York: Longmans, 1983), pp. 339–56; Murray Bookchin, *The Rise of Urbanization and the Decline of Citizenship* (San Francisco: Sierra Club, 1987); and Jonathan Schell, Introduction to *Letters from Prison and Other Essays* by Adam Michnik, trans. Maya Latynski (Berkeley and Los Angeles: University of California Press, 1985), pp. xvii–xliii.

[18] Henry A. Giroux, "Marxism and Schooling: The Limits of Radical Discourse," *Educational Theory* 34, no. 3 (Spring 1984): 126.

[19] Arendt discusses Weber's definition of the state in her essay "On Violence," in *Crises of the Republic* (New York: Harcourt, Brace, Jovanovich, 1972) 2:134–36.

[20] Plato and Aristotle are not mentioned by Ignatieff even though they have significant things to contribute to a discussion of needs.

ical participation is always self-incarceration, and freedom requires us to choose the way of metics, rootless aliens whose happiness depends on not being citizens of a polis or members of a community or having some assigned place. "I do not shut myself up in the four corners of a politeia," Aristippus gravely announces, "but am a stranger in every land." Ignatieff is concerned with moral and personal costs of being strangers. Yet for all their differences, there is a significant congruence in their political and theoretical conclusions, a congruence that challenges my choice of texts.

"Political utopias," Ignatieff asserts, "are a form of nostalgia for an imagined past projected on to the future as a wish. Whenever I try to imagine a future other than the one towards which we seem to be hurtling, I find myself dreaming a dream of the past. It is the vision of the classical polis. . ." Because utopias "never have to make their excuses to history" and have, like all dreams "a timeless immunity to disappointment in real life," we ignore inconvenient facts (such as slavery) that tarnish the dream or complicate the wish. What beckons us still is the polis's human dimension; "small, cooperative, egalitarian, self-governing and autarkic: these are the conditions of belonging that the dream of the polis has bequeathed to us."

The irony of such rampant nostalgia is that words like community, belonging, and fraternity have become so sentimentalized that we can no longer regard them as serious goals or discern the realistic possibilities of membership in modern society. Modernity has so changed the possibilities of civic solidarity that our Greek-inflected political language "stumbles behind like an overburdened porter with a mountain of old cases." We can unburden ourselves by generating a language of belonging adequate to our situation, rather than retaining one that is simply a way of "expressing nostalgia, fear and estrangement from modernity." In the grip of the polis, we think of belonging as rootedness in a small familiar place, as being tied to fixed, known, and familiar places. Yet our homes are transient places we leave in order to grow up and become ourselves, convulsive arteries of great cities, an "electric and heartless creature eternally in motion." Captivated by premodern lineaments of membership and citizenship, we think of belonging in moral terms as direct impingement on the lives of others. Yet the moral relations that exist between our income and the needs of strangers at our doors pass through the arteries of the state. Finally, caught by utopian visions, we think of belonging as "the end of yearning itself, as a state of rest and reconciliation with ourselves beyond need itself. Yet modernity and insatiability are inseparable."

To see who we are and how we should live we must use a language "adequate for the times we live in," not one that entices us to forgetfulness and escapism. To find ourselves, we must resist "losing ourselves in resignation toward the portion of life which has been allotted to us. With-

out the right language we risk becoming strangers to our better selves";
without asking the right questions we give up any possibility of discovering the right answers.[21] The point then is to liberate ourselves from the
haunting images of civic belonging bequeathed us by Athens, Rome, and
Florence. The right question is not how can America become more like
Athens, but whether there is "a language of belonging adequate to Los
Angeles?"[22] (a question for which Thomas Pynchon has an answer, as we
shall see in chapter 9).

Nostalgia as presenting the past as a present or future alternative or as
a desire to return to a former time in one's life is, Ignatieff suggests, escapism. But there is another meaning of the word present in the Greek
and still listed in contemporary dictionaries. *Nostos* was a desire to return
to one's home, family, or friends, to arrive safely from some perilous journey and from fear.[23] *Algia* (from *algos*) meant feeling pain of loss, being
troubled or distressed, grieving over some lack or separation. In these
terms, nostalgia may be less an irrational refusal to adapt and adjust to a
modernity in which we must give up all ideas of cooperative egalitarian
self-governing communities, than a cry of pain, an instinct for cultural
and personal identity and a refusal to accept euphemisms. If our homes
are indeed transient temporary places, then it is perhaps better to admit
with Aristippus that we are strangers everywhere. If we leave home purportedly to grow up, then we might ask if "we" do, or whether, on the
contrary, leaving home (both metaphorically and literally) makes "us" all
the more susceptible to a romantic communitarianism, which we are
warned to resist in the name of realism and liberty.

Ignatieff thinks we need a language "adequate" to our times, and his
book is an experiment in that direction. Although I am not sure who the
"we" is or what he means by adequate,[24] or how he thinks language functions, he is surely right that ignorance of the imperatives that shape our
thought and action is suicidal. But there is also a "need" to be untimely,
not to reify the present or even adjust to it, but to render political and
theoretical critiques of what we are being asked to adjust to, who is doing
the asking, and why they are doing it at all. If Nietzsche is right that we
"remain necessarily strangers to ourselves," if, as he says, "we *must* mis-

[21] Michael Ignatieff, *The Needs of Strangers* (New York: Viking Press, 1984), pp. 107,
138, 141, 142.

[22] The force of the question is rhetorical, for he follows it with "Put like that the answer
can only seem to be no," which however quickly becomes a maybe.

[23] The man famed for his homecoming is, of course, Odysseus. Such returns are always
fraught, for the home and homecomer are different. In Odysseus's case the breach is not
beyond repair, though the cost is great violence. With Agamemnon, matters are beyond
repair; because the home is no longer a home, the homecomer no longer fits.

[24] Adequate can mean fully adequate or barely adequate: Ignatieff clearly means the former, I am suggesting it is the latter.

take ourselves,"[25] if the assumption of epistemological and moral progress upon which our beliefs in superior self-understanding and our grasp
of the past is exaggerated and self-serving, then we cannot "privilege" our
vantage point on the past or present even if our investigation of both
inevitably starts from our prejudgements. Nietzsche thought the meaning
of classical studies for our time is precisely their untimeliness, their acting
"counter to our time and thereby acting on our time and, let us hope, for
the benefit of a time to come."[26]

Such untimely timeliness characterizes such "utopian" works as Plato's
Republic and More's *Utopia*. In neither case does their utopianism simply
consist of nostalgia for an imagined past, though Plato perhaps and More
certainly admired the archaic polis and early Christian communities respectively. Both works make the obvious, everyday, natural, necessary,
the omnipresently "modern" seem contrived, absurd, flagrantly unjust,
passé and incomprehensible. By inverting the real[27] and imaginary, in
making "natural" divisions and hierarchies appear as historical conventions sanctioned only by the self-serving legitimizing myths of those in
power, they politicize what had been regarded as outside or beyond political decision. In this, and in the vision of some alternative future, utopianism has an emancipatory impulse.

Thus critiques of utopianism run the risk of inadvertently reifying the
present and of purging the emancipatory rhetoric characteristic of much
political theory (including thinkers such as Burke). In these terms one
could read Ignatieff's critique of nostalgia and utopianism, together with
his counsel to adapt, as a symptom of and argument for political and
theoretical retrenchment.[28] Even more justly could one interpret

[25] "It is not possible for us to describe our own archive, since it is from within these rules
that we speak, since it is that which gives to what we can say . . . its mode of appearance,
its forms of existence and coexistence, its system of accumulation, historicity and disap-
pearance." Michel Foucault, *Archeology of Knowledge*, trans. A. M. Sheridan Smith (New
York: Pantheon, 1972), p. 130.

[26] Nietzsche, *The Genealogy of Morals*, trans. Francis Golffing (Garden City, N.Y.: Doubleday, 1956), p. 149, and "On the Uses and Disadvantages of History for Life," in *Untimely Meditations*, trans. R. J. Hollingdale (Cambridge: Routledge and Kegan Paul, 1983),
p. 60. The new American productions of Greek tragedy, Arthur Holmberg suggests, "go
backward by going forward. They recapture the essence of Greek tragedy, not by donning
white sheets and aping marble statues, but by finding vital equivalents that give the texts a
modern, syncopated voice" "Greek Tragedy in a New Mask Speaks to Today's Audiences,"
in *New York Times* (March 1, 1987): section 2, p. 1.

[27] Here is Martha Graham: "It was inevitable that I choreographed the Greeks . . .
They're alive in all of us. Modern man is timid, but the Greeks were realists. We hide from
the truth. The Greeks stared life in the face. They knew it was wild and bitter and beautiful.
I was never interested in creating pretty pictures. I wanted to use dance to explore the hidden
landscape of the soul, so I turned to the Greeks." Quoted in Holmberg, *ibid.*

[28] This is not entirely fair. Ignatieff offers us a kind of relevant utopianism in the final

14

Holmes's repudiation of participatory politics and classical political theory in favor of modern politics and social theory as a kind of theoretical and political timidity.[29]

The question is, Why such retrenchment now? Why these critiques of the polis and classical political theory? What is happening in the polity and academy to legitimate and give force to such arguments? One can readily understand why the calling of a society that deprives a substantial majority of its population of full citizenship "democratic" seems hypocritical at best, though it is worth distinguishing Greek slavery from our own, acknowledging the uncertain evidence about the standing of women in Athens (and their apparently greater power at Sparta), containing our sense of superiority, and being sure that what we are contrasting Athens with really is as it seems. But why the debunking of what seems most admirable about Athenian life: its participatory ideals, its concept of public life, the questions posed about that life by its poets and philosophers? Is this simply a scholarly commitment to truth over mythology and to realism over utopianism or is it a countermyth with its own selective memory and implicit utopianism of the present? If we were to examine these respective myths in the light of Nietzsche's distinctions in the *Uses and Disadvantages of History for Life*, which would be life-sustaining and which not? If, as Nietzsche suggests, there are no innocent readings of history (which is not to say all readings are equally "guilty"), what is the political agenda contained or presupposed in the critique of the polis and what image of political theory is being explicitly or implicitly defended against the classical model? Can we see the critique of the participatory aspects of Athenian public life as part of the repudiation of 1960s activism, which, at least up to 1968 and in the Port Huron Statement, leaned so heavily on the tradition of civic republicanism?[30]

But there are some good reasons for such retrenchment given the forms political and theoretical boldness has taken in our century (though whether timidity is the proper response to boldness is another matter). There are good reasons too for being skeptical about regarding the Greeks as a moment of archaic and natural innocence, a moment of pure presence and self-presence. We cannot go back to the Greeks, not only because "the Greeks" is often a misleading projection, but because "going back" is never an option given the distinctiveness of modernity as defined by the demythologizing of society with its division of the sacred and profane, work and home, public and private; the privatization of religion and growth of the territorial nation-state with its bureaucratic ad-

---

pages of his book. The problem is not with these sentiments, but how disconnected they are from the rest of the book.

[29] This is a possible implication of Holmes's argument; it is not entailed by it.

[30] See James Miller, *Democracy in the Streets* (New York: Simon and Schuster, 1987).

ministration; the dominance of capitalist rationality and triumph of specialized science based on rigorous quantitative procedures and manipulative mentality; the disassociation of art from politics, rise of mass politics, and debasement of democracy; the shrinkage or transformation of kinship units, proceduralism of law and justice, and triumph of what Jacques Ellul calls "technique" in fact and as ideology; the development of a world economy, the "computer revolution," and the professionalization of knowledge and the role of experts.[31]

Ignatieff and Holmes are right to insist that we have no choice but to confront the intellectual and institutional forces that shape our lives as citizens and as scholars (though I think Greek tragedy and classical political theory can help us do that). Evasion is no substitute for analysis; nor is rancor for critique. If we are to understand ourselves as interpretative beings, we must recognize the traditions that have made us who we are, the stories in which we play a part, and the prejudgments, interests, and reasons that initially draw us to a text or text analogue. As Gadamer, among others, has argued, understanding is necessarily a matter of self-understanding. That means that changes in how we understand ourselves (including ourselves as interpreters of texts) alter how we understand a text or culture even as our interpretation of that culture alters our sense of self and the prejudices that animated our initial inquiry.[32] This (always incomplete) historical consciousness requires both an awareness of the strangeness or otherness of that which we are trying to understand and an assumption of commonality[33] sufficient to engender mutual interrogation.[34]

In these terms, ignoring the historical conditions of the polis and the political theory that emerged in it provides the opportunity for false familiarity and easy idealization. Regarding the Athenian city-state or clas-

[31] The list is drawn from Holmes; one could add the imminent prospect of environmental catastrophe (including environmentally caused diseases) and the possibility of thermonuclear "war."

[32] "Whether he wants to or not, the ethnologist accepts into his discourse the premises of ethnocentrism at the very moment when he is employed in denouncing them. This is absolutely necessary and everyone must give in to it. The question is how one gives into it, whether one borrows from a heritage the resources necessary for deconstruction of that heritage itself." Jacques Derrida, "Structure, Sign and Play in the Discourse of the Human Sciences," in *The Structuralist Controversy: The Languages of Criticism and the Sciences of Man*, ed. Richard Macksey and Eugenio Donato (Baltimore: Johns Hopkins University Press, 1972), p. 252. On the relationship between hermeneutics and Derrida, see David Hoy, "Jacques Derrida" in the mistitled *The Return of Grand Theory in the Human Sciences*, ed. Quentin Skinner (Cambridge: Cambridge University Press, 1985), pp. 50–54.

[33] This parallels the distance and proximity of spectators in the theater to the actions performed before them.

[34] As Gadamer recognizes, it is not clear how we discover that there is a difference between our own customary linguistic usage and that of the texts we address.

sical political theories as near perfection tempts us to suppose that by "applying" them we would somehow become cured or redeemed, even though those texts themselves warn us about technical applications and the limits of using "texts" as repositories of truth and value.

But why do we suppose that the Greeks, above all others, are so available either as exemplars (as with Strauss and Arendt), or as object lessons (as with Holmes)? Why the "temptation of transparency" to use a phrase of Vidal-Naquet. Perhaps it has something to do with the Greeks' self-conception that what they were about was perfectly, even brutally clear and distinct. That this is not the case is suggested by Vidal-Naquet's and Vernant's efforts to restore Greek rationality to its historical setting[35] and their insistence on the historical uniqueness of Greek tragedy,[36] from which they conclude that "a century of Hellenic studies has succeeded to a great extent in moving Greece farther away from us rather than bringing it closer."[37] Perhaps Holmes and Ignatieff are simply making a similar point about political theory.

But there is an irony in all this. The defamiliarizing of the "old" Greece and the repudiation of traditional treatments of "the Greeks" it had sustained have led to a "new" Greece and interpretations in which the tragedians and sophists anticipated contemporary literary views and strategies. The "classical" Greece of proportion, harmony, reason, pristine democracy, and heroic achievement is replaced by a Greece of fissures, turbulence, discontinuities, and dismemberments. The serene order of the polis and the triumph of reason is replaced by a drama that interrogates the "normal" polarities and hierarchies of Greek culture, those for instance between sanity and madness, Greek and barbarian, men and women, self and other. In place of political communities we have cities riven by class conflict, dynastic strife, and the waywardness of language and sexuality. Increasingly the subjects of recent scholarship include generational conflict, slavery, mysogyny, eroticism, the sophists on language. Increasingly critics are more inclined than they were to expose the way a text fails to "work" or to establish its message despite its rhetorical strategies intended to obscure its partiality. Here is the triumph of Dionysus over Apollo and of Nietzsche over Wilamowitz.[38]

[35] That means "giving back to reason its turbulence and aggression" (Vidal-Naquet quoting Bachelard in *The Black Hunter: Forms of Thought and Forms of Society in the Greek World* (Baltimore: Johns Hopkins University Press, 1986), p. 249.

[36] See Vernant's "Le Moment historique de la tragedie en Grèce-essai d'interpretations," in Macksey and Donato, *The Structuralist Controversy*, pp. 345–49.

[37] In *The Black Hunter*, p. 252.

[38] Angus Paul ("Appreciation Grows for the Complexity and Expanse of Ancient Greek Culture," *The Chronicle of Higher Education* [March 25, 1987]: 6) thinks the new Greece closer to reality.

In this book I want to tell both stories at once, or at least not tell just one of them. Substantively that means, for instance, a concern with justice in the *Oresteia* and with dismemberment of the male body politic in the *Bacchae*, or more generally with the way tragedy helps constitute a democratic polity and challenges the democratic credentials of that polity. In terms of interpretative controversies, it means that, while I usually suppose that what a modern critic regards as a text working against itself is part of the text's purposeful education of the critic, I am aware that such a strategy has its pitfalls—an unhermenuetic hypostasizing of "the text, insulating the text from critique by preemptively incorporating criticism as part of the author's purpose and the resuscitation of "the" author. Because I do not think there need be an opposition between authority and liberty, I am interested in the ways texts empower their readers to join in the collective construction of meaning.

In terms of the book's structure telling both stories at once means treating writers both in conventional sequence (Aeschylus, Sophocles, Euripides, Thucydides, Socrates, and Plato), and turning back on that sequence to compare Aeschylus and Plato on justice, Sophocles and Socrates on identity, and (more conventionally) Euripides and Thucydides on membership (or dismemberment). Necessarily this places extra burdens on the transitions between chapters because they must elaborate the argument of the previous chapter and anticipate the one that follows, illustrate tragedy's influence on theory, refer to the modernism—postmodernism debate, and carry out a series of comparisons on the three substantive issues. Finally it means that my substantive and theoretical commitments remain constructive and humanistic though chastened by Foucault's criticism and the events that inspired them.

PRECISELY because Michel Foucault's methodological convictions, political commitments, and substantive conclusions are so different from Ignatieff's and Holmes's, their common belief that we need to let go of the Greek polis and political theory to confront the distinctiveness of modernity or postmodernity is all the more striking. His admonition is particularly germane because it explicitly invokes the idea of a theater. Here he is in *Discipline and Punish*:

> Our society is not one of spectacle, but of surveillance; under the surface of images, one invests bodies in depth; behind the great abstraction of exchange, there continues the meticulous, concrete training of useful forces; the circuits of communication are the supports of an accumulation and a centralization of knowledge; the play of signs defines the anchorages of power; it is not that the beautiful totality of the individual is amputated, repressed, altered by our so-

cial order, it is rather that the individual is carefully fabricated in it, according to whole technique of forces and bodies. We are much less Greek than we believe. We are neither in the amphitheatre, nor on the stage, but in the panoptic machine, invested by its effects of power, which we bring to ourselves since we are part of its mechanism.[39]

We are neither actors nor spectators in the theater but organized subjects who are seen, known, observed, and controlled by specialists, administrators, and managers, whether scientists, wardens, psychiatrists, physicians, or teachers. Synoptic visibility (exemplified by Bentham's panopticon) and individualizing visibility (the elaborately detailed observation of individual habits) have constituted the individual as simultaneously an object of inquiry and a target of power. Because such visibility is unidirectional, and because we cannot know whether anyone is actually in the central observation tower watching us, we internalize the "gaze" and watch ourselves.

In such a world, given the workings of the disciplinary machine, what point is there in having recourse, yet again, to Greek tragedy and classical political theory and to the humanism they inspired and that informs the tradition which interprets them? To think of ourselves as an audience or as actors is to miss how we have become objects and subjects of speculating, how the spaces for action have been closed down and turned in. To accept human structures as natural, to posit essential forms, to seek permanent foundations for belief and action, or to offer norms outside of particular regimes of power by which to distinguish legitimate from illegitimate power or proclaim "the" good life, is to pretend we live in a world that is no more (if it ever was) and to obscure the world that is here now.

As this language indicates, Foucault, like Holmes, regards classical political theorists as part of the problem.[40] Indeed, Foucault explicitly directs his genealogies at what he regards as Plato's sacralizing of Socratic metaphysics. "The locus of emergence for metaphysics," Foucault writes in "Nietzsche, Genealogy, History" is "the vulgar spite of Socrates and his belief in immortality." Instead of turning against this Socratic philosophy as he was "undoubtedly" tempted to do, Plato consecrated and so was defeated by it.[41] Foucault writes of the great Platonic divide and the emergence of rationality and theory, which destroyed the pragmatic po-

[39] *Discipline and Punish*, trans. Alan Sheridan (New York: Vintage Books, 1979), p. 217.

[40] Foucault would be as critical of those theorists Holmes admires as of those he criticizes. The case of Arendt is more complicated given a number of similarities between her and Foucault.

[41] The essay is reprinted in *Language, Counter-Memory, Practice: Selected Essays and Interviews*, ed. and intro. Donald F. Bouchard (Ithaca, N.Y.: Cornell University Press, 1977), pp. 159–60.

etics of the pre-Socratic Greeks. When the sophists were defeated, the Platonic will to truth triumphed, creating its own self-perpetuating institutions and self-justifying history.[42] Seduced and overpowered by Socrates, Plato posits the finality of forms and permanent essences, leading us on a path upward to the heights of immaterial truths and inward to the domain of consciousness. His forms draw all phenomena around a single center, principle, or meaning, annihilating differences, robbing particulars of their identities by forcing them to become epiphenomenal veils for a generative ontological realm.[43] Plato is all hidden meanings and mysterious depths at the expense of surface practices and material bodies. Against this Foucault insists there is no lurking essence secreted behind appearances except perhaps the secret that essences are "fabricated in a piecemeal fashion from alien forms."[44]

Unlike Ignatieff (and perhaps Holmes),[45] Foucault's distancing of the Greeks is part of a larger critique of humanism's elaboration of the Enlightenment's hope and assertion that once liberated from the constraints of church and privilege "man" could achieve a previously denied integrity, realize the freedom inherent in his nature, and enter upon a path of increasing knowledge and self-knowledge whose intellectual and moral progress would allow him to create his own destiny. He rejects the goals and proclaimed accomplishment of autonomy, mutual recognition, dignity, and human rights together with the metaphysics of the transcendent subject that underlies them. Contrary to humanist assertions, truth cannot control power, texts are not the product of independent genius whose intention is controlling for subsequent readings, and history is not the evolution from combat and contest to universal reciprocity and the rule of law.[46]

Humanism is a theory of the "subject" in both senses of that word.[47] As such it presupposes persons as they "really are" in themselves—individuals with rights by nature or in respect of their essential humanity,[48]

[42] Michel Foucault, "The Discourse of Language," in *The Archeology of Knowledge*, pp. 215–38.

[43] *The Archeology of Knowledge*, pt. I and pt. IV, chap. 1.

[44] "Nietzsche, Genealogy, History," in *Language, Counter-Memory, Practice*, p. 142.

[45] There is a moment of confluence between Foucault and Holmes. Like Holmes, Foucault is critical of the ideal of civic virtue as found in the Greeks and the republican tradition, regarding it as complicitous with overt forms of coercion in the normalizing enterprise humanists explicitly castigate. (The point of confluence may be Weber.) But Foucault's archaeologies and genealogies have a very different ground and purpose.

[46] "Nietzsche, Genealogy, History," p. 151.

[47] See Foucault's "Afterword: The Subject and Power," in *Michel Foucault: Beyond Structuralism and Hermeneutics*, ed. Hubert L. Dreyfus and Paul Rabinow (Chicago: University of Chicago Press, 1982), pp. 208–26.

[48] "By humanism I mean the totality of discourse through which Western man is told:

apart from participation in historically specific regimes of power. It assumes there are such things as minds capable of constituting the phenomenal world and giving themselves moral laws, transcendent egos cum noumenal selves, rational beings who design and order the world. By radically historicizing "human nature" and "man"[49] Foucault transformed the subject from an independent knower whose agency controls history into a product of contingent yet historically specific sets of linguistically infused social practices that inscribe power relations on bodies.[50]

For Foucault the humanist theory of the subject presupposes epistemological as well as political and moral progress. Philosophy claims and assumes that it can discover and disclose truths by which particular regimes of power can be compared, judged, and constrained. But that is simply bad faith, a presumptive distancing from rhetoric, repeating Plato's pretensions against the sophists. "In fact,"[51] there is no truth outside a regime of power and so no way truth can fix the limits of legitimate power. For Foucault, the question is, "What type of power is susceptible of producing discourses of truth that in a society such as ours are endowed with such potent effects?" In every society there are manifold relations of power that permeate, characterize, and constitute the social body. These relations of power cannot themselves be established, consolidated, or implemented without the production, accumulation, circulation, and function of discourse. Power is exercised through a specific economy of discourses of truth. "We are subjected to the production of truth through power and we cannot exercise power except through the production of truth." Although this is the case for every society, our society organizes the relationship between power, right, and truth in a specific fashion.[52]

'Even though you don't exercise power, you can still be a ruler. Better yet, the more you deny yourself the exercise of power, the more you submit to those in power, then the more this increases your sovereignty.' " This is so whether that be the sovereignty of the soul ruling the body but subject to God, consciousness ruling judgment but subjected to the necessities of truth, the individual in titular control of personal rights subject to the laws of nature and society, and basic freedom ruling within but accepting the demands of an outside world seen as "aligned with destiny." In sum, "humanism is everything in "Western civilization that restricts *the desire for power*." (The quotations are from "Revolutionary Action: 'Until Now,' " in *Language, Counter-Memory, Practice*, pp. 221–22.

[49] The "classical" example of deconstructing these ideas is still Roland Barthes' analyses of the exhibition of photographs which became a book in the late 1950s entitled *The Family of Man*. See his *Mythologies*, trans. Annette Lavers (New York: Hill and Wang, 1972), pp. 100–102.

[50] Nancy Fraser, "Foucault's Body-Language: A Post-Humanist Political Rhetoric?" *Salmagundi* 61 (Fall 1983): 56.

[51] It is not clear how Foucault can make such an assertion, what epistemological status it has.

[52] See Foucault's "Two Lectures," in *Power/Knowledge: Selected Interviews and Other*

The distinctively modern regime or power-knowledge is exercised through disciplinary mechanisms that constitute and institute norms of health, sanity, stability, and citizenship (as opposed to disease, insanity, chaos, and delinquency). These disciplinary mechanisms cannot be assimilated to older juridical definitions of power such as we find in Hobbes, nor adequately analyzed in terms of class domination, although there is indeed a "class" of experts who define what is abnormal and supervise our carceral institutions. Thus power is not a possession, property, or privilege that operates from the top down. It does not impose itself on subjects through the threat of violence by an intermittently present agent of the sovereign. It is local rather than centralized, productive rather than restraining or repressive, continuously circulating (as does blood or electrical current), extending to even the furthest extremities.

In these terms the dominated or disciplined and the dominating or disciplinarians are equally part of a network of power relations that spin a web of control over the most intimate recesses of everyday life. The network operates as much by self-surveillance and over those who have not (yet) transgressed established norms or laws as by surveillance over those who have. Because of the visibility of the self to agents of normalization, all of us strive to present "ourselves" as responsible agents for whom treatment is unnecessary. Thus we discipline any impulses or inclinations, any passions or pleasures that do not fit within the accepted boundaries of normal behavior. We trap, deflect, and incarcerate them before they become visible even to ourselves. This preemptive interiorization of norms means that we become the conduit for remaking ourselves into the subjects the human sciences study and constitute.

Humanists assume that the discourse of a discipline—criminality, madness, sickness—is centered around an essential object outside discourse to which the discourse refers and to which, if accurate, it represents. In contrast, Foucault insists that there is no object prior to or outside of a discursive formation, It is not, for him, a matter of speaking the truth about the object but being within a regime of truth in which what is said is recognized as a claim about which truth or falsehood is appropriately decided.[53] "I should like to know," Foucault writes in the foreword to the English edition of *The Order of Things*, "whether the subjects responsible for scientific discourse are not determined in their situation, their function, their perceptive capacity, and their practical possibilities by conditions that dominate and even overwhelm them." His concern with scientific discourse is from the point of view of "the rules that come into play

---

Writings, 1972–1977, ed. Colin Gordon (New York: Pantheon, 1980), pp. 93–94, and "Truth and Power," in the same volume, pp. 109–33.

[53] See *Archaeology of Knowledge*, chap. 2, and the appendix "The Discourse on Language," pp. 224–25.

in the very existence of such discourse; what conditions did Linnaeus . . . have to fulfill, not to make his discourse coherent and true in general, but to give it, at the time when it was written and accepted, value and practical application as a scientific discourse."[54]

As part of his repudiation of humanism, Foucault rejects any leading role for humanist ("representative," "general," or "universal") intellectuals. In opposition to them and their global (totalizing, unitary, universal) theories, he offers the specific intellectual and genealogies.[55] Whether persons of general culture or disciplinary specialists, humanists pretend to be the conscience/consciousness of "humanity" and to be outside of regimes of power even as their position makes them conduits for the extension and development of the postmodern regime of disciplinary power. Whereas global theories or unitary discourses such as Marxism and psychoanalysis[56] filter, hierarchize, and order knowledges in the name of truth, genealogies disinter the local, discontinuous, disqualified, illegitimate knowledges (of the psychiatric patient, criminal, or inmate) from the anonymity of functionalizing history and politically self-serving reconstructions of the past. Whereas theories and traditional histories seek unity and stability and speak in evolutionary or teleological terms, genealogies look to and for disruptions and struggle, variety and difference, contingency and surprise. Theories posit givens, draw cognitive maps, rely on "metahistorical deployment of ideal "significations"" and discover immobile forms that precede that external world of accident and succession. Genealogy reveals cultural practices as ungrounded except in terms of prior, equally contingent, historically instituted practices. By exposing the constructed character of "man," "humanity," "human nature," and

[54] *The Order of Things* (New York: Vintage Books, 1973), p. xiv.

[55] As Marx posited the withering away of the state, Foucault sees the withering away of state power and with it the withering away of the state (i.e., general) intellectual. As he argues that resistance must be local (to be resistance), so he argues for the role of the "specific" or particular intellectual.

[56] The genealogist or specific intellectual supports the insurrection of subjugted discourses by which Foucault means two things: "the historical contents" that have been buried and disguised in a functionalist coherence of normal systemization; and the "set of knowledges that have been disqualified as inadequate to their task or insufficiently elaborated; naive knowledges, located low down on the hierarchy, beneath the required level of cognition and scientificity." Because global discourses or totalized theories filter, hierarchize, and order knowledges in the name of truth, they are part of the problem. Especially when their normalizing is done under the banner of liberation or democracy, they make the problem worse. Paradoxically, "participatory" democratic discourse is the most seductive of all because it appears to be most sympathetic to marginal groups and sections of the self. Although these groups will continue to be examined, measured, and prescribed for the proscribed form, they will be literally disarmed. Nor will increased reflexivity help alleviate the problem or resolve the paradox, since reflexivity experts define maturity, reason, and sanity and, by doing so, bring the self under further control (see *Power/Knowledge*, pp. 81–82).

"self," the genealogist or specific intellectual honors, if not provides space for, subjugated peoples and discourses, those marginal subordinated and secret voices that have been reduced to a murmur beneath the clamor of the dominant discourse. The specific intellectual does not seek to speak for a new humanity or emancipatory class but instead engages in guerrilla warfare against the dominant form of knowledge production *and* any putatively hegemonic intellectuals who offer themselves as liberatory guides from such domination.[57]

Many things could be and have been said about Foucault's method of analysis and his conclusions, about the arguments he makes and refuses to make, the purported inconsistency between the world he describes and his own actions in it, and about his idea of local resistance which seems to be, at most, a momentary interruption in the otherwise hegemonic deployment of power-knowledge. But what concerns me is his attitude toward the texts and themes of this book. Foucault insists we are in the panopticon, not the theater, and that Plato is the paradigmatic totalizing theorist.

Yet, as this suggests, even as Foucault warns us against false analogies induced by Hellenic romanticism he, very much like Arendt and Strauss, "uses" the Greeks as a diagnostic aid to clarify the character and contours of modern theory and society. Whether considering history or truth, rationality, the play of discursive formations, or the desiring subject, he regards studying the Greeks as a way of "getting free of oneself."[58] He begins his study of sexuality with them so that we can see our own with fresh eyes and posits a Platonic divide on the far side of which technologies of thought were inseparable from truth and goodness and epistemology was linked to politics and practical philosophy. His aim is to help us see the beginnings of a totalizing order of things so as to locate our practices and institutions that have partly escaped totalization. And the last (unpublished) project of his life on discourse and truth is a detailed study of *parrhēsia*, frankness in speaking the truth.

But for all this, Foucault never discusses[59] Greek tragedy even when (as in *The Uses of Pleasure*) one might expect him to do so, and the passing references he does make, such as the one in the *Discipline and Punish*, are dismissive. Moreover, his whole project denies the existence of the natu-

[57] *Power/Knowledge*, pp. 82–86, and "Nietzsche, Genealogy, History."

[58] Foucault in *The Uses of Pleasure: The History of Sexuality*, trans. Robert Hurley (New York: Patheon Books, 1985), 2:8. Although Foucault uses the Greeks to reveal differences that undermine the obviousness and certain of the present he is anxious to avoid any nostalgia that would present the past as an alternative. On Foucault's relationship to the Greeks, see Mark Poster, "Foucault and the Tyranny of Greece," in *Foucault: A Critical Reader*, ed. David Hoy (Oxford: Basil Blackwell, 1986), p. 209.

[59] He does in his survey of truth telling.

ral order Aeschylus and Sophocles assume,[60] although the latter is aware that some do not believe in such an order[61] and that its structure stands revealed only to blind prophets favored by Apollo.[62] Furthermore, Foucault does not think in terms of unfolding dramas whose plot "weaves together great speeches and actions of heroic characters into a pattern of fate" but sees clashes as among kinds of discourse.[63] Nor does he have much sympathy for "traditional" political theory, regarding it as impotent in its outmoded reliance on centralized ideas of power and all too potent in its reinforcement of prevalent structures of domination and in legitimating the pretensions of universal intellectuals.

Given all this and more, why strain to make connections Foucault does not make or even denies? Why use his project to frame my own?

There are a number of reasons why. For one thing, discussing the affinities between Foucault and tragedy is a way of introducing Greek tragedy and classical political theory read in its terms to those otherwise inclined to dismiss the latter as irrelevant in a postmodern era. It also allows me to dramatize those features of Foucault's project that are more general than his insistence on the distinctiveness of our carceral society would indicate. For another thing, I think Greek tragedy anticipates certain of Foucault's concerns (which is not surprising given the significance of Nietzsche and Heidegger for him), and that classical political theory understood against a background of tragedy "problematizes" Foucault's equation of theory, centralization, totalization, and normalization. Finally, the dilemmas Greek tragedy bequeathed to classical theory are analogous to the ones Foucault presents for contemporary political theory.

It is unclear, to say the least, whether and how one can, on Foucault's account, distinguish just from unjust regimes. It is perfectly clear that, for him, any narrative that moves from darkness and chaos to light and freedom, from disease, madness, and transgression to health, sanity, and salvation, or from monstrosity to normalcy is suspect, subject to genealogical critique. Yet the *Oresteia* seems to do precisely that. Orestes becomes purified, Argos is rescued from corruption and injustice, and women are returned to their "normal" place and powers. Yet the trilogy also enables us to see the way power orders reality, simultaneously shaping in-

---

[60] Not everyone agrees with my assertion. See, for instance, Cedric Whitman, *Sophocles: A Study of Heroic Humanism* (Cambridge, Mass.: Harvard University Press, 1951).

[61] Or so I will argue in chapter 4 when discussing the chorus's "Why shall I dance?"

[62] It is as if only a god could stand outside and apart from a particular regime of power.

[63] John Rajchman characterizes *I Pierre Reviere* as "a story without heroes, villians or fate, a battle without a strategy. The power involved is not the power of the characters but of the discourses devised to describe them" (*Michel Foucault: The Freedom of Philosophy* [New York: Columbia University Press, 1985], p. 70).

stitutions, practices, and conceptions of knowledge that exclude and subordinate some forces and aspects of the "self" while including others. We see how a "democratic" regime, like the Athens of the *Eumenides*, which strives for inclusiveness and celebrates the incorporation of previously warring parties into a unity that respects their diversity, nevertheless establishes a center, thereby creating literal and metaphorical spaces that bound respectability. The Athenians in the play are road builders and boundary drawers who create a civilized space against the press of infinite nature and establish a political discourse that delimits who and what can be recognized within its sphere. Because the *Oresteia* insists on the need for such boundaries and spaces and celebrates the establishment of political discourse, it differs from Foucault. But in the way the *Eumenides* establishes them and in its recognition of the limits of what it celebrates, the play provides a mediating vision in the debate between Foucault and his humanist critics.

In that debate we are given a choice between the archaeology of disciplinary society and democratic aspirations, between repudiating every imaginable ideal as just one more extension of the present system and generating yet again a single vision of "the" good society. As I shall argue in chapter 3, I think the *Oresteia* provides the political language and substantive intimations for a vision of democratic life that, as William Connolly puts it in reference to Foucault, consciously maintains a tension between "affirming the legitimacy of limits and conventions essential to democratic politics" and "exposing and opposing the modern drift toward rationalization, normalization and dependency." In recognizing the intractable tensions between the "drive to disturb forces of normalization and the quest to sustain preconditions of democratic life," this vision "might show how each, properly understood, is a precondition and a limit to the other."[64]

The parallels are far more striking between the *Oedipus Tyrannos*'s portrait of fate and freedom and Foucault's discussion of discursive formations and how individuals simultaneously undergo and exercise power.[65] Oedipus's life is shaped jointly by his god-ordained fate and by his character—that is, by the "characteristic" way in which he thinks, speaks, and acts. Although his destiny is realized despite his intentions and without his knowledge, it is still his fate in the double sense that it belongs to him alone and that it was his actions that brought it about. He is not a self-made man as he presumes when he castigates Teiresias's de-

---

[64] William E. Connolly, *Politics and Ambiguity* (Madison: University of Wisconsin Press, 1987), pp. 107–8.

[65] "They are not only its inert or consenting target, they are always also the elements of its articulation. In other words, individuals are the vehicles or power, not its point of application" (*Power/Knowledge*, p. 98).

pendence on Apollo, in contrast to his own unaided intellectual prowess. We cannot, as he supposes when he calls himself a child of chance, construct another identity for ourselves any more than we can liberate ourselves by developing our self-consciousness until we and the world become utterly transparent. Nor can we achieve mastery without blindness or uncritically accept the value and desirability of knowledge as it "functions under the sign of the 'will to truth' within the humanistic project, that is, as it is presumed to 'assure' liberty, progress and human fulfillment."[66]

Oedipus's intellectual hubris is chastened as Foucault chastens the emancipatory hopes and beliefs in epistemological and moral enlightenment that characterizes putatively self-constituting subjects. Foucault talks of a "double system of reference"[67] that suspends all certitude, of being trapped within the positive context of language, labor, and life, of being defined by articulations about which we can never achieve some final narrative. Sophocles portrays human beings as riddles to themselves and to others, as grasping for certainties that elude and then turn back on the most talented among them. In a comment about the play that recalls Foucault's critique of humanism, Simon Goldhill says that the *Oedipus Tyrannos* challenges "not only fifth century or modern claims for the rigour, certainty and exhaustiveness of man's intellectual progress, but also the security of the reading process itself with its aim of finding, and delimiting, the precise, fixed and absolute sense of a text, a word. Athenian tragedy questions . . . the place and role of man in the order of things. . . ."[68] "Do not seek to be master in every way" (*Panta mē boulou kratein*, 1522) says Creon to Oedipus. "Do not," Foucault might say, "think to be the author of a text."

Goldhill's statement is even more apropos for the *Bacchae* than for the *Oedipus Tyrannos*. In Euripides' play literal readings of events, fixed understandings, closed-mindedness, and single angles of vision imprison the man who would imprison others.[69] Pentheus rigidly adheres to the normalizing polarities and hierarchies of his culture (those between men and

[66] Paul Bové, *Intellectuals and Power* (New York: Columbia University Press, 1986), p. 14.

[67] In *The Order of Things*.

[68] Simon Goldhill, *Reading Greek Tragedy* (New York: Cambridge University Press, 1986), p. 221.

[69] "What is fascinating about prisons is that, for once, power doesn't hide or mask itself; it reveals itself as tyranny pursued into the tiniest details; it is cynical and at the same time pure and entirely 'justified,' because its practice can be totally formulated within the framework of morality. Its brutal tyranny consequently appears as the serene domination of Good over Evil, of order over disorder." These lines (from *Intellectuals and Power*, p. 210) can be applied with almost equal appropriateness to Pentheus and the *Bacchae*; or so I will argue in chapter 5.

women, Greek and barbarian, self and other, reason and madness, pollution and purity, inside and outside, imprisonment and freedom and despises Dionysus because he does not. The young king regards politics as a matter of command, membership as a matter of obedience, and order as discipline. Because he does, he becomes a virtual slave to Dionysus, is dismembered, and creates havoc in the order he thinks himself protecting. Rejecting the words and experience of others and the other in himself, he murderously projects himself onto a world he has symbolically reduced to rubble even before the earthquake scene.

But perhaps the point of the play is even more radical—that every interpretation of a play is as much a projection as is every interpretation of Dionysus in it. Perhaps there is no more a single audience witnessing the drama at Athens than there is a single audience witnessing Dionysus's demonstration of his divinity on stage. Indeed, the mere fact that there are multiple audiences—the one assembled in the theater at Athens, the other being the chorus as an audience watching the play within the play—may make the spectators conscious "that they are viewing and interpreting the god's actions through a sense of subjective and unreliable perspectives and performances.[70] The question is, Can there be definitive performances? Is there some "objective" perspective outside the play even if there is none in it? Or is it the case that divine or poetic representations are partial projections that manifest an impulse to imprison what we cannot understand? Is the resistance to Dionysus in the play analogous to our possible resistance to the play's decentering ironies, which demand that we constantly turn back on our own readings?[71]

The possibility that no single perspective or final reading is possible echoes the contemporary repudiation of Hegel's belief that absolute undistorted knowledge is achievable through Reason's reflections on itself and the ultimate identity of subject and object. Like analytic philosophers such as Rorty, Quine, and Goodman, Foucault denies that there are certain truths or facts upon which knowledge can be unequivocally founded. Instead, like them, he argues that what creates a fact or knowledge is always relative to a theory, a specific system of representation, or a regime of power. In some respects the *Bacchae*'s treatment of *sophia* can be read as a dramatization of this position (as I will argue in chapter 5). Virtually every character in the contest for power we see on stage defines wisdom differently. (In the case of the chorus of Asian bacchants, the definition

[70] The quote is from Helene Foley *Ritual Irony: Poetry and Sacrifice in Euripides* (Ithaca, N.Y.: Cornell University Press, 1985), p. 222. For reasons I give in chapter 8, I think this is true of the *Republic* as well.

[71] This does not mean there are no standards by which competing interpretations of the "same" text can be evaluated. It only means that there is no single standard regardless of context.

changes as their vulnerability changes.) The effect is not only to leave us uncertain about what *sophia* means but to dramatize how conceptions of wisdom and knowledge are articulated within a particular political and epistemological regime.

Part of Foucault's power lies in his immanent critique of humanism. Nothing has more moral force within that critique than his claim that modern society, rather than honoring diversity and liberty (as Holmes presumes it does), marginalizes those deemed abnormal and controls through self-surveillance all eccentricities of behavior or deviant self-expression. Modern society no less than the society it claims to have superseded is defined by polarities, which become hierarchies sustained in and through a rhetoric of liberation. Foucault's genealogies are meant to disrupt this comforting self-serving rhetoric while decentering the historical metaphysics that legitimates it.[72] In many respects that is what Greek tragedy did at Athens.

In the theater of Dionysus, during the festival honoring the god who confounded the divisions and inequalities deemed central to public life,[73] tragedy put the city's dearly bought cultural accommodations on trial before itself. There and then the putatively normal and natural stood revealed as fictive imperatives that more often than not entailed violation of nature, city, household, and self. From inside the polis tragedy questioned the divisions between inside and outside. Part of the city's order, it "problematized" the idea of order, contesting as it constructed, challenging what it helped to sustain, and presenting transgression, paradoxes, and archaisms to disrupt civic teleologies which it eventually reaffirmed. Tragedy played "outside the ordered table of resemblances,[74] creating internal disturbances, strategically questioning the political and intellectual tradition with the tools that tradition supplied,[75] even providing competing versions of culture's constituting myths and narratives.

Like Foucault, tragedy does not present otherness as a disease to be

---

[72] "His very outrageousness in refusing standard humanist virtues, narrative conventions and political categories provides just the jolt we occasionally need in order to dereify our usual patterns of self-interpretation and keep alive our sense that, just possibly, they may not tell the whole story" (Fraser, "Foucault's Body-Language," p. 75).

[73] Foucault sees himself as doing something analogous. "In the second part of my work, I have studied the objectivizing of the subject in what I shall call 'dividing practices.' The subject is either divided inside himself or divided from others. This process objectivizes him. Examples are the mad and the sane, the sick and the healthy, the criminals and the 'good boys' " ("The Subject and Power," the afterword to *Michel Foucault: Beyond Structuralism and Hermeneutics*, by Hubert L. Dreyfus and Paul Rabinow [Chicago: The University of Chicago Press, 1982], p. 208).

[74] The phrase is Foucault's from "Theatrum Philosophicum," in *Language, Counter-Memory, Practice*.

[75] Derrida, *Writing and Difference* (Chicago: University of Chicago Press, 1978), p. 36.

cured but leaves the other as other. The great Sophoclean heroes and heroines remain liminal figures, saviors and polluters, touching gods and beasts at once. They do not instigate a third term in which warring principles are fully subsumed and silenced. Even the achievement of justice in the *Oresteia* is not a matter of progressive incorporation that discards the "primitivism" of the earlier world and play. And the *Antigone*'s celebration of *technai*, which brought men and mastery and the creation of the city, is hardly an unalloyed triumph. As the chorus makes clear, mastery is an assault and a violation for the same reason Foucault gives when he speaks of discourse as a violence we do to the world.

To the degree tragedy confronted its audience with the fictive aspects of its otherwise lived past and warned of the mind's propensity for theoretical closure, it was itself a genealogical activity. But it was also a warning about genealogy's insufficiencies. The tragedians tend to portray discourses that fix, define, center, and ground us as simultaneously closing us off from other possible modes of speaking and acting and giving us place and identity.[76] Characters in the plays are trapped in webs partly of their own inadvertent devising, which also, in the best of circumstances, empower them. Bound by and to their "character" and their history, they are limited in their capacities of perception and reflection, attached to particular blindnesses in which they have no small stake. Yet they (and the audience perhaps more so) are able to see their blindness and so draw upon and extend the modes of discourse and practices that would otherwise simply ensnare them.

To think this way is to both recognize how insidious the division between inside and outside can be and to see that we may not be able to live without it or the social "facts" it describes. Insofar as we care most for those with whom we share a common life, a life that constitutes our being including our capacity for freedom and deliberation, there will be those who are with us and those who are not, those who are like us and those who are different. Of course, differences need not, ought not—and, given contemporary weaponry, cannot—be allowed to translate into what Dostoevski's Grand Inquisitor calls the "craving for community worship" for which men have "slain each other with the sword." And there may be times when such divisions become incidental, as in the reconciliation between Priam and Achilles, which is what I shall call a "Theoretical Moment."

In certain respects the tragedians are, like Foucault, suspicious of any theoretical impulse. They warn about the tyranny of mind with its pas-

---

[76] See Connolly's discussion of the "paradox of articulation" in his *Politics and Ambiguity*. I think Connolly is right about the paradox, but I am not sure Foucault saw it as clearly, at least in his more "theoretical" writings. Of course, Nietzsche did, in large part, I am arguing, because of his profound knowledge of Greek tragedy.

sion to transform enigmas into problems with solutions, dissolve mystery, and impose one voice on debate. There is Agamemnon gagging Iphigenia, Oedipus boasting of his self-generating intellectual prowess, Pentheus vainly imprisoning what he sees as other and anarchic. It is at least suggestive that Dionysus, the god of tragedy and a democratic god (in the sense of rejecting hierarchies based on gender, class, and race) is antitheoretical in his distrust of intellectual ordering and the restraints of reason. It has been argued that there are no theories of democracy in classical Athens (with the possible exception of Protagoras's in Plato's dialogue), because the Athenians had democratic practices.[77] It may also be true that they had no such theory because theory reduces what it makes intelligible.

But in other respects the tragedians legitimate the impulse while theorists like Thucydides and Plato incorporate the suspicion. If true, then classical political theorists themselves anticipate the criticism Foucault levels at theory. They may even provide an example of theorizing that is not totalizing, and offer an immanent critique of the general intellectuals he supposes them to be. That such theorizing emerges as an extension of democratic politics makes perfect sense.

[77] That is the argument of Donald Kagan, *The Great Dialogue: History of Greek Political Thought from Homer to Polybius* (New York: The Free Press, 1965), chap. 5.

TWO

The Road Not Taken

IN THE opening scene of the *Eumenides*, the Priestess refers to the Athenians[1] as road builders (*keleuthopoioi*) who, in honor of Apollo, "transformed a wilderness into a land no longer wild" (924–25). Literally *keleuthos* means road, track, or path on land or sea; metaphorically it indicates a way of life. (The word can also mean journey, voyage, or a way of walking.) This suggests that the Athenians have, in alliance with the god, defined a way of life as well as a human place; that they have charted a moral and political wilderness as well as a physical one. Where before darkness and confusion reined, there is now light and order. When Athena establishes the Areopagus to stand with her in the determination of justice, she and her citizens are completing a path begun by their ancestors and retraced by Orestes. The founding of the city is nothing less than the creation of a cosmogony.[2] Or so it seems.

The language and imagery of paths and ways, of journeys and gaits, of boundaries and definitions is familiar in Greek poetry and philosophy. Oedipus fulfills the oracle at the crossroads, is marked (literally and metaphorically) by his gait, and transgresses the most sacred natural boundaries. In the *Bacchae* Dionysus too is a traveler coming home (to rescue the honor of his mother), and is a confounder of cultural demarcations. Thucydides' Pericles boasts that the Athenians have compelled every sea and land to be the highway of (or more precisely grant access to) their daring, and the *Republic* is a path upward from the Piraeus to the theory of the Forms. Finally the idea of a journey reminds us of the *theōros*, who was a traveler sent to witness the practices of other *poleis* or an ambassador to Delphic Apollo, and of *nostos* with its meaning of returning home after a perilous voyage.

---

[1] She identifies the Athenians as Hephastus's sons (line 10) which echoes the beginning of Clytaemnestra's speech explaining how she knew of Troy's fall (281).

[2] On the *Oresteia* as the creation of a cosmogony, see Nancy S. Rabinowitz, "From Force to Persuasion: Aeschylus's *Oresteia* as Cosmogonic Myth," *Ramus* 10, no. 2 (1981): 159–91. Traditionally, she argues, cosmogonies move "from mixed and undifferentiated matter to an ordered world. Creation is thus a process of separation and organization of formerly confused elements. Just as traditionally, however, chaos continues to exist on the *borders* of the newly created world; and there is always the danger that chaos may erupt and challenge the newborn order" (p. 159). I will return to this issue at the end of chapter 3 when I discuss the trilogy's concluding scene.

No sooner is the Priestess finished celebrating the peaceful transfer of authority (*oude pros bian tinos*) from an older female goddess to a younger male god and the civilizing of the wilderness than she is confronted by the wild Furies. Their fearsome presence interrupts the scene's serenity, compromises the narrative of an orderly transfer of power between generations and sexes, and raises questions about who and what is excluded from the triumph of civilization the trilogy purportedly portrays.[3]

When the Furies complain that Orestes has escaped their net and vow to pursue him until they bind him fast, they are elaborating a set of images that have been introduced in the *Agamemnon*[4] and that work to undercut those of road building and boundary making. While the latter suggest freedom and control, nets, webs, and snares enclose and constrict, imprisoning action and strangling life itself. One might even say that men are bound by their bonds in the sense of obligated and tied up by what not only connects them to others but what also constrains them. Certainly they now appear as victims and subjects, baffled by the ambiguities of silence as well as of speech,[5] enveloped by fact and evidence, which never are quite as they seem. Trapped by the rhetorical virtuosity of his wife and by his own character, Agamemnon walks upon the rich tapestry and into a fearsome net of ruin. And he is hardly the only one caught in the play of power and powerlessness, road building, and losing one's way. There is Oedipus, who remains bound to the fate he fled; Pentheus, who would imprison all that is other but is instead enslaved to the passions and the god he would incarcerate; Thucydides' Athenians, whose boundless empire turns them into victims of the laws of power over which they have no power; Socrates, who is accused of violating the boundaries between heaven and earth and politics and philosophy; and Plato, whose *Republic* brings both impulses to their apogee without resolution.

[3] Rabinowitz, ibid., argues that the Priestess's new version of the Pythian foundation myth (which ignores Apollo's battle with Delphyne or Python and invents a new recipient of the oracle, Phoibe, who "eases the transfer of power from female to male" [p. 182]) indicates how the challenge of the Furies will be met. I think the violent transfer of power is as much covered up as overcome. This has obvious implications for how one reads the happy ending.

[4] Clytaemnestra speaks of the net with which she trapped Agamemnon, and uses nets and tapestries or robes (*heima, peplos*) as weapons. She calls the unrolled tapestry *poros*, whose metaphorical meanings include the ways in which men's minds control their surroundings. The words she uses for net at line 1382 (*amphiblēstron*) can also mean embrace and is thus an example of the way bonds are binding (on this, see Rabinowitz, ibid., pp. 173–74).

[5] John Herington, *Poetry into Drama: Early Tragedy and the Greek Poetic Tradition*, Sather Classical Lectures (Berkeley and Los Angeles: University of California Press, 1985), p. 125, speaks of the "appalling atmosphere of ambiguity and dread that shades and colors so much of the tragic landscape."

In the *Eumenides* Apollo is the champion of Orestes and the implacable enemy of the Furies. Yet his name suggests an affinity with his enemies, an affinity that elaborates the tension between achievement and transgression at the play's opening. These connections are present in Cassandra's *Apollon Apollon aguiat', apollōn emos* (1085). *Apollon* suggests one who lays waste or utterly destroys. Yet Apollo is the god of healing invoked to celebrate moments of joy and triumph. Her cry then reminds us of the unwanted darker significance that attends healing celebrations (including, presumably, the one with which the trilogy concludes).[6] And it reminds us of the simultaneity of justice and transgression, accomplishment and ruin, health and disease, insight and blindness, reason and tyranny that mark both Greek tragedy and political theory.

Perhaps the most concentrated treatment of these themes is found in the "choral ode to man" in *Antigone*. The "stage" is set by Creon's fury at the mere suggestion that the gods might be involved in the mysterious burying of Eteocles, at those citizens who continue to rear back against his "yoke," and at the guards whom he is sure have been bribed. It is after Creon's violent threats that the chorus sings men's praises.

"Many wonders (marvels, awesome things) are there, but none is more wondrous (strange, powerful, awful) than man" (*Polla ta deina, kouden anthrōpou deinoteron pelei*, 332). Humans are, at one and the same time, powerful and inventive beyond all other creatures, and destroyers as they create and of what they create, killers of what they love most, out of harmony with themselves and out of keeping with their surroundings. Awesome and terrifying, in control yet uncontrollable, they are masters of nature but unable to master themselves. This double edge recapitulates the tensions of the *Eumenides'* opening scene and is elaborated in the ode's subsequent images.

In the *Eumenides* men had built roads to tame a wilderness; here the chorus speaks of making paths through even the most turbulent seas and of wearing away the goddess Earth with ploughs. Yet Creon pilots the ship of state, Haemon speaks of the need to slacken sails in a storm, and Thebes is likened to a harbor of death. And, insofar as the sea was a symbol of elemental passions and storms of madness, Creon's speech and actions that preface the code hardly promise control.[7]

Not only can man master the sea and the land, he can snare birds, catch fish in "the twisted mesh of his nets" (to use Wycoff's translation), and yoke horses and bulls. Yet once again the boast is undercut by the image

[6] See the discussion of this point and the place of oxymora in tragedy in George B. Walsh, *The Varieties of Enchantment* (Chapel Hill: University of North Carolina Press, 1984), p. 71 and passim.

[7] There is a fine discussion of these points and of the ode in Charles Segal, "Sophocles' Praise of Man and the Conflicts of the Antigone," *Arion* 3 (1964): 46–66.

of Antigone as a bird and birds feeding on the exposed body of Eteocles; by the twisted net Creon weaves for himself and by the yoke he would impose on all those who refuse to follow his commands. Next, men are celebrated for having taught themselves language, thought, and civic sentiments. Cities, like homes, are shelters against the forces of nature. Indeed, though men cannot escape death, they can prolong life through the invention of cures for once incurable illnesses. This clever skillful creature need never face the future helpless. Yet again each claim is compromised. What good is language if men do not listen? What good is thought if men are thoughtless? Of what use is practical wisdom when excesses transform wisdom into delusions?

The chorus recognizes the moral ambiguity of the cleverness they have just praised, and when Antigone enters with the guards, the recognition assumes an "ontological" status. Reacting to what they see before them, to the strangeness of man they have been recounting, and to the necessary conjoining of progress and impiety, their mind "is split as this awful sight." The problem then is not just that unattended roads become rutted and impassable, but that the very building of them is a kind of transgression.

One could even argue that tragedy itself replicated the tension in the opening scene of the *Eumenides* and the choral ode to man. After all tragedy was an Athenian invention and, as such, an institution that helped tame the wilderness. In this aspect it too brought form to public spaces that defined it and that it helped define. Yet tragedy is distinctive in its interrogation of the achievement to which it contributes. Aristotle gives a sense of this when, in the *Poetics* (1455b), he describes the plot of a play as a combination of *desis* (binding or fettering), and *lusis* (unbinding, loosening, setting free), "which in its complex form he calls sumplokē," an interweaving which "describes the fabric, the texture of the play."[8] Contemporary critics, such as Vernant and Segal, have gone further in arguing that tragedy simultaneously validates established cultural boundaries and "problematizes" if not dissolves them. Bounded by the conventions of theater and festival, tragedy demonstrated the dangers of impiety and overconfidence within a coherent set of symbols representative of the divine and human order. Yet the violence of the action, the inversion of the "natural," the radical questioning of human and divine justice, the betrayal of trust and friendship, and the perversion of speech together with the corruption of public and private morality as a whole, all stretched the coherence of that "order" to its limits.[9] As assumed and

[8] See the discussion of this point in Froma Zeitlin, "Playing the Other: Theater, Theatricality, and the Feminine in Greek Drama," *Representations* 11 (Summer 1985): 74.

[9] The general point has been emphasized particularly by Charles Segal. See especially his *Interpreting Greek Tragedy: Myth, Poetry, Text* (Ithaca, N.Y.: Cornell University Press,

assured demarcations are confounded, confidence in what one knows and how one knows it is eroded. As settled categories dissolve or reveal themselves as distorting masks, reason loses its hold and foresight its reliability.

A similar tension exists in Plato's *Republic* suggested by a parallel between the structure of the first book of the *Republic* and the ideal state. The first interlocutor we meet is Cephalus. As a man whose life has been dedicated to gaining possessions and making money, he would belong to the lowest class, those furthest removed from power. (In this respect it is significant that Cephalus is not part of the subsequent discussions.) The second interlocutor is Polemarchus, whose view of justice as helping friends and harming enemies makes him an ideal warrior. He is, potentially, the well-bred dog, fierce to his enemies and kind to his friends, useful when guided by philosophy, dangerous when left on his own. If the symmetry between the sequence of interlocutors in book 1 and the order of the ideal city were to continue, we would expect a philosopher to be the next interlocutor. But instead we get the would-be tyrant Thrasymachus. There are several reasons for this but one has to do with the affinities between tyranny and philosophy (or what Foucault calls global theory). It is an affinity anticipated by Aeschylus's Agamemnon and Sophocles' Creon in *Antigone*.

Agamemnon must decide between sacrificing his daughter so the ships can sail and disbanding the army, thereby avoiding the sacrilegious sacrifice of his daughter. Clearly he has no innocent alternative and he knows it, at least in the beginning. But once he *has* chosen, he pretends there was no choice; having murdered Iphigenia, he forgets her. The gag he places in her mouth before the altar silences those obligations to house and respect for generation that makes a world and man whole. Having killed this innocent child, he is "free" to murder the innocent children at Troy. Having dissolved his dilemma, he cannot learn from the pain that memory of it could inspire. As Martha Nussbaum has recently argued, self-knowledge and political deliberation depend on "an honest effort to do justice to all aspects of a hard case, seeing and feeling it in all its conflicting many-sidedness."[10]

Not to do so is to ignore the ways in which human beings are powerful and vulnerable, active and passive, free yet subject to forces they do not make but which go towards making them whatever they will be praised or blamed for being. In these terms the tyrannical impulses displayed by Agamemnon after the sacrifice (but present in us all) are not simply man-

1985), p. 25 and passim; and "Greek Tragedy and Society: A Structuralist Perspective," in *Greek Tragedy and Political Theory*, ed. J. Peter Euben (Berkeley and Los Angeles: University of California Press, 1986), pp. 43–75.

[10] Martha Nussbaum, *The Fragility of Goodness: Luck and Ethics in Greek Tragedy and Philosophy* (Cambridge: Cambridge University Press, 1986), p. 45.

THE ROAD NOT TAKEN

ifestations of a desire for more but are, also, rage at the vulnerability and passivity that thwarts human power. Time and again tragedy's characters (and cities) reject, turn away from, or seek to resolve in transcendent unity the complexity of life and thought evident in Agamemnon's dilemma. When they "succeed," they live an impoverished life and a dangerous one too. Ignoring what they push aside or behind, they embrace a part as if it were the whole.

Tragedy also portrays the attractions of simplifying, harmonizing, and freeing oneself from the guilt and remorse imposed by practical choices in a complex moral universe. "The impulse to create a solution to the problem of conflict," Nussbaum continues, is "present within tragedy as a human possibility." Alongside the tragic view, tragedy also discloses "the origins of the denial of that view. These two views illuminate and define one another, so that we have not fully understood the 'tragic view' if we have not understood why it has been found intolerably painful by certain ambitious rational beings."[11]

Creon has good reason to be preoccupied with order. Thebes has barely survived a civil war in which brother slew brother. Authority is uncertain, relief is mingled with continued apprehension. But the legitimate concern with order goes too far and order becomes everything. As it does, "politics" becomes a matter of command and obedience and Creon becomes the only voice listening only to itself, the only one with wisdom among others whom he assumes are self-centered and self-aggrandizing. As he pares down and pushes away one group after another (he will not be ruled by women, by the young, by his fellow citizens, or even by the gods until he has second thoughts after Teiresias leaves), he isolates and disempowers himself. The man who insists on total power to maintain complete order is powerless to save the city and is, instead, its active destroyer. Seeking mastery, he winds up a helpless victim. Creon's fate gives substance to Arendt's claim (based on her reading of the Greeks) that power is necessarily collective and that a political order presupposed a plurality of voices and points of view.[12] It also gives substance to the idea that the impulse toward tyranny comes not simply from what is basest in us, but from what is most admirable[13]—our drive for political and intellectual

---

[11] Ibid., p. 50.

[12] Her view of power is put forth in *The Human Condition* (Chicago: University of Chicago Press, 1974), pt. 5, sections 27–28, pp. 192–207, and in her essay "On Violence," in *Crises of the Republic* (New York: Harcourt, Brace, Jovanovich, 1972), 2: 134–55.

[13] Here is Ivan in Dostoevski's story of the Grand Inquisitor: "Why can there not be among them one martyr oppressed by the great sorrow and loving humanity? You see, only suppose that there was one such man among all those who desire nothing but filthy material gain—if there's only one like my old inquisitor, who had himself eaten roots in the desert and made frenzied efforts to subdue his flesh to make himself free and perfect" (*The Grand Inquisitor on the Nature of Man*, trans. Constance Garnett in the Library of Liberal Arts edition [Indianapolis, Ind.: Bobbs-Merrill, 1945]).

order, our power to define and bound the world in ways that provide both certainty and security. No doubt Creon illustrates the base motives Aristotle attributed to tyrants in the *Politics*.[14] But to leave it at that is to simplify the problem of tyranny and miss its affinities with philosophy and political theory as that is presented and represented by the *Republic*.

The problem Creon confronts, and the temptation to which he succumbs, confronts and tempts political theory as well. Theory arises, and is a response to, periods of political and intellectual disorder, when what were once thought to be natural and god-sanctioned boundaries and categories come to seem contrived, if not perverse.[15] Like Creon, the challenge is to reconstitute an order; like Creon, the temptation is to believe order is all and you alone can establish it.

One can read the *Republic* as an attempt to impose form (or forms) on a disintegrating polis and the moral chaos embodied in the sophistic "enlightenment." Certainly the assertion that Plato was so overwhelmed by the pathology of disorder that he had recourse to implausible metaphysics and totalitarian politics is familiar enough. But this is at best half the story, for we can say about the *Republic* what Nussbaum says about tragedy—that it presents the tyrannical impulse toward certainty and security as a possibility, but that alongside it is an immanent critique of that possibility. There are two views of philosophy in the *Republic*, the one practiced by Socrates and the interlocutors, the other the vision of philosophy they agree upon in the course of their discussion. Each illuminates, defines, and interrogates the other. If we have not understood the force and attractions of one, we will not understand the force and seductiveness of the other. All this suggests that the tension we find in the *Eumenides*, the choral ode, and tragedy reappears in political theory or philosophy.

THE CHAPTERS that follow will explore these themes by considering three substantive issues: justice, identity, and membership, and, through them, the relationship between tragedy and theory. My approach is to pair chapters comparing a tragedy with a theory. Thus justice is the subject of chapter 3 on the *Oresteia* and 8 on the *Republic*; identity is the topic of chapters 4 on the *Oedipus Tyrannos* and 7 on the *Apology of*

---

[14] 1313a17–1316b27. But as Aristotle suggests, tyranny is not always or simply a term of condemnation.

[15] Michael Walzer (writing about sixteenth- and seventeenth-century England) describes the disorder as a "slow erosion of the old symbols, a wasting away of the feelings they once evoked, an increasingly disjointed and inconsistent expression of political ideas, a nervous insistence upon the old units and reference—all this accompanied, willy nilly, by a more and more arbitrary and extravagant manipulation of them until finally the units cease to be acceptable as intellectual givens and the references cease to be meaningful" ("On the Role of Symbolism in Political Thought," *Political Science Quarterly* 82 [June 1967]: 198).

Socrates; membership (or rather "dismembership") is the concern of chapters 5 on the *Bacchae* and 6 on Thucydides' *History*. Although individual chapters and pairings focus on one issue, the other issues and pairings are always present by way of context and by implication. Let me elaborate.

The *Oresteia* is about justice—about where, how, why, and by whom boundaries between spheres of activity, principles, and social groups are rightly conceived and instituted. It presents justice as the noblest achievement of civilization and Athens as the most civilized city. It is Athens that provides impetus and place for otherwise warring principles or forces to join in a unity that enhances the distinctive contribution of each to the whole. Moreover, a just man, woman, or city, unlike an Agamemnon who obliterates his daughter's pitiful cries from hearing and heart, is committed not only to order but to the recognition of what that order necessarily silences and sacrifices. Justice is "morally" precarious because of such exclusions; it is "politically"[16] so because it depends on reconciling passions that threaten to split it asunder. Thus justice must be continually rewon and reconstituted.[17]

The *Republic* is also about justice; about where, who, why, and by whom boundaries between spheres of activity and social categories are rightly conceived and instituted. Much of the dialogue is an effort to define what is rightly common and what is one's own and the degree to which class, gender, and wealth are relevant categories in the assignment and exercise of power. Once again justice provides impetus and place for otherwise antagonistic forces (whether in the soul or state) to enhance both the social efficiency and moral efficacy of the community. For reasons analogous to those found in the *Oresteia*, the establishment of justice in the *Republic* is precarious.

Like justice, identity is a matter of boundaries and distinctions. "Who" someone "is" is a matter of their distinctiveness, of how they "characteristically" speak and act, how they present themselves. "Action and speech," Hannah Arendt writes, "contain an answer to the question asked of every newcomer: 'Who are you?' " In acting and speaking, men and women "show who they are, reveal actively their unique personal identities and thus make their appearance in the human world." One's identity is implicit in everything one says and does but is almost never the product of willful purpose. On the contrary, "it is more than likely that

---

[16] I put morally and politically in quotes because the distinction that seems obvious to us was not to the Greeks.

[17] This does not preclude the *Oresteia* from being mysogynist, although I think the play helps create a sensibility able to see that (much as American commitments to equality provide a language in which inequalities *can* be attacked even if, for various reasons, they are not).

the 'who' which appears so clearly and unmistakenly to others, remains hidden from the person himself, like the daimon in Greek religion which accompanies each man throughout his life, always looking over his shoulder from behind and thus visible only to those he [or she] encounters."[18]

One's identity also involves where one can "normally" be found or discovered. To identify someone is to "place" them in a location or story, to recognize and name them, to "re-member" who they are and where they fit in some larger scheme as mortals and citizens, men and women, parents and children, Greeks or barbarians, Athenians or Thebans. To identify someone is a claim to have knowledge of who they are (as recognize implies) and where they come from, what Oedipus does not know about himself.

A just man or women, whether in the *Oresteia* or *Republic*, is able to identify things and others rightly and to judge where they stand in relation to each other. To recognize (realize and acknowledge) specific others in relation to oneself is to speak and listen to them in ways that respect them as distinctive sources of experience, meaning, and value even as one sees aspects of oneself in them. This is what *Antigone*'s Creon, *Agamemnon*'s Argos, and the Athenians at Melos did not do. Because they did not, their political and moral landscape became flat and undifferentiated. Everything seemed comparable with everything else; each character and every action seemed part of a homogeneous system of mechanical revenge that denies distinct identities.[19] In this sense the absence of justice is also the loss of identity, a connection made chillingly obvious in the concentration camps.

Whereas questions of identity are present in the *Oresteia*, they are "foregrounded" in the *Oedipus Tyrannos*. That play is about "who" we are, the ways in which we fashion our own identities and have them given to us, how it is we come to think about ourselves as fashioners of our identities, and why, as a result, we act in the ways we do. More concretely, it is concerned with who we are as beings born in particular times and places, to particular parents and members of distinct communities.

Oedipus, of course, does not know who his people or parents are. Ignorant of his origins and beginnings, he does not know where he comes from or where he is going (in particular and in general), and so what he is doing. He supposes himself the son of Polybus and Merope, then glories in the prospect of being the offspring of Tyche, only to discover in "the end" that he is the son of his wife, the murderer of his father, and the brother of his daughters. By collapsing all difference into a perverse unity

---

[18] Arendt, *The Human Condition*, pp. 178–80.

[19] "Metaphors," George Walsh writes, "proliferate and combine in the *Agamemnon*, they produce a network of likeness and associations that make everything seem comparable to everything else" (*The Varieties of Enchantment*, p. 73).

of being, this always three-footed man has compressed past, present, and future in the staff that is his constant support and his fate.

If Bernard Knox is right, then the play is also about the political identity of Athens. "Oedipus Tyrannos then is more than an individual tragic hero. In his title, tyrannos, in the nature and basis of his power, in his character, and in the mode of his dramatic action, he resembles Athens, the city which aimed to become . . . the tyrannos of Greece.[20] Knox goes on to argue that because Athens was the center of Greek intellectual life, the question, Who is Oedipus? becomes two questions: Who are the Athenians and Who is man? That, of course, is the answer to the sphinx's question and the subject of the choral ode in *Antigone*.

I think the play is also about the identity of tragedy. It calls attention to what tragedy is, the preconditions of its performance and the ways in which human beings ineffectively but persistently construct words to capture its lessons. Tragedy was a spectacle performed before an audience of spectators. The *Oedipus Tyrannos* is notable for the pervasiveness of its sight imagery and for the way a character, Oedipus, refers to and offers himself as a spectacle to the audience in the play. This has a double effect; it creates something like a play within a play and, through a kind of inversion, reminds the audience watching that they too will be actors judged by audiences in their capacity as actors outside the theater. Because tragedy was also part of a festival honoring the gods, the chorus's reflections on prideful men who disregard gods and justice—"If deeds like this are held in honor why should I join the sacred dance" (*ei gar hai toiaide praxeis timiai, ti dei me choreuein* 895–96)—call attention to the context of tragedy's performance and what religious skepticism means for it. Finally, Oedipus's calm assumption and then aggressive assertion of his capacity to create a consistent harmonious world impervious to the intrusion of tragedy fail. He (and we) can no more insulate himself than he can run away from the fate his character provides. The irony of the attempt and the force of its failure suggest two things: our knowledge of the world depends on a knowledge of the self; and self-knowledge remains elusive, except perhaps for blind men out of power.

In the opening lines of the *Apology* Socrates complains that his accusers have argued so persuasively that they almost made him forget his own identity (*egō d'oun kai autos hup autōn oligou emautou epelathomēn, outō pitheanōs elegon*). What follows is a defense against his accusers and

---

[20] In *Oedipus at Thebes* (New York: W. W. Norton, 1970), p. 99. I think Knox's identification of Oedipus with Athens too direct and his identification of Thebes with Athens overstated for reasons Froma Zeitlin gives in "Thebes: Theater of Self and Society in Athenian Drama," in Euben, *Greek Tragedy and Political Theory*, pp. 101–41.

an effort to define "who" he is, for others and for himself.[21] Because what is characteristic of and distinctive to Socrates is the kind of life he leads (and the sort of death he now chooses), his identity involves the practice and fate of philosophy. But almost immediately Socrates reverses the challenge and puts Athens and politics on trial. Then the question is no longer who is Socrates and the nature of his philosophical activity, but who are the Athenians and what is the nature of political activity? Socrates castigates his compatriots for their failure to live up to their own self-understanding and criticizes their political practices. He (and philosophy) urges the Athenians to consider their actions in terms of their ideals and, insofar as those ideals are themselves embedded in a corrupt conception of politics, to reconsider the understanding of politics as well. In these terms philosophy and politics are defined in terms of and against each other, and Socrates' identity is defined in terms of the tensions between them. Socrates comes to understand himself (and political philosophy) as the culmination *and* chief critic of "the" Athenian political and intellectual tradition as that was shaped by tragedy. Like Oedipus, he comes to see something about his parentage—that Athens is father to philosophy, even if philosophy and the city may have to go their separate ways.

Of course, Oedipus and Socrates are men of very different temperaments who find themselves in quite different circumstances.[22] Yet for all their differences the two "share the same god [Apollo] in the same function of search and discovery."[23] Each is possessed with seeking the truth amid appearance, pretense, and mere plausibility no matter what the cost to themselves. Both investigate and question, seeking to clarify and to reveal, driven on by the injunction (and warning) "know thyself," which they transform from platitude to precept. As they do, both rediscover their mortality, partiality, and origins—one as the son of Laius and Jocasta, the other as a son of Athens. Challenged to solve Apollo's riddles (Who is the murderer of Laius? and How can a man sure only of his ignorance be most wise?), each becomes the gods' spokesman. And though Socrates does not pollute Athens the way Oedipus did Thebes, he

---

[21] The *Apology* is about "who" Socrates is in Arendt's sense but with this difference: he, like Achilles, chooses the conditions of his death and so, to a degree others cannot, he can tell his own story.

[22] The issue is complicated by the fact that Oedipus is a character in a way that Socrates is not (although Socrates *is* a character in a drama written by Plato). Because Oedipus hardly "speaks for" Sophocles, it is possible for a disparity between Oedipus and Socrates to unite Sophocles and Socrates. (In the less "historical" dialogues such as the *Republic*, where Socrates is more of a character and less of a spokesman for Plato, the matter is more complicated still.

[23] Alister Cameron, *The Identity of Oedipus the King* (New York: New York University Press, 1968), p. 18.

too is regarded as violating natural boundaries. Finally, although Socrates does not kill his father[24] or marry his mother, he does confound his city's division between public and private by refusing to be political in the accepted ways and places.[25]

In the *Oresteia* and *Republic* justice entails reconciling otherwise warring parties and principles into a whole that enhances the respective powers of each. In the *Oedipus Tyrannos* and *Apology*, identity emerges in an answer to the question, Who are you? To identify someone is, as I have said, to define what distinguishes them from others: their character and characteristics, their words and deeds, the place and people that gave them life. But identity is not simply a matter of distinguishing someone from others; it is also to identify them with the others from whom they are being distinguished. For who we are is as much a matter of describing the community we belong to as the traits or actions that separate us from others in that community. Identity then is a matter of singularity and plurality, of standing with as well as standing apart, of political membership.

To be a member of a just community is to belong to a whole that enhances the respective powers of each it has helped shape through education and participation in the community's affairs. It is to give one a place and home where one's words and deeds are honored in life and commemorated in death, a community, in Tocqueville's phrase, or the dead, living, and unborn. The *Bacchae* is about being a member: in the political community of mythical Thebes, in the ecstatic community led by Dionysus, in the community of onlookers in the theater of Dionysus, and in the democratic community of Athens.

But the central dramatic image of the play is not the granting of membership to a group (such as the Furies), or a generous conception of membership (as in the concluding festival in the *Oresteia*), but the dismembership of Pentheus and Thebes. Pentheus is a young king who defines membership as obedience and defies the god (even when the signs of his divinity are incontrovertible) in part because of that definition. He is also literal-minded, blind to the hidden meaning of words and the symbolic significance of actions. This too is an aspect of his unyielding conception of membership, which suggests that our ideas of belonging and community are tied to the richness or poverty with which we read the world.

Like Pentheus, Thebes is a city divided against itself, trapped by categorical oppositions that actually categorize nothing, by divisions which

---

[24] But the *Crito* does raise the question of patricide since the laws call themselves Socrates' parents.

[25] There is another dimension to this comparison. If Knox is right in arguing that Oedipus's character is that of Athens, then the comparison between Oedipus and Socrates (as well as that between Sophocles and Socrates) is also a comparison between political philosophy on one hand and Athenian politics and tragedy on the other.

turn out to be artificial yet dangerous, by polarities that presuppose an identity, and by hierarchies that collapse with a breath of resistance or imagination. Thebes has no place for Dionysus or for theater, and so no space or prescribed time when it can "interrogate" its normalizing practices and discourse.

The play not only focuses on the actual dismemberment of Pentheus and Thebes. It is also concerned with membership in an ecstatic community, and with the potential dismemberment of the community of spectators as well as an Athenian community exhausted by a protracted war.

Dismemberment occurs when the forces and principles united in the *Oresteia* revert to annihilating each other, as at Argos in the *Agamemnon*. The *Bacchae* inverts the closing scene of the trilogy. In it and in mythical Thebes instinctive forces and primitive drives surge up through the legal and political structure, itself now an overlay of hollow forms and trite pieties, to destroy the city.

More dramatically, dismemberment of a body or body politic involves a violent rending of whole into parts. It evokes images of civil war, madness and death, of identities confounded or lost. While Oedipus is recognizably the same man at the end of the *Oedipus Tyrannos* as he was in the beginning, Pentheus is utterly transformed. "We see in his costume and madness," William Arrowsmith writes, "not merely his complete humiliation but the total loss of identity the change implies."[26] The same is true of Athens as portrayed by Thucydides.

Thucydides' portrait of the civil war at Corcyra provides a vividly concentrated image of dismemberment under the pitiless pounding of battle and war. The moral bankruptcy, frenzied passions, and limitless carnage that surface there with such ferocity disclose the underside of civilization and the eventual outcome of those heroic achievements of mind and deed that give the world human impress. It also discloses what the absence of justice and the loss of identity means for individuals and cities.

The *stasis* at Corcyra is connected with the fate of Athens. The civil war there is dramatically and linguistically linked to the plague at Athens. The plague is itself an implicit commentary on the funeral oration and establishes an analogy between the corruption or dismemberment of the body and of the body politic. In addition, the later *stasis* at Athens is the only other convulsion to receive extended treatment.[27] That Athens is the animating power and principal subject of the *History* recalls the (now) Eumenides' prayer (976–77) that "Civil War fattening on men's ruin shall

[26] This is from his introduction to the *Bacchae*, (New York: Washington Square Press, 1969), p. 152.

[27] Whether Thucydides is right about Athens is another matter. A good case can be made that it was more factionalized before Pericles' death than Thucydides suggests and that it was less factionalized (and more stable) after his death than he indicates.

not thunder in our city" (Lattimore's translation) and Knox's claim that the tyranny in *Oedipus Tyrannos* is that of Athens. These road builders who have tamed what was wild, making every sea and land the highway of their daring, are no more able to keep the wild outside than Pentheus was in the *Bacchae*.

The Corcyrean revolution is tied not only to the fate of Athens but to that of the entire Hellenic world. It was, we are told, a preview of the brutal excesses that later revolutions would refine with perverse ingenuity. So what we see here is a disease that worsens as its infection spreads. More than that, Corcyra is a crucial stage in the continuing collapse of the admittedly imperfect Hellenic unity in the Persian wars. When that war ended, war between the Greek cities began. As this war continued, war within cities began, eventually becoming a war of all against all. As everyone became a potential enemy, the only trustworthy friend was one-self and the only sane party was a party of one. When Plato suggests that we are often our own worst enemies (never more so than when seeking domination), it is a coda to Thucydides' story of the dismemberment of Hellas summed up and anticipated by Corcyra.

The Corcyrean revolution is the occasion for Thucydides' most general and direct statement about war, human nature, and civilization. In part of that statement he talks about the way language too became dismembered. So one could interpret Thucydides' *History* as an effort to maintain the integrity of language against the temptation to instrumentalize it in the way religion, family, party, and rhetoric were during the civil war. Or, to put it more accurately, one could argue that Thucydides is trying to sustain conditions within the text that make political deliberation and moral discourse possible outside it, whether among his readers or future actors. In this sense he is trying to repair, in the context of his work, the frayed moral discourse that shapes the initial debate between Corcyra and Corinth, a discourse that is barely present at Mytilene and Plataea and has disappeared by the time of Corcyra and Melos.[28]

THROUGH and alongside my consideration of justice, identity, and dismembership I want to make two arguments: one about the continuities between Greek tragedy and classical political theory; the other about the "usefulness" of such theory when approached through tragedy for "grounding" contemporary theory. Both arguments are initially implausible.

The first argument has to confront the uncomfortable fact that Thucydides defines his project in opposition to the poets; Socrates indicts them

[28] See the subtle discussion of this point in James Boyd White, *When Words Lose Their Meaning* (Chicago: University of Chicago Press, 1984), chap. 3.

for their ignorance and insists, against them, that no harm can come to a good man; and Plato banishes poetry from the ideal state (except under the most stringent conditions) while presenting a fully intelligible cosmos overseen by fully moral gods. In this world no one would be confronted by contradictory obligations as was Agamemnon, be urged to matricide as was Orestes, commit incest and patricide as Oedipus did, or be dismembered by his mother as was Pentheus.

It also has to confront the fact that tragedy was a formal part of public life, whereas political theory was not, and that drama evolved as a democratic institution, whereas political theory arose as a critique of its corruption. In addition, for all its exploration of questions about mortality, fate, freedom, and wisdom, tragedy remained tied to the politics of a specific human community. With Thucydides, Socrates, and Plato, these ties become as much a subject for critical reflection as a precondition for it. Finally, although tragedy was self-reflective, it was so only implicitly and indirectly. History is at least part of Thucydides' subject, and philosophy is clearly a central preoccupation of the *Apology* and *Republic*. Political theorists are metatheorists in ways the classical tragedians are not metadramatists.

Although I will challenge the interpretation of the *History, Apology,* and *Republic* that I think exaggerates the differences between tragedy and theory, as well as the view of political theory such exaggerations sustain, I have no intention of explaining these differences away. Rather I will consider them in terms of my discussion of identity. If identity is a matter of describing the community to which one belongs and the characteristics that distinguish one within it, then one can say that classical political theorists defined their enterprise in terms of their relationship to tragedy. Only if we recognize how pervasive an influence tragedy was can we appreciate how much theory took its form, content, and status from the critique of tragedy.

The second argument must confront the sorts of objections raised by Holmes and Ignatieff. Given massive changes in social structure, moral sentiments, and political practices, justice, identity, and membership mean different things for us than they did for the Greeks.[29] For instance, the force of the *Bacchae*'s image of dismemberment is less arresting for us because being "civilized," we find ritual sacrifice of the kind associated with Dionysian ritual appalling.[30] No doubt we find Empedocles' descrip-

[29] One could say the same for our understanding of justice in which men and women uprooted from place and people are seen as unmediated individuals who must be treated equally and impartially, and of identity that is conceived either in these deracinated terms or as discursively constructed.

[30] The tearing to pieces (*sparagmos*) and eating raw meat (*ōmophagia*) of a goat fawn or bull was a ritual element in Dionysiac worship. It was intended to bring the worshiper as

tion of the Cosmos as ruled by Strife, which dismembers, and Love, which reassembles what has been torn apart, as quaint,[31] and Aristotle's likening of analysis and synthesis to the sacrifice of an ox[32] as a primitive residue. But most importantly, we regard political membership as largely a matter of laws and procedures, rights and entitlements, voluntary participation and cross-cutting pressures. Whereas their language was one of friendship and fraternity, ours is one of contract and self-interest. "Liberal society, Michael Walzer wrote some years ago, "is conceived as a voluntary association of private men, egoists and families of egoists, a world not of friends and comrades but of strangers."[33] Whereas we insist on a distinction between state and society in order to subject the state to social control and free society and its individual members from the restraints of active citizenship and patriotic fervor, the Greeks knew no such distinction. Finally, whereas they regarded analogies between the body and "body politic" as natural (as in the *Republic*'s analogy between the city and soul), most of us regard the phrase as a literary conceit, and so lose the language of mortality (but not growth) to think about political matters.[34]

Because our conception of political membership is less demanding (or less liberal); because we tend to regard politics as, in Robert Dahl's words, a "remote, alien and unrewarding activity"; and because, as Ignatieff and Walzer remind us, the distinction between friend and stranger has become politically attenuated, we are not particularly moved or defined by oppositions between citizens and foreigners, insiders and outsiders. But the *Bacchae* counts on the assumed naturalness of such polarities in order to problematize them. The contest between Pentheus and Dionysus is, among other things, a contest over the status of conventional Greek polarities and hierarchies that Pentheus defends (but eventually undermines) and Dionysus dissolves.[35] It is a contest over who does and who

---

close as possible to the life, power, and liberation of wild nature and to the other worshipers. (See the footnote on pp. 41–42 in Geoffrey S. Kirk's edition of the *Bacchae* (Englewood Cliffs, N.J.: Prentice-Hall, 1970).

[31] See principally Diels-Kranz B20 but also B128 and B137 (*Fragmente der Vorsokratiker* [Berlin: Weidman, 1954]).

[32] See also Aristotle's discussion of the polis in terms of dismemberment and membership in the *Politics*, 1253a19–23 (the *Republic* carries the analogy forward at 462c–d).

[33] *Obligations: Essays on Disobedience, War and Citizenship* (Cambridge, Mass.: Harvard University Press, 1970), p. 113.

[34] The loss is compounded by the fact that we so often isolate those who are infirm, diseased, aged, or handicapped, as if to distance any sign of mortality. Our convenience in this regard is matched by professionals who earn their living and prestige by supervising institutions to house such people.

[35] This is a momentary occurrence, part of a ritual practice. The Dionysian is a glimpse and an instant, not a world.

does not belong to which sort of communities, over the place of class and gender in a city committed to *isonomia*, the sharing of political power.[36]

Given such differences, *how* could I and why do I choose Euripides' *Bacchae* to think about membership (or the *Oresteia* to think about justice or the *Oedipus Tyrannos* to think about identity)? Why not a more modern, familiar text?

One reason is that the etymological field of our word "membership" provides a resource for understanding the *Bacchae*, just as the play is a resource for understanding the limits of our ideas about membership. For instance, in English, "member" suggests the male sex organ and so dismemberment raises issues of sexual politics, a central issue in the play. Or again, membership and dismemberment suggest "re-membering" not only in the sense of recalling, but of reconstructing or renewing a community. So to talk about dismemberment is to talk about memory and recollection (what Cadmus does with Pentheus's body), about "reminding" and "bearing in mind" (in both senses of the phrase). Because Dionysus is the god of forgetting and the dominating figure in the play, the *Bacchae* can be interpreted as a rumination on Kundera's oft-quoted line, "The struggle of man against power is the struggle of memory against forgetting."[37]

I also think a Greek tragedy such as the *Bacchae* provides terms in which to reassess both the polarities of gender, class, ethnicity, and status that still define our collective lives *and* the now fashionable rejection of all such distinctions and divisions.[38] Moreover, the play takes some of our fondest, noblest aspirations, such as liberation and objectivity, shows their power, attractiveness, and necessity, but also their powerlessness, partiality, and fictiveness. Against and with Foucault, it implies that liberation, like false consciousness, can be given up only at the risk of becoming a slave and only embraced at the risk of being a tyrant. It presents "objectivity," the view of the world as an object grasped by a reasoning subject whose intellectual prowess depends on distance and dispassion, as both an ideal and as an assault on the world, the city, and the self.

None of this is meant to deny tragedy's historical distinctiveness (though that assertion itself presumes a commonality sufficient to note the

---

[36] See Helene P. Foley, *Ritual Irony: Poetry and Sacrifice in Euripides* (Ithaca, N.Y.: Cornell University Press, 1985), chap. 5.

[37] *The Book of Laughter and Forgetting* (trans. Michael Henry Heim (New York: Penguin, 1981), p. 113.

[38] There are many echoes of the *Bacchae* in Foucault's concerns with normalization, discipline, prisons, and even archaeology. That is not surprising given how important the *Bacchae* was to Nietzsche and Nietzsche is for Foucault. But the play is just as harsh on some of Foucault's embrace of "the other." (It is an embrace Foucault himself drew back from at the end of his life.)

difference). Indeed, I want to insist on it. If we are, as Nietzsche insisted, bound to misunderstand ourselves, then it is precisely the *Bacchae*'s (or *Oresteia*'s or *Oedipus Tyrannos*'s) untimeliness that recommends it. To the extent that we learn what we need through suffering its lack, then dramatizing that lack may help us articulate the need. True, the terms of articulation must, in the end, be "our" own as is the sensibility we bring to the play. But through engagement with "it," we may be able to redefine the terms of articulation and the collectivity doing the articulating. More concretely, I think the *Bacchae* (and other tragedies) dramatize the limits of our political discourse, disclosing the exclusions it sustains and the parts of our lives it misdescribes or fails to recognize. This might free us, if just a little, from Kundera's prison and Foucault's disciplinary society.

It is because the language of rights is so congenial that it cannot be of much help here, however essential it may be in other respects. It is too much embedded in our institutions, academic and otherwise, too much part of the dominant discourse in political theory and so too much the arbiter of what is good politics and good political philosophy.

In fact, liberal discourse may have helped impoverish our language and experience of solidarity with the paradoxical result that ideas of membership are bifurcated into the abstract language of rights, which regards communitarianism as primitive and a sentimentalized idea of community as beyond difference. The *Bacchae* dramatizes this bifurcation, revealing how polarities (such as between rights and belonging, authority and liberty, individual and community) share an inner attraction and affinity that enables them to be related to each other in the first place. It also dramatizes how it is that oppositions turn into each other and why it is that what we banish returns with such explosive power. In terms of the play it is not at all surprising that bureaucratic structures, contractual sentiments that extend to private life in the form of prenuptial agreements or sexual health cards, and the further isolation of work (computer piece work) and leisure (video cassette recorders) should enhance the attractiveness of religious cults and the power of those who would turn the "city" into a cult.

In Euripidean terms the issue is finding a way to honor "Dionysus," since efforts to exclude him bring mutilation. The point is not to "revive" Greek tragedy, whatever that could mean. It is to ask whether there is some cultural analogue where the god can make his public appearance and genealogy be institutionalized as it was with tragedy. That would require a citizenry made powerful enough by democratic participation to confront the political and "ontological" tensions of their mortality: their strangeness as depicted in the choral ode in *Antigone*; their unique capacity to build roads, yet be bound by nets as in the *Oresteia*; and their capacity to answer the sphinx and save themselves only to miss what is intimate and obvious as in the *Oedipus Tyrannos*.[39] And it would require a conception of literature as having public responsibilities for educating a democratic citizenry.

LITTLE IN OUR experience of theater prepares us for the place of drama in Athenian collective life. For us drama is a literary genre or form of entertainment that we choose from an array of recreational opportunities. The choice itself is thought to have no political or moral dimensions but to be simply a matter of individual preference. Nor is drama a collective experience beyond the moment of performance. We enter and leave the theater as strangers. Any bond created by the experience of the play is a temporarily shared suffering fractured at the play's end.

Furthermore, our dramas are written, performed, produced, acted, and studied by professionals. The idea of a great general being our most distinguished playwright (or the reverse) strikes us as an odd confusion of sensibilities and vocations. All of this is because drama is not, for us, an integral part of an absorbing public life. We bring neither the experience of democratic participants to the theater, nor the political wisdom informed by drama to the common deliberations of an assembly. Indeed, for "us" theater is an activity for the few. Finally, we have institutionally insulated the pursuit of political ends from dramatic representation and the asking of philosophical questions from either. Hence we must do without any publicly shared communal mode either for representing political conflict or for subjecting politics to philosophical interrogation.[40]

The situation in fifth-century Athens was quite different. That difference is implied by the etymology of theater.[41] *Theatrōn* was a place for seeing, a physical space set aside for dramatic representation. It also designated the community of onlookers or spectators, *hoi theatai*. Theater was thus a place where the Athenians became a community through

[39] The only one who knows all is Teiresias and he is blind, outside the city with its centers of power, and dependent on another.

[40] See the remarks by Alasdair MacIntyre, *After Virtue* (Notre Dame, Ind.: University of Notre Dame Press, 1981), p. 129.

[41] Theater and theory have a common root. The Greek *thea* means see, sight, gaze, look upon, behold, admire, and contemplate. As a feminine noun, *thea* suggests a view or thing seen, a sight or a spectacle. It is related to verb *theaomai*, to gaze at, to behold, especially with a sense of wonder and admiration. This is not limited to physical vision but can include mental activity as it does in the *Republic* (582c) and in the *Theateus* (155d) where Plato connects philosophy with wonder: *mala gar philosophou touto to pathos to thaumazdein* (see also Aristotle's *Metaphysics*, 928b12). I have traced the origins of theory in my "Creatures of a Day: Thought and Action in Thucydides," in *Political Theory and Praxis: New Perspectives*, ed. T. Ball (Minneapolis: University of Minnesota Press, 1977), pp. 32–38. On the Indo-European root of theater and theory, see Julius Pokorny, *Indogermanische etymologisches Wörterbuch* (Bern and Munich: Francke, 1959).

common response and developed a shared sense of responsibility. Indeed tragedy, unlike its predecessor, the dithyrambic chorus, was from the beginning, "a celebration of the polis as a whole . . . and not of its competitive parts."[42]

As this implies, tragedy was a public event and a political institution. It was performed before and for the public, largely by the public, and judged by citizens it helped educate to the task of judgment. Because plays were public events, their meanings, unlike those of our own plays, were interjected into the polis itself through the context of performance and festival. For the duration of that festival the city turned itself into a theater watching itself as an object of representation on stage.[43]

What the assembled citizenry witnessed was its past political choices, institutional forms, and cultural practices "problematized" in the situations, themes, and characters on stage. This is obviously and directly so in the *Eumenides* where the audience of potential jurors watch the creation of a jury; what Albert Cook calls the imagined scene and actual scene are thus most congruent without being identical.[44] But it is also, if less literally, the case with the *Oedipus Tyrannos* and the *Bacchae*.

The *Oresteia* makes unmistaken references to the newly concluded Argive alliance by which the Athenians first challenged Spartan hegemony in Greece and to the revolution of 462–461 in which the democratic party led by Ephialtes (who was latter killed) and Pericles curtailed the prerogatives and power of the Areopagus.[45] As the Assembly assumed greater sovereignty over what had been a local, sacred, or secretive authority, there was a shift in the locus and understanding of power. Where power had resided in the prowess of individual men, it was now collective and could be derived from the citizens assembled in the Ekklesia, the theater, or the hoplite phalanx.[46] As the archonship was opened to the second

[42] John J. Winkler, "The Ephebes' Song: *Tragoidia* and *Polis*," *Representations* (Summer 1985): 26–62.

[43] See Jean-Pierre Vernant, "Tensions and Ambiguities in Greek Tragedy," in *Interpretation*, ed. Charles S. Singleton (Baltimore: Johns Hopkins University Press, 1969), pp. 107–8.

[44] Albert Cook, *Enactment: Greek Tragedy* (Chicago: Swallow Press, 1971), chap. 2, esp. pp. 33–34.

[45] Anaximenes, a fourth-century historian, claimed that Ephialtes brought the objects on which Solon's legislation was inscribed from the Acropolis down to the Agora and Council chamber, which, if true, suggests the "publicizing" of the law. See his "Philippica" in *Die Fragmente der griechischen Historiker*, ed. F. Jacoby (Berlin: Weidman, 1922), 72, F. 13.

[46] In the hoplite phalanx each soldier was immediately dependent for his survival and power on those next to him. Any break in the line meant defeat for all. Greek politics and morality were similar; it was the visible dependence of each on the others that, at its best, empowered all to maintain the line, not against some foreign enemy, but against the temptations to simplify the world. See Simon Goldhill's remarks on the transformation of individual prowess into collective power (in his *Reading Greek Tragedy*, p. 145).

property class, the easy identification of status with office no longer obtained. Because the saving victory at Salamis was a naval one, the poor who manned the ships with such courage could now make political claims for power on grounds previously thought to be innate to the *aristoi*.[47] Of course none of these transformations contemporary with the *Oresteia* went unchallenged. For instance, some Athenians apparently sought Spartan intervention against the rising power of the demos, which suggests what other evidence corroborates—that the city was close to civil war. Given this context it is not surprising that the *Oresteia* is preoccupied with the foundations of a political order, with the establishment of a just harmony between otherwise warring factions and principles. Nor is it incidental that the trilogy's closing tableau with the entire citizenry on stage, consecrating the justice established by their goodness, follows the Furies warning about civil war. It is as if the playwright was reminding his audience of how far it has fallen from the common dedication displayed at Salamis, of how wide a gulf now separated the "ideal" from the actual.

But even the *Oresteia* with its dramatization of Athenian past and present political controversies does not debate those issues as the Assembly might. Aeschylus does not take sides on questions that had, in their particularity, already been decided anyway.[48] In this sense the trilogy is less propaganda than the setting of previous actions in a context that helped the collectivity better appreciate what is was doing to itself and to others.[49] When the audience watches the juridical function on stage it performs outside the theater, it is not so much judging a case as judging the qualities of mind and character that constitute sound judgment. Here, as

---

[47] On the crucial role of the Persian War in the development of a self-conscious political identity centering around the idea of freedom, see Christian Meier, *Die Entstehung des Begriffs "Demokratie": Vier Prolegomena zu einer historischen Theorie* (Frankfurt: Suhrkamp, 1970), Kurt Raaflaub, *Die Entdeckung der Freiheit: Zur historischen Semantik und Gesellschaftsgeschichte eines politischen Grundgegriffs der Griechen*, Vestigia: Beitrage zur alten Geschichte 37 (Munich: Beck, 1985), and my essay "The Battle of Salamis and the Origins of Political Theory," *Political Theory* 14, no. 3 (1986): 359–90.

[48] The questions of taking sides and voting become important themes in the *Eumenides*. Here as with other issues, highly particular events or issues take on much larger meaning in terms of the trilogy as a whole. Literal or narrow meanings become more inclusive without discarding the earlier and other significations. Thus, the meaning of justice ranges from legal decision to cosmological reconciliation. On this issue, see Michael Gagarin, *Aeschylean Drama* (Berkeley and Los Angeles: University of California Press, 1976); E. Fraenkel, *Aeschylus: Agamemnon* (New York: Oxford University Press, 1950), 1: 27–29, 270–72, 294; and Eric A. Havelock, *The Greek Concept of Justice* (Cambridge, Mass.: Harvard University Press, 1978), pp. 280–89.

[49] See the discussion of this point by E. R. Dodds, "Morals and Politics in the Oresteia," *Proceedings of the Cambridge Philological Society* n.s. 6 (1960): 19–31.

in most tragedies, the tension between imagined and actual scene creates a space for questioning and reflections.

By interweaving mythical Argos and legendary heroes with stories of Athens' ancient founding and contemporary politics, Aeschylus establishes a balance between proximity and distance that puts events of his time and place in a perspective more complete than any available to the same audience in their role as political actors. Distance from the particular present provides a general context of understanding. But the obvious parallels between the mythical story and present politics mean that issues retain their particularity and urgency. This balance allowed the citizen-audience to see themselves as both freely choosing actors-protagonists responsible for their deeds, and suffering victims afflicted by family curses, blindness, pride, chance, and fate.[50] In sum, by clothing contemporary political debate in the costume of a legendary but still living past, Aeschylus provides those in the audience with a magnified image of their lives.[51]

Something similar can be said about the *Oedipus Tyrannos*, although the absence of Athens on stage and the play's uncertain allusions to contemporary politics makes contextualization more subject to our own prejudices about empire and power than is the case with the *Oresteia*. Sophocles may well have shared the "optimism, ethusiasm, curiosity, love of adventure and love of experiment" of his compatriots.[52] But if Knox is right in identifying Oedipus with Athens and regarding Athens as the home for "the idea that man was capable of full understanding and eventual domination of his environment" and given Pericles' strategy of uprooting citizens from their land for refuge behind the city's walls as well as his citizenship laws, which rigidly distinguished between insiders and outsiders, it is not surprising that thirty-two years after the *Oresteia* we have a play about identity. In a time of expanding political and intellectual horizons, of empire and sophistic skepticism, coordinates of place and time become hard to see and harder to draw. Like the Athenians,

---

[50] That is why in the *Eumenides*, Athena represents the continued presence of inherited guilt even as the play celebrates the polis as a realm of freedom. E. R. Dodds, *The Greeks and the Irrational* (Boston: Beacon Press, 1954), pp. 33–34, and Ulrich von Wilamowitz-Moellendorff, *Griechische Tragoedien* (Berlin: Weidmannsche Buchhandlung, 1909), p. 18, argue that citizenship was regarded as a wider circle of blood relations such that the same connection of generations would apply to the polis. According to Wilamovitz, "Es war die Zeit des Geschlechterstaates wo der Einzelne nicht auf sich stand, sondern immer ein Glied seiner Sippe blieb, oder seines Staates; den die Burgerschaft war immer der betrachtete sich doch als einen weiteren Kreis von Blutsverwandten."

[51] Despite these specific references and the final scenes at Athens, this is an image in a drama, not a historical representation.

[52] W. G. Forrest, *The Emergence of Greek Democracy* (New York: McGraw-Hill, 1970), p. 36.

Oedipus is a traveler; like the younger sophists, he along with Jocasta questions the veracity of oracles. He is also, in his contest with Teiresias, a representative of the kind of knowledge we might call empirical, analytic, and objective. That such knowledge has its value is evidenced by Oedipus's ability to answer the sphinx's riddle: What is four-footed in the morning, two-footed in the afternoon, and three-footed in the evening?[53] That such knowledge is also a kind of blindness is clear from Oedipus's inability to see that as a man who requires a staff to walk he is an exception to that answer but is *the* answer to the new riddle, Who killed Laius? The abstract knowledge that enabled him to see continuity amid differences disables him from seeing the particular circumstances of his life. One could put the same point in terms of Oedipus's two crimes, incest and patricide. Incest is being too close to one's own, too attached to what is particular and intimate, whereas patricide, the killing of one's past and legacy is, like the deracinating methods of science, too remote from what is close at hand. This problem of unity and diversity is at once "personal," political, and epistemological.

The *Bacchae* too is concerned with the status of knowledge and the presence of skepticism as well as with contemporary Athenian politics. Virtually every character in the *Bacchae* claims that his or her speech and action are *sophos*. Yet the word itself has many meanings[54] and those meanings are different for different characters and for the same character (at different times).[55] These repeated invocations of *sophos* and *sophia* indicate the banality of the term and of the traditional Greek moral precepts that rely on it. Indeed such precepts are often contradicted by the actions of those who mouth them or are pronounced by those (such as the chorus of Asian bacchants) who hate the polis these precepts purportedly sustain. Yet the play not only exposes the triteness of accepted moral pieties; it also raises questions about the sophistic manipulation of them. To put it politically, the play is as unsympathetic to the claims of a revanchist aristocracy as it is to those of a demagogic democracy, as critical of the punitive aggressiveness of Athenian "neoconservatives" as of the "radicalness" of classical "deconstructors."

The waywardness of moral language in the play is paralleled by the

[53] Of course both his success and his failure are Apollo-aided.

[54] The meaning of *sophia* ranges from animal cunning, techne, and cleverness (either in the sense of an agile mind or one too agile for its own good, i.e., merely clever), to knowledge of one's character and the necessities of life and death. It is contrasted with *amathia*, which describes someone who is untaught and unteachable, crude and coarse, with a tendency toward ungovernable violence and cruelty. (On this whole issue, see Arrowsmith's introduction to the *Bacchae* [New York: Washington Square Press, 1969] pp. 150–51.)

[55] In Foucault's terms, wisdom and knowledge have meaning only within a particular regime of power.

political dismemberment of Thebes and, indirectly, of Athens. It may or may not be of significance that the *Bacchae*, one of Euripides' last three plays, was written in voluntary exile or that he left Athens "bitter and broken in spirit."[56] Nor can we say for sure that he looked back from "the fringe of the Hellenic world to the collapse of the Athenian empire whose power and confidence fostered the development of tragedy."[57] But I do think that the *Bacchae* reflects the terrible political and social desperation and war-weariness of fifth-century Hellas[58] and is, in consequence, reflecting on what it means to belong to communities whose members are exhausted by principles they anyhow betray, whose traditional grounds for action and thought misrepresent the world as much as they represent it, and whose individual members denigrate commitments beyond those of the moment.[59]

As a political institution, tragedy was part of and helped to shape the democratization of Athenian life. Drama was an important means by which knowledge, values, and reasoning became elements of a common culture.[60] As a form of public speech, it opened public life to debate, discussion, and criticism while helping to qualify citizens to participate intelligently in them. This was unlike predemocratic Athens where speech has been preserved as private tokens of power in aristocratic family traditions, exclusive rituals, or formulaic statements. It is also different from antidemocratic arrangements where large segments of the population are excluded from the knowledge that comes from living a public life and where this enforced ignorance becomes a justification for their continued exclusion. Rotation in office and rule by lot presumed a degree of political wisdom which tragedy helped supply. In this sense it was a significant source of democratic political education, indeed more democratic than most of the other "democratic" institutions at Athens given the inclusiveness of Dionysian rituals and the presence of metics and perhaps women in the theater. If true, then the context of tragedy together with its content, which often brought "marginalized" people on stage, dra-

---

[56] Arrowsmith from his introduction to his edition of the *Bacchae*, p. 147.

[57] Charles Segal, *Dionysias Poetics and Euripedes' Bacchae* (Princeton: Princeton University Press, 1982), p. 3.

[58] Arrowsmith again, this time from "The Criticism of Greek Tragedy," *The Tulane Drama Review* 3 (1959): 35.

[59] For detailed discussions of the relationship between the factionalism at Athens and dismemberment in the play, see Hermann Rodich, *Die Euripideische Tragodie: Untersuchungen zu ihrer Tragik* (Heidelberg: C. Winter, 1968), and Hans Diller, "Die Bakchen und ihre Stellung im Spatwerk des Euripides," in *Euripides*, ed. Ernst-Richard Schwinge, Wege der Forschung 89 (Darmstadt, 1968).

[60] See Jean-Pierre Vernant, *The Origins of Greek Thought* (Ithaca, N.Y.: Cornell University Press, 1982), chap. 4, esp. pp. 49–51.

matized the necessity of democratic normalization and the need to disrupt the hegemony of such norms in the name of democracy.[61]

In at least one respect, tragedy was a political institution unlike any other. In saying that, I do not mean to deny the influence of the law courts or assembly deliberations on the form and content of tragedy. What I do mean is that tragedy's distance from the urgency of daily decisions—which drove the council, assembly and juries—allowed it to develop a uniquely "theoretical" perspective.[62] This can be seen by the inclusiveness of its understanding, its preoccupation with the status of knowledge, its interrogation of otherwise unquestioned categories and demarcations, and its self-reflectiveness.

Tragedy was part of the road building that defined a human space. By portraying the establishment and disestablishment of boundaries around and between spheres of activities, drama provided an opportunity for men (and perhaps women) to reflect on themselves as definers and redefiners, as boundary creators and boundary violators. Freed from the urgencies of making immediate decisions, as in other institutional settings, tragedy encouraged its citizen-audience to think more inclusively about the general pattern implicit in their actions. In this way it was a theoretical as well as political institution.

Drama was also a theoretical act and institution in the sense that the theater was an occasion, place, and way for theoretical considerations to become relevant to practical affairs without violating the contingency and irony of action. This was possible because the citizen-audience became simultaneously spectators and actors. As spectators of the action in the play they could see a whole denied those who enact their parts and who were therefore bound to the particular. But as political actors they could take part in a whole they can only partially know, thus imitating the actors on stage. This double vision is the foundation for Aeschylus's view that suffering brings wisdom and wisdom suffering, of Sophoclean irony, and for Socrates' dictum that ignorance is the foundation of knowledge. It is also a reason why tragedy has been called "the epistemological form par excellence." Various characters act out, live through, and sometimes overcome the consequences of having clung to a partial view of the world and themselves. What they learn, and what we learn from them, is pre-

[61] See William Connolly's discussion of Foucault and democracy in *Politics and Ambiguity* (Madison: University of Wisconsin Press, 1987), chaps. 1 and 7. As J. K. Davies points out in *Democracy and Classical Greece* (Glasgow: Fontana, 1978), p. 109, the production of a tragedy was, like the obligation to commission and command a trireme for a year, a liturgy that redistributed wealth to the poorer people who formed the choruses and crewed the ships.

[62] Christian Meier makes a similar argument in his *Die Entstehung des Politischen bei den Griechen* (Frankfurt: Suhrkamp, 1980).

cisely the epistemological complexity of the world: its recalcitrance to single standpoints or simple dualities. Although tragedy charts "a *path* from ignorance to knowledge, deception to revelation, misunderstanding to recognition,"[63] what is known, revealed, and recognized is the problematic character of the achievement.

This tension is paralleled by the tragedian's critical and conservative stance toward the tensions of his culture. Drama both embodied and defined the cultural and political tensions it portrayed. To the degree tragedy embodied these tensions, it was fully part of the city and looked outward toward the audience as did the actors on stage. In this sense, and like them, it was precluded by limits of time and place from knowing the full context of its own undertaking. But to the degree tragedy defined rather than embodied these tensions, it looked down on the actors in the political arena as the audience did the actors on the stage. In this respect the dramatist could claim a privileged understanding of collective life, though to the extent his plays educated his audience to share his insight, it was a privilege shared with his community. Without separating his activity or thought from that of his fellow citizens, the tragedian achieved what was at one and the same time a unique distance from, and integration with, the sustaining visions of his polis. In this, as in other ways, they anticipated the intellectual endeavor and the ultimate dilemma of their Athenian theoretical successors.[64]

Tragedy was theoretical not only because it pushed citizens to an inclusive understanding of their collective lives, and provided a systematic understanding of justice and corruption. It was also theoretical in the scope and kind of cultural critique it offered.

To the degree that tragedy was an established institution that drew its stories from an established mythical tradition, it was conservative rather than radical. Yet part of what is conserved was a tradition of critical discourse. Moreover, the seemingly minor innovation tragedians made within that mythical tradition could have radical implications. Indeed, it was precisely because tragedy was an established institution that it was able to disestablish the city's self-understanding within the confines of ritual, theater, and stage.

Finally, tragedy was theoretical in its self-reflectiveness. Insofar as it dramatized the problematic aspects of collective life in which it partici-

---

[63] The phrase and claim are Froma Zeitlin's ("Playing the Other," p. 72). Later (p. 79) she talks about the paradox that while theater necessarily resorts to artifice "it can also better represent the larger world outside as it more nearly is, subject to the deceptions, the gaps in knowledge, the tangled necessities, and all the tensions and conflicts of a complex existence."

[64] The previous paragraphs are adapted from my introduction to *Greek Tragedy and Political Theory*.

pated, tragedy explored its own preconditions, place, and future. When it considered the ironies of speech and action (as do these plays), it was also, indirectly, considering itself as a form of speech and action. Concerned with the interplay of passion and reason, tragedy not only sought a balance that enhanced both on stage, it provided an example of such balance in its very form. Probing the shaping force of institutions and traditions, tragedy was itself a political institution and part of a tradition. Educating the judgment of the community (Detienne calls them "les maîtres de verité"), tragedy sought to nurture an audience capable of appreciating what is was and did.

Not only is tragedy theoretical; theory is also dramatic (and tragic). Tragedy evoked and provoked its audience into participating in the task of deconstructing and reconstructing a world that was both familiar and other. It awakened and enlivened the mind and heart, arousing emotions and reason rather than drugging them, as most textbooks do.[65] Showing people learning to change, tragedy helped its audience see the need to do the same: seeing the connection between belief and action on stage, the audience could recognize how its own ideas shape its beliefs and actions.[66] The characters we see on stage, searching for the right thing to say and do in difficult circumstances, help us interpret our own difficulties. We are invited to assess Agamemnon, Oedipus, and Pentheus for ourselves to see their limitations and the circumstances that call them forth, to realize with them or because of them how hard it is to know what to do. Tragedy does not so much provide us with a solution as insist on the depth of the problems and the dangers of a "problem-solving" mentality.

Much of what I have said about tragedy can be said about Thucydides' *History* and Plato's dialogues. For example, Thucydides' *History* draws us into the experience of trying to make sense of an event first in one way, then in another, but never wholly succeeding. By constructing a text that replicates the difficulties for the reader that he faced as a historian describing and making sense of his world, Thucydides presents for us the problem of trying to reconstitute and comprehend collective experience. In most of the Platonic dialogues we see characters and ideas evolving as

[65] But even tragedy's awakening is selective. Texts that invigorate the mind in some respects may pacify it in others; they may distract and lead us away from "the" world even as they seem to lead us back into it." That is one reason why Nietzsche saw texts as facts of power rather than of democratic exchange. In Edward Said's words: "They compel attention away from the world even as their beginning intention as texts, coupled with the inherent authoritarianism of the authorial authority . . . makes for sustained power"; see *The World, the Text and the Critic* (Cambridge, Mass.: Harvard University Press, 1983), pp. 45–46. For a defense of reading as a form of democratic exchange, see White, *When Words Lose Their Meaning*, chap. 1.

[66] My argument (and some of my language) comes from Nussbaum.

the interlocutors search with Socrates for the right thing to say or do in the dialogue and the world outside it. As with tragedy, we are invited to become an interlocutor ourselves, judging the argument and the characters who make them (including Socrates). And though the *Republic* has many admonitions against arousing the passions tragedy arouses and offers "solutions" as tragedy does not, it too relies on specific passions and qualifies many of its confident conclusions.

THIS BOOK ends not with a discussion of Aristotle's response to Plato's views on politics, philosophy, and poetry or with a comparison of Athenian with American democracy and theater or with an extended discussion of "Grand Theory," but with a study of a contemporary American novel, *The Crying of Lot 49*. Pynchon invites a comparison with Greek tragedy by naming his central character Oedipa,[67] but that alone would hardly be enough for the novel to carry the burden of concluding a book on Greek tragedy and political theory, especially since the name is just one clue in a book full of clues that do not add up or add up in contradictory ways. Why then do I make such an unconventional choice?

One reason is that I find Pynchon's portrait of America generally compelling and his preoccupations typical of our most perceptive cultural critics. If the question we bring to our investigation of classical texts are framed or inspired by the crisis of our time, then studying Pynchon's novel is a way of studying the context out of which those questions arise and take shape. More particularly, that portrait helps explain my choice of subject and texts, my treatment of them, and the structure of the book as a whole.

A second reason is that Pynchon teaches us how to read both the novel itself and the framing culture in "political" ways. For instance, *The Crying of Lot 49* implies that interpreting a novel or cultural legacy requires the active participation of the reader-citizen. Without such participation both the novel and culture will become subject to single interpretations and homogeneous readings. It is not, as Barthes[68] argues, that the author must die for the reader to live, but that the author must empower his or her readers, making them equal contributors in constituting "the" text's

---

[67] But one must be cautious, for Pynchon parodies the erudition his text demands. Moreover, as one would expect in a work concerned with entropy, there is more than one story to be told. Given the work's affinities with Melville and especially Henry Adams, one could discuss it as a distinctively American novel. Given its religious imagery, one could regard the novel as theology or even a theodicy.

[68] The object of Barthes' concern is with the "tyrannical" concentration on the person, life, tastes, and passions of the author, prominent in "ordinary culture." See his essay, "The Death of the Author," in *Image, Music, Text*, essays selected and translated by Stephen Heath (New York: Hill and Wang, 1977), pp. 142–48.

meaning. Because Pynchon has helped teach me how to read the works discussed in this book, my reading of his novel might be considered a methodological coda.

A third reason is the reverse of the second: the playwrights and theorists discussed in subsequent chapters also help me read Pynchon. If I am right in believing that Pynchon offers us a perceptive portrait of contemporary American culture, and teaches us how to read and reclaim a cultural legacy, and if Greek tragedy and classical political theory understood in its terms add depth to both the portrait and the teaching, then I have indicated one way in which the authors considered in this book can help "illuminate" the discursive practices and institutional forms that continue to shape or misshape our individual and collective lives.

Given Foucault's critique of the enlightenment, the sometimes ironic, often futile efforts of various characters in tragedy to "bring things to light" and the pervasive sight imagery in both the plays and theories, I had better say something about what sort of illumination I have in mind. I do not mean to offer a single well-lighted path which, to paraphrase Stanley Fish, moves forward in the hope and belief that all that was once obscure will now be clear again. That ignores the warnings of tragedy and of theory as I interpret them and misses Pynchon's point about entropy. What I intended is to offer some "untimely" mediations. But because "our" time is one that dismisses classical texts or the standard readings of them *and* canonizes both those texts and those readings as essential for saving "Western Culture," the untimeliness will move in two directions. Pynchon will, once more, be a teacher here. He warns us not to romanticize outsiders, decentered play or genealogy, even as he insists that those outsiders may be the only hope for renewing America; he is himself a master of such play and a genealogist truer to Nietzsche than many of Nietzsche's proclaimed followers.

A fourth reason for choosing Pynchon is that he dramatizes the costs of modernity Holmes ignores, anticipates Ignatieff's challenge to find a language of community adequate to Los Angeles, and echoes Foucault.[69] Like Ignatieff, Pynchon is uneasy with utopianism at least insofar as it posits a single voice to replace the voice it finds repellent or creates yet another binary opposition. But unlike Ignatieff, he also sees the potential need for utopian visions to energize systems that dismiss them. More fundamentally, Pynchon suggests that calling something utopian or someone nostalgic presumes that one knows what has been, is now, and will occur, and that one can, without much fuss, draw a clear line between fact and

[69] Pynchon is as fascinated by Los Angeles as he is repelled by it. He may even be suggesting that since L.A. has become America, any redemption must begin there. It matters that his novel never leaves California.

fiction, beginnings and endings. But if the historical ontology upon which such distinctions depend is unpersuasive, then "nostalgic" and "utopian" may be accusations that beg the question. Where Ignatieff sees homes as transient places we leave in order to grow up, Pynchon sees tract homes; where Ignatieff talks positively about the "arteries" of big cities, Pynchon sees those arteries as clogged with killer cars and narcotics and the cities themselves populated by isolates such as the Inamorati Anonymous and by outcasts like Tristero.

One could describe *The Crying of Lot 49* as existing on the cusp between modernity and postmodernity[70] and so, as Vernant says about Greek tragedy, looking in two directions at once. Thus, one finds Foucauldian themes and methods—normalization, genealogy, microdomination, the capillary nature of power, knowledge as embedded in regimes of power, the disciplinary construction of the self—but they are warnings about what might happen, not conclusions about what has happened. The novel dramatizes how the self is systematically drawn into the orbit of social discipline and so why paranoia, the constant sense of being under the surveillance of others, is our paradigmatic mental "illness." Yet Tristero might really exist, and if it does, Oedipa is not paranoid. The novel makes us suspicious of liberation but its possibility cannot be excluded and belief in it may be essential for action. "We" must look at the world in its immediate particularity, yet that world *may* manifest a transcendence the signs of which *may* be everywhere if they are not put there by others or by our own hallucinations. We see what is lost, subjected, and marginalized by the construction of traditional history, yet such histories sometimes save us from incapacitating madness. Global theories are entropic but their absence may be as well and so the wholesale dismissal of political theory will not do either politically or epistemologically.

A fifth reason for ending with Pynchon lies in the way he elaborates the images of road building. In the novel roads do not differentiate a human world from the wild untamed world outside as they do in the *Oresteia*. Instead, roads obliterate all distinctions, crisscrossing boundaries in a predatory urban sprawl. Nor do these roads lead from Argos and corruption to Athens and justice, but rather to death, paranoia, or, at best, the uncertainty of Tristero. Our highways kill those who drive on them, decimate the land through which they are built, and, by destroying cemeteries, desecrate the peoples already wasted by progress. Creon would kill Polyneices the second time by forbidding his burial. We would kill the Indians twice and with them our own past as well. Nor do these highways

---

70 I think *Gravity's Rainbow* may well be a "postmodern novel" but *The Crying of Lot 49* seems to me more traditional. Perhaps here too we have an example of a middle term.

honor any god, though there are "signs" of some unseen design behind what may or may not be random developments.

In the *Oresteia*, road building is counterposed to images of nets and snares. Similar images appear in *The Crying of Lot 49*. Oedipa is trapped in a tower of her mind, woven into a tapestry, subject to some plot of her own inadvertent devising or the purposeful devising of others.

Penultimately, the novel recapitulates the substantive concerns of the book—justice, identity, and membership—as they appear in the plays and theories. Like the *Oresteia*, it is concerned to find place and hearing for different voices within a whole that respects the integrity of the parts and with reclaiming a legacy however cursed it may be. Like the *Oedipus Tyrannos* it begins with a mystery about a dead man, which turns into a quest for meaning knowledge and identity. As the protagonists look for clues in order to reverse the plague that afflicts their respective homelands, they find that surface meaning—in Oedipa's case, the world of Muzak and Tupperware—covers an underside of violation. Both the novel and the *Bacchae* are about membership and dismemberment. Both bring fluidity, precariousness, and sudden reversibility to the "safe fortified heavily defended walls of whatever Thebes each of us inhabits." Both focus on the "necessary interaction between 'officially affirmed and officially negated patterns,' between approved, normative values and marginal, suppressed anti-values in the construction of human society and human socialization," while revealing and symbolically enacting these contradictions in their art.[71]

Thucydides' *History*, like *The Crying of Lot 49*, portrays a world "speeding" up until its protagonists cannot make sense of, let alone direct the overwhelming particularities and rush of events that inundate them. The two competing paradigms in the *History*, that of political and intellectual power as described and exemplified in the funeral oration and the plague-stasis, become the shifting parameters that frame Oedipa's thought and actions. Like Socrates, Oedipa walks among her fellow citizens asking questions they do not ask (or even know to be questions), being skeptical of the answers they do not question, acknowledging her ignorance. By recognizing their mortality, they acknowledge their need for others and that the need can never be fully met anymore than their respective quests can be ended. Both understand that the world (or the world Oedipa thinks she is in) is a world of deprivation and need. Few of their compatriots know that; fewer still are able to confront it; but all are somehow maimed by it. That is the special wisdom Oedipa and Socrates

[71] Segal, *Dionysiac Poetics*, pp. 259, 274, 329. The phrase he quotes is from George Devereux, *From Anxiety to Method in the Behavioral Sciences* (The Hague: Mouton, 1967), p. 212.

have and it is their persistent courage in the face of it that defines their character and their fate. With Oedipa we see why and how an ordinary person becomes philosophical.[72] One might even say that, with her, we get a glimpse of what Socratic philosophy would look like in modern or postmodern dress.

In the *Republic* Socrates draws his interlocutors toward transcendence; from the beginning Oedipa thinks she sees evidence of transcendent meaning. As she actively pursues it, her initially banal world takes on depth and seriousness, much as the characters and positions in book 1 of the *Republic* do as Socrates follows the path upward from the Piraeus to the theory of the Forms. Of course, Oedipa is not sure there are paths that carry one upward out of the dark night, with its intimidating plethora of clues, to clarity, order, and meaning. She suspects that such hope is but one more drug, an LSD of the mind, like her husband, Mucho, who thought all the world spoke in his voice. But I think analogous doubts are present in the *Republic* too.

Finally, I choose Pynchon because his inviting a comparison with Greek tragedy shows us how to "use" such tragedy as the tragedians "used" mythological stories, characters, and cities like Argos and Thebes—as "other" places, which, despite their distance, reveal possibilities in this place. Perhaps presenting America as both distant and proximate to ancient tragedy allows Pynchon to create interpretive energy against entropic criticism.

Because "this" place is contemporary America, Pynchon's portrait of our culture establishes a context of performance from which we address Greek tragedy and classical political theory. As such it helps set the terms for contemporary political theory. Echoing, but also departing from Foucault, Pynchon seems to believe that foundations and grounding are preconditions for diversity (and for genealogy), *and* that every foundation and ground (like Creon, Oedipus, Pentheus, and perhaps theory itself) are potentially tyrannical. His "answer," insofar as he has "one," lies in the way he teaches us to read the novel and act in the world outside it. We must participate in the construction of the novel's meaning, thus sharing power with the "author," just as we must participate in elaborating the legacy of America. Pierce Inverarity, like Thomas Pynchon, left us a will; it is up to us to execute it. Leaving Winthrop Tremaine and his ready-to-wear back-to-school SS uniforms, Oedipa declaims: "You're chicken, she told herself, snapping her seat belt. This is America, you live in it, you let it happen."[73]

---

[72] She could, of course, imitate the men in her life who opt out and run away. But that is no real choice since what they run away from runs after them. There is no escaping plots; even suicide won't do, as the death of and voluminous literature on Marilyn Monroe attest.

[73] *The Crying of Lot 49* (New York: Bantam Books, 1967), p. 112.

PART II
GREEK TRAGEDY AND POLITICAL THEORY

THREE

Justice and the *Oresteia*

THIS CHAPTER is concerned with the idea of justice in the *Oresteia*.[1] Thus it will analyze what the characters in the play and the play as a whole understand justice to be and the status they accord it in public life. Given tragedy's status as a public institution, the chapter will consider how its form and content sustained and helped constitute justice in the polis. Because the dramatist was a political educator, as I suggested in the previous chapter, I will also have something to say about the sort of educator he was.[2]

As previously noted, any discussion of justice must also be about identity and dismemberment. Thus many of the themes considered here such as inheritance, homecoming, exile, tyranny, freedom, and sexual politics will reappear in chapter 4 and especially chapter 5, since the *Bacchae's* ending is, I will suggest, an explicit contrast to the ending of the *Oresteia* (even when we take account of Zeitlin's argument).

My focus on justice is not only a preface to the other tragedies, it also introduces the chapters on Thucydides, Socrates, and especially the *Republic*. Despite the charge of moral and metaphysical ignorance Socrates levels at the dramatists in the *Republic*, that dialogue and Aeschylus's trilogy both center on a similar understanding of justice that, in each instance, their structure helps define.

AS WE SAW in chapter 2, the path toward justice leads from Argos to Athens via Delphi. It is a path where perversions and corruption are set right,[3] where once-stifled speech and ominous silence assume their proper role, and where strangled action is freed from the grip of the house's

---

[1] "It is plain to the most casual reader that dike (justice) is a central notion of the trilogy" (C. W. MacLeod, "Politics and the Oresteia," *Journal of Hellenic Studies* 102 [1982]: 133). "The primary issue in the *Oresteia* is, of course, justice" (Froma Zeitlin, "The Dynamics of Misogyny: Myth and Mythmaking in the Oresteia," *Arethusa* 11 [1978]: 161).

[2] I do not mean to exaggerate: to the degree that political education was a matter of living a public life, it was necessarily mutual and collective in process and aim. The playwright helped define, sustain, and extrapolate a collective legacy. This is particularly true of Aeschylus. In this regard it is significant that the *Oresteia* ends with the whole people of Athens on stage. The gifts of ancestors must be deserved and their victories rewon by the citizenry as a whole.

[3] At *Eumenides* 995, Athena calls it "the straight path of righteousness."

curse. It is a path of integration and of resolution hard won over many obstacles, long in coming, divine as well as human. To follow the road toward the achievement of justice, we must see what stood in its way at Argos.

The *Oresteia* develops as a series of confrontations between characters and forces on both divine and human planes.[4] There are a number of such oppositions, each with an integrity of its own and a place in reinforcing or modifying all others. It is not necessary to deal with all of them. Two illustrations should be sufficient to indicate how these tensions and their resolution involve the most fundamental issues of justice, action, and politics.

Throughout the trilogy, men and women are in conflict. Apollo wishes to banish the Furies, Artemis demands perverse sacrifice when her father's eagles devour the innocent unborn young of a pregnant hare, Zeus is at odds with Moira, Agamemnon murders his daughter, Clytaemnestra her husband, and Orestes his mother.

In the *Libation Bearers* the chorus sings of the excesses of men and women. They refer first to the *hypertolmon andros phronēma* ("the bold recklessness") (594–95) which drives them beyond the proper boundaries of action and place.[5] Agamemnon is such a man. Though Zeus's avenger against Paris's violation of laws of guest friendship, he is, as a male committed to conquest and heroic glory,[6] one who goes to excess, destroying daughter and wife, the household, the polis, and the balance of nature itself. In sacrificing his daughter, Agamemnon assaults her mother and his wife and thus the *oikos* as a whole. Setting out to avenge a wrong done to his house, he becomes an unwitting accomplice in his enemy's crime, as punisher and punished join in an unrecognized conspiracy of common violation.[7]

Destruction extends to the city as well. Prior to the herald's entry an-

[4] Two particularly good analyses of this are those by H.D.F. Kitto, *Form and Meaning in Drama* (New York: Barnes and Noble, 1970), chaps. 1–3; and Karl Reinhardt, *Aischylos als Regisseur und Theologe* (Bern: A. Francke, 1949), pp. 151–52.

[5] My analysis here owes much to John H. Finley, Jr., particularly his *Pindar and Aeschylus* (Cambridge, Mass.: Harvard University Press, 1955).

[6] Critics have been reluctant to see Agamemnon as heroic. I think the issue is not so much Agamemnon as the reckless pride that characterizes heroes. In this regard the "thinning out" of the trilogy's later characters (Electra as opposed to Clytaemnestra, Orestes in contrast to Agamemnon) has the rhetorical effect of moralizing and collectivizing the heroic ethic. By moralizing I mean bringing moral criticisms to bear against the propensities that are necessarily part of that ethic; by collectivizing I mean presenting the entire citizenry of Athens as "properly" heroic.

[7] The common fate of victors and vanquished is shown throughout the *Oresteia*, perhaps most powerfully by the common fate of the captive slave Cassandra and the captor King Agamemnon.

nouncing the victory at Troy, the chorus laments the sorrows suffered by each Argive home for the sake of Menelaus's single sorrow. To revenge the loss of a wanton wife, the city has lost its young men and their king has become the willing partner of Ares, god of war, "money changer of dead bodies."

> Those they sent forth they knew;
> now, in place of the young men
> urns and ashes are carried home
> to the houses of the fighters.
>
> (*Agamemnon* 433–36)

With the city's sons dead, the chorus of old men is impotent to prevent the murder of their returning king, to intervene when it happens, or to punish the usurping mannish-woman murderer. Hearing the king's cries, they speak severally rather than as one, their separateness providing sign and voice to the political disarray at Argos.

Finally, the sacrifice of Iphigenia is part of Agamemnon's destroying the balance of nature. The chorus's description of his dilemma and the sacrifice that resolves it is preceded by the great hymn to Zeus with its gnomic "from wisdom comes suffering," all part of the longest *parodos* in extant Greek tragedy.

> Zeus who guided men to think,
> who has laid it down that wisdom
> comes alone through suffering.
> Still drop by drop there falls upon the heart in sleep's
> place sorrow and remembered pain; against
> our pleasures we are made temperate.
> From the gods who sit in grandeur
> grace comes somehow violent.
>
> (179–83)

They pray to Zeus because they can find no prospect of good winning out in the end despite their repeated pleas; because they see no healing for their pain or easing of their perplexity; and because they cannot go on and tell this awful tale without assurance that it has some meaning in an as yet unrevealed context which they cannot fathom. The tale is of Agamemnon's dilemma; either disband the host and abandon the expedition (thereby facing the wrath of Zeus for leaving Paris unpunished and of his allies who lust for glory) or commit impious sacrifice destroying what is most dear and closest to him. He must choose between fatherhood and kingship, between the glory of his house and glory for his army.

For a moment he is poised between the alternatives and knows well the cost of each. In the beginning he seems to be for Iphigenia.

My fate is hard (heavy, oppressive, burdensome) if I disobey,
And hard if I slaughter (massacre, sacrifice,)
the child who is the pride (glory, delight) of my house,
with streaming virginal blood polluting (defiling, staining)
these father's hands hard by the altar.

(206–10)

But he quickly changes his mind and chooses the glory and wealth of war and battle over that of his house. Having decided for one side of the dilemma, he wipes out the memory of the other and of the dilemma itself.[8]

But when he had donned the yoke of necessity
he changed, and from the heart the breath came bitter
and sacrilegious utterly infidel,
to warp a will now to be stopped at nothing.
The sickening of men's minds, tough,
reckless in fresh cruelty brings daring. He endured then
to sacrifice his daughter
to stay the strength of war for a woman
first offering for the ships' sake.

(217–26)[9]

Now passioned for battle, the king ignores his child's supplications and cries of father. He gags her not only to prevent her uttering a curse upon the house[10] but to deprive her of speech and voice, as if by silencing her

---

[8] R. P. Winnington-Ingram thinks the description of the sacrifice so revolting that there is no real dilemma. See his "Agamemnon and the Trojan War," in *Studies in Aeschylus* (Cambridge: Cambridge University Press, 1983), pp. 82–83.

[9] See the discussion of this point in Albin Lesky, "Decision and Responsibility in the Tragedy of Aeschylus," *Journal of Hellenic Studies* 86 (1966): 78–85; Martha C. Nussbaum, *The Fragility of Goodness: Luck and Ethics in Greek Tragedy and Philosophy* (Cambridge: Cambridge University Press, 1986), chap. 2; and Suzanne Said, *La Faute Tragique* (textes à l'appoi) (Paris: Maspero, 1978).

[10] The curse Agamemnon hoped to prevent by silencing Iphigenia has already been pronounced by his uncle Thyestes and remains the unspoken framework in which the king acts. The curse was uttered after Atreus had murdered Thyestes' children, serving their flesh to him as revenge for his having seduced his wife. So even before the present perversion, this is a house where eagles devour their own innocent young and illicit couplings issue in evil and impiety. In these terms Agamemnon's sacrifice of his daughter is part of a murderous pattern of transgression and revenge that ensnares the house. His deed activates the spirit of vengeance dormant since the first murder of innocents. Although from the standpoint of hereditary pollution Agamemnon is guilty before the sacrifice, it is just to pay the penalty only when he has committed a similar crime and incurred guilt in his own right. Though a member of an accursed family and thus predisposed toward evil, the king is not predestined. The choice may be harder for him than for others; in some sense it may even be an impossible one. Yet he does the deed and cannot escape responsibility for it or for how he lives with its aftermath. In "choosing" to sacrifice his daughter, Agamemnon simultaneously dons the

he can obliterate memory of her and his crime. (When he returns from Troy, he does not mention Iphigenia though the carpet scene and murder recapitulates and inverts the earlier sacrifice.)[11] He has her lifted for sacrifice "as you might a goat" with her saffron mantle, a symbol of marriage, trailing to the ground. For Iphigenia the sacrifice is a *proteleia* (line 226), a rite or ceremony performed before a marriage is consummated. Like the virgin maidens of Troy, her only husband is death. And Agamemnon, by killing his daughter, kills part of himself and becomes, like his daughter, a consort of death.

Finally, Agamemnon destroys the balance of nature. From his sacrifice of Iphigenia he takes a "bitter sacrilegious heart" to Troy where his uncontrolled passion for revenge vents itself indiscriminately on things sacred and mortal, innocent and guilty. This is made clear by Clytaemnestra's pretended fear (which is her secret hope)[12] that the Greeks have violated what they should not; by the chorus's indirect warning about those who, in their great daring, "trample down the delicacy of things inviolable"; and by the herald's report.

Gone are (the Trojan) altars, the sacred places of the gods
and the seed of her land has been wasted utterly.
With such a yoke as this he [Agamemnon] has gripped the neck of Troy.
(*Agamemnon*, 527–29)

Here, as elsewhere in the trilogy, birth and fruitfulness have been murdered, the rich fecundity of the world struck down, and the gods dishonored by perverse sacrifice. As with the murders of Thyestes' children and of Iphigenia, and the coming murder of Agamemnon, intertwining images of marriage, sacrifice, and death cast a net around the action of the play.[13]

Clearly there is something noble about the heroic ethic. Its expansive-

---

yoke of necessity, reactivates the curse, and reveals his patrimony. From then on he loses his freedom and sense of judgment.

[11] Nor is he aware of the excesses he has committed at Troy even though he himself likens his victory to that of a wild lion glutting his hunger on princely blood. (On the importance of the lion image and the parable of the lion, see B.M.W. Knox, "The Lion in the House," *Classical Philology* 47 [1954]: 17–25.) Moreover, he says nothing about the death of his compatriots (whom he denigrates), though he refers to urns and ashes, an image that recalls the king as a partner of Ares in the destruction of Argos. Finally, to the chorus's warning that "you will learn in time which of your citizens have been honest, which unfitting guardians of the city," he too confidently responds that he is fully capable of discerning the envious and insincere and healing any infection in the city (*nosou*, the word translated "infection," can also mean a sickness in the mind, hence madness).

[12] See Hugh Lloyd-Jones, "The Guilt of Agamemnon," *Classical Quarterly* n.s. 12 (1962): 193.

[13] See the discussion in Ann Lebeck, *The Oresteia: A Study in Language and Structure*, pt. 1 (Cambridge, Mass.: Center for Hellenic Studies and Harvard University Press, 1971), and Kitto, *Form and Meaning*, p. 17.

ness is liberating; its drive to test the outer reaches of human capacity is noble and inspiring. Yet it is also a constant temptation to see others and the world as sheer potentiality, as obstacles to be conquered or instruments to be used. Thus driven, men are possessed by a warlike spirit that generates a power of its own, beyond specific objectives, righteous vengeance, or even remembrance. This once-loving father who wept at the mere thought of harming the delight of his house becomes a man who knows neither tears nor his daughter.

Heroism disconnects men from some vital center, some hold or limit that otherwise reminds them that their desire for domination is madness. Uprooting them from the hold of place, it drives them beyond what they can know, see, and judge. Thus driven, men such as Agamemnon kill innocents and forget the dead, trample down the sacred altars of the gods and walk as gods upon rich tapestries the color of congealed blood. The end of this path, as opposed to those built by the Athenians in the *Eumenides*, is ignominious death—Agamemnon murdered by his wife while taking a bath.

There is a lively debate over whether Agamemnon had any choice, whether he put on the yoke of necessity or had it put upon him by the gods or fate. Stated this way, the issue is wrongly posed. For Agamemnon both chooses necessity and Zeus's necessity chooses him. Being the kind of man he is, he chooses as he does, for men act from the necessity of their nature and as the god compels them.[14] Moreover, what matters more than the choice is what happens to Agamemnon after he chooses. And what happens is that he becomes a changed man, unable to recognize that part of himself and the world he had cherished just a moment before. Now blinded, he becomes one-sided, partial, unjust.

In this trilogy as in the *Oedipus Tyrannos*, blindness is a subject and a challenge. Insofar as drama provided a setting and opportunity for its audience to attain an impartiality precluded by the press of daily decisions, it helped those spectators to an insight otherwise unachievable. To the extent that tragedy enabled those in the theater to recognize voices and forces otherwise marginalized, silenced, or denied, it stood as a reminder of what it means to choose and think about choice in the way Agamemnon did. "The essence of tragedy," Helen Bacon writes, "is the moment of concentrated awareness of irreversibility, of that which nothing can undo, in the light of which life, for any survivors on stage and off, including the audience, will henceforth be lived."[15]

[14] See William Arrowsmith, "The Criticism of Greek Tragedy," *The Tulane Drama Review* 3 (1959): 31–57.
[15] Helen Bacon, "Aeschylus," in *Ancient Writers: Volume I*, ed. T. James Luce (New York: Charles Scribner and Sons, 1982), p. 108.

If the temptation of men is the passion for high daring which takes too little account of house, nurture, and female, the vice of women exalts marriage and household at the expense of the masculine force for movement and glory. The chorus that sang of men's pride goes on to speak of "the desperate passions of women without scruple."

> The female force, the desperate
> love crams its resisted way
> to gain total victory
> over the wedded unions of beasts and men.
> (*Libation Bearers*, 599–602)[16]

As Agamemnon leaves his proper place too long, destroying both an inner balance and balance of obligation, so does Clytaemnestra and with similar results. In part this is due to the corruption of Argos, which consumes its citizens and leaders. But in part Clytaemnestra's anger at her daughter's death and long-absent mate transforms her, as the sacrifice of Iphigenia transformed her husband. And as that sacrifice made Agamemnon and Paris unintended accomplices in a violation of the household, so too the king and queen unwittingly join forces to complete the task. Avenging the death of her daughter in the household's name, Clytaemnestra goes on to commit adultery, banish her son, and treat her other daughter like a slave. It is as if her movement out of the household into the city and the power she now has is an excess comparable with that of Agamemnon's. With both, situation and character conspire to drive them beyond justice. In the queen's case this involves confounding the public and private in a way that perverts them both. As a woman who is no woman and a mother who is no mother in a household which is no longer a household, she destroys private life for public ambition. As a ruler who is no ruler but a tyrant, she chokes the space of public action by intimidating political speech and so destroys the polis for "private" revenge.

But it is important to remember that these "mistakes" are not hers alone. Although, unlike the other women in the trilogy, she does indeed act on her own—her brilliant resourcefulness is shown by the system of beacons she establishes to warn her of Agamemnon's arrival—she is also Zeus's avenger of Agamemnon's transgressions, and as she later recognizes, an instrument of the Curse that lies upon the house. Moreover, as I have suggested, what she does is importantly a response to what Agamemnon has done to her. His choice for glory at the expense of house and

---

[16] See the discussion of the entire chorus in Aya Betensky, "Aeschylus' Oresteia: The Power of Clytaemnestra," *Ramus* 7 (1978): 21–22.

family is an assault on the wife-mother-woman whose dignity resides there.

Because of his choice and this assault, Clytaemnestra moves out of the household to assume her husband's place. There is nothing wrong with a queen temporarily donning the mantle of power in her husband's absence. But this queen seems to want something more—to continue to rule even when he returns. That is why Clytaemnestra and her speech block Agamemnon's way when he turns to enter the house and resume his rightful authority. Now she will murder him not only to avenge Iphigenia and her initially fearful loneliness,[17] not simply because she is jealous of Cassandra or loves Aegisthus or merely as Zeus's vehicle for punishing Agamemnon's transgressions or as a member of an accursed house, but also because she envies him as a man.[18]

That is why this woman with a man-counseling heart is not content to kill him without first showing her strength in battle with him. To triumph over the conqueror of Troy is a victory that "justifies" her claim to rule. The battleground is the crimson carpet.[19] Indeed the entire carpet scene is replete with words of conflict: *machēs* (940) suggests both single combat and battle between armies; *nikasthai* (941) means victory, conquest, or getting the upper hand; *dērios* (942) too suggests a fight or contest; and *katestrammai* (956) means to be subdued or reduced by another.[20]

Again like her husband, Clytaemnestra not only assaults the household and city, she destroys the balance of nature. Her actions, like those of her husband, are manifestations of a world pushed out of joint by displaced passion and misplaced energy. The point is indelibly made in her speech gloating over the body of her dead husband. Recounting the deed she uses an image stunning for its sacrilegious parody of ritual forms and twists of cult language.[21]

[17] Here and elsewhere I interpret Clytaemnestra's words as indicating feelings that were once genuine but have been transformed into their opposites. Brian Vickers (*Towards Greek Tragedy* [New York: Longman, 1973], pp. 348–88) argues that Clytaemnestra no longer knows what she is or how she feels, and thus her words are double ironies that say what is true even when she does not intend them to.

[18] Here I follow the argument of R. P. Winnington-Ingram in "Clytaemnestra and the Vote of Athena," *Journal of Hellenic Studies* 68 (1948): 130–47. A comment by Christopher Lasch is apropos: "As social life becomes more and more warlike and barbaric, personal relations which ostensibly provide relief from these conditions take on the character of combat." See *The Culture of Narcissism* (New York: W. W. Norton, 1978), p. 30.

[19] The final confrontation between Orestes and Clytaemnestra is similarly warlike. See the discussion in Thomas G. Rosenmeyer, *The Art of Aeschylus* (Berkeley and Los Angeles: University of California Press, 1982), p. 205.

[20] When (330–47) Clytaemnestra voices hope that the victorious Greeks do not take their revenge too far, her evocation of the passions and details of war suggests a woman with an intuitive grasp of what it means to be a warrior.

[21] The parody is all the more significant if Albert Cook is right that "every tragedy sym-

As he died he spattered me with the dark red
and violent driven rain of bitter savored blood
to make me glad, as gardens stand among the showers
of God in glory at the birthtime of the buds.

(*Agamemnon* 1389–92)

Whatever longing she had for her husband has become a lust for revenge, as if his death provides the sexual gratification denied her by his life away from home. This unnatural consummation of marriage, this wedding of death and blood to life and birth, proclaims a ruthless daring that places the natural order in jeopardy and perverts the ritual of Greek sacrifice. Through the expression of guilt and remorse at the necessity of sacrificing life according to the will of the gods, men showed their deeply rooted respect for life.[22] But Clytaemnestra shows no remorse.

Like the heroic ethic, the life of the household and the dignity of those who sustain it are essential to a fully human life. The house is a space in which the continuity of generations is maintained. But the triumph of the *oikos* is as dangerous as the victory of the heroic ethic. That is because exclusive preoccupation with instinctive attachment, ancient traditions, and biological life is too confining an ethos for living a fully just life. Its intensity precludes resolution of the dilemmas that it generates, and its narrow attachment to generation and life itself disregards more comprehensive activities and realms. In these terms, heroism and home, men and women need each other as conditions of their distinctive integrity. Each without the other is myopic and incomplete.[23] In the absence of reciprocity each goes to extremes and excess, thereby overthrowing house, city, and nature. To flourish, men and women must limit and complement each other. Mutuality is what justice means and what a rightly ordered polis enshrines (though that is not the literal meaning of *dikē*).

Political justice must also resolve the conflict between what is old, traditional, and inherited and what is young, new, innovative, and chosen. In some respects this second tension is a variant of the first. For if women embody reverence for what is continuous, local, and inherited, and if men

---

bolically reproduces a sacrificial pattern" in the sense that the audience is purged by going through the representation of the sufferings on stage. See his *Enactment: Greek Tragedy* (Chicago: Swallow Press, 1971), p. 120.

[22] The point is made by Walter Burkert, "Greek Tragedy and Sacrificial Ritual," *Greek, Roman and Byzantine Studies* 7 (1966): 87–120.

[23] Aeschylus was hardly a "feminist" (though it is possible to conclude from the *Oresteia* that the only way to insure reciprocity between heroism and location is by men and women sharing both). But one could argue that he is intent on reestablishing the "feminine" as an essential aspect of collective life against the domination of the polis; that the reciprocity he counsels is not a mask for domination; and that, as I will argue later, if recast in nongender terms, the argument has real force.

are committed to what is new, far-flung, and chosen, then the tension between the old and new is already implicit in the tension between men and women. This impression is strengthened by the fact that the divine antagonists are again the Furies (older gods championing the ancient religion of the hearth and female) and Apollo (spokesman for the younger gods, the new religion of the polis and the male). But in this second opposition, the fatal bond is between generations—Agamemnon and Iphigenia; Orestes, Electra and Clytaemnestra; Zeus and Kronos. This different alignment of foes presents somewhat different issues.

The central character in this conflict is Orestes, the son sent at Apollo's behest to avenge a male, his father, by killing a female, his mother. Orestes' dilemma presents the past and inheritance as both blessing and curse. On the one hand, his deed and search for purification are undertaken not only to rehabilitate his dishonored father, but to escape the intense sorrow and deprivation of homelessness. As Orestes makes clear, the successful reclaiming of his inheritance as citizen, phratry member, and heir to his father's estates amounts to a rebirth that restores him to wholeness and protects him from the exile's fate of unmourned and forgotten death. The image of the lopped off member withering into nothing suggests that without his inheritance Orestes is a nonentity.[24] Yet with it he is cursed. For inheritance and the past, particularly his inheritance and his past, are an unbearable burden. The yoke of death and revenge infecting the house of Atreus is his legacy fully as much as the lustral waters that restore him to his ancestral religion. Orestes is trapped by the net of his inheritance, which alone gives significance to his life.

The past is a necessity that makes freedom possible, in the same way that the community provides identity for individuals and the play a structure that defines character (in both senses). What is new and innovative must be built on the still-living foundations of what is old and inherited. As something chosen and created, the polis threatens ancient and established ways even as it draws strength from them. A just city gives full and free assent to such ways, which it nevertheless elaborates and reconstitutes. Unlike the unconfined daring of Thucydides' Athenians, those in the *Eumenides* are still patient with their inheritance. At the play's end the Athenians are continuing the task begun in the opening scene when, in alliance with Apollo, they created a civilization out of a wilderness. But the ending, though tied to the beginning, enlarges and changes what was initiated. For now the Athenians are allied with Athena, a goddess who is both female and male and respectful of old and young alike.

[24] John Jones, *On Aristotle and Greek Tragedy* (New York: Oxford University Press, 1962), p. 98. I will argue (in chapter 7) that Socrates understood the relationship between philosophy and Athens in similar terms.

Athena reconciles past, present, and future through instituting the new court that gives place to the Furies. Through her good offices once antagonistic forces and characters are partnered in a manner that enhances the exercise of their respective prerogatives. By her guidance each is able to achieve an efficacy unattainable in their singularity and opposition. It is Athena who shows how the ancient traditions are salutary boundaries for the "reckless pride" of mortals, how inheritance is a necessary limit on the striving for innovation, and how the dark instinctive passions of age-old Furies invigorate dreams of ideality, equity, and balance.[25] As a dialogue between the contemporary city and its formative legend, tragedy itself is a way of healing the breach between generations.

These examples suggest that injustice in the broadest sense is pushing one's claims too far, seeking mastery and domination instead of recognizing the legitimacy of what is other. Injustice is a part masquerading as the whole, like some tyrant claiming absolute sovereignty precluding the participation of others. For instance, both Apollo and the Furies claim to be the exclusive arbiter of the trilogy's conflicts. Like Agamemnon and Clytaemnestra each seeks to banish the other, unaware that in opposing what seems opposed they also oppose themselves. For the world of men and women cannot exist without them both. Each has a rightful share in a whole that their just reciprocity alone completes. Claiming too much for themselves and recognizing too little in their adversaries, both dishonor justice and destroy the balance of nature.

If I am right about these examples and Aeschylus's idea of injustice, then the acquittal of Orestes does not represent the triumph of what is new, male, progressive,[26] civilized,[27] rational, enlightened, and the *polis* over what is old, feminine, regressive, primitive, irrational, Archaic, and the *oikos*. Nor is it a case of the male representing unbinding (will), center, Greek, order, future, rule, and clarity triumphing over the female as

---

[25] The point is made by Robert Fagles in his translation of the *Oresteia* (New York: Bantam Books, 1977), p. 13. I have relied primarily on three translations of the trilogy, adding my own emendations when necessary. They are: Richmond Lattimore's (Chicago: University of Chicago Press, 1953), Hugh Lloyd-Jones's (Englewood Cliffs, N.J.: Prentice-Hall, 1970), and Henry Weir Smyth's (Loeb Classical Library, Cambridge, Mass.: Harvard University Press, 1926). Where feasible I use the Lattimore version both because it is the most widely read and because it (along with the Fagles translation) is unsurpassed in capturing the trilogy's poetry.

[26] George Thomson argues that Aeschylus "regarded the subordination of women, quite correctly, as an indispensable condition of democracy" (see his *Aeschylus and Athens* [New York: Haskell House, 1972], p. 288). Thomson gives a "progressivist" interpretation of the *Oresteia*.

[27] The Furies are "childish and barbarous," the "dark race of the world" before "it won Hellenic culture." Apollo "stands for everything the Furies are not: Hellenism, civilization, intellect and enlightenment" (Richmond Lattimore in his introduction to the *Oresteia*, pp. 30–31.

binding (fate), limit (frontier, interior), Barbarian, chaos, unruly (misrule), and obscurity (riddle).[28] In the play Apollo does not win[29] any more than the Furies lose. Something else and different is happening. What that something is depends on how we understand the character and arguments of the male Apollo (as well as of Clytaemnestra,[30] the unnatural woman, and of Athena, the virgin father-born goddess who opts for the male).

Apollo is harsh and intransigent. He would obliterate the Furies if he could and argues for the male—that he is the only true parent—in a way that eliminates the very idea of matricide.[31] In part this harshness is due to the fact that Apollo's oracle must be fulfilled.[32] But it is not clear why the realization of that oracle necessarily demands the posture and tone he takes. No doubt his bluntness and threats establish an important contrast to the words and persuasion of Athena and may even be a necessary dramatic and theological condition for them. Still, one could argue that Apollo's intransigence is counterproductive;[33] that it is Athena and her ways, not he and his, that actually bring the oracle to pass.

[28] The contrasts are taken from Zeitlin's "Misogyny," p. 171. For a very different view, see Arlene Saxonhouse, "Aeschylus' Oresteia: Misogyny, Filogyny and Justice," *Women and Politics* 4, no. 2 (Summer 1984): 11–32. It is possible to argue both that Aeschylus is trying to preserve the "feminine" against its increasing relegation by the male city *and* that this preservation must be understood in terms of an earlier reversal of power which he rationalizes. In any case, it is a male writer's conception of "femininity" that we are talking about. (Although I am and will be critical of some of Zeitlin's conclusions, I am not directly confronting the terms in which she makes her argument.)

[29] Few contemporary critics claim Apollo "wins." Even Zeitlin who argues that Apollo's "interests are ratified by Athena" agrees that the god is "superseded (but not fully denied)" and that the *Eumenides* "modifies and diminishes the role of Delphic Apollo as the sole arbiter of the Oresteian dilemma in favor of a larger, more inclusive transaction" ("Misogyny," pp. 151, 167, and 172).

[30] It makes a great deal of difference whether one regards Clytaemnestra as a woman villified for refusing to conform to male definitions and power, or as a woman who has adopted the worst in the masculine drive for glory. What one makes of her unmotherliness toward Electra and Orestes is equally crucial. (Her response to the "news" of the latter's "death" contrasts markedly with that of the nurse.) One could argue, as some contemporary feminists do about women who enter the economic and political life to outmale men, that she has forsaken the distinctive dignity of what women have traditionally done for the worst of what men do. The danger, of course, is seeing biology as destiny.

[31] There is a question of whether Clytaemnestra can be made to stand for women and how much the plausibility of Apollo's argument depends on the particular circumstances of her mothering. She is called a woman who is no woman, a wife who is not wife, and, in Electra's words, a mother "whose heart is all unmotherly to her children" (*Libation Bearers*, 190–91). Moreover, it appears that Clytaemnestra never suckled Orestes (though she claims she did), and in fact sent him into exile as if he were a transient in her body. Also, she fails to recognize him when he returns. Apparently Apollo takes the perverse for the norm.

[32] For the reasons why, see Deborah H. Roberts, *Apollo and His Oracle in the Oresteia* (Gottingen: Vandenhoeck and Ruprecht, 1984).

[33] See the discussion of Oliver Taplin, *Greek Tragedy in Action* (Berkeley and Los Ange-

There are other reasons for being uneasy about the opposition between the Furies and Apollo and so the argument that one is victorious over the other. For one thing there is nothing in all surviving Greek tragedy like Apollo's unheralded entry and his silent and unnoticed exit.[34] For another thing, both god and goddesses share a number of characteristics in addition to their common intransigence and partiality. Both remain tied to the old idea of vengeance, disparage an intimate relationship, and are indifferent to extenuating circumstances when it suits their purposes. Both are also morally bivalent. As I indicated in chapter 2, Apollo is called healer and savior, but destroys Cassandra as he did the Greeks at Troy. The Furies are as much sustainers of civilization, pious dread of authority, and punishers of pride and violent outrage by men against their own, as they are uncivilized, outrageous violators.

This bivalance suggests a further commonality: both change their scope of concern in the trilogy, and so the relationship between them changes as well. Apollo sends the avenging Atreidae against Troy and the plague against the avenging Greeks, destroys the Trojan Cassandra, and sends someone who will avenge her death as well as that of Agamemnon.[35] Thus he is not just for the male and often works with the Furies. For their part the Furies are not always opposed to the new gods or preoccupied with matricide. This is not to deny their evolving identification with a rigid law of retribution which they construe narrowly as the punishment of consanguinous murder, or the fact that they appear indifferent to Clytaemnestra's crime (for which, as they point out, she had been paid), or their obliviousness to the constraints that drove her son to his. But they have previously been described as executors of Zeus's justice and as avengers with wider duties. Orestes is afraid of his father's Furies if he should fail to avenge his death; the curse of Atreus's house is identified with the Furies whom Cassandra sees dancing on the roof where the watchman once lay; the gods send the Furies in response to the cry of eagles, and the army dispatched to Troy is likened to a Fury. None of these punishments involve matricide; not all pertain to kindred murder. Thus, when in the *Eumenides* (269–71) the Furies enlarge their concerns from matricide to any dishonor to god, guest, and parent, it is, as so much else in the trilogy, restoration more than "progress." This expanded concern reunites them with Zeus, who is precisely the god responsible for upholding the principles they mention as their new responsibility.

---

les: University of California Press, 1978), pp. 38–39, and Winnington-Ingram, "Studies in Aeschylus," p. 147 (cf. Roberts, "Apollo in the Oresteia," in *Apollo and his Oracle*, chap. 3).

[34] Roberts, *Apollo*, p. 70.

[35] See the discussion in Winnington-Ingram, "Clytaemnestra and the Vote of Athena," in his *Studies in Aeschylus*, pp. 101–31.

There is a further reason why the opposition between Apollo and the Furies is too unsubtle and the assumption that he triumphs leaves out half the story. We are made aware not only of Apollo's moral deficiencies but his political ones as well. The god accepts Orestes as a suppliant and gives him sanctuary, but it is only a temporary refuge. He purifies the matricide yet this is merely a first step. Most important, though he is a codefendant and primary pleader in the case, he does not win it. Depending upon how one reads the text, the vote is either tied or the jury of Athenian males actually votes *for* the Furies and the female. What the vote suggests is that as far as human beings are concerned, men and women are equal, or, at the least, mortals cannot decide otherwise. True the goddess Athena is for the male and that is of the utmost importance for the play and as a statement about the marginality of female citizens. But it is also important to remember that she is for the male when the existence of the polis is at stake and that the female she votes against is a woman whose claims to be a woman are suspect and whose actions are (partly) a response to the transgressions of her husband.

Finally there is a reason of a different kind for being skeptical about the *Oresteia*'s endorsement of Apollo the male. There is external, though inconclusive, evidence that the Athenians regarded Apollo as pro-Spartan at precisely the time Athens was turning away from its onetime ally to that ally's foe, Argos. Moreover, Apollo had given bad—some thought traitorous—advice to the Greeks at the approach of the Persian armies in 480 B.C. Finally, some Athenians were apparently critical of what they regarded as the meddling of the god in their internal politics. A god so mistrusted is unlikely to be regarded as a fountain of wisdom about the place of women in procreation or in the polis.

Even if we accept Apollo's assertion that the child shares the blood only with "him who mounts," whereas the mother receives the alien seed as nurse and stranger or hostess (*xenē*) to the stranger-guest (*xenos*), it does not necessarily denigrate motherhood. For one thing, his argument inverts the conventional view that man belongs to culture and woman to nature. Here the woman has the cultural function of hospitality and nurture whereas the man has the "natural" function of mounting. For another thing, given that the trilogy presents bonds of hospitality as at least as sacred as those of blood (the presiding god is Zeus Xenios), the ultimate transgression is not a violation of the blood tie but Clytaemnestra's murder of a husband as a king. Finally there is the problematic connection between birth and nurture as illustrated by the nurse and the Furies. Neither has actually given birth, yet both give life in the form of nurture. Although the Furies are foreign guests at Athens and so lack any blood ties, they give a second life to the land, people, and the laws of the city. Their transformation, which emphasizes nurture performed by females who are not blood relatives, legitimates Orestes' acquittal, breaks the cycle of vengeance, and prepares for the final scene of healing and release.[36]

In the end Apollo alone is as partial as a world that excludes him. His views, and the forces associated with him, are essential to civilized life only when they are completed, complemented, and incorporated in a larger whole whose legitimacy he does not recognize and would destroy. If he *is* associated with what is male, enlightenment, civilization, rationality, progress, and the polis, then these are as compromised as he is. In these terms Aeschylus is not trying to drag us out of archaic pessimism or embody it, but doing both and so something different from either.[37] Here, as in the trilogy as a whole, the point is not suppression or supersession but incorporation and inclusion.

In these terms justice has four attributes. First, it involves the reconciliation of diversities into a restored yet new city. But insofar as reconciliation connotes mere acceptance (as when we say someone was reconciled to their fate) rather than active collaboration, it is too passive. For justice requires the active complementarity of reciprocity. This second characteristic connotes a continuous though imprecisely defined sharing of authority and mutuality of decision; although it does not posit equality of power, it does preclude domination. Third, justice requires recognition both in the sense of acknowledging the legitimacy of another and in the sense of perceiving something or someone as the same as previously known. In the former case, recognition implies the necessity of taking others into account or giving them due consideration and honor as Athena does with the Furies and Orestes. (She greets them with equal respect and treats them both respectfully throughout the trial.) In the latter instance, recognition is an act of identification, as when Electra recognizes her brother, or Clytaemnestra her avenging son, or Athens its tribulation in the portrait of mythical Argos. Finally, justice demands judgment rather than the mechanical cycle of vengeance that marked the *Agamemnon* and threatened the existence of house and city. Judgment is a question of balance and proportion, of evidence and reflection, of looking backward and forward. It involves the capacity to see things from another's point of view and so accept the human condition of plurality—and to practice what Hannah Arendt calls representative or political

[36] Helen Bacon, "Aeschylus," pp. 149–50.

[37] Thus I am not wholly convinced by E. R. Dodds (in *The Greeks and the Irrational* [Boston: Beacon Press, 1954], p. 40) when he argues that Aeschylus's purpose was "not to lead his fellow-countrymen back into [the archaic world], but, on the contrary, to lead them through it and out of it. This he sought to do, not like Euripides by casting doubt on its reality through intellectual and moral argument, but by showing it to be capable of a higher interpretation, and, in the *Eumenides*, by showing it transformed into the new world of rational justice."

thinking.[38] And, as we shall see, judgment is the faculty that responds to and evaluates action (including drama as a political act).

The discovery of this last element of justice is made by Electra. Its importance is emphasized by Orestes' speech after murdering his mother.[39]

When told by the chorus to pray for the "coming of some man or more than one" to avenge her father, Electra interrupts, asking them, "Do you mean a *dikastēs* or *dikēphoros*?" (*Libation Bearers*, 120). *Dikēphoros*— a bringer of retribution or reciprocal killer—is no new word. The herald used it in referring to Agamemnon's overthrow of Troy (*Agamemnon*, 525), and Aegisthus mentions it (*Agamemnon*, 1525–27). But *dikastēs* is a new word and means one who will judge. (In Athens a *dikast* is a juryman who brings justice.) By this distinction Electra asks what has been previously unaskable—Is retribution just?—and points the way out of the narrow legalism of revenge enunciated by the chorus.[40]

That same question concerns Orestes as he contemplates the act he must do and later reflects back on the act he has done. Unlike either of his parents, he is aware that what he must do is a crime as great as the crime it avenges and that the old conception of *dikē*—like for like—involves an unending cycle of bloodshed. (Both Agamemnon and Clytaemnestra think their crime is an end to past crimes and a new, cleansed beginning.) Confronting his mother and his impending matricide, Orestes cries "Wrong was the murder that you did, wrong is the fate you now suffer" (*Libation Bearers*, 930).[41]

Orestes' point of view is broader than that of his parents. He understands his act more generally than they did theirs. And this difference in perspective is related to the meaning of justice. For all four elements of justice require and promote an inclusive understanding of human action

---

[38] See her essay, "Truth and Politics" in *Between Past and Future* (New York: The Viking Press, 1968), pp. 241–43.

[39] It is significant that this liberating distinction is made by a woman.

[40] See the discussion of this point in Kitto, *Form and Meaning*, pp. 40–41; Havelock, *Greek Concept of Justice*, p. 289; and Anthony J. Podlecki, *The Political Background of Aeschylean Tragedy* (Ann Arbor: University of Michigan Press, 1966), chap. 5.

[41] Orestes stands over his dead mother as she stood over her slain husband. But this similarity merely heightens the disparity of attitude. Orestes begins politically—"Beyond the two tyrants of our land"—only afterward turning to their private wrongs, whereas Clytaemnestra does the reverse. Moreover, Orestes offers no lurid account of the actual murder. Furthermore, whereas Clytaemnestra was indifferent to public judgment (cf. *Agamemnon*, 1403) Orestes invites it. (This concern with judgment was introduced by Electra's distinction between *dikastēs* and *dikēphoros*, mentioned previously.) In addition, Orestes does not glory in his deed as his mother did. His victory is "polluted and has no pride" (1017). Finally, the son lacks the mother's self-righteousness. He knows, as she did not, that no one can murder and then peacefully enjoy the fruits of the crime. He never claims that his act will heal the festering wounds or break the cycle of revenge. On the contrary, he sees "not how this thing will end."

and relations. One figure in the drama shows and embodies this breadth of vision and justice—the goddess Athena. It is she who unites male and female, new and old. Although she herself is a young goddess and opts for the male, she, unlike Apollo, shows great respect to the older gods and decides for Orestes only in the end and when the existence of the polis is at stake.[42] And even then she does not excuse his deed for no one can be allowed to undo the deeds of the past. Instead she completes the process of purification, thereby returning to him his capacity to act, which would otherwise be confined to a single deed from whose consequences he could never recover.[43]

Not only does she bring the warring factions together, she shares her power with others while doing so. When asked to judge between the Furies of Clytaemnestra and Apollo-Orestes, she institutes the Areopagus, a human court, to assist her in the decision.[44] She goes on to instruct these twelve best citizens and all her citizens to bear witness to the trial, the following confrontation, and the ultimate reconciliation with the Furies. In this way Athena teaches the jurors, the audience in the play, and the Athenian audience watching the play what justice is and how it must be lived.[45]

But from another point of view it is not Athena who teaches, but Aeschylus himself inspired by the goddess. For what Athena does in the play, Aeschylus does through it. This is not only a matter of drama instructing men in civic virtue through explicit content. It also involves an affinity between dramatic form and political justice.

[42] But Athena, like Clytaemnestra, is a sexually ambiguous figure. "Everything that Clytaemnestra's nature demanded and her sex forbade Athena is free to do by virtue of her godhead." She is a god-goddess to Clytaemnestra's man-woman and her masculinity wins praise and worship while Clytaemnestra's leads to disaster. See Winnington-Ingram, "Clytaemnestra and the Vote of Athena," pp. 44–45. Although Christian Meier (*Die Entstehung des Politischen bei den Griechen* [Frankfurt: Suhrkamp, 1980]) agrees with me that the *Oresteia* is about the foundations of a political order and that both the Furies and Apollo are irresponsible in their intransigence, he disagrees about the role of Athena whose intervention he regards as simply an extension of the partisan controversy rather than as a means for its resolution.

[43] See Hannah Arendt, *The Human Condition* (Chicago: University of Chicago Press, 1974), pp. 236–43.

[44] Aeschylus identifies the court with the Athenian people as a whole (lines 566, 638, 775, 997, 1010). While the Areopagus is the "best of citizens (*astōn . . . ta beltata*) that is to emphasize not that they are superior, but they perfectly represent the city"; see MacLeod, "Politics and the Oresteia," p. 127.

[45] The trial scene itself has been characterized as a farce and burlesque intended to suggest the limitations of Athenian legal practices (see Lebeck, *The Oresteia*, chap. 14). I think these views rest on (1) a too-narrow reading of the "trial"; (2) an inaccurate assumption that blood guilt is here being replaced by legal debate, rational decisions, and principles of equity; (3) an overemphasis on the trial scene as the turning point in the trilogy; and (4) a misreading of the significance of the tie vote and Athena's intervention.

JUSTICE EXISTS when men and women are part of a whole larger than themselves. To think and act justly requires acknowledging the need for a unity of difference. A just polis is the setting where such diversity is duly recognized and the inevitable conflicts created by it are muted without violation. As part of the polis, drama both defines this achievement and participates in it. I have already argued that it does so in content; I now want to show how dramatic form seconds the substantive teachings on justice. This involves indicating how the structure of tragedy itself exemplifies justice; of how reconciliation, reciprocity, recognition, and judgment operate amid the layered tension between intelligence and passion, limits and action, political discourse and poetry, wisdom and suffering, and the *Eumenides* and the *Agamemnon*.

Especially in the *Agamemnon*, passion's destructiveness is everywhere, disrupting house, city, and cosmos. Each actor seeks an end to the reign of limitless passion by asserting his or her passion as definitive while preempting that of others. Each seeks to be sovereign and so force others to be lifeless or apathetic. But this is no solution either in the *Agamemnon* or in Greek society generally. For passionate action is the necessary condition for the excellence of word and deed Greeks regarded as distinctive to human life. Only the preeminent man or city could make a name for itself and so live beyond its time and place. They alone had a second life in the songs and stories of the poets and in the actions their storied greatness inspired in future generations. The brilliance of their words and deeds revealed the spark of divinity in men, pushing aside the darkness that shrouds those who lack the courage or opportunity to act before others in the light of day. Those silent and nameless ones pass their days in obscurity and leave no mark on the world they so briefly inhabit.[46] "The best of men," Heraclitus wrote, "choose one thing rather than all else; everlasting fame among mortal men. The majority are satisfied, like well-fed cattle."[47]

Moreover, passion and action (like the Furies and "mankind" in the choral ode on man) have a double capacity for violence and renewal, death and birth, obliteration and making known, consuming and empowering.[48] In the corrupt polis of Argos every act, however liberating, is itself a transgression that brings suffering to the actor and community. That is the dilemma of Orestes, who is aware that his act is a crime before he

---

[46] Thus women's, Chicano, or black history is partly an attempt to rescue those consigned to oblivion by bringing them "before the public."

[47] Frag. 29 in Kathleen Freeman, *Ancilla to the Pre-Socratic Philosophers* (Oxford: Basil Blackwell, 1948), p. 26.

[48] See Fagles, *Oresteia*, p. 14, and Albin Lesky, "Decision and Responsibility in the Tragedy of Aeschylus," *Journal of Hellenic Studies* 86 (1966): 78–85, who writes "It was Aeschylus who discovered the problem of the uncertainty of human action."

commits it, but also knows that it must be done.[49] A just polis seems immune to this dualism. Certainly the Athens we see on stage at the end of the *Eumenides* shows (or at least indicates) men and women as partners in sustaining a whole that gives identity and dignity to each, rather than as victims of each other's actions. Similarly young and old are not warring factions but mutual participants in a collectivity that communalizes the burdens of action while providing object and limit for passion. In Athens the deeds of children do not murder those of parents but enlarge them. Freed from the mechanical cycle of revenge and the life-destroying passions that paralyzed action in the *Agamemnon*, these Athenians will participate in framing their own destiny in conjunction with the gods. Yet even a just city is composed of mortals and thus of potentially warring forces. Athens too must rely on those passions and actions whose destructiveness we have seen in the *Agamemnon*. Although the just polis does offer respite from injustice and corruption, it is only a respite. Even if it can turn ruinous forces toward good, the dual capacity of passion and action remains.[50] That is why all resolution is but temporary.

It is also why all endings are also beginnings. As long as men are both doers and victims, actors and analysts of action, free and constrained—that is, as long as they live human lives—no final escape from contingency is possible. For to act is to begin something new and unexpected even for the actor himself or herself.[51] Action initiates a chain of further action and reaction whose ending cannot be predicted and whose consequences disturb established practices. One's act is like one's child: you give birth to it, it is yours, and you are responsible for it. Yet it has a life of its own that frustrates the best intentions. For no matter how free an initial act

---

[49] The point is made by the chorus in the *Libation Bearers* (313–14) when they say: "Who acts, shall endure. So speaks the voice of age-old wisdom" (*Drasanti pathein, trigerōn mythos tade phōnei*). In the particular context, endure (*pathein*) means to suffer in pain and as victim. But in terms of the trilogy as a whole (though it is not in the literal meaning of the Greek) endure suggests "live on in memory" such that only by acting do men create stories in which they survive their physical demise. All three meanings are present when Orestes turn to Pylades and asks *ti drasō* ("What shall I do?") (*Drasō* like *drasanti*, comes from the Doric *dran*, which means to act and from which "drama" derives.) In English his question is really three questions: How shall or should I act? How can I bear the suffering that awaits me? How will I be remembered for the deed I am about to commit?

[50] That even the best of lives is mixed with unhappiness is said by Achilles in the reconciliation scene with Priam (Homer, *Iliad*, 24. 525–30).

[51] See Arendt, *The Human Condition*, p. 169; her essay "What is Freedom," in *Between Past and Future*, pp. 143–72; and James Redfield, *Nature and Culture in the Iliad: The Tragedy of Hector* (Chicago: University of Chicago Press, 1975), p. 64: "The success or failure of an action is known only by its results, and since every result leads to a further result, the final result is never before us. . . . The actor commits himself to the future and thus never knows his own act; since the future is without limit, there is no moment when the results are in."

may be, the fact that people live among other acting beings insures that the meaning and reality of what an actor does escapes his or her understanding and control. And that means that one's deeds take on a life of their own, working themselves out over time and space as did the curse of the house of Atreus. In sum, the irony of action, with its bifurcated moral potentialities, is present whenever human beings live together.

It is drama that makes this irony and the more general duality it exemplifies vivid, intelligible, and bearable. By telling a story with a beginning, a middle, and an end it provides a finitude for action that is essential to judgment yet is never so clearly present outside of drama. Similarly, it displays the potency of passion within safe boundaries by depicting madness and excess within the structure of theater, stage, and poetic form. In this way tragedy illuminates the darkest passions as spur and foundation of its own enterprise, the polis, justice, and wisdom. It extends the idea of reciprocity (and justice) from a sharing of authority between men and women, past and present, to a sharing between passion and "reason." Once more justice requires that each be an enhancing limit on the other. Thus enlightenment, even when joined with friendship and goodwill, is insufficient to unite citizens in a harmonious community without the aid of those passions represented by the Furies. That is why (in the *Eumenides*) Athena compensates for the new benevolence of the Furies, now the Eumenides. When they had threatened desolation, she spoke of fruitfulness. Now when they sing a song of benediction, she responds in solemn counterpoint, calling them by their old name as if to remind her citizens that their hard-won and new-found justice must incorporate the instinctive passions that men and women forget in moments of intellectual achievement.

The need for, and meaning of, reciprocity between passion and intelligence is elaborated by a parallel need for reciprocity between poetry and political discourse. Once more it is possible to see how the justice extolled in the trilogy is reiterated in its dramatic form.

The dense poetry of the *Agamemnon* creates an oppressive atmosphere that is both claustrophobic and boundless.[52] In that play men are silent or reduced to abortive and deceitful speech. Yet at the same time speech seems unfocused, too full of meanings the speakers cannot understand, as if the world lacks firm center and coherence. Metaphors, images, and omens have endless associations and create unintended ironies that split human discourse into fragments, concealing rather than revealing the meaning of events. Word and deed have parted company. For instance the chorus's thoughts in the *Agamemnon* are bifurcated into intentional meanings and unselfconscious significance. More than that, their resis-

---

[52] Fagles, *Orestia*, p. 44.

tance to the prophecies of Calchas and Cassandra suggest that they have a stake in this separation and the ignorance it sustains. It is only after a fact they cannot avoid—the king's murder—that they begin an unqualified search for clear speech and interpreters. Only then does the knowledge they unconsciously possess and indirectly express become a direct and clear statement.[53] This movement from obscurity to clarity reaches its culmination in the institutionalization of political discourse at Athens. Compared with the enigmatic utterances of the *Agamemnon*, the *Eumenides* is notable for simplicity of expression (outside of the less frequent choruses). Here there is no tangled net of language to stunt speech. No deceit or irony persists in polluting discourse. Word and deed are joined, revealing the actors to each other and reestablishing previously severed relations.

There is no doubt that the triumphs of clarity over obscurity and of persuasion over force are represented as a stupendous achievement.[54] Without it, human enterprise would be doomed to failure, the Furies lament already repeated (776–92, 808–24) would go on endlessly, the cycle of revenge would continue until Argos and Atreus' house were no more and rational discourse could not exist.[55] Yet the achievement is misunderstood if seen as part of the permanent triumph of the polis over the earlier world of the *Agamemnon*.[56] As the chorus in *Antigone* reminds us, as the Priestess's song interrupted by the Furies suggests, as road making is circumscribed by nets, and as Apollo is wrong to regard the Furies as primitive relics of a vanished order rather than pillars of all governments including Zeus's, so must this victory of clear speech and persuasion be

[53] Lebeck, *The Oresteia*, gives a masterful analysis of this process.

[54] For Rosenmeyer (*The Art of Aeschylus*) there is no such achievement because language has been transparent throughout. He finds no "tenuous connections with secret reverberations and rebellious second thoughts" in Aeschylus as one does in Sophocles and Euripides. "The immediacy of Aeschylean speech is, therefore, a last vestige of public communication, of a rhetoric that stays, at every step, in tune with its listeners" (p. 86). In almost diametrically opposite terms, Simon Goldhill, *Language, Sexuality, Narrative: The Oresteia* (Cambridge: Cambridge University Press, 1984), emphasizes "the text's plurality, its openness to the production of meaning, its 'textuality' " (p. 4).

[55] Nancy Rabinowitz argues that persuasion is "the only weapon that can justify the Olympian victory and make it permanent. . . . The appeal to the goddess Peitho breaks the Erinyes' pattern of lament and marks the beginning of rational discourse; thus when reason supplants force, the chain of killing can be broken, for there are no remnants of the old hostility lingering on to undermine the new order" ("From Force to Persuasion: Aeschylus' *Oresteia* as Cosmogonic Myth," *Ramus* 10, no. 2 [1981]: 183). As my argument makes clear, I do not share this sense of permanence.

[56] E. R. Dodds, "Morals and Politics in the Oresteia," *Proceedings of the Cambridge Philological Society* n.s. 6 (1960): 19–31, argues persuasively for Argos being a corrupt polis rather than a prepolitical state organization left behind by a progressive evolution to the classical city-state.

similarly qualified. (It is interesting that Athena reminds us that persuasion ultimately depends on Zeus's thunderbolt.) We know such exclusive claims threaten justice, the polis, and drama itself.

If all this is true, then the transparency of the *Eumenides* represents both a gain in clarity *and* a loss of meaning (or at least a temptation to forget and erase). For order requires the vivid potential of disorder; the relative abstractness of political discourse requires both distance from and dependence on the primal passions and compact poetry of the earlier play and world. This is what the *Oresteia* both shows and does in its insistence that political and linguistic order must simultaneously sustain and constrain the conflicting passions that are the substance of public life. The polis (and tragedy) cannot exist without engaging these passions, which are its source of energy, the spring of patriotism, and the foundations of its dignity. Yet it can barely exist with them, for its precarious unity demands the constant attention by citizens of judgment.

Similarly, while speech is a prerequisite for a healthy political life, silence too has its assigned place. In the first two plays, silence is almost always a strategem, or a consequence of intimidation. But once speech is righted, silence too can resume its proper place. Thus twice (1035, 1038) in the final passages of the *Eumenides* the female escort speaks of silent blessing and reverence. Because the polis is founded on such reverence, the implication is that public speech rests on what is sacred and unspeakable, that the world of the *Eumenides* presupposes that of the *Agamemnon*, and that politics relies on passions inarticulate within its realm of discourse. Thus, although there are things inappropriate for or dangerous to such discourse, they are nevertheless fundamental to it. In his position as poet and political educator, the dramatist reminds the citizens of the silent foundations of their speech. By expressing the deepest instincts and passions within the boundaries of his drama, he articulates their powerful and essential presence in public, yet at a distance from the assembly and agora.

If political and dramatic forms are a reduction necessary for life, and if in our need for patterned intelligibility and judgment we construct stories that sacrifice complexity, then dramatic form must point outside itself for the same reasons that political justice in the polis can never be finally achieved but is always in the imperfect process of achievement. Like the Socratic philosophy that they inspire, drama and political justice involve a search made possible by a form whose incompleteness calls itself into question. This is one reason why I do not regard the ending of the *Eumenides* as a triumph of speech, reason, and justice over the rightly jettisoned "primitivism" of the *Agamemnon*.

I do not mean to interpret away the joyful reconciliation that marks the trilogy's close and restores the balance of nature. The final scene of previously malevolent life-destroying forces now gracious and generative, of men and women brought together in mutually sustaining embrace, and of the divine Furies sharing authority with the august Areopagus is truly awesome. Robes once strewn beneath and draped around the victim Agamemnon, displayed by his son Orestes to justify his deed and by Apollo to justify his, are now carried by the female chorus to consecrate the polis. When these women twice speak of silent blessing and reverence, even the *Agamemnon* and *Eumenides* seem to have made peace with each other. Finally, and most impressively, there are the old and new gods reunited, not in destruction (as they were at Troy), but in giving life to Athens. Now, at last, the world has been set right; humankind has found healing and release.

Nor would I deny the enormous claims Aeschylus makes for the polis; it is nothing less than the greatest achievement of human thought and action, a singular yet collective culmination of mankind's search for freedom, order, and justice. A righteous city is the end (telos, culmination, completion) of human striving, the place where all true paths lead, the welcoming home as distinct from the abortive homecomings of the first two plays. In it all claims, principles, and individuals are given place, part, and purpose in an inclusive yet bounded community of differences. As the trilogy is larger than any single play or character, so the polis is more than the individuals who compose it. But for all this, the final reconciliation does not and cannot obliterate what has gone before. To imagine that it could misses the point of tragedy, politics, and justice and blunts one of the most sharply etched teachings of drama—that wisdom comes only with grief and remembered pain.

The world of the *Agamemnon* remains a living presence at the trilogy's end not only as an omnipresent image of corruption and alternative to justice, but as the suffered preface to the political wisdom of the *Oresteia* as a whole. To suppose that world wholly discredited by the concluding celebration misses the meaning of the gnomic *pathei mathos*, that wisdom comes through suffering. For Aeschylus, the violent kindness of the gods decrees that humans must suffer and that from this suffering, though against their will, comes the wisdom of discretion.[57] The passions men have and the trials they experience because of them are the most powerful teachers of political wisdom and the firmest support for political justice. Without them, intelligence and understanding are impotent.

Thus suffering can hardly be relegated to a previous, less-civilized age or play. If this is true, then it becomes the task of the poet-dramatist not merely to display suffering or instill it in his audience, but to show this

[57] What men learn is that they can only learn through the consequences of their acts when the hitherto hidden significance of their "doings" is revealed.

inescapable connection between pain and passion on the one hand and the achievement of wisdom and justice on the other. That is why the Furies must not be banished, and why Athena, founding the city, echoes their sentiments.

In the *Agamemnon* human suffering is particularly intense. Men and women collide with a recalcitrant reality under a double yoke of necessity—their own nature and a world they did not make. Here suffering is barren, an affliction that constricts understanding rather than enlarging it (though Clytaemnestra does come to recognize the working of the curse). Only in the just city (Athens at the end of the *Eumenides*) is suffering liberated from fruitless reproduction. There it becomes the foundation for a mode of political thought and judgment alert to the meaning of human power *and* mortality. And it is tragedy's part in this city that makes the point and assists in the deed. On the one hand, the *Oresteia* presents the polis as an awesome achievement and encourages the citizenry to recognize their greatness as it is displayed on stage. But on the other hand, because this presentation is idealized, the spectators become aware of the discrepancy between the drama's vision of order and the political disarray of the contemporary city. The distance between the two emphasizes the precarious nature of what has been gained and the constant proximity of loss. This recognition reinforces what the similarity-contrast of the *Agamemnon* and *Eumenides* has already made clear: that others like us have been defeated in the struggle with primal chaos, and our fate may be like theirs. When we feel for them, we become aware of our own limitations.[58] By reminding us of our mortality in the midst of celebrating human power, tragedy maintains the suffering necessary for wisdom. Thus the *Oresteia* does not end suffering but collectivizes it through the medium of dramatic performance. Drama itself may even replace part of the experience of suffering and thus become a source of wisdom. But the wisdom drama offers about individual and collective mortality, the dangers of pride, the contingent nature of politics, the fragility of justice, and the moral opacity of action brings suffering in its wake. Thus suffering brings wisdom and wisdom suffering.

If this analysis is fair, then the joyous finale of the trilogy is neither as joyful nor as final as it appears. The memory of earlier plays and the discrepancy between poetic vision and political realities penetrate the celebrations of the city's founding in the same way Greek sacrifice joined festive joy with the horror of death.[59] However powerful the final hymns of benediction, they cannot wholly seal off the memory of death, perver-

[58] Cassandra is the pivotal character here. Speaking of her, Wilamowitz says her knowledge is "her special sorrow" (*Griechische Tragoedien* [Berlin: Weidmannsche Buchhandlung, 1909], p. 41).

[59] Burkert, "Greek Tragedy and Sacrificial Ritual," p. 106.

sion, violence, and disease that dominated the earlier portions of the drama. Despite its "happy" ending, "reading the *Oresteia* makes one afraid for one's life."[60]

Especially one's collective life. For an Athenian watching the play it is this life that is dramatized and hangs in the balance. His city has embarked on radical domestic reforms and foreign adventures. Political passions are intense, and civil war threatens. As the pull of immoderate demands unravels the tightly woven fabric of communal life, citizens treat each other as Apollo and the Furies did. Each side claims exclusive privilege at the expense of others and of the whole. By dramatizing this crisis, the *Oresteia* puts the city on trial before itself. The judgment Athena asks citizen-jurors to render in the drama becomes paradigmatic for the one spectators are expected to render on the actors, actions, and the play they see before them. These in turn become paradigmatic for the citizen-actors outside of the play and theater. And as Athena is the political educator in the trilogy, so Aeschylus is through it. Inspired by the goddess and assuming the Solonic mantle of poet-sage, the playwright joins with both the goddess and lawgiver in contributing to his city's political self-education, its wisdom, and its justice. By making the tensions and sheer formlessness of human life lucid and thus intelligible without slighting the contingency of politics, the permeability of human constructs, the irony of action, or the duality of passion, Aeschylus seconds the prodigious integration of life his trilogy commends. Insisting that men and women recognize their inevitable subjection to the contradictions of existence, his reflection on politics and justice allows them to understand their predicament and, in that understanding, find a strength of character, mind, and action to sustain a distinctively human life. So is the promise of Hephastus's sons realized in Athens and in tragedy.

A NOTE ON MISOGYNY AND METHOD

There is a catch to all this. Insofar as road building is associated with a male god who is compromised in the drama, the play encourages us to "interrogate" the paths it prescribes, the accommodations it accepts, and the adequacy of the road building as a metaphor for the creation of politics and justice.

Let me address this issue by looking again at the themes of sexual politics in the *Oresteia* from a slightly different standpoint.[61]

---

[60] This sentence concludes Brian Vicker's analysis of the *Oresteia* in *Towards Greek Tragedy*, p. 425.

[61] I am less concerned with issues raised by generational conflict (such as disinheritance, exile) for two reasons: it receives less critical attention than gender issues and because I will deal with them in the next chapter.

Critics agree that Clytaemnestra and the world she rules are character-ized by disorder and perversion. Boundaries are transgressed, distinctions obliterated, norms violated, rightful heirarchies ignored or inverted. Nothing is as it seems; no one is as they appear to be; all walk too firmly upon a glass surface that can shatter and mortally wound at any moment and in a second. Clytaemnestra herself is a baffling mixture; a life-giving mother who is a killing monster, a mannish woman whose beacon is a dark flame and whose words of love suggest murderous embrace.[62]

But they disagree about Aeschylus's (or the play's) attitude toward Cly-taemnestra and women. Winningham-Ingram[63] considers the trilogy a protest against the tragic status of Athenian women. Brian Vickers argues that Aeschylus "exorcises" the unnatural Clytaemnestra with "a sus-tained concentration of moral disapproval rarely equaled in literature,"[64] John Jones insists that "even the simplest Athenian in Aeschylus' audi-ence" would have seen Clytaemnestra's sexual and ritual noncompliance with the socioreligious norm as the central fact about her and the play,[65] while Froma Zeitlin regards the *Oresteia* as "the decisive model for the future legitimation of [misogyny] in Western thought."[66]

I do not wish to comment on this controversy any more than I have already except to raise a final question about justice in the *Oresteia* and introduce an interpretative principle I elaborate in chapter 8.

It seems to me that Aeschylus "uses" the politics of gender and sexu-ality to make "larger" points about "the" human condition.[67] Of course, it matters that he dramatizes those points about justice, tyranny, stasis, and transgression by focusing on a woman who refuses prescribed roles,

[62] The net with which Clytaemnestra trapped Agamemnon (*amphiblēstron*) can also mean embrace; *paiein* means both to strike and to have sexual intercourse with; the robes are bridal robes. (On this double set of references, see Rabinowitz, "From Force to Persua-sion," pp. 173–74.)

[63] "Clytaemnestra and the Vote of Athena," p. 146.

[64] *Towards Greek Tragedy*, p. 423.

[65] He would have seen it because "he lived in a society where women had no public life to live, neither political nor sacerdotal nor military, and where their private self was sup-posed to find fulfillment and a complete exhaustion of resources in sustaining the larger family life in which it was enveloped." *On Aristotle and Greek Tragedy* (New York: Oxford University Press, 1962), p. 118.

[66] "Misogyny," p. 150. Zeitlin argues that the pacification of women is an ideological effort to solve the dilemma of the inextricable connections between female fertility and fe-male sexuality by making women subordinate to men within the family in patriarchal mar-riage and the family subordinate to the city (pp. 159, 172). Along similar lines, see Mary O'Brien, *The Politics of Reproduction* (London: Routledge and Kegan Paul, 1983), pp. 145–46.

[67] Kathy Ferguson does something similar in *The Feminist Case against Bureaucracy* (Philadelphia: Temple University Press, 1984). I use quotations here to indicate (what is perhaps obvious) that such words presuppose a politics if not a theory.

who first challenges and then triumphs over her husband. But the larger question the play provokes is whether Aeschylus's understanding of justice, with its acknowledgment of hierarchy, acceptance of normalization, and the boundaries necessary for political "health" are persuasive if "we" do not make it gender specific. True, Clytaemnestra is directly described or indirectly linked to *deinos* words,[68] and so likened to a monster. But as the last chapter's consideration of the choral ode on man indicates, this double capacity for creation and destruction is not limited to women, but characterizes "civilization" itself. In these terms, Clytaemnestra's conquering of time and space through the brilliantly ingenious system of beacons and her equally brilliant strategy in conquering Agamemnon is a warning against human presumption made more vivid by her being a woman but not exclusively about her.

It is also true that the trilogy can be interpreted as commending the sexual division of labor and the continued political marginalization of women. Even so, this does not address the question of whether Aeschylus is right in commending the mutual dependence of location and heroism. Does the trilogy provide significant ways of thinking about the relationship between public and private life or foreign and "domestic" politics? Of course, none of us lives in an *oikos* or a *polis*. Nor are we likely to have to choose between leading an army and sacrificing our children. But in less dramatic terms there are many who must balance the ties of place and parenting with work and politics, who try to stay whole amid demands that threaten to pull that whole apart, and who try, as best they can, to honor the things that, for the moment at least, they have been forced to choose against.

Even if Aeschylus is a misogynist, the trilogy helps us see why misogyny is unjust and the limits of the values it ends up reconstituting. It does this not only by dramatizing the process of normalization, but by providing us with a principle of justice that bids us to see the inconsistency of application much as the incomplete liberal critique of patriarchy nevertheless provided a language (of consent, rights and liberty) that feminists have used to extend the critique well beyond its initial intentions.[69] Put another way, we could say that the play invites us to augment its principle of justice by creating a more inclusive political structure and cultural narrative than "it" contains. At the same time that this enlarged framework provides a vantage point to see the limits of the *Oresteia*'s more exclusive frame, the trilogy warns against this movement toward inclusiveness in terms analogous to those it brings against the heroic impulse for "going

[68] See the discussion in Betensky, "Aeschylus' Oresteia," p. 21.

[69] This argument has been made by Carole Pateman in "Women and Consent," *Political Theory* 8, no. 2 (1981): 149–68.

too far." The encouragement of generality and the warning against the loss generality entails reappears in the *Apology* and *Crito* as a tension between philosophy and Socrates on the one hand and politics and Athens on the other.

Perhaps all texts reveal their incompleteness and are, to that extent, failures. Or, to put it less polemically, perhaps they point away from themselves to something their form cannot capture.[70] What is distinctive about Greek tragedy[71] is that completeness and form are its subject and that it treats that subject in ways that allow the participation of otherwise subjugated knowledges.

Wisdom from suffering (*pathei mathos*) is not an exclusively intellectual claim. Rather it suggests that passional reaction (the suffering itself) is, in Martha Nussbaum's words, "a partial constituent of the character's correct understanding of his situation as a human being. . . . There is a kind of knowing that works by suffering because suffering is the appropriate acknowledgement of the way human life in their cases, is." This is an occasion and way of living that cannot, even in principle, be grasped by intellect alone.[72] Thus, the kind of intellect tragedy encourages is one mindful of incoherence, respectful of the contradictoriness of experience, and conscious that questions about justice and politics do not yield their significance to terse hypotheses. Because political knowledge remains embedded in plot and characterization, such knowledge is necessarily allusive and imitative rather than explicit and determinative.[73] It does not so much solve problems as deepen our understanding of them and of the delusions of problem solving. Making our dilemmas vivid, the *Oresteia* draws us toward the stage as participants in the struggle to create meaning and sense about a world that outruns our advances and overflows our categories. The "success" of the trilogy is measured not in the number of propositions it proves, but in the number of illuminations it provokes, in the horizons it widens, and in its effectiveness in making us think harder and act differently.[74]

Of course, we do confront problems, foremost among them being a

[70] How this happens is discussed by Stanley E. Fish in *Self-Consuming Artifacts: The Experience of Seventeenth-Century Literature* (Berkeley and Los Angeles: University of California Press, 1972), chap. I and appendix.

[71] It is distinctive though not unique, as I shall argue in chapter 9 on *The Crying of Lot 49*.

[72] Nussbaum, *The Fragility of Goodness*, pp. 45–46. She opposes this poetic knowledge to philosophical knowledge more unequivocally than I will in chapter 8.

[73] See Sheldon Wolin, "Political Theory as a Vocation," in *Machiavelli and the Nature of Political Thought*, ed. Martin Fleisher (New York: Atheneum, 1972), pp. 23–75, esp. pp. 45–46, and my discussion of the essay in the introduction to *Greek Tragedy and Political Theory*.

[74] Fish is here (*Artifacts*, p. 8) talking about what he calls a "teacher-dialectician."

determination of who "we" are as persons and citizens. It is who we are that enables us to discover elided dimensions in modern (or postmodern) and ancient materials, not serially or instrumentally but simultaneously, often unexpectedly, sometimes shockingly. There is no method here, nor much concern about method except perhaps to insist that methodists invariably discount their own points of departure precisely when they are most sure of their newness and most contemptuous of what they do not see before them.

FOUR

Identity and the
Oedipus Tyrannos

PEOPLE'S IDENTITIES are revealed by the way they move and hold themselves, by their speech and deeds and by the character and fate that seems theirs alone. When we identify "who" people are, we invariably distinguish them from others by enumerating those characteristics that make them who they are rather than someone else. That is why Pericles as well as Socrates contrast their steadfastness with the "situational ethics" of their opponents and why calling someone a chameleon is a moral epithet. We often begin our identification by "naming" the person, perhaps echoing the Greek belief that a person's name (say Oedipus or Pentheus) is an omen and oracle of identity, then placing them in some narrative that mentions their parents and ancestors, where they come from and now belong, and where they stand in the world. In these terms, to identify someone is to locate them within a set of coordinates of time and space.

As this suggests, to identify someone is not just to distinguish them from others; it is also to identify them with others. Identity is a matter of standing with as well as standing apart, of community as well as individuality. "Who" we are is disclosed by our singularity amidst a condition of plurality; it involves describing what makes us different and the shared life in which those differences can be noted and understood.[1] Although our political discourse insists on an opposition between community and individuality or authority and freedom, identity seems to require that we undersand particularity by reference to those others with whom we share a history and a life. Diversity presupposes unity just as distinctiveness does belonging.[2] At least one etymology of freedom defines a free man or

---

[1] How much we share and the nature of that sharing obviously varies from culture to culture. In what we like to call a pluralistic society, any single sharing must compete with other duties or obligations. Of course, the intensity of involvement varies as well. In the polis a man was simultaneously a member of a household and city. Insofar as he thought of himself as a Hellene (rather than a barbarian) he might claim a cultural identity as well. More abstractly still he might regard himself as being of a certain race (in Hesiod's sense), or as living at a particular time (as Thucydides does) or as sharing a common mortality.

[2] "Only when difference has its home, when the need for belonging in all its murderous intensity has been assuaged, can our common identity begin to find its voice" (Michael Ignatieff, *The Needs of Strangers* [New York: Viking Press, 1984], p. 131).

woman as someone who lives among those with whom they share a common origin.[3]

To say that one's identity is defined against others is to suggest that Oedipus's character is delineated in opposition to the other characters in the play *and* as part of the community of action and narrative in which those antagonisms, seen at first as insurmountable differences, disclose unrecognized uniformities. Thus, "who" Oedipus is is delimited by the confrontations we hear about (with the drunken Corinthian, Apollo at Delphi, and Laius at the crossroads) and the ones we see (with Creon, Teiresias, and the old shepherd). From one point of view, each confrontation distinguishes Oedipus as a monstrous exception, unique, resembling no one. But from another point of view, much about his temperament, especially his anger, is mirrored in those he is distinguished from. In a discussion of Oedipus, René Girard argues that antagonists caught up in a sacrificial crisis "invariably believe themselves separated by insurmountable differences" which "in reality" reveal an "illusion of rigid differentiation within a pattern of ever-expanding uniformity."[4] But the characters on stage are only the most immediate community in terms of which Oedipus's character is defined. There is also the chorus "representing" mythical Thebes (and perhaps Athenian spectators), the audience in the theater of Dionysus watching the play, and all subsequent audiences of readers or watchers. In each case "who" Oedipus is—the community in terms of which he is defined—is, appropriately enough, overlapping and historically distinct. This not only raises problems of interpretation (especially the "hermeneutic" problem), it replicates what Zeitlin calls "the unstable arithmetic of the self" which "the" play dramatizes. This arithmetic is, paradoxically, both the "subject" of the play and a warning against the construction of a single subject.[5]

[3] See Emile Benveniste, *Indo-European Language and Society* (Coral Gables, Fla., University of Miami Press, 1973), bk. 3, chap. 3. Hugh Lloyd-Jones, in his introduction to the reprint of Karl Reinhardt's *Sophocles* (Oxford: Basil Blackwell, 1979), p. 2, notes that "Sophocles' deities offer no comfort to man, and when they lead his fate to a point where he recognizes what he is, it is his discovery that he is abandoned and alone that makes him realize his human condition.... Sophocles' tragic characters are lone, uprooted, exiled creatures.... But the violent uprooting would not be so painful if the roots were not so deep."

[4] René Girard, *Violence and the Sacred*, trans. Patrick Gregory (Baltimore: The Johns Hopkins University Press, 1977), pp. 78–79. Girard writes about "the violent elimination of differences between the antagonists, their total identity . . ." (p. 72), whereas I want to maintain the distinctiveness within the identity.

[5] Girard argues that though the full burden of guilt finally settles on Oedipus, it could just as well settle on Teiresias or Creon, which means that there is no true guilt or innocence, except that "in the case of the 'true' guilt no voice is raised to protest any aspect of the charge. A particular version of events succeeds in imposing itself; it loses its polemical nature in becoming the acknowledged basis of the myth, in becoming the myth itself" (*Vio-*

If we think about identity in these ways, then the loss of identity entails two seemingly opposed but actually complementary conditions: sameness and isolation. Sameness erases distinctions between people, leaving them part of an undifferentiated mass. As unseen and unrecognized figures, such men and women merge into the background, passive victims of others or adjuncts of "Nature" or "History." That is why Oedipus so fiercely insists that his fate, however horrific, is his and his alone. Isolation and exile leave us dissociated from those who gave us life and those whose power empowers us, facing the prospect of an unremembered and unmourned death. Here is Hannah Arendt writing about modern exile: "We lost our home, the familiarity of daily life, lost our occupation which means the confidence that we are of some use in the world. We lost our language which means the naturalness of reactions, the simplicity of gestures, the unaffected expression of feelings."[6] Perhaps this helps explain why Orestes risked all to reclaim his place in Argos and why the punishment of exile Oedipus unknowingly calls down upon himself is a punishment that fits the crime.

Oedipus the patricide and committer of incest is "the slayer of distinctions" and the father of "formless duplications, sinister repetitions, a dark mixture of unnamable things."[7] Violating natural boundaries, he collapses what should be distinct and plural into a perverse singularity. He is one where he should be many and many where he should be one, out of place and too much in the same place. He supposes himself self-generated and autonomous, standing above and outside the forces that constrain lesser men.[8] And in a sense he is and does; but it is not the sense he supposes. Rather than being a homeless exile who has achieved his place and power through the force of unaided intellect and freely chosen action, he is very much at home, fulfilling his fate because of his intellect. He thinks he has mastered the world's distinctions when, in fact, he operates amidst interchangeable kinship terms: brother, father, husband,

---

lence, p. 78). As helpful as I find Girard's reading, I think it misreads the character of Creon, the exchange with Teiresias, and where "Oedipus" "stands" at the end. And I am not wholly persuaded by its genealogical reading of guilt and innocence. Of course, Girard's project is larger than the play.

[6] From "We Refugees," in *The Jew as Pariah: Jewish Identity and Politics in the Modern Age*, ed. Ron Feldman (New York: Grove Press, 1978), pp. 55–56. In various essays, Kundera talks about the suspended state of a person in an occupied country while Said regards the permanent state of exile as the source of the critic's radicalization. Between them they pose a dilemma present in this play and in the *Apology* and *Crito*.

[7] Girard, *Violence*, pp. 74–75.

[8] Oedipus takes himself to be the child of chance ("But I take myself to be Fortune's fortunate child" [egō d'emauton paida tēs Tychēs nemon, 1080]). The connection between *nemo* and *nomos* makes explicit what is implicit in Oedipus's assumption: that he is a law unto himself, absolutely free, unconstrained, with all possibilities within his grasp.

children, bride, wife, and mother.[9] In this sense the generation destroying plague has been in Thebes long before it takes a public toll. His own disease is symbolized in the circularity of his life, the way in which his journey has doubled back on itself, closing in on him until he returns to the very beginning: his mother's bed.

In this Oedipus is paradigmatically Theban, for Thebes, as Froma Zeitlin argues, "has no means of establishing a viable system of relations and differences either within the city or without, or between the self and any other." Because it cannot incorporate outsiders, the city oscillates between extremes of "rigid inclusions and exclusions on the one hand and radical confusions on the other," unable to "generate new structures and new progeny." In the *Oresteia* the cycle of vengeance was at long last broken. Orestes was restored and Argos was liberated from tyranny. But in Thebes no such salvation is possible. Here the past is tyrant and the new only seems so as "each generation looks backward to its ruin."[10]

Incest is a political disease as much as a familial one. As an unnatural mixing of what should remain separate, with its promiscuous exchange of identities, and in its creation of sameness, incest seems a political disease to which democracies are particularly susceptible. At least Plato seems to think so in book 8 of the *Republic* where democracy is characterized as destroying any stable sense of self and place. In democracies ruler and ruled, old and young, father and sons, citizens and foreigners, teachers and students, men and women revel in scandalous equivalence.[11] Plato's complaint that democracies are afflicted by a political Oedipal complex has been echoed by contemporary critics of mass society, who also identify democracies with an "unstable arithmetic of the self."[12] All being equal to each other and to nothing at all eventually leads to rule by a tyrant and what is tyrannical in us.

Given this we can give a specifically political dimension to Zeitlin's argument about Thebes being "the other place" where Athens plays out the dangers of self-assertion. It is also possible to see it as the place where a democracy confronts its other or underside in the form of arguments by conservative critics against what they regard as social, economic and political leveling. We might go further and suggest that Thebes is also the place where antipolitics is explored, if we agree with Aristotle that the

---

[9] Lines 1405–7. See the discussion of his loss of differentiation in Simon Goldhill, *Reading Greek Tragedy* (New York: Cambridge University Press, 1986), pp. 215–16.

[10] "Thebes: Theater of Self and Society in Athenian Drama," in *Greek Tragedy and Political Theory*, ed. J. Peter Euben (Berkeley and Los Angeles: University of California Press, 1986), pp. 121–22, 126.

[11] See the *Republic*, 556b–d, and Vincent Farenga, "The Paradigmatic Tyrant: Greek Tyranny and the Ideology of the Proper," *Helios*, 8, no. 1 (1981): 6–7.

[12] The phrase is Zeitlin's ("Thebes," p. 130).

polis is a unity of differences and a plurality made possible by a shared commitment to a common life. Then incest becomes a crime against politics, a view shared by Thomas Pynchon for whom incest (or entropy) is a crime against America.

Questions of identity seem, inevitably, to raise questions about identity, about how it is we become who we are. What forces, internal and external, shape our actions and wants, our speech and our gestures? In what sense and under what circumstances are we initiators, complicitors, or simply victims of our character and our destiny? Can we tell our own story or must we leave it, necessarily, to others to say and portray "who" we are? To what degree can we understand how identities are formed, our own and others, as persons and as cultures? The latter question and the issue as a whole is raised in the sphinx's question, which is not only What is man? but Can man be defined by men?[13] One answer is that as self-conscious largely autonomous beings possessing a unified will and stable self we can, to a large degree, define ourselves and control the consequences of our action and the meaning of our lives. Although we begin in situations we do not choose and as partial beings, we can, through reason, therapy, revolutionary praxis, will, or prayer transform our situation and so ourselves. The other answer is that we are socially constructed individuals or historically constructed subjects who lack any fixed identity apart from the institutional matrices and forms of discourse that shape regimes of power-knowledge we are largely unable to consciously control and completely unable to judge outside their own terms.

But whatever one's view on this matter, there is a prior question here. Why is it that questions about identity arise at all? Vernant's answer about the Greeks is that they became aware of the need to choose between the values of an archaic tribal past preserved in mythic form and the new political and juridical reality of the emerging city-state. Caught between these two points the new subject was born from a double or split consciousness and from the feeling of contradictions dividing man against himself.[14] Vernant not only helps explain the institutional place, structure, and themes of Greek tragedy; he also helps us understand why *Oedipus Tyrannos* was (and still is) regarded as the paradigmatic Greek tragedy.

What is implied in the notion of "choosing" between systems of value[15]

[13] That is Farenga's elaboration of the question in "The Paradigmatic Tyrant," p. 20.

[14] See Vernant's "Greek Tragedy: Problems of Interpretation," in *The Structuralist Controversy*, ed. Richard Macksey and Eugenio Donato (Baltimore: Johns Hopkins University Press, 1972), pp. 273–89, and "Intimations of the Will in Greek Tragedy," in *Tragedy and Myth in Ancient Greece*, by Vernant and Vidal-Naquet (Atlantic Highlands, N.J.: Humanities Press, 1981), pp. 28–62.

[15] On how this is possible, see Alasdair MacIntyre, "Relativism, Power and Philosophy,"

and dramatized in the play is that the issue of identity is both a political and an epistemological one. Oedipus is a knower and a thinker. His outstanding characteristic is his (seemingly) powerful mind and the decisiveness of his actions. He analyzes problems before others know there is one and acts on his analyses before any remedy occurs to them or where they are hesitant. Indeed, insofar as Oedipus is a tyrant, or comes to act as one, it is a tyranny of mind. At least from the exchange with Teiresias afterward, Oedipus fits Knox's description of the *anthrōpos tyrannos*, "man the master of the universe, self-taught and self-made ruler who has the capacity to . . . 'conquer complete happiness and prosperity.' "

Identity as an epistemological issue is dramatized in the play's treatment of its pervasive sight imagery. Because the Greeks regarded sight as the source of knowing and the basis of inquiry[16] to deny the equation, as the *Oedipus Tyrannos* does, is to raise questions about the ground or foundation of knowledge. Among other things, it undermines the secure position of the "spectators" "watching" in the "theater" (literally "the place of watching"). As Goldhill asks: "What could it mean for a spectator to watch or listen to a play which seems to equate sight and ignorance?"[17] I would add: What does it mean to consider the problem of identity through a public institution that relies on role playing, acting, masks, and disguises? What should we make of the fact that Oedipus is the "Corinthian" stranger playing the part of the Theban king, the son of the queen playing the role of her husband, the brother of the royal children playing the role of father? This raises the specter (or possibility) that the answer to the question What is Oedipus's identity? is that he can never be said to have any.[18] It also poses uncertainties about political theory, given the original meaning of theory as vision and journey.

Many of these themes as well as the problem of identity itself have been present as background in previous chapters. The issue of homecoming is broached in chapter 1 by Ignatieff's redefinition of home, his insistence that we confront modern homelessness in all its aspects, and his search for a language of belonging unweighted by republican baggage and Greek nostalgia. It is elaborated in chapter 2 and 3 with the story of Orestes' reclaiming of an inheritance which is both a curse and a precondition for

---

in *Proceedings and Addresses of the American Philosophical Association* (Newark, Del.: University of Delaware Press, 1985), pp. 5–22.

[16] See the discussion of sight and knowledge in Bruno Snell, *The Discovery of Mind*, trans. T. C. Rosenmeyer (Cambridge, Mass.: Harvard University Press, 1953), pp. 4–5.

[17] *Reading Greek Tragedy*, p. 220. He goes on to argue that the *Oedipus Tyrannos* challenged "not only fifth century or modern claims for the rigour, certainty and exhaustiveness of man's intellectual progress, but also the security of the reading process itself with its aim of defining and delimiting the precise, fixed and absolute sense of a text, a word" (p. 221). I will return to this point in chapter 9 when comparing the play with *The Crying of Lot 49*.

[18] That is Farenga's suggestion in "The Paradigmatic Tyrant," p. 15.

his becoming whole and powerful. In the *Oresteia* the conflict is resolved by having what is new, chosen, and innovative build upon what is old, earthbound, and given. But at Thebes and with Oedipus the "new" is neither chosen nor innovative but rejects a past it unknowingly replicates.[19]

The problem of identity, of "who" we are or have become, is an animating question in Foucault's investigations of how the modern subject has been constituted. Significant parts of his critique of liberation, traditional history, global theorizing, and authorship are anticipated by this play, which questions the self's status as an object and subject of knowledge and "the place and role of man in the order of things."[20]

Oedipus is the civilizing hero whose every achievement reflects "the ambiguity of man's power to control his world and manage his life by intelligence."[21] A ploughman who plows forbidden fields, a hunter who tracks himself in the abstract language of cause and inference, a pilot at home in an unnatural harbor that wrecks the secure ship, a physician unable to diagnose his own unspeakable illness, and a knower ignorant of the fundamental facts of his existence, his name, place, and birth, Oedipus does not know who he is, where he is, or what he is doing to himself and others. This man of unparalleled intelligence is a creature of the wild. He organizes, divides, and orders things, events, and eventually people, yet violates the most sacred boundaries, caught in a net woven jointly by his acts and Apollo.

This point and language recall the paradox of "man's" civilizing power implicit in my discussion of Holmes's view of modernity and explicit in my discussion of the choral ode to man in *Antigone*. If nothing walks stranger than man, what man walks more strangely than Oedipus? What

---

[19] In this, Thebes is like Argos in the *Agamemnon* where each avenger (until Orestes) is sure they have ended the cycle of revenge they are in fact perpetuating. Speaking about Oedipus, Creon, and Teiresias, Girard argues that all are drawn "unwittingly into the structure of violent reciprocity—which they always think they are outside of because they all initially come from the outside and mistake this position and temporary advantage for a permanent and fundamental superiority. . . . Each party progresses rapidly in uncovering the truth about the other, without ever recognizing the truth about himself. Each sees in the other the usurper of a legitimacy that he thinks he is defending, but that he is in fact undermining" (*Violence*, pp. 69, 71).

[20] Although Goldhill (*Reading Greek Tragedy*, p. 221) makes the comment about Greek tragedy as a whole, he says it in his discussion of *Oedipus Tyrannos*.

[21] Charles Segal, *Tragedy and Civilization: An Interpretation of Sophocles* (Cambridge, Mass.: Harvard University Press, 1981), p. 232. He is a *pharmakos* and scapegoat. In Greek *pharmakon* means both poison and the antidote to poison, both sickness and cure, anyone (or any substance) capable of doing an extraordinarily good or evil action according to the circumstances (dosage). On Oedipus as a *pharmakon*, see Segal, chap. 7; Girard, *Violence*, chap. 3 and 4; and Vernant, "Ambiguity and Reversal," in *Tragedy and Myth*, pp. 100–106.

man is less of a stranger when he supposes himself to be most strange even when he is most at home? If the Ode's "lesson" is that progress is also transgression, who better demonstrates it than the hero savior and foremost of men who is also the polluter most hated by the gods? Who is more the *pharmakos*, healer and disease, than Oedipus? And what about him is more *pharmakos* than his mind and intellect? The mind that saved Thebes from the sphinx is also a mind oblivious to what it is saying, seeing, and doing.

This doubleness is presented in the *Eumenides'* opening scene as I discussed it in chapter 3. The Athenians are road builders who tame a wilderness. With the god's help and in his honor they create a human space and identity by establishing literal and metaphorical boundaries against the undifferentiated realm of nature, the unindividuated realm of the beasts, and the boundlessness of time, space, and deed. But as we saw, this is too neat and only half the story. In the *Oresteia* the other half is represented by the presence of the Furies at the shrine and, more generally, by the imagery of nets and binding. In the context of the *Oedipus Tyrannos* the Priestess's locution in referring to the Athenians as Hephastus's sons takes on particular significance. The god's lameness not only suggests an underside to triumph being celebrated, it has a pointed relevance for a play about a lame hero. It is as if there is some symbiosis between Oedipus's way of walking and his intellect, between his stoop and his stature.

The play suggests that in the end and for all our efforts the most carefully wrought boundaries are breached by the men most responsible for building them. Such men are law breakers as well as law makers, transgressors of demarcations they jointly consecrate with the gods, capable of barbarous cruelty within the civilized space that marks their presence. Whether in civil war at Corcyra or with Oedipus, the outside is also inside. The wild cannot be finally banished for it lies, if not in our being, then in our politics. Oedipus commits patricide in the desolate place where the roads meet. There, in no man's land, between cities, he refuses to be pushed off the road and so kills his father. But he commits incest not in the wild but in the city, in his house, in his very bed. Patricide and incest, the prohibitions against which were thought to separate humans from beasts, are committed by this greatest of men who collapses space and time into perverse singularity.

The same themes are posed in a set of puns on Oedipus's name. In Greek *dipous* means two-footed while *oi* is an exclamation of pain, grief, pity, or astonishment. Thus Oedipus (*oi-dipous*) already contains a clue to his identity and his fate. This is complicated by another set of puns that play on "I know" (*oida*), as when the priest says to Oedipus "perhaps you know" (*oistha pou*) (line 43). The word *pou* with an accent means "where"; but without it (as here) it means "anywhere," "somewhere," "perhaps," "I suppose." Thus the grief in his name is connected with the indeterminacy of knowledge and his uncertainty of place. There is more still. Later (1038) when the messenger expresses ignorance about the origins of Oedipus's name and suggests that more could be learned from the man who gave the child to him, he begins with *ouk oid'; ho dous*, a probable echo of Oedipus's name which is the topic of discussion. Now *ho dous* also spells "roads" and so the king's identity, pain, and ignorance have to do with the roads he has taken and not taken.[22] He has taken the road from Corinth to avoid the crime the road he takes leads him to. At the crossroads he chooses a way of life and a way of death. In the *Gorgias* Socrates pictures the judges of the underworld conducting their tribunal in a meadow at the crossroads. One road leads to the isles of the blest, the other to Tartarus (524a2–4). The choice is decisive and final; and the evidence of the right choice is available. For Oedipus the "choice" is equally decisive but the evidence is not there. He must choose without knowing the end and in ignorance that each choice is a strand in a fabric that traps him in a net of ruin.

THE PLAY and this chapter is about the identity of Oedipus as a member of the house of Laius, as a citizen of Thebes, and as a mortal whose evolving desire for absolute sovereignty and self-engendering (which the acts of patricide and incest imply) transgresses the boundaries between men and god.[23] It is also about the identity of men and women as searchers for identity.

Other tragic characters discover themselves in the sense of coming to realize the true situation in which they had acted in ignorance. But only Oedipus is looking for himself when he finds himself; only in this play is the finding of the self the whole action rather than a product of it.[24] Certainly few if any characters pursue, hunt for, and search out an answer to the question, Who am I? more relentlessly. Dismissing the warnings of Teiresias, Jocasta, and the old shepherd to cease questioning, Oedipus pushes on until he discovers who he is as son, citizen, and mortal. Responding to Jocasta's "god keep you from knowing who you are" (which, typically, he misconstrues, thinking it a slur on his birth), the king concludes: "Being born as I am, I could never prove false to who I am and not search out the secret of my birth to the end" (1084–85). Driven by external and internal forces, by his fate and his character, by the god and

[22] See Goldhill, *Reading Greek Tragedy*, pp. 216–18, and Vernant, "Ambiguity and Reversal," pp. 96–97, on how the puns work in detail.

[23] See the discussion in Zeitlin, "Thebes," pp. 122–23.

[24] Alister Cameron, *The Identity of Oedipus the King* (New York: New York University Press, 1968), pp. 51–55.

his own actions, Oedipus seeks his true identity only to receive for his efforts untold agonies, which he is compelled to recognize are his own doing.[25] In the end, Oedipus realizes that mortals cannot control their fate in the sense of taking it in their own hands and making it anything they wish. This does not mean that his fate is simply given or passively received,[26] still less that he is morally exonerated from the consequences of deeds done in ignorance. It does mean that his fate becomes real only through the action of his character, that he is made by the destiny he helps fashion. In Joel Schwartz's words, Oedipus's "part is apportioned, but he 'plays' his part. . . . If the god is the author of Oedipus's script, Oedipus is, so to speak, the method actor who has found himself in the part."[27]

It is because men are victims as well as shapers of their fate that human life retains an opacity immune to the greatest minds and most decisive actors. Recognition of this is, as both Sophocles and Socrates suggest, an acknowledgment of mortality and so the foundation of human knowledge.

The idea that mortals are, despite their prowess, victims of barely discernible forces, which they nevertheless precipitate and constitute, is hard for an exceptional man like Oedipus to bear. For those who regard riddles as problems to be solved, enigmas are intolerable. But Oedipus is hardly alone in this impatience. Although we do not live with the dramatic dualities of tyrant-king, husband-son, and savior-pollutor, we too are often strangers to what is most intimate to us and among those we should know best. Like Oedipus we sometimes live amid unsuspected and unsought ironies that bifurcate life and action. Such limitations disturb the comforts of daily life and everyday plausibility, leaving us unsure of identities conferred by house, position, friends, and city. If a man as talented and perceptive as Oedipus can be so wrong about so much, how can we be sure that we know who we are and what we are doing (or about our

---

[25] Ibid., p. xvix.

[26] Thomas Gould in his three essays on "The Innocence of Oedipus: The Philosophers on Oedipus the King," *Arion* 4, no. 3 (1965): 363–86; 4, no. 4 (1965): 582–611; and no. 4 (1966): 478–525, emphasizes the innocence of Oedipus and thus the unwarranted character of his fate. He is right to criticize those who make Oedipus guilty and so leave the play without moral complexity or perplexity. But he goes too far; the language of guilt and innocence are simply not subtle enough.

[27] The fact that Sophocles restructured the Oedipus myth and that tragedy was regarded as a mode of political education supports the idea that our fate does not descend on us from outside as some pregiven destiny. Joel Schwartz discusses the issue of fate and choice in terms of the relationship between authority and freedom, neither of which "is possible without the other." Later he argues that Sophocles' relationship to existing materials and authorities is recapitulated by Oedipus's relation to his *daimon* ("Human Action and Political Action in *Oedipus Tyrannos*," in Euben, *Greek Tragedy and Political Theory*, pp. 189 and 204). The quote is from pp. 203–4.

interpretation of the play)? If he has transgressed the boundaries of nature he above all seemed to understand so well, what is our condition? If he has so confounded appearance and reality, what makes us so sure of the realities that guide our life and thought?[28] "If Oedipus has a hamartia," William Arrowsmith writes, "it is not a sin or flaw but the ungovernable tragic ignorance of all men: We do not know who we are or who fathered us but go, blinded by life and hope toward a wisdom bitter as the gates of hell. The cost of action is suffering and heroism is the anguished acceptance of our own identities forged in action and pain in a world we never made."[29]

The play is also about the identity of Athens. Knox regards the correspondence between Oedipus and Athens as direct and extensive. For him Oedipus's title, tyrannos; the nature and basis of his power; the forcefulness with which he imposes that power on others and on circumstances; his restless energy and intellectual audacity; his unyielding courage, self-reliance and dismissal of compromise; his insistence on clear and complete knowledge and impatience with half truths, all make Oedipus a "microcosm" and "symbolic representative of Periclean Athens." Because Oedipus "resembles the citizen audience watching the play the spectators in the theater of Dionysus are looking down at themselves in barely disguised mythical garb."[30] And when Oedipus finally "falls," they see "in symbolic, prophetic, riddling terms" the fall toward which Athens was forcing its way with all the uncompromising logic, initiative, and daring that brought it to the pinnacle of worldly power.[31]

---

[28] Charles Segal, "The Music of the Sphinx: The Problem of Language in *Oedipus Tyrannus*," in *Contemporary Literary Hermeneutics and the Interpretation of Classical Texts*, ed. Stephanus Kresic (Ottawa: University of Ottawa Press, 1981), p. 162.

[29] "The Criticism of Greek Tragedy," *The Tulane Drama Review* 3 (1959): 51.

[30] *Oedipus at Thebes: Sophocles' Tragic Hero and His Time* (New York: W. W. Norton, 1971), pp. 107, 99. Although I think Knox is helpful, I have three caveats. The first is a warning about taking tragedies as strict allegories with clear correspondences between action in the theater and actions outside it. The second (which is an extension of the first) is my agreement with Zeitlin's argument about "Thebes" and Athens. In her terms Knox's book would be better titled "Oedipus at Thebes: The Oedipus Tyrannos at Athens." The third caveat has to do with *tyrannos*. A tyrant was not yet unambiguously what Aristotle came to describe in the *Politics*, although it began to have pejorative connotations after the Persian Wars. In its neutral meaning a tyrant was simply one who came to power by his own devices rather than by normal hereditary succession. By the time of this play the word had probably lost its neutral sense, although there would be some who looked back at Pisistratus's tyranny as a golden age.

[31] For Knox the quest for secular knowledge, rational principles, and mastery is self-defeating. Oedipus's and Jocasta's successive changes of attitude toward the gods and oracles are "symbolic of the mental agonies of a generation that abandoned a traditional order of belief with a hopeful vision of an intelligible universe only to find itself at last facing an incomprehensible future with a desperation thinly disguised as recklessness" (*Oedipus at Thebes*, p. 168).

The *Oedipus Tyrannos* is also concerned with the identity of tragedy. To a certain extent this can be said about every play. If theater was a public institution concerned with the political, moral, and religious foundations of polis life, drama was necessarily concerned with its own context of performance. If the tragedians were political educators in the ways I argue in chapter 2, then they were almost surely preoccupied with the political and intellectual condition of their audience. Occasionally, as in the trial scene of the *Eumenides,* the audience is specifically invited to reflect on an activity that was an important part of their contemporary lives. But Aeschylus does not make theater or tragedy the direct subject of his trilogy as I think Sophocles does in his consideration of sophistic skepticism and in his use of theatrical language.

As the play progresses, Oedipus follows Jocasta's lead in dismissing Apollo's oracle. If the oracle cannot be credited, then there is no point in believing in prophecy as a whole or the god whose authority legitimates it. The chorus balks at such skepticism, in part because they recognize that if men rather than the gods are the measure of all things, then Oedipus's sufferings are without any higher meaning. But there is another reason for their refusal to support a king to whom they have so far been loyal. Because drama is part of a festival honoring the gods, any disrespect toward them leaves tragedy with an uncertain place and purpose.[32] If Jocasta and Oedipus are right in their growing skepticism,[33] then the chorus has no reason to "join in sacred dance to honor the gods" (894–5). Moreover, to the extent that dance symbolizes rituals in general, including those essential to polis life as a whole, what the chorus envisages

---

[32] Cedric Whitman, in his *Sophocles: A Study in Heroic Humanism* (Cambridge, Mass.: Harvard University Press, 1951), and in his review of Knox's *Oedipus at Thebes, American Journal of Philology* 80 (1959): 76–80, disagrees with my interpretation. His disagreement is part of a reading of the play that emphasizes the separation between Sophocles and the chorus and the identification of Oedipus and Sophocles. Whitman is right on the first point but overstates the second. While the chorus is not the playwright's mouthpiece but a dramatic character, partly inside and partly outside the action, it is not faithless, or unthinkingly pious. That they are confused by their dual allegiance to the god and their king seems to me perfectly appropriate given the immediate situation and their general status as actors partly removed from the action and therefore sensitive to the demands of gods and men. Also it seems to me plausible that Oedipus's behavior now and what they learn about his behavior before should be the occasion for these reflections on tyrants even if they do not fully apply to him. On the whole issue, see R. P. Winningham-Ingram, *Sophocles* (New York: Cambridge University Press, 1980), chap. 7 and 8.

[33] As the play progresses, Oedipus's thoughts and deeds become increasingly disengaged from explicit deference to Apollo until, following Jocasta's lead, he dismisses the god's oracle. If Laius was killed by several men as reported rather than by one as prophesied, then Oedipus could not have killed his father as the god predicted. And if the oracle cannot be credited, then there is no point in believing in prophecy as a whole or in the god whose authority legitimates it.

is not just the end of tragedy but the end to the polis itself. If skepticism should triumph, there may be dancing on the wild mountainside (1091–93) but not in the communal spaces of the city.[34]

But if man is not the measure, are the gods? Or, to put the question another way, is Sophocles endorsing the conservative complaint that men must obey limits by repudiating their intellectual power and political daring? Any answer has obvious consequences for how we view Oedipus, Athens, and the play's overall "message."

The issue is posed in the *agōn* between Teiresias and Oedipus. On the one side is the God's seer whose knowledge is divinely inspired; on the other a man whose knowledge comes from reasoning. Lacking sight, Teiresias has insight based on the descriptions others give him of the omens he must read and about which he must speak enigmatically. Oedipus has his sight, depends only on himself to solve riddles, and brings all to light in unambiguous speech. Clearly Teiresias is right and Oedipus wrong about the latter's parentage, deeds, and the killer of Laius. But that does not mean that the play fully endorses him at the expense of Oedipus. Rather the play repudiates neither character but incorporates both kinds of knowledge in a whole more inclusive than either. Like Oedipus, drama shapes and integrates experience, directly in the case of the mythical tradition, indirectly in the case of the self-understanding of its contemporary audience for whom that tradition was a store of shared wisdom. But it does so in an un-Oedipean way. Instead of trying to solve problems, it deepens them; instead of taking sides, it indicates the limits of one-sidedness. In order to do this, the play "speaks" in the "voice" of Oedipus and of Teiresias. It speaks and hears poetically and discursively, ironically and directly, mysteriously and literally, prophetically and rationally. Only such a discourse can preserve, present, and embody human knowledge while remaining faithful both to the enigmatic quality of the world and to the need to map and bound it. Even then there is no guarantee of evading bitter sorrows. To suppose otherwise is to suppose that men and women can be precisely defined and measured. Because they cannot, "man" cannot be "the measure of all things." But he (and she) is *a* measure. That, I think, is *a* message of this play and of drama as an institution.

The play's concern for the identity of tragedy is also evident in its "theatricality."[35] The *Oedipus Tyrannos* calls attention to itself as presenting

[34] On this, see Segal, *Tragedy and Civilization*, chap. 7. Thucydides provides the right epitaph. During the revolution at Corcyra men no longer respected the gods or justice. Living only for the moment, the killing of fathers seemed unworthy of special mention.

[35] On the notion of "theatricality," see Charles Segal, "Time, Theater and Knowledge in the Tragedy of Oedipus," in *Edipo. Il teatro greco e la cultura europea; Atti del convegno internazionale*, ed. B. Gentili and R. Proetagostini (Rome: Ateneo, 1986), pp. 459–89; and

a spectacle for an audience through its elaborate language of sight, in the dramatically culminating act of self-blinding, and by the way it presents its hero as a paradigm to be looked upon (1193). The messenger, reporting that Oedipus shouted for the doors to be unbarred so he can be seen by all, ends his speech with "Soon you will see a spectacle (*theama*) to waken pity even in the horror of it" (1295). Then when the blind Oedipus comes on stage he is greeted by the chorus's "This is a terrible sight (*idein*, from *eidō*) for men to see." In its concluding speech the chorus asks us to "behold (*leusset'*) this Oedipus" as proof that no mortal should be counted happy until he has passed the final limits of his life secure from pain.

Not only are we reminded that the action is a spectacle; we are reminded of tragedy's political function. Oedipus insists that his self-discovery and self-revelation be public and so he emerges out of the house into the light of day and the orchestra of the theater. At this moment Oedipus's search for self-knowledge and identity becomes explicitly part of the city's collective endeavor to attain self-knowledge and identity through the medium of tragedy. It is tragedy that gives substance to Pericles' boast that no people could equal the Athenians in their love of wisdom and action. As the existence and place of tragedy suggest, no people has asked Who are we? and What are we doing? with such persistence. Whether through tragedy in the theater, Socrates in the Agora, or (more contentiously) Plato in the Academy, they above all others sought to define themselves as citizens, mortals, and thinkers.[36]

THE OEDIPUS we first see is godlike and god-respecting. He stands before us a great king, a protector and patriarch of his people (the first word of the play is children). Emerging from the palace he finds suppliant citizens sitting before him as others are before the shrines of Apollo and Athena. But the priest does not identify Oedipus with the gods, judging him instead "the first of men in the recurring crisis of this life and in the relation between mortals and gods" (334), and the king himself promises to do all Apollo commands, calling himself the gods' ally. Here is a man

---

David Seale, *Vision and Stagecraft in Sophocles* (London: Croom Helm, 1982), p. 245 and passim.

[36] I think this so even when that theory was critical of democracy. Hannah Arendt argues that the idea of inner freedom and feeling free are derivative, in the sense that they presuppose a retreat from a world where freedom was denied. See "What is Freedom," in *Between Past and Future* (New York: Viking Press, 1968), pp. 145–46. I think the same true of political theory. Even when antidemocratic, it remained parasitic on the experience and practice of democratic Athens. I also happen to think Socrates and Plato understood that fact.

who knows himself to be one, and who honors the boundaries between mortality and divinity.

Yet there are several disconcerting aspects to the scene. For one thing there is the implicit equation of Oedipus with Apollo and Athena. That equation is reinforced by the priest's appeal to the king, a reversal of the usual order of things,[37] and emphasized by the former's use of words meaning mastery, power, and rule. It is also reinforced later when, having taken over the search for Laius's murderer, Oedipus speaks like a god and prophet; he will reveal the truth and will bring things to light.[38] Of course, Oedipus is chosen by the gods; but he is hardly favored by them. He is indeed Apollo's ally, but not in the way he imagines or desires. The equation itself keeps changing; Oedipus as equal to the gods and as equal to nothing.

For another thing there are the repeated references to "I,"[39] which prepare us for a man whose character dominates others and all that follows. As it turns out no god predicts that the investigation will prove successful or that Jocasta will kill herself or that Oedipus will blind himself. Oedipus sets the penalty, calls the witnesses, conducts the investigations, renders the verdict, and executes the punishment.[40] Even his soon-expressed self-lessness is self-referential. *He* pities those before him; *he* knows the story they came to tell before they told it; *he* knows they are sick, "yet there is not one of you, sick though you are, that is as sick as I myself." Although they each have a single sorrow his spirit groans "for the city and myself and you at once." *He* has given many tears to the plague; *he* found the one remedy; *he* sent Creon to Apollo so *he* could save the city; *he* is impatient; *he* will do all the Gods commands (58–77).

Then there is the paternal language, which is, to say the least, "problematic" given the fact that Oedipus has killed his own father, is brother to the children he fathered, and is patriarch to a city withered by the "black Death which grows rich in groaning lamentation." Moreover, be-

[37] As Karl Reinhardt argues in *Sophocles* (New York: Barnes and Noble, 1959).

[38] See the introduction to *Oedipus the King* by Stephen Berg and Diskin Clay (New York: Oxford University Press, 1978). As R.G.A. Buxton argues, it is because of Oedipus's power of sight that he threatens to blur the distinctions between god and man. The blindness of prophets is a way of reestablishing the boundaries in different terms ("Blindness and Limits: Sophocles and the Logic of Myth," *Journal of Hellenic Studies* 100 [1980]: 22–37).

[39] I do not want to moralize; Oedipus has accomplished great things and he is fully entitled to remind others of those achievements. It is the total scene that matters here.

[40] Cameron (*The Identity of Oedipus the King*, p. 56) talks about the play's "tremendous concentration on the self." Not only did Oedipus kill his father and marry his mother, but "in the process of searching for himself, condemned himself, cursed himself, nearly killed the man closest to him, virtually sent his wife and mother to her death." In his ignorance "he acted against himself in every conceivable way and then, as if that were not enough, when he found who he was, blinded himself."

cause not all who sit before him are literally children, the paternal language he uses establishes a general link between the political situation and the family horror and allows him to identify himself with the city as a whole, an identification typical of tyrants.[41]

Finally, there is the plague itself. An imponderable danger that appears out of nowhere, it kills indiscriminately, without regard to character. Its presence emphasizes the collective nature of the disease and, presumably, of the cure. For these and other reasons plagues are the ultimate test for political leaders, whether they be leaders of mythical Thebes or of Athens. Some cities, like "Thebes" are plagued in the ways Zeitlin enumerates in her discussion of it as "the other place"; no new beginnings, no real children or parents, only stillborn births. "If," as Hannah Arendt claims, "action as beginning corresponds to the fact of birth, if it is the actualization of the human condition of natality,"[42] then the political dimension of the plague remains in "Thebes" even after its physical dimension subsides.

Yet all this is more counterpoint than principal theme, more anticipation than statement. The Oedipus we see here seems, on balance, to deserve the reknown and honor he has received. Unlike tyrants who secret themselves, monopolize power, and look first to their own private good, Oedipus makes a point of coming outside to hear the suppliants, rejects Creon's suggestion that Apollo's oracle be repeated in private, listens to the advice of others, calls an assembly, and willingly shares authority with his brother-in-law and wife.

One can also interpret Oedipus's compassion more favorably. He feels the community's pain, willingly assumes its burdens, and draws to himself as the symbol of collectivity the disease they feel in their separate bodies. His tender concern here anticipates his loving but impotent concern for his helpless daughters at the play's end. Such symmetry is evidence for what we come to see repeatedly: that despite altered circumstances and new knowledge Oedipus remains at the end the kind of man he was at the beginning.

Even in the opening scene we can see that Oedipus is, and knows himself to be, an intelligent and decisive man. Although he sends Creon to Delphi and for Teiresias, he is, nevertheless, sure of himself and of his judgments, confident that what he knows is most worth knowing. Not only does the king already know what others tell him, he has already done what they would have him do. Once he hears the oracle's reply, he acts swiftly and speaks forcefully. After cross-examining his brother-in-law (and uncle) about the circumstances of Laius's death and the aborted in-

---

[41] Arlene Saxonhouse, "The Tyranny of Reason in the World of the Polis," *American Political Science Review* 82, no. 4 (1988): 1261–75.

[42] *The Human Condition*, p. 178.

vestigation of it, he proclaims a decree whose ferocity is only matched by its irony.

The decree is significant beyond its specific content and dramatic irony. Its rhythm is a microcosm of the play's movement as a whole and it reveals another side of Oedipus's character. Oedipus starts calmly enough, but his words against the unknown pollutor gather momentum and fury until they explode in a terrible imprecation that goes far beyond the initial sentence of exile. Never imagining that he is calling down the appalling penalties on himself, Oedipus prays that the "killer's life be consumed in evil and wretchedness" (248–49). Adding loss of rights, misery, and poverty to the gods' demand of purification, Oedipus unknowingly, yet true to his character, goes beyond anything Apollo ordained and so makes his own fate worse than it need be. His "self revenge is foreshown in the gathering vehemence of his self-conviction."[43]

So intense does the irony become that, like those in the chorus who prefer fulfillment of the dread oracle to the collapse of cosmic order its falsity would entail, we prefer to believe that Oedipus subconsciously knows what he is saying rather than accept the possibility that human beings can live in a world where "the first of men in mortal ways and wisest in ways of god" is so completely deluded by a plausible but misconstrued reality. When his boast, "It is I who will start afresh and bring the criminal to life" (132) can also mean, "I shall discover myself as the criminal,"[44] when he assures the chorus that the curse extends to all even "if it should turn out that the culprit is my guest here, sharing my hearth" (250), and when he proclaims himself the surrogate son of the dead king, we can hardly believe that a man of such extraordinary gifts is missing the obvious significance of his words. And when he three times (123, 225, 293) mishears or misquotes what he has just heard about there being bandits and instead refers to the killers in the singular, we are convinced that Oedipus is transparently attempting to deceive us rather than unknowingly deceiving himself.[45]

Why is Oedipus deceived and self-deceived? Why is this brilliant man who bested the riddling sphinx and saved Thebes so ignorant of who he

---

[43] Seale, *Vision and Stagecraft*, p. 221.

[44] See Jean-Pierre Vernant's discussion of this line in "Ambiguity and Reversal: On the Enigmatic Structure of Oedipus Rex," in Vernant and Vidal-Naquet, *Tragedy and Myth in Ancient Greece*, p. 92.

[45] Berg and Clay (*Oedipus the King*, p. 13) argue that his "slip" in making "robbers" singular and his close identification with Laius are not so much manifestations of Oedipus's subconscious as a sign that the language and action of the play are not his alone. At these moments his "disease breaks through the surface of the play; when the illusory world on stage is disrupted by the demonic forces" that guide the action along and throughout.

is and what he is doing? And is there some connection between his brilliance and his ignorance?

Oedipus understood man's changing yet single identity from four-footed childhood through two-footed maturity to three-footed old age. Where others saw only difference and discontinuity, he was able to see morning, noon, and evening as one day and one life.[46] Where they lived amid particularity and observed distinctions, he, as a stranger who has left his family and home, is able to think more abstractly, generally, and analytically. Unencumbered by the baggage of specific time and place, Oedipus's more inclusive vision enables him to organize the world and so act decisively in it where others are hesitant and seek the counsel of others.

Of course, such baggage is what defines who we are as members of a household and city and as mortals, and this is where Oedipus gets into trouble. He does not see if or how he fits in the abstract answer "man" he gives to the sphinx.[47] In fact, he does not fit and fits all too well. He is excepted from the riddle and the answer because his own yoked feet were one, and because, in all likelihood, he relies on a staff (or third foot) when by "nature" he should need two. The riddle is "Oedipian" and Oedipus the perfect respondent because his assimilation of time and difference, the fact that he occupies two generations at once, suggests his perversion of the trigenerational structure of life. He has not lived in a progress of years, but on a coincident plane of diachrony and synchrony. In other words, Oedipus's unique intellectual ability is commensurate on the familial level with his acts of patricide and incest.[48]

So Oedipus is helmsman, path finder, puzzle solver, knower, guide, and liberator and so a wanderer, pursuing false trails, confused himself and confusing others, without shelter or home at the very hearth where he belongs. It is as if uncertainty of place yields a mind able to discern hidden abstract truths at the cost of understanding immediate and intimate realities. Especially for heroes, each riddle has an answer that is a further riddle; each victory obscures the defeat within it. Oedipus saved Thebes; yet that success was preface to a vile pollution that now jeopardizes what was won.

In addition to his sincere desire to rid Thebes of the plague, Oedipus has two other reasons for making the curse so severe and extending it to

[46] Saxonhouse, "The Tyranny of Reason."

[47] The sphinx herself is a monstrous mixture of human and animal, joining in one form different biological categories of bird, lion, and woman. So what we have is an unnatural conflation of differences questioning an unnatural conflation of differences. In these terms, Oedipus can answer the sphinx because he is like her.

[48] Zeitlin, "Theater of Self and Society," pp. 126–28; and Segal, "Time, Theater and Knowledge," p. 7.

his own house. First, as becomes clear later, he suspects that Creon was party to the murder and is therefore a threat to him now. Second, he associates himself "with the oracle and takes the side of the dead king" and so enhances the legitimacy of his rule. Oedipus has acceded to power outside the normal line of succession, on the basis of his individual exploits. (In fact, of course, no one is a more legitimate ruler than Oedipus.) But that leaves him vulnerable in times of crisis when new exploits are called for to justify his position. The plague is such a time. Until he hears Creon's report of the oracle, he claims to be a stranger to the story of Laius's death and so to his part of Thebes's history. But by identifying himself with Laius he retroactively inserts himself into that history and becomes more fully in fiction what he unknowingly is in fact.

It is typical that Oedipus pronounces the curse precipitously, before he has yet heard from Teiresias who "most often sees what Apollo sees." When the old prophet appears Oedipus greets him with respect and hope,[49] calling him "one versed in everything, things teachable and things not to be spoken, things of the heavens and earth-creeping things" (300–301). Joining his fellow citizens kneeling in supplication before Teiresias as they had previously kneeled before him, Oedipus pleads with the prophet to champion the city against the plague. Given what he knows, Teiresias is sorry to be here and reluctant to speak. It is not unconcern with "the law and city that reared him" that makes Teiresias hold his tongue. Still less is it some desire to wrest power from Oedipus. Rather, Apollo's spokesman cannot satisfy the contradictory demands Oedipus unknowingly imposes on him—to "save yourself, the city, and me."

Finally goaded by Oedipus's slanderous accusations, Teiresias is forced to say what kingly anger cannot hear, "You yourself are the pollutor of the city" (353). Oedipus is at first incredulous and thinks the old man mad, then is furious and thinks him a conspirator with Creon; finally, he is contemptuous, reminding everyone that it was he, not the god-aided prophet, who solved the sphinx's riddle and so saved Thebes. (The Priest had emphasized that Oedipus's triumph was god-aided.)

> But I, Oedipus, who knew nothing,
> I thought it out for myself without the help of birds.
> And this is the man you think to exile,
> So you may find a place close by Creon's heart.
>
> (397–401)

---

[49] A number of commentators assert that the play compromises Teiresias. The claim is that the seer displays an all too human fit of temper, that Sophocles knew that most prophecies in circulation were fraudulent in his time, and that he was skeptical of them and their prostitution for political ends. It seems to me such claims are belied by the great respect both Oedipus and the chorus show Teiresias. Nothing I can find in the play compromises the prophet's integrity, including his outburst against the abusive king.

Clearly, Oedipus has been provoked. The seer's words seem so preposterous that only jealousy and ill will could possibly explain them. Yet Oedipus is wrong about Teiresias and wrong about Creon. The fact that he is wrong and the way he is wrong says something about the intellectual talent that defines his character and his fate.

Oedipus is initially presented to us as a benign ruler whose easy confidence in his intellectual competence and political power allows him to share authority with Creon and Jocasta and receive the oracle's message in public. But once he supposes himself challenged, he becomes increasingly tyrannical, disinclined to observe the pieties he earlier endorsed. As his sure sense of command becomes frustrated, his mastery of situations here and later turns to the mastering of anyone who appears to be either a threat or an obstacle to his plans or his power.[50] As the new riddles Who is the murderer of Laius? and Who am I? refuse to yield, Oedipus becomes more unyielding. Losing control he becomes more controlling, denying others the right to speak or not hearing them when they do.[51] And he assumes like Creon of *Antigone* that his failures are due to the venality of others.[52]

Oedipus's once admirable celerity of mind has become impulsiveness and impatience; his decisiveness, thoughtlessness; his sense of mastery, intolerance of opposition. Although Oedipus lets Teiresias go and yields to the entreaties of Jocasta and lets Creon live, his quickness to anger and the self-righteousness of his rage disclose again a consequence of the deracinated knowledge that "characterizes" him. It is such knowledge that he flaunts in his contest with Teiresias and that he now assumes enabled him to vanquish the sphinx unaided by any god. It was his reasoning, not the seer's divinely inspired insight, that revealed nature's secrets and brought him victory.

Of course, this man who has made nature yield its secrets is secretly the most unnatural of men. He who will dismiss prophecy is the living demonstration of its truth. This brilliant man who exemplifies human reason is living proof of the limits of rationality and the presence of the divine.[53]

That Oedipus is quick to misjudge and to anger makes what had been counterpoint a principle theme. From what we learn about Laius and from what we see here, Oedipus is truly his father's son and, by that to-

---

[50] Much the same sentiments are sometimes expressed by urban planners.

[51] Thus Oedipus's self-blinding and his desire to strike out his ears are particularly appropriate responses.

[52] Knox, *Oedipus at Thebes*, p. 48.

[53] As Richmond Lattimore says, for a man of great intelligence Oedipus makes disastrous mistakes—he rushes to Delphi and then rushes away indignant and when he leaves he is so sure of his assumptions that he does the two things he should never do—kill someone old enough to be his father and marry someone old enough to be his mother. See *The Poetry of Greek Tragedy* (Baltimore: Johns Hopkins University Press, 1958), chap. 4.

ken, a man capable of doing what Teiresias says he has done. Moreover, Oedipus's anger at Teiresias reminds us of his anger at being dishonored by Apollo, while his near killing of Creon, someone to whom he is closely bound by public and private affiliation, comes close to repeating the patricide. Finally, the present connection between Oedipus's impatience and ignorance has a previous history as well. Hearing a drunken Corinthian's assertion that he was not the son of Merope and Polybus but a *plastos* (bastard, counterfeit, fabrication), Oedipus goes to Apollo to discover the truth about his origins and his identity. But Apollo does not say who his parents are, only that he would kill his father and marry his mother. At both Corinth and Delphi, Oedipus assumed he understood his circumstances and the god. He was wrong then as he is now about Creon and Teiresias.

If Oedipus had been less certain of his interpretations and less inclined to dismiss the interpretation of others, he might have asked why Apollo's seer could not or did not answer the sphinx's riddle. His boast forces us to ask it for him. When we do, we not only recognize the sphinx as Apollo's instrument, but realize that the present contest between the prophet and king is a scarcely veiled confrontation between the greatest of mortals and the god immanent in the play's action.

One thing in the *agōn* between Teiresias and Oedipus rivets the latter's attention and temporarily interrupts his diatribe: mention of his parents. Oedipus does not know who they are and thus who he is. Teiresias's first mention of them escapes comment.

> You have your eyes but see not your own evil,
> nor where you live, nor whom you live with.
> Do you know your parents?
>
> (415–17)

But the second mention stops the king cold: "What parents? Who are they of all the world." To the seer's "This day will give you parents and break your heart," Oedipus responds, "You and your riddles." This riddle will be harder for Oedipus to solve than uncovering the murderer of Laius or answering the sphinx, because the answer to his third riddle contains the true answer to the other two. Oedipus's search for his origins and the understanding of what he has done are inseparable from his learning his place as a mortal between the beasts and gods. The revelation of who he is as a particular man and who men are as mortals is embedded in a "debate" about the veracity of oracles and the relevance of the gods.

The last half of *Oedipus Tyrannos* is a roller coaster of proud assertions that oracles are false and men autonomous shapers of their own destiny, and abject fear that oracles are true and men mere playthings of the gods. This alternation of escalating hope and boldness with growing despair and trepidation culminates in Jocasta and Oedipus denying the pertinence if not the existence of the gods *and* the latter's claim to be one. It is only resolved when this equal of the gods is also seen as equal to nothing; when the king stands forth revealed as the unwitting but full partner of the god in his own destiny, neither autonomous nor a puppet.

The oscillation takes place against the chorus's desperate steadfastness in the face first of intimations, then of mounting evidence that the king is indeed the murderer of Laius and the vile pollutor of house and city. They are steadfast because they would never find fault with a man whose wisdom saved them unless there was proof beyond all doubt (508–9). Later they reiterate their support, vigorously reassuring Oedipus of their loyalty after he interprets their pleas for Creon as a wish for his banishment or death.

These protestations are sincere and consistent. Yet there is a disharmonious counterpoint, sung *sotto voce*, which inflects their sentiments of love with foreboding. In one sense it is introduced before they speak a word. In the opening scene there is an implied contrast between the priest's emphasis on Oedipus's god-aided intelligence and the king's sleighting of such help. The contrast is more explicit in the juxtaposition of the chorus's elaborate prayers to Zeus, Athena, Artemis, Dionysus, and especially Apollo for clarity and release with Oedipus's angry boast that he came alone to solve the riddle by his unaided wit. The first choral ode brings out the contrast and counterpoint even more strongly. Now the chorus admits confusion—they do not know who to believe or what to say—and the ode bears them out. They deny the Seer's exceptional wisdom, because, compared to all-knowing Zeus and Apollo, mortals are relatively equal in their capacity to judge things of the world. Yet they had previously called Teiresias the "godly prophet . . . in whom alone of all mankind truth is native" (299), and the invocation of Apollo here recalls that accolade and fact. They go on to claim that if any man is superior in wisdom it is Oedipus; and if any deny his superiority and find fault with him they must prove it "beyond all doubt" (508).

By the second choral ode their doubts have increased (virtually in proportion to their king's and queen's doubts about the oracle's veracity). The previously muted dissonance becomes louder and more insistent as they intuitively understand the growing discrepancy between Oedipus and the gods, a discrepancy that forces them to choose between their beloved king who has earned their loyalty and the gods' oracles that pronounce him guilty. Given this division, they are unable to embrace either side. That is why they remain baffled and vacillate between accepting their king's doom and later joining him in exultant speculation about his supposedly divine parentage (1089–1109).

All this uncertainty is manifest in the ode. Although it is about Oedipus, it is not wholly about him; although it illuminates part of his situation, it does not simply apply to him. Oedipus is at most ambiguously tyrannical as tyranny is here defined. And though he is "guilty" of intellectual pride and transgressing the boundaries between god and men, he is also the good king who benefits the city and whose disastrous actions were done in ignorance.

In the ode the chorus sings of piety, tyranny, and pride. They pray to be always righteous in word and deed, mindful of those heaven-begotten eternal laws that light men's way amid the darkness of ignorance and forgetfulness. It is disobeying these laws that breeds a prideful tyranny in men, a reckless vanity that leads them to surfeits of hope which are but preludes to ruin. But the god-fearing man of ambition who protects the city is worthy of emulation and protected by the gods. Such a man is not haughty. Nor does he outrage god's holy law. Unlike the tyrant pride and prideful tyrant, he does not disdain immortal powers. Heeding the shrines of the gods, he heeds justice.

But where men are blasphemous and in desperation lay hands on holy things by claiming more than their share of glory, where they proclaim oracles mere wind and Delphic vision blind, where hearts no longer know Apollo and refuse to reverence the gods, and where the order of the universe is denied and the unseen pattern of men's lives are dismissed because they are beyond human comprehension, there no tragic poet sings. When impiety is honored, "why should I join in sacred dance to honor the gods" (894–95)?

But the chorus is not only concerned for itself and tragedy; they are also concerned for Oedipus. These champions of the king who continue to honor him even when he is dishonorable would rather the horrible oracles be fulfilled than that the gods be proved wrong. If oracles are false, then Oedipus's whole life is nonsense, since he has lived it in faithfulness to them. If his horrible deeds are nothing but inexplicable coincidence and Oedipus himself is simply a monstrous biological freak of nature whose incest and patricide are as meaningless as the indiscriminate mating and killing of birds and beasts, then his and our cries of agony become "an echoless sound in an indifferent universe."[54]

For the chorus as for us, this is too terrible a fate to contemplate. Fortunately for their sanity and for ours there is an echo, and so what Oedipus has done can be referred to a force outside himself and his deeds, something beyond clear understanding—the prophecy itself. In sum, it is worse for Oedipus to suffer less without meaning than to suffer horribly with it, even if, as mortals, the whole meaning escapes us. The wisdom of

[54] Knox, *Oedipus at Thebes*, p. 44.

suffering comes too late, except perhaps for the audience who learns this wisdom watching the play.[55]

In contrast to the chorus's evolving apprehensiveness are the wildly vacillating responses of Oedipus and Jocasta. Entering just in time to help the chorus prevent Oedipus's killing Creon, Jocasta joins them in chastising this private quarrel, which preempts concern for public affliction. Discovering that a prophecy lies behind the squabbling and the king's anger, she reassures Oedipus by recounting the oracle given Laius that he would be killed by his son. Because Laius was murdered by foreign robbers and the ankle-pierced son was cast out on a barren hillside and left to die, it is clear that the oracle is false and that prophecy (though not Apollo) can be safely disregarded. But her attempt to assuage her husband (son) has the opposite effect. He begins to glimpse the truth that has so far eluded, avoided, and spared him. Her disproof of oracles is his proof of them.

> As you spoke a shadowy memory crossed my mind
> which unhinges me and drives me mad.
>
> (726–27)

As Jocasta answers his queries with details, Oedipus's fear grows along with his insight. Suddenly recognizing the god-given design in his life, he realizes that, in his ignorance, he has cursed himself and, in his darkness, missed the seer's sight.

One detail gives him hope and on it he builds a world. Jocasta spoke in the plural and he is but one. To resolve the discrepancy and thus establish his innocence (or guilt) once and for all, Oedipus has Jocasta send for the one surviving witness of Laius's murder. The queen remains unworried. For no matter what this witness says, she knows that her child is dead and so the oracle is false. "From now on where oracles are concerned, I would not waste a second thought on any" (858).

Oedipus directs Jocasta to send for the lone witness to Laius's murder. But instead of the old shepherd appearing, a stranger from Corinth enters to announce the death of Oedipus's "father." The sheer unexpectedness of his entrance (all previous entrances have been anticipated) indicates the growing waywardness of the action in contrast with the planned appearances of Teiresias and Creon.[56] This sense of losing control is heightened by Oedipus's conspicuous absence, by the incongruously buoyant mood of the messenger, by Jocasta's supplication to Apollo which both suggests how much her "skepticism" is part of a desperate defense against the threat of the oracle's truth and recalls Apollo's previous dishonoring of

[55] For a detailed discussion of this point, see in Winningham-Ingram, *Sophocles*, chap. 7.
[56] See Seale, *Vision and Stagecraft*, p. 237.

her husband-son. It is manifest too by the fluctuating elation and despair which, though already present, now assume full form and force.

The messenger is joyful because he brings to Oedipus and his house small pain (the death of Oedipus's "father" Polybus) and much happiness, for Oedipus has been chosen king of Corinth. Of course, both Jocasta (to whom the news is first told) and Oedipus (whom she quickly calls on stage) are indifferent to the honor but exult in the pain.

Armed by the messenger's assurance that Polybus is truly dead, Jocasta exclaims "O Oracles of the Gods, where are you now" (945). Learning the news, Oedipus joins her in triumphant chorus.

> O dear Jocasta, why should one
> look to the Pythian hearth
> or to the birds screaming overhead?
> (964–66)

The oracles are as dead as his father, and utterly worthless. When Oedipus suddenly remembers the prediction and expresses the fear that he would marry his still living "mother" Merope, he is reassured by his real mother, to whom he is married, that he has no need to worry.

> Why should men fear since chance prevails in everything
> and true forsight reckons nothing clearly?
> Best to live unthinkingly, day to day, as one can.
> (977–79)

Sleeping with their mothers invades all men's dreams, says this mother whose son's dream is their shared nightmare. Only "he to whom such things are nothing bears life most easily." As for oracles, they are but empty words, unworthy of respect or attention. There is no rule to things, no order behind the random actions of our lives, no past prediction that constrains men now or in future. Men and women make their own lives unencumbered by superstitious fears and god-ordained fate. Our limits are only dreams which, once conquered, leave us free of bonds and bounds.[57]

But the elation is short-lived. The paean to human power and freedom becomes a prelude to the shattering truth, which reveals unholy bonds forged irrevocably by god and destiny. Jocasta is the first to see it. As the messenger reveals that Polybus is not Oedipus's real father and that he, the messenger, received Oedipus as an ankle-bound child from one of

---

[57] "Oedipus' irreverent cry 'why should one look to the Pythian hearth' . . . is not ultimately rebuked by the play's events, not because the oracles were false, but because even though true, they are of no use to man. If, owing to man's limited insight, divine truth only deceives and misleads, then man is fully justified in turning away from prophecy." See Laszlo Versenyi, *Man's Measure* (Albany: SUNY Press, 1974), pp. 230–31.

Laius's men at Cithaeron pass, Jocasta begs the king to desist from his hunt for birth and being. Seeing the full truth, she pleads with her husband-son, "For the love of god let us have no more questioning" (1069) (or "I pray that you do not come to know yourself"). But the king, in ecstasy at the prospect of knowing the circumstances of his birth, forgets the fears that tormented him but a moment ago. He does not listen to Jocasta and wrongly attributes her pain, her "may you never know who you are," and her hasty departure to fear that he is not of royal blood. As with Teiresias and Creon before, Oedipus wrongly assigns self-serving motives by misinterpreting the actions of others who wish to aid him as disguised attacks on his authority.

So close to the truth, Oedipus is constitutionally and characterologically incapable of hearing, let alone heeding, admonitions of caution: "With such clues I could not fail to bring my birth to light"; "I will not obey for I am driven mad with the passion to know clearly"; "Being born such as I am, I could never prove to be other and so not seek out my birth to the end" (1950, 1965, 1984–85). The drive to know clearly is transformed into near hysterical imaginings as he supposes himself the child of *Tyche*, sui generis and self-made; and the chorus, responding to his frenzy (and mistaking this new impiety as piety), supposes him a child of the gods. But he is not the child of the gods but of Jocasta and Laius. He is not some force of nature with space and time as his family, but a violator of nature, family, and the city of his birth. He thinks himself free of all human responsibilities, able to live as he likes and for the moment, while in fact no one is less free or living less as he likes than he.

But not for long. The old shepherd enters in a scene reminiscent of Oedipus's earlier confrontation with Teiresias. Both old men know what we know, both attempt to keep that knowledge hidden through a silence that infuriates the king. Oedipus has the herdsman seized as if to grasp forcibly the truth that has so long eluded him.

With Oedipus, the Corinthian, and the Theban herdsman on stage, we are watching a repeat of the meeting on Mount Cithaeron long ago. The paths of Oedipus's life have finally and truly come together. His search at an end, the ironies of his life dissipated, Oedipus can join the oppositions of his life "in conscious and agonized union rather than unconscious coincidence."[58] Yet the long sought unity of understanding merely presages disintegration. As the three men leave the stage the image is of the whole world wholly shattered.[59]

Now, when the herdsman confirms the seer's words, Oedipus has no choice but to believe that he is indeed the killer of his father, the husband

---

[58] Segal, "The Music of the Sphinx," p. 161.
[59] Seale, *Vision and Stagecraft*, p. 245.

of his mother, and the polluter of Thebes. The oracles are fulfilled and the most glorious of men and vanquisher of the sphinx is the equal of nothing. Banished by his own decree, he is fated to wander in exile, a helpless beggar, the power and majesty of kingship forever behind him. The finder is the thing found, the revealer the thing revealed, the actor the sufferer, the seeker the thing sought.[60]

The play does not end with Oedipus's initial acknowledgment of transgression and request for banishment. There are still some 350 lines left, and in them the former king is not just reduced to zero. In fact, for all of what he now knows and despite radically altered circumstances, he remains, as I suggested before, very much the man he has always been. What the last section of the drama does is to reestablish, more confidently, the balance with which the play began. There is evidence for this in Oedipus's new relationship to Creon, in his act of self-blinding, and in his attitude toward his fate. Each item elaborates the others and together they return us to the question of identity.

After blinding himself, Oedipus both commands (*episkēptō*, which is the word he uses in unknowingly cursing himself in line 252) and pleads (*prostrepsomai*, which can mean turning toward a god or coming near [e.g., an enemy]) with Creon to burn Jocasta, exile him, and take care of his daughters (1446–67). The simultaneity of suppliant-master continues until the end when, having directed Creon to exile him but refusing the new ruler's request to give up his children, the latter has to remind Oedipus that striving to be master in all things has been his downfall (*Panta mē boulou kratein; kai gar hakratēsas ou soi tōi biōi xynespeto*, 1523).

Just when the doubleness that has so far afflicted Oedipus's speech and actions is dissolved, they reappear as "ontological" dualities of power and powerlessness analogous to those presented by the choral ode to man in *Antigone*. As Oedipus discovers who he is, he discovers that men and women remain riddles to themselves, creating new ones while answering the old, in a continuous rhythm of remembrance and forgetting. Living with riddles that cannot be fully answered or finally resolved is not a fault to be remedied, it is simply a condition of being human. As particular beings, our identities are established by specific attachments and places that constitute our being *and* preclude our knowing ourselves as others and the gods do. Like the Heisenberg Uncertainty Principle, which holds that the position and speed of an electron cannot be measured simultaneously because of the effects of the observer on the observed, we cannot measure the meaning of what we say and do because it is difficult to determine whether or not what we see and hear is our projection on the

---

[60] Knox, *Oedipus at Thebes*, p. 131 and passim.

"data." Intelligence can illuminate the darkest secrets only at the cost of obscuring other, equally dark secrets.

The ode describes human beings as strange in the double sense of wondrous, awesome, and powerful *and* terrible, awful, and violent. In part this doubleness derives from our mediating position between beasts and gods. Having affinities with both means that we are always divided between our divinity and bestiality. Here is Vernant: "When man decides, like Oedipus, to carry the enquiry into what he is as far as it can go, he discovers himself to be enigmatic, without consistency, without any domain of his own or any fixed point of attachment, with no defined essence oscillating between being the equal of the gods and the equal of nothing at all."[61] Seeing the world from both high and low, humans confront a double-faceted reality about which they cannot help but speak ironically.[62] By enabling the audience to recognize these dualities in the theater, tragedy enables the citizenry to recognize their presence outside it. But it also reminds the spectators that the wisdom they have gained through their understanding of Oedipus's condition is not attainable in their case. No one should be as certain as Oedipus. Only the gods know for sure and they, as Heraclitus said about Apollo but might have said about Oedipus Tyrannos, "neither speak nor conceal but give signs" (*sēmainei*).[63]

To put it in Gadamer's terms: "Self-understanding can no longer be integrally related to a complete self-transparency in the sense of a full presence of ourselves to ourselves." That is because self-understanding is a "path whose completion is a clear impossibility. If there is an entire dimension of unilluminated unconscious; if all of our actions, wishes, drives, decision, and modes of conduct (and so the totality of our human social existence) are based on the obscure and veiled dimension of the connotations of our animality; if all our conscious representations can be

---

[61] "Ambiguity and Reversal," p. 110. ("His real greatness," Vernant concludes, "consists in the very thing that expresses his enigmatic nature: his questioning.")

[62] The point is made in the play's use of language which has both intellectual or animal connotations. Thus Oedipus tracks down (or hunts) *and* searches out Laius's killer.

The language of high and low gives philosophical dimension to Machiavelli's discussion of the theorist as a landscape painter (in the beginning of the *Prince*) able to see the low *and* high in ways that neither the prince nor the people can. It also lends support for those who think the *Prince* partly ironic and for those who would interpret it as a drama in which the prince plays a part in a script written and directed by Machiavelli.

[63] *Ho anax ou to manteion esti to en Delphois, oute legei oute kruptei alla sēmainei* (Heraclitus, B93): "Giving signs turns the questioner back upon himself, beguiling his aspirations toward clear vision, refusing to guarantee that fallible humanity can interpret the signs correctly." Delphi thus confronts man with his frailty as do the plays of Sophocles. Both "convey a sense of the inscrutibility of the gods and of man's inability to fully grasp their will in time to avert disaster" (Reinhardt, *Sophocles* [1959], p. 136). *Sēmainei* indicates both evidence from which rational deductions may be made and mysterious marks of supernatural intervention.

masks, pretexts, under which our vital energy or our social interests pursue their own goals in an unconscious way; if all the insights we have, as obvious and evident as they may be, are threatened by such doubt; then self-understanding cannot designate any patent self-transparency of our human existence. We have to repudiate the illusion of completely illuminating the darkness of our motivations and tendencies."[64]

The double meaning of *deinos*, the mediating position of human beings, the impossibility of self-transparency, the tension between commanding and begging, remembrance and forgetting, prescience and ignorance, come to light in Oedipus's self-blinding and the acceptance of responsibility for his fate the explanation of that act calls forth.

The self-blinding is an act of self-assertion, of self-mutilation and self-abnegation. In its excess and its forcefulness, it is paradigmatic of the man and expressive of his character. It also proves him to be the son of a woman who committed suicide and a father whose fierce will would yield neither to the oracle nor to the stranger at the crossroads. In its dramatic ferocity the self-blinding echoes the equally fierce curse Oedipus called down upon himself. Now as then, he makes things worse for himself than they need be and would make them worse still.

> If there were a means to choke off the source of hearing,
> I would not have stayed my hand from totally locking up
> my miserable body seeing and hearing nothing:
> If my mind could be put beyond reach
> of hurt and misery, that would be sweetest.
>
> (1386–90)[65]

But neither blindness nor deafness provide such sweetness. Instead of banishing the hurts, the succeeding lines are a long apostrophe of them. Shut up inside, the pain is more vivid than ever. Absence of present worldly distractions intensifies remembrance of things past. It also contracts the world, creating a space of suffocating viscosity, perhaps the most appropriate punishment for a man who committed incest.

The self-blinding is *his* way of dramatizing the lesson that blindness lies at the heart of sight and *his* chosen punishment for eyes that saw what they should not have seen and failed to see what most needed seeing. In

[64] "Hermeneutics as Practical Philosophy," in *Reason in the Age of Science*, trans. Frederick G. Lawrence (Cambridge, Mass.: MIT Press, 1983), pp. 103–4. (Gadamer goes on to insist that we cannot simply accept this condition.)

[65] Oedipus will not hear Teiresias and calls the seer blind in ears, mind, and eyes, while the prophet turns the line back on Oedipus (at 372–73). The three terms correspond to Oedipus's response to the first mention of Laius (105). Again Oedipus refuses to hear Creon (543–44) until he arrives at the point of dreadful hearing (1169–70). At 1437 he says, "Drive me from here with all due speed to where I may not hear a human voice." The line and image is discussed by Segal, "The Music of the Sphinx, " pp. 159–60.

the act of self-blinding, Oedipus not only accepts responsibility for what he has done, he seizes it, insisting that the deeds done are his alone ("no man but I can bear my evil doom"). When the chorus castigates his self-blinding, Oedipus emphatically defends it: "What I have done here was best done; do not tell me otherwise, give me no further counsel" (1370–71).

The self-blinding also unites Oedipus with the blind seer Teiresias and, as such, is a symbolic acceptance of the fact that the knowledge he had was, as Socrates says in the *Apology* of his knowledge, only human. This does not mean Oedipus should have stopped searching for who he was or that ignorance is bliss. He could not have stopped without betraying himself, without ceasing to be who he was. He should not have stopped because ignorance is as dangerous if not more dangerous than knowledge. The prudent and pious Creon, who might well have stopped or never even started, seems, when compared with Oedipus, to be like Heraclitus's sleepwalkers or well-fed cattle.[66] Still, continuing as he did, Oedipus uncovers a light so dazzling that only the blind can bear it. It seems that human intelligence, perhaps especially an intelligence unknowingly formed by its origins in space and time, comes to grief.[67] When Oedipus says "If I had eyes, I do not know if I could stand the sight," he gives an ironic twist to the cave parable in the *Republic*. It is as if singleness of form, with its taming of ambiguity, requires self-mutilation and blindness. This possibility is all the more intriguing if I am right about the special relationship between philosophy and tyranny.

The self-blinding not only unites Oedipus with Teiresias, it also unites him with the god who he recognizes has been his unseen companion throughout his life. Asked by the chorus to identify the divine presence (*daimonōn*) that urged him to the extreme of self-blinding, the king answers:

> It was Apollo my friends, Apollo
> who brought my bitter sorrow to its completion
> But the hand that struck me was mine alone.
>
> (1329–31)

---

[66] Reinhardt argues that Creon is an anti-Oedipus. He is lucid, cautious, and overly pious, without "deep roots" or lofty aspirations; has no drives except those he can consciously control, and no relationships except those that can be calculated and entered on a balance sheet. There is nothing tragic about him; he is a foil for Oedipus (Reinhardt, *Sophocles* [1959], p. 111).

[67] There is, of course, a paradox in putting it this way. Tragedy does overcome mysterious forces by situating them within its own ordering process and "rational" schema. "If tragedy is a negation of the possibility of a systematic order of knowledge, how is it that it is itself one of the finest examples of this supposedly impossible order?" See Timothy Reiss, *Tragedy and Truth* (New Haven: Yale University Press, 1960), p. 21.

All his life the god had been spurring him on.[68] But only now does he realize that he and Apollo have together molded his fate; that although he acted in ignorance, everything he did was his, in the double sense that it belonged to him and was profoundly expressive of his character.[69] This recognition is a discovery "about himself that is scarcely less crucial than the discovery of his identity."[70]

With this recognition Oedipus joins the audience in becoming a spectator of his own tragedy while they, in turn, participate in his discovery that the beginning of knowledge is ignorance.

THIS IS, of course, Socrates' view in the *Apology*. I exaggerated when I said that no one pursued the question of his own identity as intensely and persistently as Oedipus. As I indicated in chapter 2, he has a rival: "Socrates" in Plato's *Apology* and *Crito*. And however different the two may be, they nevertheless share a special relationship to Apollo and a passion to uncover the truth no matter what the cost. Moreover, although Socrates does not pollute the city, what he says and where he says it is regarded as a violation of proper boundaries and separations. Although he brings no plague, he is accused of corrupting the youth, of impiety, and of discarding the proper awe for the natural order of things by claiming to know what is above and below the earth. Although he does not kill his father the king and marry his mother, Socrates confounds the city's structuring of private and public life by refusing to be a citizen as others are, and by refusing to do politics in the places where they do it. The *Apology*, like the *Oedipus Tyrannos*, is about being strange in one's own place, and being alien among those with whom one should be closest. And both reveal characters who refuse to betray their identity even at the cost of what appears to be self-destruction.

Like the play, the *Apology* and *Crito* are concerned with the question of identity, with "who" Socrates and Athens are and how philosophy and politics should be defined. If Socrates defines his vocation "in terms of" its relationship to Athenian politics, and if Knox is right in suggesting that the *Oedipus Tyrannos* is about the identity of Athens as well as that of Oedipus, then Athens provides a middle term for the comparison between

---

[68] The god continues to lead him even now. The messenger relating the events in the palace preceding Oedipus's self-blinding tells of how the king was led by an invisible god to where his mother hung herself and of the prodigious feats of strength he performed in forcing his way into the room by bending the bolts out of their sockets.

[69] This is summed up by Heraclitus's aphorism "*Ethos anthrōpōn daimōn*" whose dual reading "character is destiny" and "destiny is character" is a central theme of the play. See the discussion in Vidal-Naquet and Vernant, "Ambiguity and Reversal," in *Tragedy and Myth*, and Winningham-Ingram, *Sophocles*, p. 177.

[70] Cameron, *Identity*, p. 115.

the play and dialogue even as both of them provide competing representations of "who" Athens is.[71]

Of course, "in terms of" does not necessarily mean imitation. It may
mean reconsideration, augmentation, or even rejection. What it must
mean is engagement—that explicitly or implicitly Socrates understands
the task of philosophy as criticizing, purging, and perhaps replacing the
form and content of tragedy and the tragedian as the political educator
of the city. For instance, when in the *Apology* (30d) Socrates proclaims
death, exile, deprivation, and disenfranchisement minor evils (as compared with accusing a man unjustly), he apparently[72] dissolves the tragedy of Oedipus. Similarly, when, as in the *Crito*, he dismisses Crito's concern with particular attachments and obligations (to friends and
children), he appears to embrace those abstractions that blinded Oedipus
to the truth of who he was.

The tyranny of mind as dramatized in the *Oedipus Tyrannos* has obvious relevance to political theorizing. A good argument can be made that
political theory was "born" and is reborn in times of cultural crisis; that
its raison d'être is the reconstitution of political discourse and life.[73] Yet
theory's capacity to save us from the "sphinx" seems to depend on a de-
racination that, like Agamemnon's going to Troy to avenge one injustice
only to commit another, creates a plague as life-threatening as the one it
ended. Like *Antigone*'s Creon, theory may aim to save politics from itself
but, also like him, it contains an impulse toward intellectual and political
exclusiveness that, if uninterrogated and unchecked, leads to an emphasis
on order at the expense of politics.[74] That is especially challenging if one
takes democracy as seriously as Joseph Tussman does. "The democrat,
when democracy was a creed that mattered" argued that men and women
"have deliberative and moral potentiality and that given the proper education and environment each could take his [or her] place in the deliber-

[71] Oedipus is a character in Sophocles' play and, as such, no more a spokesman for the
playwright than the chorus whose later ruminations contain oblique criticisms of him. Thus
the differences that separate Socrates and Oedipus (and so Socrates and Athens as "represented" by Oedipus) do not necessarily separate Socrates and Sophocles (and the Athens *he*
and the play as a whole "represent"). It may even be that the differences between the former
point to affinities between the latter, which would suggest an affinity between especially this
tragedy and Socratic political theory.

[72] I say "seems" here and in the next sentence because I think Socrates is alert to the issue.
Indeed, I will argue in chapter 7 that much of the *Apology* and *Crito* revolves around it.

[73] I have argued this at length in my essay "The Battle of Salamis and the Origins of
Political Theory," *Political Theory* 14, no. 3 (1986): 359–90.

[74] Perhaps this underlies Machiavelli's claim that while one man is necessary for founding,
a lasting foundation needs the sharing of power and authority. In this case, as in others,
Machiavelli "politicizes" dilemmas that are posed theoretically by more philosophically ori-
ented theorists.

ative forum and share the responsibilities of sovereignty" not simply to get more but "primarily in order to develop his [or her] deliberative and moral character and to achieve the dignity of being a ruler of the society in which he [or she] is a member. For this is the genuine democratic urge, impervious to all the cornucopias of the most benevolent paternalism," whether of a Theban king or a Platonic philospher.[75]

The road from *Oedipus Tyrannos* leads in many directions: to Thucydides (via Knox), to the *Apology* as we have seen, and to Plato. But there are two other roads: one that leads to the *Bacchae*, the other to Los Angeles.

However unjustified Oedipus's punishment may be, and however harsh the play's judgment of human intelligence may appear, the *Oedipus Tyrannos* is not simply a play of despair. The waywardness of its action and the miscommunication that marks so much of its speech are partly (but not wholly) redeemed by the continuous presence of the gods; by the undoubted existence of an inclusive order, however enigmatic; and by the nobility of its "fallen" hero. And for all the play's warnings about Athenian excess, the polis remains a vital realm of speech and action, mitigating the metaphysical homelessness that afflicts and distinguishes us from other species and from the gods.

In the *Bacchae* there is no such redemption or certain order, no comparable hero, no polis to mediate "metaphysical" homelessness. In the *Oedipus Tyrannos* the king chooses to mutilate himself in punishment for recognized transgressions. In the *Bacchae* Pentheus is dismembered by his mother while playing a peeping Tom. Whereas questions of identity (as well as of justice, knowledge, and speech) are enigmatic in Sophocles' play, they are simply confused in the *Bacchae*. That such confusion exists in a play about the god of theater raises the issue of tragedy's place in the polis even more forcefully than did the *Oedipus Tyrannos*.

The other road leads from Oedipus to Oedipa, from Sophocles' Thebes-Athens to Pynchon's America. Once more the concern is with unity and diversity now in terms of entropy and narcissism. Once again the danger is the mania for certainty, singularity, and closure *and* the romanticization of openness, structurelessness, and randomness, which Pynchon regards as a corollary rather than opposite of certainty. With him, in America, roads have become highways that kill twice over, murdering the drivers who use them and being built through cemeteries, obliterating signs of mortality, desecrating the American past, the land, the Indians yet again. Pynchon fears that America will become like Zeitlin's Thebes: oscillating between rigid inclusions and exclusions on the one

---

[75] *Obligation and the Body Politic* (New York: Oxford University Press, 1960), p. 105.

hand and radical confusions on the other, unable to generate new structures and new progeny. His image for this is the used-car lot with its endless trade-ins of dented malfunctioning versions of the self for another just as futureless projection of someone else's life. "As if it were the most natural thing. To Mucho it was horrible. Endless, convoluted incest."[76]

[76] *The Crying of Lot 49* (New York: Bantam Books, 1967), p. 5.

FIVE

Membership and "Dismembership" in the *Bacchae*

THE THEME of membership and dismembering has been background for the discussion of justice in the *Oresteia* and identity in the *Oedipus Tyrannos*. The trilogy presents justice as the bringing together of forces and principles that create a whole larger than but respectful of the parts that constitute it. Under the aegis of Athena, men and women, old and young, and gods and mortals find place and purpose in a common endeavor, while the instinctive or passional basis of politics and wisdom are recognized and similarly honored. The Furies find a home below as the literal and metaphorical foundation of public life. Here at last is relief from the suffering of previous plays and earlier times.

There is no talk of justice in the *Bacchae*, except talk that identifies it with the vengeance the *Oresteia* rejects. In this play, instinctive forces and primitive drives surge up through the legal and political structure,[1] itself now an overlay of hollow forms and trite pieties, to destroy the polis. Instead of respecting diverse parts, the city dishonors aspects essential for its own composition and completion, with disorder and tyrannical authority as a result. Instead of reciprocity, we have dismemberment; in place of diversity within unity, we have on the one hand the isolation of Pentheus, the disintegration of Cadmus's house, and the fragmentation of the city; on the other, an ecstatic community of Bacchants that ignores all distinctions. In opposition to the *Eumenides*, passions run wild as intelligence denies their legitimacy while mirroring their excesses. In the *Bacchae*, the Bacchants echo the Furies but are never made part of the city. Instead they dance with joy at its demise.

The contrast between the *Oresteia* and the *Bacchae* is most vivid when we compare their final scenes. The *Eumenides* ends with a sacred procession of all citizens consecrating the establishment of justice. In the *Bacchae*, father and daughter are forced apart by the god to face their separate fates. In her grief at parting and impending isolation, Agave asks where she can go and to whom she can turn, to which Cadmus can only respond: "I do not know my child. Your father can be of no help to you"

---

[1] See the discussion of this point in Marilyn Arthur, "The Choral Odes of the *Bacchae* of Euripides," *Yale Classical Studies* 22 (1972): 69–70.

(*ouk oida teknon; mikros epikouros patēr*, 1368). There is no healing or relief here, only "a wisdom bitter as the gates of hell."

The inversion of the *Oresteia*'s final scene and vision goes beyond the collapse of Cadmus's house or even the collapse of Thebes. We have seen how, as road builders, the Athenians tame a wilderness, establishing boundaries and demarcations against the amorphousness of an otherwise undifferentiated nature. The road they build leads to justice, to Athens, and to civilization. Dionysus's punishment of Cadmus is the undoing of civilization. By transforming him into a serpent, the god is reversing the civilizing act, because the founding act of Thebes is the slaying of the serpent. Not only does the god thereby remove the foundation of the city, he robs Cadmus of the one thing he has left: the visible sign of great deeds, his name, reputation, and identity. Denying the possibility of imperishable glory (the Homeric *kleos aphthiton*), Dionysus rejects the idea of worldly immortality that had been the spur to wisdom (but which the chorus of Asian Bacchants now regard as overreaching ambition). Such denial is tantamount to reinserting men into the cycle of nature against which their distinctively human identity as speakers and actors was initially affirmed. The end of Cadmus's house is the end of Thebes, the end of heroism, and the "dismembering of civilization itself."[2]

Membership and dismembership were also background for my discussion of identity in the *Oedipus Tyrannos*. As I argued there, any answer to the question Who am I? entails situating someone as a "member" of a particular community that provides a context for their characteristic deeds and statements. It was precisely knowledge of place and parents that Oedipus lacked. While the absence of such knowledge may have aided him in giving the abstract answer to the sphinx's riddle, it also precluded him from recognizing the special significance of the riddle for his own life. To say that one's identity entails situating oneself as "a" member of a particular community implies that membership is always a matter of being with others, of plurality as well as singularity. This is what Creon (in the *Antigone*) forgets when he proclaims himself master of disorder and equates himself with the city. Oedipus falls victim to the same seduction too, though not immediately or in quite the same way.

If membership, like identity, presupposes plurality or standing apart as well as standing with or community, then the loss of identity, the simultaneous erosion of difference and unity, is a form of dismemberment.

---

[2] Charles Balestri, "The *Bacchae*," in *Homer to Brecht: The European Epic and Dramatic Tradition*, ed. Michael Seidel and Edward Mendelson (New Haven: Yale University Press, 1977), p. 211. See also Charles Segal, *Dionysiac Poetics and Euripides' Bacchae* (Princeton: Princeton University Press, 1982), p. 305, and Hannah Arendt's discussion of eternity and immortality in *The Human Condition* (Chicago: University of Chicago Press, 1974), section 3.

Whether figurative or literal, collective or individual, political or physical, dismemberment destroys completeness and continuity until what has been whole and coherent is scattered, torn apart, unrecognizable. Pentheus, isolated from those who could sustain and constrain him, is helpless before the god's machinations. Utterly seduced by what he thinks he despises and would imprison as other, he vacillates between hypermasculinity and coquettish effeminacy,[3] double-sightedness and single-mindedness. In this he is politically and psychologically dismembered long before he is dismembered physically and ritually. Here is a man (or boy) without character—unformed, inconstant, tyrannical.

It is his dismemberment that forms the dramatic center of Euripides' *Bacchae*. And it is the futile effort of his grandfather to re-member him that poses the central political question of the play. Near the end of the drama, Cadmus, the founder of Thebes, enters with pieces of Pentheus's body. The young ruler of the city has just been torn limb from limb by his mother, Agave, Cadmus's daughter. Blinded and empowered by Dionysus, she has (with her Maenad accomplices), mistaken her son for a lion and dismembered him with her bare hands. The old man, exhausted by his search for the scattered pieces of the body, with his life dissolving before him and all his achievements about to be undone, has yet to bring his still-frenzied child back to reality and to a "sorrow beyond measure, comprehension, or bearing" (1244). Before him stands a mother displaying her dead son's head as a trophy, demanding the glory usually reserved for men. She cannot understand her father's joylessness at her victorious hunt; but we can. Facing all this and more, the old man tries, as best he can, to restore his daughter to sanity, to reassemble the body of his grandson, and to make sense of his now-shattered life and woesome fate. Here is the beginning of his description and lament for his dead grandson, for Thebes, and for his house. I think it is also Euripides' description and lament for his city scattered by a factionalism borne of war and empire.

> This was Pentheus
> whose body, after long and weary searchings
> I painfully assembled from Cithaeron's glens
> where it lay, scattered in shreds, dismembered (*diasparakton*)[4]

---

[3] In English "member" suggests the male sex organ, which is appropriate since The *Bacchae* raises questions about masculinity, about the way the male body politic maintains gender divisions, and about the relationship between Dionysus, tragedy, and the liberation of women from traditional domestic tasks and subordinate political status.

[4] *Diasparakton* means to tear to pieces, rend asunder (*dia-sparasso*), transgress or separate (*dia-spao*). It is etymologically connected with *sparagmos*, the tearing or mangling of a body, but also spasms, and metaphorically to attack savagely without human limits. *Sparagmos* is central in Dionysian ritual.

throughout the forest, no two pieces
in a single place.

(1217–20)[5]

Later, and now sane, Agave joins her father in restoring Pentheus's head to his body: "as best as we can we shall make him whole again."[6]

This chapter is about membership and dismembership in the *Bacchae*. It is concerned with what it means to live within a particular circle of belief, action, and commitment; what happens when one is excluded from that circle or marginalized within it; and what occurs when the circle loses its form and center. The chapter will focus on the fate of Pentheus. But Pentheus is not simply a man; he is the king of Thebes. Thus, his figurative then literal dismemberment is also that of the city he rules. Dismemberment means madness, civil war, and death, being torn apart or driven asunder, displaced from the language of one's ancestors, parted from all for which one cares, being forced, as Cadmus is, to search for a unity of being and understanding amid scattered lives and disconnected thoughts.

Because the action takes place in mythical Thebes and involved Cadmus—not, as in the *Oresteia*, at Athens where it concerns practices in which the audience directly participated—we need to recall Zeitlin's argument that Thebes is a conceptual category in the Athenian theater that provides a negative model to Athens' manifest image of itself. It is the "other" place where questions of polis, self, and family are acted out in an imagined rather than a "real" city. Within the theater Athens is not a tragic space, but the scene where theater can and does escape the tragic, where reconciliation and transformation are still possible as they are not in the closed entropic society of Thebes. In these terms Thebes is literally a trope for imprisonment, exile, and death in contrast to Athens, a place of freedom and regeneration. Thebes may stand as a warning to Athens, unsurprisingly so given the general dimension of the issues tragedy raises. It may also be a preventive medicine, again unsurprisingly given tragedy's role as a mode of political education. But it is misleading to identify Athens with Thebes. I think Zeitlin is right, but that with the *Bacchae* the dramatic setting and the setting of the drama close in on each other more than in the *Oedipus Tyrannos*.[7] What is the evidence for that?

---

[5] The translation is William Arrowsmith's in *The Complete Greek Tragedies* ed. David Grene and Richmond Lattimore (New York: Washington Square Press, 1968), p. 216.

[6] This is part of Arrowsmith's reconstruction of a lost part of the play. With an almost too perfect irony, this section of the text is mutilated.

[7] This closing-in means that the issue of re-membering, in the double sense of re-constructing citizenship and recalling (re-collecting, re-minding) the foundation upon which citizenship had initially been constituted, reflects a concern with contemporary Athenian factionalism.

Some have offered biographical considerations, contrasting Sophocles' position as an Athenian general with Euripides' self-imposed exile. More compelling, I think is what seems a pointed repudiation of the *Oresteia*'s concluding vision.[8] If, as several critics have argued, the *Oresteia* had achieved classic status, then inverting its concluding vision would have special significance. Perhaps Euripides is suggesting that the vision was idealistic if not fictive to begin with, that the world embodied in it never was and cannot be. Or perhaps it is a world that once was but is and can be no longer. In either case continual obeisance to it can only engender a nostalgia that blinds men to contemporary realities and sours them for any action except romantic reaction or revolutionary excess.[9] The inversion might also have signaled a new cultural narrative. If our ability to sustain political practices and institutions is tied to our ability to tell stories that secure continuity between who we are now and events, actions, and characters that have preceded and shaped us, then the *Bacchae*'s story suggests both discontinuity between the present and the received perception of the past and a reshaping of the past in terms of the present. Both the discontinuity and the reshaping alter the sense of who "we" are and what it means to be a member of the "new" political community, as well as of the audience which is that community in the theater.[10]

Although turning the *Bacchae* (or any tragedy) into a commentary of its times is reductive, let me, nevertheless, put the point "historically." I think the *Bacchae* takes apart traditional stories of the past with their, by now, trite pieties *and* the sophistic critique of them.[11] What it dramatizes in a condensed and accelerated form is the erosion of old myths and forms, a wasting away of the feeling they once evoked, an increasingly disjointed and inconsistent expression of ideas, a nervous insistence upon

[8] On the relationship between the trilogy and the *Bacchae*, see in general J. de Romilly, *L'evolution du pathetique d'Eschyle a Euripide* (Paris: Presses Universitaire de France, 1961). (But cf. Meier, *Die Entstehung des Politischen bei den Griechen* [Frankfurt: Suhrkamp, 1980], chap. 3, on the Eumenides.)

[9] These criticisms echo those made by Holmes and Ignatieff against the idealization of classical texts and the polis. I think one could find other parallels between Euripides' position in the mythological tradition and toward the political dilemmas of his time and Ignatieff's position toward "the Western tradition" and the politics of our time.

[10] On the relationship between the arrangements in the theater and in the structure of authority in the polis as a whole, see John J. Winkler, "The Ephebes' Song' *Tragoidia* and *Polis*," *Representations* (Summer 1985): 26–62. On narrative and politics, see William Adams, "History, Interpretation and the Politics of Theory," *Polity* 2, no. 1 (Fall 1988): 45–66.

[11] On how this works in the ode and exchanges between Teiresias and Cadmus, see Karl Diechgraber's essay, "Die Kadmos-Tiresiasszene in Euripides Bakchen," *Hermes* 70 (1935): 322–49. For how the sophistic debates in the play become a disguised form of war, which solves absolutely nothing, see Hans Strohm, *Euripides: Interpretationen sur dramatischen Form*, Zemata 15 (Munich: Beck, 1957).

the old forms and references together with more and more arbitrary and extravagant manipulation of them until "the units cease to be accepted as intellectual givens and the references cease to be meaningful."[12]

A second bit of evidence connecting mythical Thebes and Athens lies in Cadmus's fate pronounced by Dionysus at the play's end. The old man is doomed to lead a huge barbarian host against Hellas. An Athenian audience might well take that as a reference to the Persian invasion of 490 and 480 B.C. where, at Marathon, Salamis, and Plataea, the Athenians or Athenian-led allies defeated the invaders including Thebes, which had "Medized." Particularly the naval victory at Salamis was regarded by most Athenians as a foundation of their democracy.[13] To link the disintegration of Thebes as a city to the prophecy that Cadmus will lead an assault on Hellas, and to connect both to the founding triumph of Athenian democracy, need not mean Athens is following Thebes's example— unless, of course, one reads Thucydides' description of the civil war at Corcyra as a historical analogue to the dismemberment of Pentheus and Thebes.

That is exactly what I propose to do in the next two chapters. It is on this reading that the two pieces of evidence I have offered become evidence for my qualification of Zeitlin's thesis rather than further substantiation of it.

In terms of the *History*'s architecture, the *stasis*[14] at Corcyra is introduced by the plague. It is the plague that establishes a parallel between the disintegration of the physical body and the body politic. In these terms, Pericles' speech following the plague is a political version of Cadmus's efforts to put his grandson's body back together again. Although Pericles is more successful than Cadmus, he is not wholly so; and the incompleteness of the city's recovery foreshadows Thucydides' discussion of *stasis* at Athens, after Corcyra the most elaborate discussion of the subject in the *History*.

During the civil war at Corcyra, men lived for the moment and only for revenge. With ungovernable passions bursting all bounds and bonds, they behaved with unprecedented savagery and excess. (Thucydides goes on to

[12] Michael Walzer, "On the Role of Symbolism in Political Thought," *Political Science Quarterly* 82 (June 1967): 198. Walzer is talking about seventeenth-century England, not classical Athens.

[13] I have argued this at length in my essay, "The Battle of Salamis and the Origins of Political Theory," *Political Theory* 14, no. 3 (1986): 359–90.

[14] There is a connection between *stasis* and *ek-stasis* (ecstasy) which means being put out of place or kind or, more generally, an overpowering emotion or state of sudden intense rapturous delight or religious frenzy associated with Dionysus. (*Ek* means out of, away from, or beyond.) The general connection between these meanings or ecstatic and stasis is suggested by Thucydides' portrait of civil war and M. I. Finley's essay, "Athenian Demagogues," *Past and Present* 21 (April 1962): 3–24.

say that Corcyra became a precedent whose brutality was refined by later conflagrations.) Factionalism escalated until each man became a faction unto himself, and the city (and the possibility of an audience) all but disappeared. At Corcyra, reason and wisdom became animal cunning and mere cleverness, as each man tried to hunt, trap, and dominate his enemies, who increased as trust decreased. Ignoring tradition, law, morality, and religion, or using them as a means to confound an enemy and so advance their power, men refused to "recognize" (in both senses) kinship as a stronger tie than party, and so, like Agave, Dionysus, and the intention of Pentheus, they killed their own.

To kill one's kin was a form of self-destruction more terrible than personal death, because it meant destroying those sacred bonds that defined one's identity in life and in death. To violate them is to tear oneself apart.[15]

Thucydides also says that words themselves were casualties of civil war (3.82). The *Bacchae* dramatizes Thucydides's claim by showing how the various characters on stage disagree about or manipulate words for knowledge and wisdom, especially *sophia*. Although everyone uses such words, they mean different things by them, change their conception of them to suit their immediate situation, or act in ways that contradict their initial proclamations. Because every protestation that someone or some statement is "wise" becomes compromised by the subsequent action of the play, the audience is left uncertain about what knowledge or wisdom is and whether anyone in the play has "it" rather than some self-serving version of it.[16] And what is true of *sophia* and *phronēsis* is true of "Dionysus." Every representation of him is an attempt to coopt, if not imprison, him. Neither the sophistries of Teiresias, the utilitarianism of Cadmus, the intellectual aggressiveness of Pentheus, nor the riddling language of the god's initiates provides a full conception of knowledge or a reliable understanding of the play's action, or is fully able to "capture" the god. Like Creon in *Antigone* and Oedipus in *Oedipus Tyrannos*, each turns their single point of view into a world whose initial consistency or surface plausibility is revealed as more projection than reality.

Thucydides presumes there to be an invariant language by which lin-

---

[15] Balestri discusses the significance of this in his essay ("The *Bacchae*," p. 197).

[16] The meaning of *sophos* and *sophia* range from the animal cunning one needs to be a successful hunter, to techne, cleverness (whether "mere" cleverness or something more substantial), to knowledge of one's character and the larger necessities that define "the" human condition. As a craft it includes the skill of the playwright (as exemplified by the *Bacchae* or the play within the play), and stands in contrast to "artlessness." As cleverness, *sophos* words can indicate either an agile mind or one that is too agile for its own good. In the latter instance wisdom is a false wisdom, a kind of craftiness or flashy brilliance without substance.

guistic dismemberment can be identified and described.[17] I am not sure Euripides agrees. So the question becomes whether there is some "objective" perspective "outside" the play, some standpoint from which to distinguish appearance and reality or judge contending claims, or whether, on the contrary, every perspective or definition is an assault against and a projection onto the world.

In dramatizing the contested character of concepts like "knowledge" and "wisdom," Euripides emphasizes the epistemological dimension of tragedy present in the *Oedipus Tyrannos*. Here the contest is between Pentheus and Dionysus rather than Teiresias and Oedipus, but the issues are analogous: How is it that men and women come to know? Pentheus, like Oedipus, is, on the surface (and only there), dogmatically empirical and analytic, certain that what he sees is the only reality worth seeing. Dionysus offers a different way of knowing—suspension of reason with its rigid controls, letting oneself go so passion and ecstasy can teach what the mind denies or forbids. This knowledge is not a matter of purging the self of bias by following rigidly prescribed methods until one possesses knowledge, but of merging self and the world until knowledge possesses you. Once again, as in the *Oedipus Tyrannos*, epistemological questions are related to the tension between political unity and diversity. Dionysus rejects the kind of "analysis"[18] upon which Pentheus relies and transcends the polarities of class, gender, and status around which the young king organizes his life and rule.

The way the *Bacchae* emphasizes these issues suggests that the corruption of common discourse, of which the manipulation of knowledge words is a sign and symptom, provides a linguistic analogue to the physical and political dismemberment of Pentheus, of mythical Thebes, and, given Thucydides, of Athens and Hellas as well. It also suggests that knowledge and wisdom take on whatever meaning they have only within a specific form of discourse (political, ritual, analytic, or ecstatic). In so doing, the play dramatizes Foucault's point about power-knowledge.

Although mythical Thebes is the play's theatrical setting, that setting is itself set in Athens. The *Bacchae* was not only performed in the Theater of Dionysus, it is about Dionysus and theatrical performance. Thus, the play makes the patron of tragedy into the subject of tragedy, thereby

---

[17] This is the argument of Nicole Loraux in her "Thucydides et la sédition dans les mots," *Quaderni di Storia* 23 (January-June 1986): 95–134.

[18] As Aristotle for one believed, analysis is a kind of dismemberment. The question is whether reassembling what has been taken apart enhances or diminishes the "object" and the "mind." In the play Cadmus tries to reassemble Pentheus's body but he cannot bring his grandson back to life or even to a semblance of life. Machiavelli's discussion of corruption, crisis, and renewal seems to me a thoughtful reflection on this subject.

dramatizing its own beginnings, foundations, and prospects.[19] This "metatragic" dimension of the *Bacchae* is suggested by the play's self-consciousness about its properties and conventions and by the way it uses Thebes's reception of Dionysus to dramatize the paradoxical place of drama in Athenian society. In this respect the play's metatragic concerns are a third bit of evidence bringing Athens and "Thebes" closer together.

The self-consciousness is clearest in the robing scene where Dionysus dresses Pentheus up as a woman. There Dionysus becomes more explicitly what he had been all along: writer, director, costumer, choreographer, and "masked" actor in a play that "stars" Pentheus. In the *Oedipus Tyrannos*, the king has had Apollo as his constant but unseen and aloof companion and was, in Joel Schwartz's phrase, the method actor who found his part in Apollo's script. In the *Bacchae*, both relationships are more immediate; the god is the young king's constant companion, and we virtually see him writing the script. It is true that the god gives the king every opportunity to mitigate his intransigence, and in that sense Pentheus has a choice about what will happen. By the robing scene, however, Dionysus is pulling all the strings, and the young king has become his dancing puppet.

Thebes is unable to find a place for Dionysus until it is too late. That is because of what "Thebes" means in the Athenian theater and because of Dionysus. He is, as we shall discover in detail, a god who in his person and in the kind of worship he inspires transcends the normalizing polarities of gender, class, and position that define the male body politic. Given that fact and the impossibility of ignoring him, how is Dionysus to be honored without destroying the polis? How does one bring what is boundless and multiform into the bounded form of theater, play, and city? How does one contain a god, especially this god, within civic and aesthetic structures without compromising him or exploding those structures? The answer is drama, which dismembers the city on stage within an institutionalized ritual and makes it whole again, doing in Athens what Cadmus could not do at Thebes. Dramatic performances honoring the god represent his special powers of healing and bring that healing to an audience that is for the moment put in touch with the untapped energy and rejuvenation that lie in madness and disorder. It is tragedy that reveals the god's many homes and faces, that discloses an identity greater than any simple enumeration of his disguises and poses: lion, snake, bull, beast, man, and divinity.

In the end, the *Bacchae* is less about whether "Thebes" can incorporate

---

[19] I am not suggesting that this is the primary focus of the play. Rather, the situation is analogous to Socratic dialogues where the nature of dialogue is always an issue alongside of a specific substantive concern like justice, courage, or piety.

the Dionysian than about whether Athens can continue to provide space and voice to elements that are hostile to civic life through the medium of tragic performance. More pointedly, the issue is whether a democracy can continue to sustain itself against its own contradictions and exclusions. How can a city dedicated to *isonomia* continue to exclude so many from participation and power? Why exactly is Athens different from Pentheus or Thebes? What does it mean to be a member of a polis, or an audience, or a ritual celebration?

These are the themes and questions that will guide my discussion of the *Bacchae*. I will divide the play into three sections: from the prologue through the moment before the first confrontation between Dionysus and Pentheus; from that first exchange through the robing scene, after which the king is led to the mountain and his death; and from the report of Pentheus's dismemberment to the final parting of Agave and Cadmus. In each section I will offer an interpretation of the particular themes introduced within it and suggest the way those themes build cumulatively toward the end of the play and Euripides' understanding of political membership and dismembering. I want to show how the various issues are situated within a dramatic whole and how each successive section of the play deepens (often by confounding) what has gone before. If I am successful, we will be left with a tapestry that leaves us uncertain about how to hang it and how to view it.

THE *Bacchae* opens with Dionysus proclaiming his divinity against the slanderous denials of his mother's sisters. In anger and in reprisal he has driven these and all the women of Thebes out of their houses and minds. Rich and poor alike have left their domestic chores to wander in the wild until the land of his birth gives Dionysus's mysteries and his mother due honor. When and if his worship is accepted by the people of Thebes, he will move on to reveal himself to men and women in other lands.

> But if the men of Thebes attempt to force
> my Bacchae from the mountain by threat of arms,
> I shall lead my Maenad army into the field against them
> (50–53)

That seems unnecessary since the first men of Thebes we meet intend no such thing. Cadmus and Teiresias are already dressed as Bacchants prepared to join the revels on the mountain now that their worship of the god has allowed them to throw away old age. But as it turns out, they are the only male worshipers of the god and the only men of Thebes who will *not* try to force the Maenads from the mountain. "Only we see clearly and are wise" Teiresias claims. "All the others are perverse and blind" (*monoi gar eu phronoumen, oi d'alloi kakōs*, 196). Unlike those who shun the god or suppose divinity is granted by mortals, they know that human wisdom (*sophizomestha*) is as nothing to the gods whose being it cannot capture.

> Rather we are the heirs of immemorial custom
> allowed by age and handed down to us
> by our fathers. No mere argument can dislodge them
> whatever sophistries this clever age invents.
>
> (200–203)

As they are about to leave, Pentheus rushes toward them in a wild, distracted and agitated (*eptoētai*) state, which makes Cadmus fear that the young king has yet another innovation (*neōteron*) in mind. In fact, Pentheus has just heard about what he supposes to be a pretend god and of the Theban women leaving home for what he supposes to be an orgy. His response is typical of the man: a dismissal of Dionysus's divinity, which no evidence can amend; a projection of his imagination onto the world whose evidence he otherwise rejects; and a resort to threats of force expressed in the language of hunting, trapping, imprisoning, binding, encircling. He not only rejects the god's divinity but threatens to cut off his head.

The king's agitation only increases when he recognizes his grandfather and the old seer decked out in Bacchic costumes. He orders his grandfather to put down the thyrsus and accuses Teiresias of supporting the new god to line his own pockets. The king is only restrained from jailing the seer because of the latter's old age, which is precisely what the old man no longer feels when he worships the god.

Teiresias's response begins by distinguishing the seeming wisdom of the glib man from the genuine wisdom of the sane man and good citizen. He goes on to extol the benefits of Dionysian worship: the gift of wine, which provides suffering mankind with forgetfulness; the gift of prophecy; and, what should attract Pentheus, the god's usefulness in war. Finally, he warns the young king not to exaggerate the importance of force in ruling human lives. Pentheus must renounce his false wisdom, which is the product of a diseased mind, and honor the god as kings themselves enjoy being honored.

Cadmus seconds Teiresias, but less harshly. He invites his grandson to dwell with them within the traditional ways rather than reject those ways and so isolate himself in thoughtless thought. And even if Dionysus is not really a god, it is useful to propagate the divinity of a family member. After cajoling and offering utilitarian reasons, Cadmus warns Pentheus by reminding him of his cousin Actaeon's fate. He, too, shunned a god and was torn limb from limb by his own dogs. Given the kind of man he is, Pentheus does not hear, see, or understand the story for what it is—a foreshadowing of his own fate. He remains unmoved and intransigent, ordering his men to capture "the effeminate stranger."

After the characters leave, the chorus elaborates the benefits of Dionysus and praises the life far from the unconstrained rantings of a false wisdom which can only breed strife and disaster. For them, wisdom demands the life of apolitical quiet (*hēsuchia*). Only such a life can preserve the houses and sanity of men from being shaken to their foundations.

> Mere cleverness is not wisdom (*to sophon d' ou sophia*)
> Nor is aspiring to be more than human.
> Briefly we live. Briefly,
> then die. Wherefore, I say
> he who hunts a glory, he who tracks
> some boundless, superhuman dream,
> will lose what is secure and close at hand.
> Such men are mad; their counsels evil.
>
> (395–401)

Dionysus has no love for heroes striving for immortal glory. Rather, he loves the goddess Peace who grants men prosperity and preserves the young. And he himself provides for rich and poor alike wine-induced forgetfulness and an escape, however temporary, to a place where all is ripeness, joy, and unconstrained worship. But he despises those who despise his gifts, those who scorn simple wisdom and common practice. Whatever is acceptable to the common people (*plēthos*)[20] is the appropriate standard of belief and action.

These four hundred lines set the stage for the psychological and physical dismemberment of Pentheus, the political dismemberment of Thebes, and the symbolic dismemberment of Athens. Already we see men and women divided within and against each other, espousing principles that have lost their meaning and hold. The moral injunctions are repeated so often that they become mere cant, a mask whose permanent features disguise shifting sense and purpose (as the meaning of Dionysus's mask changes during the play). Or they seem verbal stratagems to befuddle an opponent, as at Corcyra. Traditional pieties are either incoherent (which suggests something about the tradition), or perfectly coherent but perfectly trite and so perfectly irrelevant. Characters are unwitting accomplices in advancing positions they explicitly repudiate and generating actions they otherwise castigate.

[20] According to Liddell, Scott, and Jones, *Greek-English Lexicon*, 9th ed. (Oxford: Oxford University Press, 1940), *plēthos* has a range of meanings from a great number, mass, throng, or crowd to the greater part of a main body (hence the people of the commons) to government of the people, i.e., democracy.

141

CHAPTER 5

Teiresias seems to say and do all the right things. He has accepted the god, advises the king to do likewise, and is appalled at the blasphemies that greet his advice. Yet this man who dismisses the new sophistic learning gives sophistic lectures, his syntax imitates an orator's poem, and he offers rationalistic explanations of religion similar to those of Prodicus, Protagoras, and Democritus.[21] Whereas the Teiresias who confronts Creon (in *Antigone*) is Apollo's spokesman, mouthing terrible truths he "reads" in the flight of birds and the unaccountable extinguishing of sacred fire, this Teiresias who strips away the mysteries of the superhuman world and flattens the mythical landscape until everything is domesticated and manageable.[22] Pentheus may be the only one who physically tries to imprison Dionysus, but in his own way Teiresias, too, tries to capture and use the god. Linking Dionysus to other Olympian deities (Demeter, Ares, and Apollo), he would constrain him "within the limits of intelligible logos and publicly useful mythos."[23] Teiresias then would bring Dionysus into the city on the city's terms, thereby imposing a permanent form on the god's fluidity, ordinariness on his ecstasy, and logic on the contradictions that are essential to his nature. For all his dressing up and plans to dance, Teiresias shares little with the god, whereas Pentheus, who ostensibly rejects him completely, shares everything with him.

There may also be more of an affinity between Teiresias and Pentheus than at first appears. Given the sophistic tone and arguments the seer makes, the young king's cynicism and impatience are to be expected. As an old wise man, Teiresias is symbolically, if not literally, the young man's teacher, and is to that degree responsible for his charge.[24] Plato's *Gorgias* makes the same point.[25]

Gorgias is, by and large, a conventionally moral man. He continues to believe in traditional conceptions of goodness and justice despite the potentially explosive implications of the way he teaches and the substance of his teaching. His conventionalism stands in stark contrast to the radical

[21] See the discussion in Segal, *Dionysiac Poetics*, chap. 8, section IV.

[22] The point as well as some of the language comes from Thomas Rosenmeyer, *The Masks of Tragedy* (Austin: University of Texas Press, 1963), pp. 18–19.

[23] Segal, *Dionysiac Poetics*, p. 303.

[24] This theme is present in other of Euripides's plays. In the *Orestes*, for instance, older men such as Menelaus and Tyndareus (Orestes' uncle and grandfather) provide no example or instruction for the young man. On the contrary, they are part of the problem. (I have discussed this in "Political Corruption in Euripides' *Orestes*," in *Greek Tragedy and Political Theory*, ed. J. Peter Euben (Berkeley and Los Angeles: University of California Press, 1986), chap. 9.

[25] Jeanne Roux, in her edition of the *Bacchae*, vol. I (Lyon: Université de Lyon, 1970), argues that Pentheus represents "le sophiste dans le cité, à l'exaltation de la raison," whereas Dionysus represents the country of "l'exaltation de la déraison." She regards each force as presented with equal power and so gives far greater stature to Pentheus than I do.

142

naturalism of his student Callicles. Yet he is nonetheless responsible for the young aggressive politician (and for Polus). At least that is what the progression of the argument and the dramatic structure of the dialogue indicate. One could say that Callicles is the logical and existential conclusion of the arguments Gorgias makes but whose full implications he does not fully understand. As he does come to understand them, he becomes something of an ally of Socrates. Pentheus is Callicles to Teiresias's Gorgias.[26]

Pentheus also resembles *Antigone*'s Creon.[27] Through a combination of circumstances and character both become morally and politically isolated. As we saw, Creon pares away affiliations and support, whereas Pentheus distances himself from others by pushing them away (Cadmus and Teiresias), refusing to recognize who they are (Dionysus) or what they say (the messengers and those for whom they speak). Creon finds himself alone and helpless; Pentheus imprisons himself even as he attempts to imprison others. Both are powerless because of their definition of power and create chaos because of their definition of order. They do not listen, and they cannot hear, and so inadvertently exclude what might make them whole. Inexperienced (though older, Creon is a new king), they ignore the experience of others. Creon will not listen to his son, ignored the qualms of the otherwise obedient chorus, is furious at the mere suggestion that the gods had a hand in the burials, is defiant with Teiresias, and condemns Antigone out of hand. Pentheus listens to no one and rejects the divine presence. Like Creon, his political language is one of command and obedience.

Like Creon, Pentheus attributes the worst motives to his opponents and the best to himself. They act from greed, self-interest, or stupidity; he acts for the common good based on knowledge of the real world. Both rulers would be master in all things, though they cannot master themselves. For both, power has become a drug and intoxicant[28] that possesses and blinds them. They regard everything that stands in their way as threatening chaos and so justify the further extension of a rigid order only they can

---

[26] Pentheus is not wholly wrong when he accuses Teiresias of embracing Dionysus for self-serving reasons. But, as is typical of the king, the charge is too literal and his response excessive.

[27] Roux is not the only one who regards Pentheus as a basically good ruler. Gilbert Norwood (*The Riddle of the* Bacchae [Manchester: Manchester University Press, 1908]), and André Rivier, *Essai sur le tragique d'Euripide* (Lausanne: F. Rouge and Cie, 1944), both regard Pentheus as a noble and respected king. Bernd Seidensticker, "Pentheus," *Poetica* 6 (1972): 35–63, uses Adorno's study of the authoritarian personality (and later American social science) to picture Pentheus as an ethnocentric protofascist.

[28] "May not the lust for power and praise be equally the course of a Dionysiac frenzy? With this Pentheus is intoxicated"; see R. P. Winnington-Ingram, *Euripides and Dionysus: An Interpretation of the Bacchae* (Amsterdam: Adolf M. Hakkert, 1969), p. 54.

insure. In their passion for control, they lose sight of what is distinctive about a political order and political power. They cannot see the power in counterorders or the opportunity in disorder. But Euripides suggests that politics cannot be a matter of command and obedience for it presupposes different points of view for the same reason Dionysus cannot be apprehended by any *one*. Nor is political power domination and control, as Pentheus's fate indicates. It includes lateral bonds of reciprocal commitments and shared ends. And political membership requires engagement, not acquiescence, a sharing of power, not the submission to it, *isonomia* and *isēgoria*, not hierarchies and silence. It also requires the existence of tragedy that, in specified times and in specific places, reveals the fictive quality of otherwise unchallenged cultural accommodations. In these terms, political dismembering suggests the disintegration of a *political* order, of *political* power, and of drama as a public institution.

But there are some differences between Creon and Pentheus despite a shared tyrannical temperament. Pentheus shows respect for the aged, is attentive to his grandfather (as we hear later), and, in pointed contrast to Creon, allows the messenger to speak freely. More important, Pentheus's lust for power and his passion for order is tied to his uncertain sexuality in a way Creon's is not. Although it is true that both men define potency as the ability to rule women and regard women's independence as the first sign of impending chaos, Creon is not prurient as Pentheus is, and there is no prospect of his becoming "effeminate." Finally, though Creon is a new king, he is not a young man. Pentheus's youth helps explain (perhaps partially excuses) his impetuosity, his lack of experience, and his literal-mindedness. It also makes him a physical double on the beardless threshold of adulthood, specifically an eighteen- to twenty-year-old citizen in military training.

As part of the passage from one social identity to another, the ephebate contained "not only training in military discipline and in civil responsibility but also rites and fictions" that dramatize what the ephebes had been (boys) and what they were in the process of becoming (men and full members of the city). They are "inbetweeners" mixing, even inventing, categories, ideals, and behavior that would be sharply opposed once they assumed manhood and citizenship.[29] What makes this ambiguity significant is the fact that the Greeks associated disguise and deception with women and with tragedy.[30] That suggests what other evidence corrobo-

[29] The argument and the quotations are from Winkler, "The Ephebes' Song," pp. 26–62. He goes on to quote the ephebic oath: "I will not disgrace these sacred weapons (hopla) and I will not desert the comrade beside me (Parastatên) wherever I shall be stationed in the battle line" (p. 27).

[30] See Froma I. Zeitlin, "Playing the Other: Theater, Theatricality, and the Feminine in Greek Drama," *Representations* 11 (Summer 1985): 63–94.

rates—that in the period immediately prior to manhood and full membership, male sexual identity was purposely and radically confounded.

In these terms, Pentheus fails the rite of passage to manhood. He never returns from the wild to the defined space of the city in one piece. When his mask *is* brought back, it is held by his mother in a horrible parody of infant male dependency.

Pentheus is not the only one who fails the rite of passage; Thebes does as well. The city refuses or cannot honor Dionysus and so provides no place for tragedy. It has a deficient understanding of manhood and so of membership. But given the context of performance, the failure of Thebes becomes a warning or challenge or prognosis about the Athenian capacity for honoring the god, sustaining tragedy, and defining manhood and membership.

The entry of Dionysus into Athens was reenacted each year by the ephebes. They were the ones who inaugurated the festival by bringing the cult statue of the god in procession from the academy (just outside the city) back to its temple and theater precinct on the southeast slope of the Acropolis. From this and other evidence it seems that the City Dionysia focused on the ephebes, that they were "physically and analytically at the center of attention," both in the play and in the physical organization of the theater.[31]

To shift attention from Pentheus to Dionysus and from Dionysus at Thebes to tragedy at Athens is justified so long as we remember that the identities of Pentheus and Dionysus, Thebes and Athens, emerge only in confrontation with each other. But it is somewhat premature in terms of the plot. Still, it is useful to summarize what has been said of and by the god up to now, so long as we observe two caveats. First, since the nature of the god is itself a significant issue in the play, no simple recitation of his attributes is likely to be adequate. Not only does he change shape, but so many contradictory traits are attributed to him that, at least until the end, he appears less as an independent entity than as a collection of projections by those who would worship, incorporate, or imprison him. Second, the *Bacchae* is as much about how to receive and honor Dionysus as it is about defining who he is, although obviously any uncertainty about the latter complicates the former.

Dionysus is the god of nature, and of fecundity without toil. As a god of nature he dissolves and so transcends conventional divisions of wealth, status, power, age, and gender. His celebrants recognize none of the usual boundaries that define self and society. Those exclusions based on oppositions between civilized and barbarian, man and beast, city and wild,

---

[31] Winkler, "The Ephebes' Song," p. 29. Beardless in contrast to the bearded actors, the chorus members were "iconographically speaking, ephebes" (p. 39).

sanity and madness, and purity and transgression are revealed as unnatural, unnecessary, and repressive. Dionysus liberates men (and especially women, as we shall see) from the monotony of ordinary life and familiar social categories. He relieves men from the burdens of civic responsibility and the weight of consciousness, from the prism and prison of rationality. Insofar as intellect keeps us from ourselves and inhibits us from letting ourselves go, to the extent that it constructs artifacts of time and space and imposes plan and shape on what is fragmentary and momentary, it thwarts impulse, instinct, and the consciousness of what it means to be a sentient being. To be reasonable and rational, to remain separated from or immune to the power of wine, dancing, and religious ecstasy, prevents us from losing our constructed identity so to discover parts of ourselves and know things that elude the most diligent analysis.

Dionysus, then, brings us all (but particularly women) out of the mundane world of routine behavior by putting us in touch with the passional springs of action and thought. Reconnected with what is elemental in life and in ourselves, we become empowered beyond physical and mental limitations, able to reach beyond ourselves and embrace what is otherwise beyond our grasp, beneath our notice, or outside the circumference of our associations. Yet, at the same time, the god helps us accept the simple life, taking pleasure in things as they are and have been done.

Dionysus is also the god of intoxication. He offers drugs that bring sweet forgetfulness of daily trials and "metaphysical" suffering. With him we escape sleepless nights, remembered failures and fears of insufficiency, isolation, and final vulnerability. At one with ourselves and at peace with others, with separations within healed and divisions between banished, the god's worshipers are fused in an ecstasy of common celebration.[32]

The promise (or seduction) of such a god and of such harmony to a generation plagued by war and civil strife is obvious. "Dionysus" promises relief from the division between generations and sexes and from war between Greeks and barbarians, Athens and Sparta, rich and poor. Here is a divinity who offers abundance amid constant loss, a young god who brings life where young mortals have been dying in combat. Here is a promise of ecstatic worship that unifies passions and person against the frenzied divisions of politics. There will be no overbearing kings or heroic strivings of actors or theorists to disturb peace and sleep. One need only give oneself over to the god, then all divisions and anxieties fade from mind and memory. As Dostoevsky and Lincoln knew, the problem of political leadership is not simply that "great" men impose their will on a

---

[32] Here and elsewhere a comparison with the close of the *Eumenides* is instructive. There too we find healing and relief but founded on remembered pain and with a division of function and place. Later I shall contrast the ending of the *Bacchae* with the final scene of the *Oresteia*.

resistant or ignorant people, but that the people impose "greatness" on them out of the deepest need for untroubled sleep and a desire to escape the burdens of consciousness and responsibility that define "civilized" life.

If Aristotle is right that a free citizen neither rules nor is ruled, then membership in a political community of mortals cannot be the same as membership in an ecstatic community led by a god. If the polis mediates between what is divine and bestial, then Dionysiac worship frees men from politics even as the god is given a place in public life in the theater.[33] The moment of anti-politics is a reminder that the polis cannot be all. That the moment is recreated within the polis suggests that it is. That both occur at once suggests something about the god and about tragedy.

PENTHUS'S MEN enter with their quarry (Dionysus disguised as a mortal) but feel no sense of triumph in the capture. Indeed, they are disconcerted by the reaction of their prey who neither fled nor fought but smilingly offered himself for arrest. They are disconcerted, too, by the fact that the jailed women have escaped, their chains untouched, the door opening of its own accord. Such miracles convince them of the god's divinity.

They do not convince Pentheus. But he is very impressed by the stranger's physical attractiveness, very curious about the god's mysteries, and very admiring (but also resentful) of the stranger's verbal skill in response to his interrogation. That interrogation is Pentheus's attempt to place the god in a set of tangible coordinates he can understand, if not control. He wants to know where the "stranger"[34] is from, which god he has brought into Hellas, what grounds (and uses) there are for believing in his new divinity, what form (*idean*) his rites take, and what is his nature (*poios*). The disguised god's response to these attempts to pin him down and give him permanent form is to insist that a divinity can take whatever form he wishes (*hopoios ēthel'*, 478). Typically, Pentheus thinks the god is avoiding the question when he is in fact answering it most truthfully. But it is not a truth the young king can understand.

That is because he cannot see and does not recognize the god in any of his manifestations, signs, or miracles. Pentheus is too literal-minded, too narrowly empirical, too preoccupied with finding evidence to support his

---

[33] Thus even the highly politicized Athenians recognized the need for respite from politics. But whereas the liberal separation of state and society is intended to grant individuals virtually permanent relief form the rigors of politics, the momentary Dionysiac transcendence of politics is meant to make us better citizens, not apolitical.

[34] I put stranger in quotes because Dionysus is far from being a stranger. He was born in Thebes and is Pentheus's cousin. But he is made a stranger by Pentheus, in the sense that the king would exclude him wherever and whenever possible.

views rather than evidence that would deepen and broaden them. He repeatedly states that the Bacchic rites include sexual intercourse even when he is told repeatedly that they do not. He would imprison the stranger even when it is clear that chains will not hold him, and he would lead an army against the women on the mountain when there is ample evidence that arms are useless against them.

Pentheus's inability to hear direct statements (let along indirect ones) is a function of his ignorance about himself and so the world outside. He is a very young man, inexperienced, labile, impatient with ambiguity and polyphony, unable to recognize the springs of his own actions, especially the element of irrationality and violence which he shares with those he persecutes. Here is the culmination of Pentheus's interrogation of Dionysus, an interrogation with striking parallels to the exchange between Teiresias and Oedipus in the *Oedipus Tyrannos*.

> *Dionysus*: [The god] is present now and sees what I endure from you.
> *Pentheus*: Where is he? I cannot see him.
> *Dionysus*: With me; but your blasphemies have made you blind.
> *Pentheus*: Seize him. He is mocking me and Thebes.
> *Dionysus*: I give you warning madman; place no chains on one
> who is sane.
> *Pentheus*: But I say chain him. I am rightfully master here.
> *Dionysus*: You do not know what you are saying. You do not
> know what you are doing. You do now know who you are.
> *Pentheus*: I am Pentheus, the son of Echion and Agave.
> *Dionysus*: Pentheus: a name that fits you perfectly.
>
> (500–508)

Though Pentheus knows his parents as Oedipus does not, he, no more than Oedipus sees the destiny in his name.[35]

One other thing is becoming clear—the king's attraction to what he so ardently rejects. There is something drawing him to his enemy, something seductive about the exclusions he so forcefully reiterates. His denial prevents him recognizing them in himself and increases their destructive potential when they explode his flimsy defenses. As Pentheus's "reluctant curiosity . . . grows into an obsession,"[36] Dionysus takes control of him rather than the other way around. It is Pentheus who is trapped, snared, and captured, not against his will and nature, but with the cooperation of those parts of him he will not acknowledge. What the king has pushed

---

[35] Pentheus (from *penthos* and *pentheō*) means mourning and lamenting, grieving and sorrowful.

[36] The phrase is G. S. Kirk's in a note to his translation (Englewood Cliffs, N.J.: Prentice-Hall, 1970), p. 63. "If Pentheus is obsessed with curiosity and desire," Winningham-Ingram writes, "the victory of Dionysus is half won already" (*Euripides and Dionysus*, p. 46).

aside and outside is lodged inside the deepest parts of his soul and character.[37]

After the exchange between Dionysus and Pentheus, the chorus calls on the god to revenge himself and them on the rabid raging beast of a king, by "quelling with death this beast of blood whose murderous insolence abuses both men and gods" (555). The god obliges by bringing an earthquake to "shake the floor of the world."

What is shaken[38] is Pentheus's house (not just his home), his authority, and his mind.[39] What he has chained is free. What he thought was a man appears as a bull, which he frantically tries to rope while his enemy sits calmly watching the spectacle of his futile labors, enjoying his escalating humiliation. Nothing makes sense, no one is where they ought to be, no form is firm.[40] Thinking to grasp the enemy that torments him, Pentheus clutches only empty hopes. Thinking the palace is on fire, he orders all his servants to bring water, but the water does nothing for a fire that no longer exists. His world is collapsing around and inside him, smashed, split asunder, dismembered. But there is still a chance that it can be reassembled and re-membered if only he will listen to what the approaching messenger saw.

What the messenger saw was the Maenads among boughs of fir and oak leaves sleeping modestly (in contrast to Pentheus's repeated assertions). Hearing the approaching herds, the women arose as one (with a discipline worthy of the best hoplite army), young and old alike. Fastening their fawnskins with writhing snakes, the new mothers among them

[37] In an essay "Dionysus in the *Bacchae*" (*Transactions of the American Philological Association* 66 (1935): 37–54, G.M.A. Grube argued that the *Bacchae* shows the Dionysiac in man becoming fiendish and evil when suppressed. Here is Dodds in a similar vein: "In the maddening of Pentheus, . . . the poet shows us the supernatural attacking the victim's personality as its weakest point, working upon and through nature, not against it. The god wins because he has an ally in the enemy's camp; the persecutor is betrayed by what he would persecute—the Dionysiac longing in himself" (*Euripides' Bacchae*, edited with a commentary, 2nd ed. [Oxford: Clarendon Press, 1960], p. 172).

[38] The contrast between things abiding unshaken or holding together (such as a house) and things falling apart or down (a form of dismemberment) runs throughout the play (see lines 348, 390, 600, 1307–8).

[39] Pentheus's attempt to confine, pin down, and imprison Dionysus has led to an explosion that tears the palace apart. What happens to the palace "foreshadows what happens next to his mind, then to his body and then to his family"; see Balestri, "The *Bacchae*," p. 204.

[40] What is crumbling to pieces is not primarily the material structure of the palace, but the spiritual and moral foundations of his house. When Pentheus emerged from the palace he "has come less from a scene of real cataclysm than from a nightmare of terrors and phantoms"; see Victor Castellani, "That Troubled House of Pentheus in Euripides' *Bacchae*," *Transactions of the American Philological Association* 106 (1976): *Euripides and Dionysus*, pp. 82–84.

suckle young gazelles and wolves. At the touch of a thyrsus against a rock, cool water bubbles up; at fennel being put in the ground, wine pours forth; at the mere scratch of the earth, milk wells up while honey streams from their wands. For the cowherds and shepherds (of which the messenger is one), these miracles of nature are proof enough of Dionysus's divinity. But not for "one of us in the habit of roaming the city, and who was therefore crafty with words" (717). In a desire to curry favor with Pentheus, he proposes that they capture Agave and bring her back to the palace. Agreeing, they try to seize her. But when the hunted see the hunters, they turn on them and the men barely escape being torn limb from limb. But the cattle they tend are not so lucky. The women who were just now suckling baby animals tear calves in two with their bare hands, while others claw heifers to pieces. Enraged bulls fall stumbling in the midst of their charge to be instantly stripped of flesh and skin. Everywhere the forest drips with blood, the ground strewn with ribs or cloven hooves.

Nor is this all. As the women sped across the field, they pillaged everything in sight, kidnapped children, and turned everything upside down. When the enraged villagers took to arms, their spears were impotent while the women's wands drew blood. And so men were routed by women.

Once more Pentheus is unable to recognize his fate foreshadowed in the story. Once more his only response is to see the humiliation (to the men of Hellas) and to use force. So he calls out the army in order to take revenge on and slaughter the women (including his mother). When the god, still patient, offers to bring the women back to Thebes without bloodshed, Pentheus dismisses it out of hand and as a ploy. His manhood and his power can be assured only by military victory. No compromise or hesitation is tolerable.

But he does hesitate when Dionysus suddenly changes tack and asks whether he would like actually to see the Bacchic revels. He is fascinated at the prospect but there is a problem; he must dress as a woman. Unsurprisingly, Pentheus is initially resistant. The resistance is softened by using manly military terms to describe his unmanly behavior. (The change of costume is likened to a tactical maneuver and his "Peeping Tomism" is called reconnoitering.) It is overcome by the prospect of seeing unrestrained sexuality. So now this man who has insisted on asserting male civic authority over women, who would force them to return to their children and domestic chores and houses where they "belong," now dresses as a woman and allows himself to be led passively through the city. The man who would rule, control, and dominate is now acted upon, a subject of control, ruled by another, as are women.[41] Now fully obsessed, he is

[41] As Zeitlin argues, "Pentheus' transformation from obstinate distancing of all that is

unaware that he has been turned inside out and into his own worst enemy, which in a sense he has been all along.

When he lavishes girlish concern about the fit of his dress, is perturbed that one of his curls has become undone, is anxious to hold the wand properly, and plays the coquette to Dionysus, the irony becomes both funny and horrific. It intensifies when this king, whose singular object has been to avoid humiliation and, who a few moments before was going to sneak through the city unseen, now insists that he be paraded in public and calls this humiliation courage. The final irony is that this mannish man who has almost incidentally threatened to kill his mother (along with the other Maenads), and has all along wanted to see her having intercourse, now desires nothing more than to be carried in her arms. He has regressed from a hoplite warrior to an ephebe initiate to a helpless infant cradled in his mother's arms.[42] And so he goes to the mountain and dismemberment at the hands of his mother.

The costuming of Pentheus makes him even more like Dionysus in appearance than he was before. The two are cousins, beardless young men, and now they are similar in dress as well. Indeed the king becomes the double of the god and a substitute for him in the ritual sacrifice that follows. The culmination of Dionysus's winter dance at Athens was the ritual dismemberment and eating of the raw flesh (*sparagmos* and *ōmophagia*) of a bull, fawn, or goat which symbolically represented the god. Such rites were thought to unite the worshipers with the potency of wild nature; assimilate beast, man, and god; and issue in the symbolic rebirth of the god. The frenzied energy necessary for the dismemberment exhausted the worshipers, readying them for mysterious union with the god.[43] When Dionysus robes Pentheus he is preparing him for the sacrifice that should lead to renewal and empowerment. That it does no such thing at Thebes is made clear at the play's end. Whether it does at Athens is unclear.

That depends on whether Pentheus's deficiencies are peculiar to him and to Thebes or are endemic to the masculine body politic or arise from "the" human condition itself. If the problem is peculiar to the young king and Thebes, then their failure becomes an edifying example for the audience of Athenian citizens. If it derives from the character of political membership in the masculine body politic then the issue becomes whether a democracy can honor what it excludes and encompass the opposed de-

---

feminine stands in contrast with Dionysus's persistent androgyny. While feminization is the emblem of Pentheus' defeat, Dionysus' effeminacy is a sign of power. The one gains power by manipulating a feminized identity while the other becomes impotent when he succumbs to it. Thus we see femininity as power and weakness" ("Playing the Other," pp. 63–64).

[42] See the discussion by Helene Foley, *Ritual Irony: Poetry and Sacrifice in Euripedes* (Ithica, N.Y.: Cornell University Press, 1985), pp. 213–14.

[43] See Rosenmeyer, *The Masks of Tragedy*, p. 141.

mands represented by civic responsibility and Dionysian frenzy. But it may also arise from the unalterable condition of mortality: old age, sleep, the reversal of fortune, the dance of life and sexuality, and death itself.[44] This possibility is raised in the choral ode on man in *Antigone*, which is echoed here when Dionysus refers to himself as *deinotatos* (861) and when he addresses Pentheus before leading him to dismemberment.

deinos su deinos kapi dein erchēi pathē,
Strange [wonderful, terrible, extraordinary, fearful] you are, strange [etc.], and strange [etc.] are the experiences you are about to meet.

(971)

In the end the *Bacchae* presents those deficiencies as rooted in all three levels. The relative importance of each, and what, if anything, can be done about our circumstances and our character depend on how we understand the play's portrait of Dionysus and the prospects for tragedy.

Like Pentheus, Dionysus changes appearance, although his alteration of shape is self-chosen. He is represented as both benign and vengeful, as a man, beast, and (later) god, and is defined differently by various characters who want or need various things from him. This fluidity of form is diachronic and synchronic. It emerges over time and reveals depths of as yet ungrasped meaning. Some of those depths appear only in the play's final scene. But one aspect of Dionysus, as the god of theater, is pointedly dramatized in the robing scene.

In some respects Dionysus has been "orchestrating" the action of the play from the beginning. But until the robing scene there is a chance that things will turn out differently—that Pentheus will see his fate in the clues offered him, or that he will, at the last minute, pull back and accept the god's offer to lead the women back without bloodshed. (Of course, if he did, he would no longer "be" Pentheus.) But in that scene Pentheus ceases to be an independent actor. Dionysus takes over center stage as he becomes director, principal actor, costumer, and producer of theatrical illusions in a play within a play. The change in costume (from king to Bacchant and then to mask alone) Dionysus brings about, anticipates the king's dismemberment, and parallels the multiplicity of unintegrated characteristics of his personality. "Torn apart emotionally as well as literally, he is also torn apart metatragically, dismembered into a sequence of costumes that end up as the empty mask, the disembodied *prosōpon* (1277)."[45]

Pentheus is torn apart because he is too rigid and too literal-minded,

[44] William Arrowsmith, "The Criticism of Greek Tragedy," in *The Tulane Drama Review* 3 (1959): 55.

[45] Segal, *Dionysiac Poetics*, pp. 248–49.

exactly what the ideal member of an audience cannot be. He is unable to see the god in the theatrical form that expresses him or to discern truth in the symbolic form that Dionysian theater and festival offer the audience and adherents.[46] It is no accident that the robing scene is full of words for seeing, sight, watching, spying, and spectator (*idein, idios, opthēs, horan, kataskopēn, theatēs*). Their immediate referent is the spectacle Pentheus anticipates seeing. The indirect one is the audience inside and outside the play watching him become the spectacle he thought to spy on at a safe distance. As Zeitlin argues that "Thebes" is an object lesson for Athens, I am arguing that Pentheus is one to the Athenian spectators in the theater. He cannot "read"[47] the world poetically and so lacks the "character" to be a member of a theatrical audience or of a democratic political community.

Rather than being a member of an audience which in other forums constitutes the citizenry, Pentheus is an isolated voyeur seeking private pleasure by spying on the practices of a community he posits as alien and other. Despite his name, he seeks to distance himself from the shared pain and suffering tragedy displays and engenders. Insofar as he is successful, he cannot participate in the healing *katharsis* the performance provides. In contrast to an (ideal) Athenian audience, which is both distant from the time and place of the action but nonetheless deeply involved in it, Pentheus is too near the action and too far from it. He is too near it because his unwilling but direct participation in the full performance of the rite "symbolically effaces the distance between spectator and actor."[48] He is too far from it because he never sees himself in "the other" or as part of some larger pattern. "Never" may be an exaggeration. Pentheus does have a moment of recognition (1119–20). But it is too little, too late, and too brief to build a case for insight. Certainly it does nothing to halt his frenzied mother from avenging the god and herself by dismembering him.

Pentheus's political and "literary" ineptness is, I think, a warning to the Athenian audience about the political significance of their literary ineptness. If tragedy is the only way the god can be made known in the city without the city imprisoning him, or he, in turn, dismembering the city, and if drama is the only "form" that is itself "open to the chaos, the ecstasy and the unmediated contradictions that are essential parts of

[46] The argument about Pentheus's literal mindedness is made by Foley, *Ritual Irony*, pp. 212, 222 and Segal, *Dionysiac Poetics*, chap. 8, esp. pp. 282–84.

[47] In Greek the word for reading is anagignōskein—to know again, recognize, distinguish, or discern. Pentheus fails in all these ways.

[48] Segal, *Dionysiac Poetics*, p. 225. He goes on to call the robing scene, "a sinister mirror image of the play's effect upon its audience, its theatai."

the god's nature,"[49] then the erosion of tragedy's context of performance, the city as audience, is an act of impiety. Or, if one prefers, the point can be put less theologically. "Dionysus" is the fluidity of experience we confront every time we leave everyday logic and the heavily defended walls of whatever Thebes we inhabit. The *Bacchae* presents itself as uniquely able to represent, recreate, and participate in that experience. Like the god in whose honor it was performed, drama makes explicit, and so subjects to reflection, categories that are normally the precondition for, rather than the object of, thought. Doing so, it brings men and women outside themselves to confront (what is now called) their socially constructed identities and those marginalized parts of their culture and selves posited as other.

The *Bacchae* imitates the god in the way its form encompasses contradictory forms. It not only employs comedic strategies for tragic effect,[50] it combines archaic formalism and archaic diction (unused since earliest tragedy) to explore radically new content. The resulting incongruity between reality drawn from ancient myth and legend and the new reality of sophistic intellectualism, "personality," and strange religious experiences has two somewhat contradictory consequences. It suggests the possibility of discovering resources of understanding in disparaged or discarded aspects of a poetic-political tradition that formed both city and theater; and it suggests the inadequacy of these older forms to comprehend (in both senses) a world it could not have imagined. Insofar as such inadequacy characterizes tragedy itself, then the *Bacchae*'s theatrical self-consciousness includes an uncertainty about the adequacy of its own form and audience to maintain the integrity of the culture.

The encompassing of contradictory forms with its resulting incongruity parallels the double vision of the action the *Bacchae* embodies and provides. When Pentheus emerged from the palace transformed into a Bacchant he sees two suns, two cities, and Dionysus as simultaneously a bull and a (disguised) man (917–20). In that (for him) rare moment of insight, he comes closest to understanding his situation and transcending his literal-mindedness.

Tragedy also imitates Dionysus in the inclusiveness of its characterization and context of performance. Although it is true that plays were written by men, that female parts were played by them, and that strong women are often portrayed in something less than admirable terms, it is remarkable how important women characters are in tragedy. Whatever else one can say about it, this seems particularly appropriate given that

[49] Ibid., p. 304.
[50] The comedic elements in the play are brilliantly discussed by Foley, *Ritual Irony*, pp. 224–34.

membership in the Dionysian rituals included women (as well as metics and slaves) as other public institutions did not. In this sense the theater was more inclusive than the assembly and so able, because of that, to raise issues that concerned the society as a whole. Dionysus was a democratic god and so it is not surprising that tragedy was perhaps the most democratic institution in Athens.[51] Whether the inclusiveness of tragedy stood as a rebuke to the undemocratic practices, I do not know. But I do think the *Bacchae* raises questions about the distribution of power and definition of membership in contemporary Athens.

Dionysus is an androgynous god as well as a democratic one. Although a vigorous young male god, he has the "languid sensuality"[52] and emotionality the Greeks associated with women. Moreover, the god is, in this play at least, predominantly the liberator of women. He frees them from the dominance of male secular authority, offering in its stead an empowering membership in a ritual community. Tragedy too has a special relationship to women. Zeitlin identifies four indispensable traits of theatrical experience: the representation of the body itself on stage; the arrangement of architectural space with its pronounced tension between inside and outside; the bringing of plots to conclusion through intrigue and deception; and the condition of theatrical mimeticism with its role playing, disguises, and representation of a self as other than it seems or knows itself to be.[53] All of these are identified with women.

The function of masking in the *Bacchae* is the final way in which this tragedy pushes its audience to reflect upon the categories and practices otherwise regarded as natural or normal. For the audience in the play, the mask of "Dionysus" is that of a man. But for the audience watching the play it is something far more complicated, the mask of a god disguised as a man who can also appear as a beast. Although there is one mask, there is more than one thing that lies behind it. That is not only because Dionysus changes shape and appearance but also because his fixed smile changes its meaning from bemusement, to calm superiority, to sneering revenge as the play unfolds. That a single appearance can hide multiple realities is an epistemological problem and an impulse toward philosophy. That a "character" can have an internal life that his place, role, and mask obscure (often without his knowledge) is a problem of "personal-

---

[51] See the discussion of Plato and Aristotle's reaction to this "fact" in Stephen G. Salkever, "Tragedy and the Education of the Demos: Aristotle's Response to Plato," in Euben, *Greek Tragedy and Political Theory*, pp. 274–303.

[52] The phrase is Zeitlin's in her essay, "Playing the Other."

[53] Ibid., pp. 68–69. This is a radically abbreviated argument of Zeitlin's own very condensed presentation. I am not fully persuaded by Zeitlin for reasons suggested by Helene P. Foley in "The Conception of Women in Athenian Drama," *Reflections on Women in Antiquity* (New York: Gordon and Breach, 1981), pp. 127–68.

ity" and an impulse toward psychology. John Jones has argued[54] that masking is a definition of what can be made humanly intelligible. It precludes penetrating the surface of things, going inside to explore inner complexity of person and psyche. But Euripides pierces the mask to create a conflict between a character's internal state and his role in the action of the drama. In challenging the continuity of dramatic convention, he is also challenging the demarcations between public and private upon which the "distinctive" status of women depended.

"Challenge" may not be the right word to describe fully what is going on. The mere presence of multiple audiences[55] to the god's theatrical demonstration of his divinity makes the spectators conscious "that they are viewing and interpreting the god's actions through a sense of subjective and unreliable perspectives and performances."[56] The next question is whether there is an "objective" and reliable perspective outside the play even if there is none in it, or whether Euripides is suggesting that all attempts to understand divine or poetic representations are projections of need and a need to imprison.

The latter is too strongly put in terms that are too modern (or postmodern). For in the end Greek tragedy reaffirmed the divisions and categories it denied in the bounded context of theater and play, although the reaffirmation could not be a return to innocence. But does the *Bacchae* conform to this pattern, or does it, despite its final restoration of traditional boundaries between man and god, do something different?

AFTER DIONYSUS LEAVES with Pentheus, the chorus calls on justice and custom to revenge themselves on this impious madman whose lawless temper flouts tradition and outrages the gods. Not his wisdom but the wisdom of humility is best and blest. Men must maintain their equilibrium by caring for ordinary things and everyday pleasures, following always the time honored path of righteousness. Anyone who refuses must be punished. Originally the chorus longed to escape from the overbearing monstrous man. As their sense of the god's presence and power increases, their sense of helplessness decreases, and they call for chastising and disciplining (*apeuthunei*) the overreaching man.[57] Once fully confident that the god is in control, they demand death. Thus they delight in the prospect of the king's dismemberment and celebrate its accomplishment.

[54] In his *On Aristotle and Greek Tragedy* (New York: Oxford University Press, 1962).

[55] There is the audience watching the play in the Athenian theater and several audiences watching the play within the play. Indeed, each character in the play constitutes an audience in the sense that they see things others do not.

[56] Foley, *Ritual Irony*, p. 222.

[57] The evolving views of the chorus are analyzed in detail by Arthur in "The Choral Odes."

It is a slave messenger who relates the horrors on the mountain. Possessed by the god, Agave ignores the pitiful cries of her now repentant son and wrenches an arm from its socket while the other Theban Bacchants join the dismemberment with shrieks of triumph. Here is Arrowsmith's vivid translation:

> One tore off an arm,
> another a foot still warm in its shoe. His ribs
> were clawed clean of flesh and every hand
> was smeared with blood as they played ball with scraps
> of Pentheus' body.
>
> (1133–36)

The mother huntress impales her son's head on her wand and carries it home in triumph, thinking it the head of a lion.

It is upon this scene that Cadmus comes, bringing his own burden, the remainder of his dismembered grandson. But he has yet another burden—helping Agave to recognize what she has done. She demands a feast but all he can offer is grief. She asks him to call the son whose head she carries so that he can be admonished for contesting with a god and witness her victory; Cadmus must make her see that the son she longs for is the empty mask she carries. In a sense he must bring up his daughter again, reminding her of who *she is*:[58] his daughter, the wife of Echion, the mother of Pentheus. It is his responsibility to restore her identity by reviving her capacity for remembering.

Up to now "re-membering" has been little more than a pun. But this exchange brings together its two meanings: recalling to mind or recollecting and becoming a member again. Apparently memory and membership help define each other. If they do then dismemberment involves a failure or absence of memory. A similar conclusion comes from the double meaning of "re-collecting"; to gather together again and be reminded of, imply each other. Both meanings are symbolically present in the collecting of Pentheus's scattered body and explain why Cadmus spent so much effort searching for each piece.

To be buried and become the subject of memory and memorial, Pentheus's body must be made whole again, just as the story of a life must have a beginning, middle, and end to be remembered. Remembrance and recollection are the only power mortals have against death, necessity, and implacable gods. Part of the horror of concentration camps, Hannah Arendt tells us, is that grief and remembrance were forbidden. This prohibition was not only due to the Nazi efforts to make death itself anonymous. And it was not only aimed at the Jews, gypsies, homosexuals, and

---

[58] I underline "she" to emphasize that along with her return to "sanity" Agave is returned to her traditional place as woman.

other inmates. It was also aimed at the Germans themselves, so they would forget their own mortality and go on in the monstrosity of supposing themselves godlike men, calmly deciding who shall live and who shall die.[59]

But there is a complication. Dionysus, the god of tragedy, is as Nietzsche reminds us also the god of forgetfulness.[60] The forgetfulness induced by wine, sleep, and religious ecstasy frees us from daily grief and metaphysical suffering. It also liberates us from socially prescribed norms, bringing peace of mind as well as community. If membership presupposed memory and, as a corollary, forgetfulness is a precondition for dismemberment, then Dionysus is the god of dismemberment and dismemberment must be a kind of blessing.

Although these equations seem borne out by the play, they are too one-dimensional. For one thing, the Bacchants who dismember Pentheus are not isolated individuals acting anarchistically but members of an ecstatic community performing rituals guided by and in honor of the god. If anything they are a countercommunity rather than an anticommunity. For another thing, one could say that by being put in touch with elemental passions repressed by convention the Bacchants are "reminded" of natural (rather than historical) "facts." It is not then a matter of remembering and forgetting but what we forget as we remember, of what is always left out in the politically sanctioned reconstruction of the past. Finally, the equation leaves one uncertain about tragedy's role in sustaining memory (and membership) and dismembering (and forgetting). In sum, and appropriately enough, we need to "transcend" the opposition between memory and forgetting too.

As we saw with Orestes and Oedipus, membership in a house and city makes us who we are. It sustains and empowers us, connecting us with a place and with a community of the dead, living, and unborn. But its prescriptions and proscriptions also confine, trap, and imprison us. In these terms, forgetfulness both disconnects us from what gives us identity and provides opportunity and space for Foucault's countermemory, genealogy, and subjugated knowledges.

That is one "message" the *Bacchae* gives and the basis of the claim it makes for tragedy as a form that incorporates remembrance and oblivion. Dramatic performance induces forgetfulness of immediate cares and specific sorrows by drawing us to the community and sorrows of mythical kings in other places. It temporarily suspends membership in a particular community and blurs the identity that community provides for a more

[59] See her *Origins of Totalitarianism* (New York: Harcourt Brace Jovanovich, 1973), p. 112, and *Eichmann in Jerusalem: A Report on the Banality of Evil* (New York: Viking Press, 1964).

[60] Agave's last wish is to be some place where no one will remind her of Dionysian rituals.

inclusive community and conception of self. In the *Iliad* Priam comes to ransom his bravest son from the man who has killed so many of his children. For a moment he and Achilles see each other not as enemies, or men of different ages and nationality, or in different circumstances, but as human beings doomed to a common fate. Inside that moment and in the midst of their grief, they both see the ravages of the war so far and still to come. Here, for an instant, they are part of a more inclusive community. It is in terms of this larger community that they see and feel something else; a joy in the beauty of the other, a joy matched by the beauty of the poetry and the structure of Homer's art, which transforms this world in flames into a lasting monument.

The *Bacchae* too is a monument to human suffering. But even more than the *Iliad*, it is also a reflection on the futility of such monumentalization. What we see in it is the bankruptcy of the culture's traditional strategies to explain suffering and relieve the pain of loss; cult, memorials, fame, and tragedy itself.[61] Evidence of this bankruptcy comes from the character of Dionysus in the play, from the symbolic significance of the punishment he visits on Cadmus, and in the parallels between the play and Thucydides' portrait of the *stasis* at Corcyra.

Near the end of the play Dionysus appears undisguised above the action to justify the punishment he had inflicted and pronounce those to come. He has destroyed the house of Cadmus and Thebes (his own house and the city of his birth) because those who should have welcomed his coming and his care blasphemed and threatened him. By doing so they transformed his potential benefits into actual maledictions that will continue in the future. Agave and her sisters will be exiled and Cadmus and his immortal wife Harmonia will be turned into serpents fated eventually to lead a barbarian host against Greece. Many Hellenic cities will be destroyed until the invaders plunder Apollo's shrine, and then they themselves will be destroyed, except for Cadmus and Harmonia whom Ares will rescue and bring to live among the blest.

Cadmus protests the punishment's harshness (*all' epexerchēi lian,* 1346)[62] insisting that "it is inappropriate for gods to resemble mortals in their violent emotions" (*orgas prepei theous ouch homoiousthai brotois,*

---

[61] "Poetry that extends memory into the future also seeks to banish the recollection of suffering by absorbing us into the oblivion brought by its involving fictional world. It makes us forget by evoking the memory of others' sorrow" (Segal, *Dionysiac Poetics*, p. 320).

[62] Epexerchei has something of the meaning of our word "overkill." Notice that Cadmus protests his fate even though he will eventually live among the blest. But by living among barbarians he is bound to lead against his own people and by being deprived of his founding deed he is losing his reputation and the immortality that comes from "memorable" deeds and works.

1348). Does the play suggest that Cadmus is right? If it does, what are the implications for tragedy performed in the god's honor?

We must be careful in even asking the question in order to avoid Christianizing Dionysus. He is beyond good and evil and to judge or define him in moral terms at the end is to repeat the attempts to domesticate him at the beginning. In addition, any judgment we do make of him must contrast the religious frenzy imposed on the rationalizing women of Thebes that leads to the violent deeds on the mountain, with the willing service of the Asian Maenads who only celebrate in song what the others do. And even then the brutality of the Theban Maenads is provoked by men who would capture, spy, or force them back into the city. Furthermore, in part the god is what we make of him. What he does and is depends on how we receive him. Finally, and most decisively, Dionysus declares that their fate was ordained or commanded (*epeneusen*, 1349) by Zeus and necessity (*anankaiōs*, 1351).

Still, Cadmus has a point. Dionysus does resemble a mortal: Pentheus. As the god distances himself from the mortal world he reveals a "Pentheus" hidden within, as the king has previously revealed a repressed Dionysus. By the end of the play Dionysus's imposition of order by a ruthless exercise of power reminds one of Pentheus whose mortality prevented him from accomplishing what the god does with ease. (Their common view of politics as repression suggests a disguised conspiracy between the tyranny of custom and innovation both in the play and outside it.) Similarly, the god is as insistent on his honor as Pentheus was on his and is as ready to revenge himself on those who slight him. Could we not, as Winningham-Ingram suggests, turn the charges leveled at Pentheus by the chorus against Dionysus? When they accuse the king of ferocity, blood, and violence or with being inhuman are "they not in fact abusing Pentheus for the possession of Dionysian traits of character?"[63] Neither shows respect for the bonds that unite men and women in families and cities (which suggests yet another unacknowledged confluence between an arid rationalism on the one hand and ecstatic religion on the other). And when we look at Dionysus's benefits they reveal an aspect that is decidedly unattractive if not repulsive: the violence and brutality of nature as symbolized by the fawns being hunted and sacrificed for their skins, the dismemberment, the escapes that are escapism, the surrender to momentary impulses, and the lust for vengeance that prevailed at Corcyra.

From one point of view the *Bacchae* presents itself as resolving the contradictions it dramatizes. It can honor Dionysus without the Dionysiac destroying the city. Tragedy neither rejects Dionysus as the Theban

[63] In *Euripides and Dionysus*, p. 80.

women do (futilely and self-destructively it turns out). Nor does it simply embrace the god as the Asian Bacchants do with their callous disregard for the polis. Rather it interrogates the norms and normalizing strategies of the culture and reaffirms their necessity. It reveals the fictive quality of the social demarcations that give a people their identity and insists that such definitions are necessary to make a people at all. Bringing up from below and from outside forces, passions, and strata otherwise ignored or excluded, it provides a more inclusive stage for reflection than do other public institutions. But it also reaffirms the need for the limits whose limits it has just displayed. And it provides both memory and forgetting in proportions that sustain rather than destroy life.[64]

From that same point of view the play as a whole offers an understanding of wisdom wider and deeper than any proposed by the characters on stage. Wisdom is a moral capacity based on experience and knowledge of the limits of experience. It is both a quality of mind and feeling, manifest in judgment and respect for the sufferings of others before implacable necessity. A wise man or woman has as much compassion as foresight. In this general sense *sophia* and *sophos* are contrasted with *amathia*.[65] *Amathia* describes one who is untaught and unteachable, crude and coarse, with a tendency toward cruelty. Such ignorance immunizes one against compassion and blinds one to common suffering. Pentheus is *amathēs* (and perhaps Dionysus as well). He does not realize that what he does to others he also does to himself.

Still from this point of view one can say that the very existence of the play as a work of art provides a sense of healing integration in tension with the dismemberment that occurs as part of the play. Indeed the more the political, moral, and spiritual world of the drama is torn apart, the more beautiful the poetry becomes. The sweetness, richness, and variety of the choral odes and poetic diction contrasts with the coarseness, brutality, and single-mindedness of the various characters in the play. As a work of art the play is a radiant center illuminating the darkness of its surroundings like the sun in the cave parable in the *Republic*.

The *Bacchae*, like Euripidean tragedy generally and perhaps all tragic art, sustains a tension between the dismembering forces it dramatizes— entropy, irrational and inexplicable sufferings, chaos—and the cohesive integrating forces that lie, ultimately, in the creative ordering and unifying energies of the work itself. If unlimited, the dramatization of tragic

---

[64] The major work on the subject is still Nietzsche, "The Uses and Disadvantages of History for Life," in *Untimely Meditations*, trans. R. J. Hillingdale (Cambridge: Routledge and Kegan Paul, 1983).

[65] My discussion of *sophos* and *amathia* draws on Arrowsmith's "Introduction to the *Bacchae*," in Grene and Lattimore, *Greek Tragedies*. (At line 480, Dionysus accuses Pentheus of *amathei* [*doxei tis amathei sopha legōn ouk eu phronein*].)

events is enervating; but in the artful elaboration from which such dramatization draws its power comes that metaphysical solace Nietzsche saw in tragedy, the absence of which Ignatieff laments in contemporary society.[66]

It may even be that in sustaining this tension between the centrifugal forces it represents on stage and the centripetal forces that lie in its own form, tragedy provides an exemplar for political membership. With its balance of diversity and unity, in the place it leaves for passion and instinct within a structure of intelligence, by the way it honors memory and forgetting in the interests of life, tragedy provides an image of reciprocity in the polity on stage.

But there is another point of view in which the claims made for tragedy in the *Bacchae* are subverted and the separation between mythical Thebes, where tragic antinomies are played out to their violent conclusions, and the audience of Athenians, who learn from but do not repeat what they see, is breaking down. I have argued here, as I did in chapter 2, that tragedy was able to "interrogate" the cultural accommodations that defined civic life. Relying on the *Bacchae*, I would restate the claim: tragedy is able to dismember and reassemble the polis as Cadmus was unable to reassemble the body of Pentheus. At least it can as long as the dramatic festival, the theater, and civic life as a whole retain their integrity. If the city (and so the audience) becomes dismembered, if Athens moves toward Corcyra, then tragedy cannot sustain the Dionysian moment. Indeed, under such circumstances the very attempt to do so may exacerbate that movement.

I wondered earlier whether Euripides, like Thucydides, presumes the existence of an uncorrupted language by which corruption can be identified and described. I am not sure he does. But I do think his own language is assaulted (or compromised) by the violence of the plot and the context of performance (Corcyra–Athens). One could say that aesthetic form absorbs the contents while simultaneously revealing the power of those contents to trouble the beauty and coherence of the aesthetic form. But in part that form is maintained only because of its distance from the context of performance. To say that is to say that the *Bacchae* is no longer a "Greek" tragedy or, less extravagantly, that it envisages the dismemberment of tragedy as previously constituted. Then the problem of membership and dismemberment would have to be presented in other terms, such as those of political theory and philosophy.

But it would be a political theory that took its agenda and its character

---

[66] I owe much of the language and these points to Segal, *Dionysiac Poetics*, pp. 340–41. Since I find the *Bacchae* even more "pessimistic" than he does, I use his argument for my own somewhat different purposes.

from Greek tragedy, especially this one. Once more Dionysus as depicted in the *Bacchae* is crucial. One the one hand Dionysus is antitheoretical. He is contemptuous of those intellectual artifacts human beings invent and pass off as nature, resents the imposition of plan and permanence on what is fragmented and momentary, and rejects evolutionary schemes that identify adulthood with moderation, the development of cognitive skills, personal independence (or differentiation), and abstract notions of fairness. His is an ecstatic community whose power and energy are drawn from animal nature, not a casual community engaged in reasoned dialogue and debate made possible by abstraction from the body. The Dionysiac is everything Plato of the *Republic* feared about tragedy and life.[67]

But there is another side to all this. In his transcendence of social conventions, prescribed polarities, and sanctioned hierarchies, and in his "positing" of a natural unity above, below, or inside particularities and divisions, Dionysus dramatizes a theoretical impulse. If I am right, then it is worth looking for ecstatic elements in Platonic "rationalism" and recognizing that totalizing theories may lie within the celebration of antitheory.

[67] See Dodds argument on Euripides as an "irrationalist" in his *The Greeks and the Irrational* (Boston: Beacon Press, 1957), pp. 186–88, 270–78.

PART III
POLITICAL THEORY AND
GREEK TRAGEDY

SIX

The Corcyrean Revolution:
Corruption, Dismemberment, and
Political Theory in
Thucydides' *History*

AT THE end of *Oresteia*, as part of the consecration of justice in the *Eumenides*, the Furies, now Kindly Ones, pray that "civil war, greedy for the ruin of cities, never strike here" (*tan d'aplēston kakōn mē pot' en polei stasin taid' epeuchomai*, 976). *Stasis* destroys common will and life and is as such the obverse of justice. In Thucydides' *History* justice is part of the rhetoric of "justification" in the initial set of speeches between Corcyra and Corinth and in the Athenian speech at Sparta. Considerations of justice are not and cannot be ignored, and that is in itself significant when one contrasts what happens to "justice" later, in the Mytilene debate, at Melos, and at Corcyra where "justice" becomes mere rhetoric, a weapon of war rather than any standard to judge it. As individual cities and Hellas as a whole become divided, considerations of justice are discounted and discarded. The road from Argos to Athens, from corruption, *stasis*, self-destruction, and confusion to health, peace, judgment, and clarity, is now a road from Athens to Melos and Corcyra. The road builders who tamed a wilderness have now made every sea and land the highway of their daring, creating an empire that knows no bounds. Partly because of that, the wild enters the heart of the city and the cycle of revenge the Areopagus transcended reappears at Melos as an implacable logic of power and empire.

Bernard Knox relies on Thucydides' portrait of Athens to argue that the issue of Oedipus's identity in the *Oedipus Tyrannos* is also the issue of the identity of the citizen audience watching the drama. Whatever uneasiness we may have about the specific identification of a mythical Theban king with contemporary Athenian history, Knox does direct us toward analogies between individual and collective identity that are helpful in understanding Greek thought. For example, if losing one's identity is, as I suggested, a matter of losing the shared life within which one's distinctiveness is recognized and affirmed, then that is what happened to individual citizens in Athens and to Athens as a city in Hellas. Pericles proclaims the city without precedent and paradigm for all Hellas. Later (at Mytilene and Melos) the Athenians contribute to the corruption of moral discourse within which claims to its distinctive status had been expressed and, by their own admission, becomes simply one more city exercising imperial sway. Once the liberator of Hellas it is now the enslaver of Greeks; once proud of its service to the common cause against Persia, Athens now rejects any reference to that service as rhetorical pretense disguising present realities.

If dismemberment is the loss of identity, then one can read the *History* as a historical narrative about Athens analogous to the story Euripides tells of Pentheus and Thebes. Like his contemporary, Thucydides presents us with a city if not a culture torn apart and unrecognizable. Although *stasis* is probably the most dramatic example of this, the Sicilian debate is equally instructive, at least insofar as we see both the stupendous power of the city displayed in the harbor and its fatal weakness displayed in the debate that decided on the expedition. That debate reveals the corruption of language, the factionalism, distrust, and self-intoxication that leads from the harbor at Athens to the harbor at Syracuse. Nothing projects the failure of enterprise or the divisions within the city more than the fact that unity of daring and deliberation that Thucydides says marked Pericles' rule is now divided between Alcibiades and Nicias.

Dismemberment is the subject of this chapter on Thucydides' *History* as it was of the previous chapter on the *Bacchae*. But I want to shift the language somewhat, from that of dismemberment to political corruption.[1] I want to shift it because, as a more recognizably political term than dismemberment, corruption signals the narrower (or more specific) conception of politics we confront in the *History* when compared with that in the plays. I will only shift the language "somewhat" because of the considerable overlap between dismemberment and corruption (indeed I will often use the terms interchangeably). That overlap reminds us that Thucydides' focus on "politics," however narrow, is still embedded in a range of associations wider than our own.

As Thucydides makes clear, corruption involves a process of decay whereby some original healthy or natural condition becomes diseased. If the corruption goes far enough the thing corrupted loses its identity. Lacking definition, the city or body becomes increasingly undifferentiated

[1] Our word "corruption" is from the Latin. I use it because its English meaning (as given in the Oxford Unabridged Dictionary) is close to the Greek word for corruption (*diaphtheiron*) and to what Thucydides means by *stasis*. (In the *Apology*, Socrates is accused of "*diaphtheiron* the youth.") I have discussed the etymology of corruption at length in an essay, "The Political Science of Political Corruption," in *Political Theory and Conceptual Change*, ed. Terence Ball, James Farr, and Russell Hanson (Cambridge: Cambridge University Press, 1988), pp. 220–46. The Greek word used in the accusation against Socrates means to destroy utterly, spoil, harm, lead astray, corrupt, ruin, bribe, or seduce.

and amorphous and so by extension anonymous. Decomposition implies loss of composure, that is, a loss of normal visage as well as a capacity to speak and act in characteristic ways.

Corruption also suggests a wasting away or wearing down and loss of vitality, both of which are causes and signs of eroded health and strength. The end of this process is decadence if not death. Decadence implies self-indulgence, luxury and excess; de-cadence points to a violation of time, as if some natural rhythm is displaced by either an artificial speeding up or slowing down of life and culture. In this sense decadence is like entropy, which involves both homogenization and loss of energy (in thermodynamics) and fragmentation and loss of energy (as in communications theory).

Corruption also implies degeneration, literally a falling away from the example of previous generations and from the life those ancestors generated. Someone who is degenerate has sunk to a lower standard of thought and action than those who have come before and so lacks the energy and power such legacies make possible. Those who are degenerate sometimes adhere to no principles at all. We say such a person or city lacks integrity.

Loss of integrity is dis-integration, a breaking apart into factions or atoms such that wholeness and coherence are lost. A disintegrating city is divided and incomplete, without center, focus, or common ends. Citizens without integrity are dishonest. Lacking an element of sound character, they become easily seduced from fidelity to the discharge of a public duty.

Corruption need not only be the absence or lack of something; it may involve the presence of some alien element that disrupts the integrity of the whole. A text becomes corrupt when through ignorance or carelessness, it was altered from its original state by later accretions and changes. In this sense corruption becomes a matter of debasement—that is, the undermining of what is basic, foundational, and fundamentally constitutive of collective life.

Thinking of corruption in this way restates the conclusions of the previous chapter, and helps us understand the *stasis* at Corcyra and appreciate the overall movement of the *History*.

THE *stasis* at Corcyra is central to both Thucydides' *History* and this book. For one thing, it connects the themes of justice, identity, and political corruption. The collapse of the first and the loss of the second provide a limiting case and paradigmatic instance of the third. Thucydides is explicit about this: what happens during the civil war there anticipates the fate of Hellas and exemplifies the overall movement of the war. For another thing, if, as I believe, political theory was invented in response to

169

such corruption and movement, Corcyra helps set the context and terms for the emergence of political theory and political philosophy.[2]

The civil war is also the occasion for one of Thucydides' rare authorial interventions and his most general remarks on the human condition.[3] It is the occasion too for his analysis of linguistic corruption, which implicitly distinguishes between his language and the corruption of language he details. In this regard his statement about words changing their meaning is analogous to the chorus's "Why shall we dance?" in the *Oedipus Tyrannos*. Both are moments when the text turns back on and into itself, while simultaneously opening itself up to reveal its principles of construction and conditions of existence. Both suggest deficiencies in self-understanding and offer an implicit standard against which distortion can be seen if not measured.

Thucydides assumes that his own words escape the corruption enveloping the words of others and that, partly for this reason, he (but not they) is capable of understanding the truth of things. The question, of course, is whether and why we should believe him. This is less a matter of class affiliation than of the degree to which the *History* is distinctively Athenian and the extent to which Corcyrean revolution displays distinctively Athenian traits now pushed to extremes. The point can be made clearer if we recall a characteristic of tragedy and look at how commentators characterize Thucydides' style.

Tragedy by its nature admits of a divided world. The very fact of dramatic representation creates a tension between what is seen and said. Because language is doubled by another mode of representation, the visual action on stage, language is constantly called into question. So tragedy, a uniquely Athenian achievement, always takes us beyond the boundaries of language to a point where "language becomes inadequate to render the experience before us on the stage or is shown as actually breaking down before that visual experience."[4] It also suspends the defining structures of the culture, forcing the mind to reach beyond them in the painful search for other principles of order very much like Cadmus's search for the pieces of Pentheus's body or in the even more painful admission that, as in the *Bacchae*, there may be no such principles. Moreover, tragedy pre-

---

[2] I have made this argument in detail in "The Battle of Salamis and the Origins of Political Theory," *Political Theory* 14, no. 3 (1986): 359–90 (Christian Meier makes a parallel one in *Die Entstehung des Politischen bei den Griechen* [Frankfurt: Suhrkamp, 1980]).

[3] I agree, however, with de Romilly that it is misleading to regard what Thucydides says as statements about human nature from which psychological laws about human action can be drawn; see her "L'utilité de l'histoire selon Thucydide," in *Histoire et historiens dans l'antiquite*, Entretiens sur l'Antiquite Classique 4 (Geneva: Vandoeuvres, 1956), pp. 41–81.

[4] Charles Segel, "Logos and Mythos: Language, Reality, and Appearance in Greek Tragedy and Plato," unpublished manuscript (p. 4).

sents terrible pollution, disturbing cruelties of the gods, mutual murders of parents and children, death or prolonged suffering of the innocent, and the triumph of the unscrupulous. Finally, the tragic situation distorts normal speech, creating paradoxes, oxymora, and ironies that signify both a loss of coherence in the world and a loss of the ability to grasp and communicate that coherence.[5] Now as long as tragedy remained a communal act and part of a religious festival, this deconstitution took place within a reaffirmation of the city's cultural accommodations and celebration of the city's gods. Where and when such affirmation was absent, when tragedy could no longer be a truly communal act and the gods disappeared, then the world becomes Corcyra. And, insofar as the gods are absent in Thucydides and his *History* is not part of a communal celebration, we need to ask about the connection between *stasis* and theory.

The "Athenianism" of Corcyra is indicated by the language critics use to characterize Thucydides' language. For instance, John Finley likens his prose style to a boxing ring in which opposite impulses constantly struggle for primacy,[6] while W. Robert Connor finds the *History* remarkable for its movement and heterogeneity, its startling juxtapositions, striking contrasts, abrupt transitions, and shattered parallelisms.[7] What he calls the "overwhelming complexity" of the work shatters "all the neat antilogies and balances of Greek and strains the language to its limits."[8] These characterizations not only recall Euripides' *Bacchae*, they also suggest a disconcerting affinity between normal Athenian politics and the *stasis* at Corcyra.

The special status Thucydides implicitly claims for his words and work during his description of civil war draws us to three issues central to the *History* and to a refinement of tragedy's relationship to theory. The first concerns the sense in which Thucydides thinks (and is right to think) of his work as a possession for all time; the second concerns whether the *History* is "based on confidence in man's powers" or whether, on the contrary, the foreknowledge it provides is "not rational prediction and control but the premonition of recurring misery and loss";[9] the third is concerned with the text's "theoretical power." Although I will discuss the

---

[5] Charles Segal, "Greek Tragedy and Society: A Structuralist Perspective," in *Greek Tragedy and Political Theory*, ed. J. Peter Euben (Berkeley and Los Angeles: University of California Press, 1986), pp. 43–75.

[6] John H. Finley, Jr., *Four States of Greek Thought* (Stanford, Calif.: Stanford University Press, 1965), p. 72.

[7] W. Robert Connor, *Thucydides* (Princeton: Princeton University Press, 1984), p. 11.

[8] W. Robert Connor, "Narrative Discourse in Thucydides," in *The Greek Historians: Literature and History* (Stanford, Calif.: Stanford University Press, 1985), p. 7.

[9] Connor, *Thucydides*, p. 31.

latter in this chapter's concluding section, let me enumerate the questions it raises by way of a preface.

By theoretical power I mean the idea of theory a text advocates, presupposes, or implies. How does this idea of theory encourage rhetorical strategies aimed at establishing the authority of various voices within the text and for the voice of the text as a whole? If there is more than one theoretical sensibility how do they interrogate, enclose, or contradict one another? What is the relationship between a text's theoretical power and its explicit analysis of political power? Does the one iterate or play off against the other? In what way does the theory's structure of argument, conception of evidence, and language point toward particular actors or situations? What and who does the theorist hope or expect to change because he or she has written in a certain way? Where is he or she in the world being analyzed, portrayed, or projected?

Theoretical power also involves the way in which a text recreates a community (or communities) between an "author" and reader that is distinct from, if not in opposition to, the larger contemporary community whose corruption or dismemberment is the occasion for theoretical reflection. As the virtues of citizenship succumb to party passion, Thucydides establishes with his readers a fellowship now impossible with his compatriots. To this community of unlimited, anonymous, necessarily individual partners, located in an unnamable place, in some undefined future and uncertain cultural context, the historian offers himself as tutor and friend, providing an experience of cultural reconstitution that can be repeated in imagination at any place and time.[10] That reconstitution stands against the relentless chaos that inevitably overwhelms moderation and life. It is this collapse of all middle ground that Corcyra portrays with such harrowing power.

It was precisely this ground that Pericles maintained and that maintained him in power. Its existence was also a precondition for tragedy, enabling the tragedians to be political educators rather than partisans, critics but not exiles. As long as the Athenian citizenry understood itself and was *an* audience instead of a series of factions who brought their partisanship into the theater, theoretical impulses retained a place in the public arena. As the citizen-audience became corrupt those impulses required other forms and forums. Putting the issue this way indicates how a discussion of Corcyra helps define the similarities and contrasts between tragedy and theory, and so more clearly delineates the idea of theoretical power.[11]

---

[10] See the discussion of this point in James Boyd White, *When Words Lose Their Meaning* (Chicago: University of Chicago Press, 1984), pp. 279–81.

[11] F. M. Cornford, *Thucydides Mythistoricus* (London: Edward Arnold, 1907), makes the most elaborate argument for the similarities between the *History* and tragedy, although

Almost all critics have come to agree with Adam Parry's judgment that the *History* is "an intensely personal and tragic work."[12] Most would also agree that Thucydides' closest affinities are to Euripides.[13] Certainly the structure of this book and the argument of the last chapter suggest as much. There are other ways in which Thucydides was influenced by a literary form that had been both his city's "unique discovery [and] characteristic medium."[14] For example: the paired speeches and specific arguments remind one of Euripides; the quality of confined intensity, dramatic juxtapositions of scenes with opposite import, the oscillation between moments of joyful exultation and disaster is especially but not only reminiscent of Sophocles; the paradigmatic status of characters who nevertheless retain their distinctive forcefulness and particular destinies is typical of tragedy as a whole; and the dialectic between *atē, pleonexia,* and ruin bears similarities to Aeschylus's theology.

Despite these and other similarities, there are two obvious differences between Thucydides and the tragedians: the *History* was conceived of as a written document[15] and historians, unlike tragedians, had no specified role in Athenian public life.

Thucydides links the distinction between momentary displays and the permanence of his own work to two other contrasts: one between mythical ornamentation, which amuses at truth's expense, and serious analysis, which aims at accuracy; the other between the conditions of oral com-

---

he concentrates on Aeschylus rather than Euripides. John H. Finley, Jr., compares Thucydides and Euripides in his *Three Essays on Thucydides* (Cambridge, Mass.: Harvard University Press, 1967), pp. 1–54, while Jacqueline de Romilly talks about judgment in Thucydides the way I talked about the role of judgment in tragedy in chapter 2 (see her *Histoire et raison chez Thucydide* [Paris: Collection d'etudes Anciennes, 1956]. Against this, see Charles Norris Cochrane, *Thucydides and the Science of History* (New York: Russell and Russell, 1965). In an essay, "Thucydides and Tragedy" (reprinted in his *Collected Essays* [Oxford: Clarendon Press, 1983], chap. 13, p. 157), Colin MacLeod writes: "I doubt if tragedy should be numbered among the literary influences on Thucydides. As an Athenian he must have absorbed it by attending the Great Dionysia; but there is no sign that he looked to it as a model, and indeed it might well be included in the categories of 'pieces for an ephemeral competition.' " And Albert Cook dismisses "the tragic vision ascribed by Cornford to Thucydides" (in his *Enactment: Greek Tragedy* [Chicago: Swallow Press, 1971], p. 67).

[12] In "Thucydides' Use of Abstract Language," *Yale French Studies* 45 (1970): 3–20.

[13] That is certainly John Finley's argument in the two works cited previously. Whereas F. M. Cornford, in *Thucydides Mythistoricus* emphasizes affinities with Aeschylus, Lowell Edmunds (in "Thucydides' Ethics as Reflected in the Description of Stasis," *Harvard Studies in Classical Philology* 79 [1975]: 73–92) and Nicole Loraux (in "Thucydides et la sedition dans les mots," *Quaderni di Storia* 23 [January-June 1986]: 95–134) have stressed his affinities with Hesiod.

[14] Finley, *Thucydides*, p. 324.

[15] On tragedy's place in the evolution from an oral to written culture, see Charles Segal, "Tragedy, Orality, Literacy," in *Oralita: Culture, Litteratura, Discourso*, ed. Bruno Bentili and Giuseppe Psioni (Urbino: Edizioni Dell'Atheneo, 1980), pp. 199–226.

position and writing. Writing (*graphein, synegrapsē*) as opposed to mere saying (*eipein, eiretai*) has a permanence and independence oral performance lacks. Because it does, it is an appropriate vehicle for discovering and representing truth, much as Pericles' independence of the demos allowed him to say what the situation required, unlike the demagogues who spoke to please the mob (*kath' hēdonēn legein*). Thucydides' claim reverses earlier beliefs that poetic speech was the only preservable speech, whereas vernacular prose had an ephemeral life in the memory of either speaker or listener. Now such prose could be put in a written volume (*ktēma*), and so "the governing word" ceases to be a "vibration heard by the ear and nourished in memory" and becomes instead a visible artifact.[16]

Of course there is another side to this independence—the absence of any established audience or prescribed institutional place. It was the peculiarity of Greek historians that they lacked both the ceremonial role and public responsibilities of the tragedians and the professional status of philosophers.[17] Nor were they thought to have any clearly defined type of knowledge to discover or transmit. (Socrates too disowns being a teacher of virtue but that is another and more complicated matter to be taken up in the next chapter.) One could of course understand them in terms of epic, drama, or, in Thucydides' case, the writings of Hippocrates. But, they, or rather Thucydides, was more than the sum of these parts, though I am arguing that tragedy was a large part of that whole. Let me now turn to that something more; to political corruption and dismemberment, to Corcyra and theoretical power.

CORCYRA is mentioned early in the *History*. In fact, the debate between Corcyra and Corinth is the first set of speeches we read and the first proximate cause offered for the war's beginning.

Epidamnus, a Corcyrean colony, had become enfeebled by factionalism and war with its barbarian neighbors. The last act before this war was the expulsion of the nobles by the people, which led the former to ally with the city's barbarian enemies. Hard pressed, the Epidamnians appealed to Corcyra, herself a rich and famous colony of Corinth, to aid in reconciling the nobles and ending the war. Rebuffed at Corcyra and after consulting Delphi, the Epidamnian ambassadors went to Corinth for similar aid. The Corinthians consented out of a sense of duty to what was, after all, their colony as well, and because they despised Corcyra's contempt for their status as the mother country about which they could do nothing given its wealth and naval strength.

---

[16] Eric A. Havelock, *The Literate Revolution in Greece and Its Cultural Consequences* (Princeton: Princeton University Press, 1982), pp. 147–48.

[17] Arnaldo Momigliano, "The Historians of the Classical Word and Their Audiences," *The American Scholar* 47 (1977–1978): 194.

When Corcyra heard about the arrival of Corinthian settlers and troops at Epidamnus, it demanded that the banished nobles be received back and that the Corinthian garrison and settlers be expelled. When Epidamnus refused, the Corcyreans besieged the city and defeated the Corinthian navy. Alarmed by massive Corinthian military preparations undertaken to avenge the defeat and its own military and political isolation, the Corcyreans turned to Athens.

They began their speech by talking about justice, their present victimization, the gratitude and goodwill the Athenians would win by supporting them, and only then mentioning the good fortune that would follow uniting the two major naval powers in Hellas. Here, then, is a golden opportunity for the Athenians to act expediently to gain power, honor, and justice at the same time. Besides, Lacedemonian jealousy makes a major war near and inevitable. They end by asserting that they are estranged from Corinth because of the latter's unjust treatment of them, that having common enemies makes Corcyra and Athens natural allies, and that she is on the sea lane to Sicily.

As with their deliberations over the fate of the Mytileneans, the Athenians hold two assemblies. In the first sentiment is for the Corinthians. Apparently the Athenians have been convinced by the Corinthian arguments: Corcyran neutrality is not a policy of consideration but of narrow self interest; the Corcyrans are violating Hellenic law; Corinth has rendered important service to Athens in times of crisis; the war is not as certain as the Corcyreans claim; and justice (by which the Corinthians mean reciprocity between great powers) demands Corinth be allowed to punish Corcyra. But in the second assembly public feeling has changed (as it would at Mytilene). The Athenians decide on a defensive alliance with Corcyra, because they desire to annex Corcyra's navy (or at least be sure no one else does), and because of the latter's geographic location in relation to Sicily.

It is of course significant that the final (though perhaps not the initial) Athenian decision ignores matters of justice, honor, gratitude, and the respect due a parent city for more immediate strategic considerations. It is equally significant that both Corcyra and Corinth find it necessary (as the Athenians at Melos do not) to use and even emphasize such moral concerns. The very fact that cities jockeyed for position by seeking to place the other in the wrong—that speakers had to be able to claim and were interested in claiming that their acts were justified if not just—shows that, at least in the beginning, *poleis* operated on terms established by a shared and comprehensible discourse.[18] At this stage each acted for a

---

[18] James Boyd White contrasts the debate between Corcyra and Corinth at Athens with the Mytilene debate to show what the collapse of this shared discourse means to the actors in the *History* (*When Words Lose Their Meaning*, pp. 60–65).

clearly defined audience. As the war and *History* proceed, this audience and shared discourse among states collapses. At Corcyra (and at Athens) it collapses within a single city. For Socrates and Plato it collapses within every individual. Thus war between states jeopardizes the discourse of international politics; civil war jeopardizes communication among citizens; war within the self jeopardizes the dialogue between me and myself that characterizes thinking itself.

Of equal importance is the fact that the careful weighing of alternatives and strategic considerations that characterizes the Athenian decision to ally with Corcyra comes to nothing. *Stasis* destroys Corcyran power, rendering her a useless ally. The irony is compounded by the parallels between the present situation of Corcyra as one of the outside forces fueling civil war at Epidamnus, and its later being the victim of such forces. Added to this irony is another: if the belief in the inevitability of war is based on general expectations analogous to those which the Athenians entertained when deciding on the alliance, and if the particular expectations were confounded, then we cannot be sure that the war need have taken place at all.

Other important matters are introduced here. The killing of fathers by sons during the civil war at Corcyra is anticipated here by the ingratitude of colonies for their mother country. Similarly, the collapse of political and moral categories there is presaged by the present disregard for traditional Greek distinctions between Hellene and barbarian, oligarch and democrat. Finally, there is the repeated mention of Corcyra's strategic location on the road to Sicily. As we know, that is the road Athens took to defeat and ruin. It is as if the ending is already present in the beginning.

For all its irony and quiet pathos, Thucydides' narrative of the *stasis* at Epidamnus is muted compared with what occurs at Corcyra and his focus on the latter here is relatively innocuous given what we witness later. This makes the present narrative a historical preface to the subsequent civil war though not an emotional or poetic one. That role is performed by the plague at Athens.

The plague caused deaths in numbers beyond memory. Its power to kill was as unprecedented as the Athenian power which it temporarily undermined. (That Thucydides claims to know the causes of that power but not of the plague is a caution against identifying his methodological modesty here with his theoretical power.)[19] As the many deaths of physicians attest, the plague defied all human art, including that of Thucydides. No skill was sufficient to understand, let alone mitigate or prevent, the dis-

---

[19] Because he does not know the plague's origins or causes, all he can do is render a clinical narrative of its symptoms and progress so others can recognize it if it should ever break out again. The question is whether this intellectual modesty applies to the *History* as a whole.

ease. Supplications and divinations were equally futile. There was no rhyme or reason why some got the disease while others did not; why some few survived while the rest perished. Indeed, the best men received the worst fate. Unsparing of themselves in the service of others, they were unspared by death. Given this discrepancy between character and destiny, and given the onslaught of the unknown and uncontrollable, men lost their capacity to resist, thereby insuring their continued victimization.

The first part of Thucydides' narrative concentrates on the plague's physical effects on the body. But as the narrative proceeds disease becomes a metaphor for the breakdown of all social restraint, that is for *stasis*. As the "disease passed all bounds, men, not knowing what was to become of them, became utterly careless of everything" (2.53).[20] Confronting a radically uncertain future they had no scruples about doing in public what they had been ashamed to do in private. "So they resolved to spend quickly and enjoy themselves, regarding their lives and riches as alike things of a day" (2.54). In such circumstances honor became a victim of instant gratification and immediate utility, lawfulness and piety the victims of apparently random connections between virtue and reward. The decay and imbalance of individual constitutions now infect the polis; the deep malaise into which men lacking spirit and hope had lapsed now characterizes the city as a whole. As the body had been divided against itself, so now is the body politic.

This is made all the more striking by the fact that the plague immediately follows Pericles' funeral oration. The celebration of human power gives way to passivity, death for known honorable cause gives way to random death by a mysterious disease; solemn rites of burial according to ancestral tradition to indecent makeshift funerals; claims to respect authority, law, and tradition to lawlessness and indifference; elaborate rhetorical construction to detailed clinical narrative, speech asserting the virtue of Athens to the plague which cancels virtue.[21]

But not entirely: even during the plague, Thucydides mentions some for whom family, friends, honor, and goodness mattered more than mere survival. No one and nothing like this survives at Corcyra.

ONE WAY to read the Corcyrean revolution is as the third play of a trilogy, the first being the Athenian debate over the fate of Mytilene, the second the Spartan acquiescence to Theban demands that Plataea be obliterated. That the debate and acquiescence are parallel, that they are done by the two major antagonists—one a democracy in constant mo-

[20] I will rely on the Crawley translation with some emendations of my own. My habit here (and elsewhere) is to elaborate meanings, a habit that, though it sometimes upsets the balance of Thucydides' prose, adds a "useful" ambiguity.

[21] This is a paraphrase from Peter Pouncey, *The Necessities of War: A Study in Thucydides' Pessimism* (New York: Columbia University Press, 1980), p. 316.

tion, the other a conservative oligarchy—is preface and justification for those generalizations about the human condition with which Thucydides concludes his description of the Corcyrean civil war.

Seeing Athenian power depleted by the plague, by continuous expenditures of men and money, and by other involvements, the Mytileneans decide to revolt, despite their independent status within the Athenian empire. They are right in believing that the Athenians are vulnerable. The presence of a Peloponnesian fleet in the Aegean and the rebellion by a large well-treated ally shook its confidence and complacency. But they are wrong to think the Athenians incapable of response. Indeed it was because of that vulnerability that the Athenians responded with such fury, initially deciding to do in anger what they did in cold calculation at Melos.

The revolt is a miserable failure. The Mytileneans are haphazard in their planning, and precipitous in their actions. They underestimate Athenian power and overestimate Spartan resourcefulness. Fortunately for them the Athenians have second thoughts about the indiscriminate cruelty of their initial sentence.[22] But the man who proposed that punishment has no such qualms. He is Cleon, "the most violent, forceful [*biaiotatos*] man at Athens and at that time by far the greatest influence on the demos" (3.36)[23] That he is the most influential because he is the most violent and the most violent because he is the most powerful says most of what needs saying about him, about the demos and city he leads, and about the context in which the Mytilenean debate takes place.

Given Thucydides' singularly explicit castigation of Cleon and his equally explicit praise of Pericles, it is disconcerting to find so many similarities between them. Like Pericles, Cleon is preeminent in the city. He too claims to be acting patriotically and uncorruptly, to be steadfast against the people's fickleness, to be forthright in calling the empire a

[22] H.D.F. Kitto, *Poiesis* (Berkeley and Los Angeles: University of California Press, 1966), pp. 294–317. Clifford Orwin, who calls these second thoughts a "massive moral hangover," is right to emphasize that the Athenians were concerned with "the justice of their decision, not its expediency"; see "The Just and the Advantageous in Thucydides: The Case of the Mytilenean Debate," *American Political Science Review* 78, no. 2 (June 1984): 485. On the strategic and political failure of the Mytileneans, see Kitto, *Poiesis*; L. Bodin, "Diodote contre Cléon," *Revue des études anciennes* 42 (1940): 36–52; A. Andrewes "The Mytilene Debate," *Phoenix* 16 (1962): 64–85; and Felix Martin Wasserman, "Post-Periclean Democracy in Action: The Mytilenean Debate (Thuc. III 37–48)," *Transactions of the American Philological Association* 87 (1956): 27–41.

[23] On the relationship between Cleon and Pericles, see Mabel Lang, "Cleon as the Anti-Pericles," *Classical Philosophy* 67, no. 3 (1972): 159–69. Commenting on the Pylos episode, she writes of the "violence, brutality, and irresponsibility of Cleon's maneuvers" which show that "he was using the people, that he thought of them as an instrument on which he played . . . and so deprived them of the self-respect and sense of responsibility which Pericles and his forerunners had so carefully built up" (p. 163).

tyranny, chastising the people for their immoderate love of rhetoric and admonishing them for their excessive confidence or excessive despair. Yet similarity merely emphasizes the contrast between the purpose and tone of their respective speeches, the policies those speeches advocate, and the idea of citizenship their respective words and lives embody.

When Pericles chastised the demos, he also praised democratic culture and institutions: when he berated the people or opposed his own resolve to their vacillations, he did so in terms that respected and even enhanced their powers of discernment. Cleon does the opposite and so enhances his power at their expense. With him steadfastness becomes stubbornness. Equating a decree (*psephisma*) with law (*nomos*) and regarding reconsideration of yesterday's judicial act as a violation of tradition, Cleon destroys the balance between past and present essential to the moderation he extols. Moreover, whereas Pericles celebrated speech as a fit prelude to decisive action and great deeds, Cleon ridicules the former, identifying anti-intellectualism with moderation, and words (as opposed to deeds) with falsehood, as if stupidity were always honest and intelligence always irresponsible.[24] Indeed when Cleon insists that all one needs to know is that the deed is done, and all one needs to do is react swiftly without deliberating, he recalls the idea of justice enunciated by the Furies in the *Oresteia*. Finally, and with telling irony, this man who arrogantly rejected Spartan peace overtures extols the Spartan virtues of moderation, unlearned loyalty, and traditional respect for the commonplace. This discrepancy between surface similarities and a deeper disjunction, together with the confounding of language that characterizes Cleon's speech, suggests a growing separation between appearance and reality and so one way in which words are changing their meaning.

In truth, Cleon, like Plato's Callicles, is the putative democrat who helps debase a democracy he then despises. That is indicated by particular things, like his contempt for traditional Athenian virtues of pity (*eleos*) and clemency (*epieikeia*) as well as by more general things, such as his attitude toward the Athenian empire. Pericles' reference to the empire as a tyranny was equivocal. The Athenians, he says, hold their empire *hos tyrannida*, which can mean either it is like but not quite a tyranny, or that it is a tyranny.[25] Cleon leaves *hos* out, so that the statement loses its ambiguity. But the issue is not only whether the Athenian empire is a tyranny but whether Athens is itself becoming a tyrannical regime with Cleon as the potential tyrant.

Remember it is Cleon who opposes speech to action, uses it to silence

---

[24] Kitto, *Poiesis*, p. 309.

[25] See Connor, *Thucydides*, p. 89, and Orwin, "Mytilenean Debate," p. 486, for the significance of Cleon calling Athens a tyranny.

others, and regards it simply in strategic terms, as a means of violence. Impugning the motives of his opponents, he forces them to defend themselves and their speaking at all before they can defend their policies. He would control if not dominate what constitutes debate as well as what is considered in it. Cleon wants to be the only voice. In this be becomes not only the rival to Diodotus but to Thucydides himself, which is perhaps one other reason why the historian bore him such animosity.

Yet for all this Cleon is not simply wrong. The Athenians are indeed too easily seduced by rhetoric, as the Sicilian adventure attests. Moreover, contempt for mere entertainment at the expense of serious reflection is one of Thucydides' own methodological strictures. Finally, there is indeed a contradiction between empire and democracy.

Although there is truth in what Cleon says, the truth is more, less and different than he supposed. For one thing, he is a master of the new wisdom he denounces, the evidence being in the very speech denouncing it.[26] For another thing, his criticism of the Mytileneans is an unwitting self-indictment of his own career and politics.[27] When he talks about the Mytileneans being so blinded by prosperity that they failed to see danger, or of their being so stupidly confident of the future that they entertain hopes beyond their powers but not beyond their ambition, or speaks of the dangers that attend sudden good fortune, he is describing his own faults and future. The irony intensifies when he proceeds to argue that if the Mytileneans had "been treated like the rest" instead of being granted special privileges, "they never would have so far forgotten themselves, human nature as surely made arrogant by consideration as it is awed by firmness" (3.39). And when this man, who regards compassion as weakness, power as violence, justice as brutality, and correct policy as self-aggrandizement, accuses the Mytileneans of confusing force and morality, the irony is complete.

In some respects, Diodotus's response to Cleon is even more disconcerting than Cleon's own speech.[28] That is because he chooses or is forced to defend the more moderate human policy in relentlessly realistic terms that anticipate the Athenian arguments at Melos. What can it mean when what seems to be the only way to save the butchery of the Mytileneans

[26] Wassermann, in his "Post-Periclean Democracy in Action," p. 32, writes that in the very speech in which Cleon "inveighs against the Athenian vogue for both displaying and enjoying the products of political oratory, [he] offers an up-to-date paradigm of rhetoric, combining features of the apotreptikon and the ketēgorikon genos as if Gorgias had been his advisor." On this issue, see R. P. Winnington-Ingram, "Ta Deonta Eipein: Cleon and Diodotus," *Institute of Classical Studies Bulletin* 12 (1965): 70–82; and Orwin, "Mytilenean Debate."

[27] Cornford, *Thucydides Mythistoricus*, pp. 150–51.

[28] The issue is how to use the Mytileneans; what we see is Cleon and Diodotus using each other, suggesting again how attitudes toward outsiders shape the relations among citizens.

prepares for the butchery of the Melians? Or that a "just" decision demands a disinterest in justice, that preventing a massacre requires disingenuousness? What do we make of the fact that Diodotus's principles often agree with Cleon's or are different but equally unpalatable? For instance, both men agree that human nature is essentially incorrigible, assert that cities and men commit violence for advantage, warn their audience against pity and gentleness, and even agree (or seem to) about the meaning of justice, although they disagree about the appropriateness of invoking it here and about the confluence of justice and expediency. Where Cleon claimed his advice was just as well as expedient, Diodotus rejects the claim, not only because Cleon unites what is necessarily opposed, but because the issues of justice and injustice, innocence and guilt have nothing to do with the matter. "We are not a court of justice," Diodotus tells his fellow citizens, "but a political assembly; and the question is not justice [dikaiōn] but to determine by deliberation [bouleuometha] how to make them useful [chrēsimōs] to us" (3.44). If this is indeed the question, then it may be more useful to put up with injustice than justly put to death those whom it is in one's interest to keep alive.

On these criteria, Diodotus argues, Cleon's policies are self-defeating. They would increase the cost of the war by making rebellious states less willing to surrender and decreasing tribute money. They would make the Athenians even more hated than they necessarily are by ignoring the opportunity to detach the demos from their oligarchic compatriots and reattach them to Athens. For Diodotus this ideological and political bond is far better insurance of support than mutual fear and suspicion.[29] Finally, in his passion for revenge, Cleon overestimates the deterrent value of punishment. Even the most severe retribution cannot still erōs (the love of action combined with the desire to get or increase our power over other men or things), elpis (the hopeful optimism that leads men to venture beyond their means, disregarding all calculations and measure), and tychē (the belief that a fortune can undo or accident will reverse present realities). Whether out of poverty and necessity, or a drive for renown, freedom, and ambition, men are courageous in the face of even the fiercest threats and examples of revenge. Cleon's policy will not work; it will only make things worse.

No doubt Diodotus means some of what he says. But there is evidence that he does not mean all, or even most of it. For one thing, there is his remark about how speeches like Cleon's force public-spirited advisors to dissimulate. For another, his distinction between the Mytilenean oli-

---

[29] On the consequences of Diodotus 's "ideologizing" of the war, see Marc Cogan, *The Human Thing* (Chicago: University Of Chicago Press, 1981), chap. 2. But see the argument by Orwin that Diodotus's view of justice does limit vengeance and even expresses "a certain sympathy of the strong for the aspirations of the weak" ("Mytilenean Debate," p. 493).

garchs who were free to choose and so responsible for the rebellion, and the demos who was compelled and thus not responsible, presents a distinction Cleon rejects and reintroduces an idea of justice different than the one Cleon proposed. Like the Furies in Aeschylus's *Eumenides*, all Cleon wants to know is if the deed was committed. That is sufficient to require immediate revenge. Like Athena, Diodotus insists on the complexity of extenuating circumstances (though unlike Athena his report of those circumstances is suspect). Justice cannot be mere reaction; it requires judgment. Certainly Diodotus regards justice as irrelevant as it is defined by Cleon. But immediately preceding his claim that they are not a court of justice, Diodotus says Cleon's "speech may have the attraction of seeming the more just in your present temper against Mytilene," which implies that in a different temper a different notion of justice might be relevant.

Here we have the most general reason why Diodotus argues as he does. As the most powerful *and* violent man at Athens, Cleon doubly sets the tone of debate. Anyone who hopes to succeed in persuading the demos must speak within the parameters he establishes. Because he has insisted that leniency can only be the product of corruption, softness, or even treason, Diodotus is forced "to cloak humane reasons in the pose of toughness even greater than that of the enemy."[30]

In the long run Diodotus's argument is self-defeating and his way of arguing is a desperate stratagem that helps bring about the inhumanity he seeks here to reverse. It is self-defeating because if, as Diodotus and Cleon agree, empire cannot help but be violent and oppressive, then a policy of indulgence will not make Athens any more secure than Cleon's policy of harsh revenge. It is a desperate stratagem because, although Diodotus apparently changes the self-understanding the Athenians have of themselves because of Cleon's speech,[31] he brings about the change through a disingenuousness that can only undermine that self-understanding.[32] Once more words and language are changing their meanings.

The question of course is not only whether Diodotus had any choice

[30] "Diodotus argues as Cleon's speech allows him to argue" (Winningham-Ingram, "Cleon and Diodotus," p. 77). As Connor points out in his *Thucydides*, Cleon is not as completely defeated as he seems to be. A resolution moved by him and passed by the assembly means more than one thousand people lose their lives and many more their land (Thuc. 3.50).

[31] Whereas Cleon encourages his fellow citizens to think of themselves as plain, blunt men who are sound and traditional but not very clever, Diodotus changes their mental picture of themselves. In his speech they have ceased being plain, blunt men of action and have become "revered counsellors fulfilling the weighty responsibilities placed upon them by their democratic constitution" (Winningham-Ingram, "Cleon and Diodotus," p. 78).

[32] For instance, Diodotus misrepresents the role of the common people in the revolt and is thereby able to distort the attitude of the democratic subjects to the empire.

but what it means for Athens, for political discourse, and to Thucydides if he did not. However one answers these questions, it seems clear that what is at stake here is not merely the fate of Mytilene or the Athenian empire, but of speech and political discourse. What is being decided upon here is not just *a* policy, but the context in which all policies will be decided upon.

Like Cleon, the Thebans at Plataea criticize speech itself. Like the most violent man at Athens, they regard language as a seduction and snare that keeps men from confronting brute facts which turn out to require brutality. Because words make us soft, susceptible to compassion, and confused about where honor and justice lie, silence (or at least extreme brevity) is a sign of toughness *and* morality. Thus the Thebans admonish their Spartan allies (as Cleon did the Athenians) to make the test deeds, not words: "Good deeds can be shortly stated but where wrong is done a wealth of language is used to disguise the hypocrisy" (3:68). Because speech veils and deforms, one needs to act without speaking, do without thinking, and concentrate on the here and now. The only real question is "Have you done anything for me lately" and that can be answered with a simple yes or no.

In fact, the Thebans use many words to insure that this remains the central question for a very good reason. As traitors to the Greek cause against Persia, their own past is highly suspect. While they deserted Sparta, the Plataeans were stalwart allies and patriots. Because the final land victory over Persia was fought there, Plataea was a symbol of common Hellenic action. So the Theban task is complex. They must reconstruct their own past to enhance their present arguments while using their present alliance to legitimate that reconstruction; and they must deconstruct the Plataean's past to undermine the latter's present moral claims on Sparta while using Plataea's present political involvements with Athens to legitimate that deconstruction. They do all this by insisting, first, that they were not responsible for their evil deeds then because they were ruled by a cabal, whereas the good they do now is freely chosen; second, that although the Plataeans were forced to be good then, they now freely choose evil.[33] In this way a speech remarkable for an elaborate syntactical structure from speakers who praise simple speech virtually "annihilates all the emotional claims which the Plataeans had offered."[34]

That the Spartans "accept" these historical revisions and the impending annihilation of Plataea is, in one sense, unexceptional. They, like the Athenians at Corcyra, side with the Thebans "who they thought would

[33] In the process, the Thebans try to identify contemporary Athens with the Persian empire, coining the word "atticize" on analogy with "medize," which is what *they* did.

[34] The phrase is Adam Parry's from his "Thucydides' Use of Abstract Language," p. 11.

be useful in the war now beginning (3.68). Certainly expediency and self-interest have their claims. But seldom have such claims come at such a cost or so completely foreshadowed a future. That is clear in the Spartan rejection of Plataean appeals.

The Plataeans invoke precisely those virtues of loyalty, traditional piety, patriotism, courage, and honor that the Greeks and Spartans themselves regarded as being preeminently (though not distinctively) Spartan. By disregarding such invocations, Sparta jeopardizes the distinctiveness of its culture and its claim to exemplary status just as the Athenians do in dismissing the desire for freedom by the Mytileneans and Melians. This is especially so, given the unique bond between the two cities. Here is Crawley's eloquent translation of the Plataean reminder of those bonds:

> Look at the sepulchres of your fathers, slain by the Medes and buried in our country, whom year by year we honored with garments and other dues . . . as friends from a friendly country and allies to our old companions in arms! . . . if you kill us and make the Plataean territory Theban, you will leave your fathers and kinsmen in a hostile soil and among their murderers, deprived of the honors which they now enjoy. What is more you will enslave the land in which the freedom of the Hellenes was won, make desolate the temples of the gods to whom they prayed before they overcame the Medes, and take away your ancestral sacrifices from those who founded and instituted them. (3.58)

That is why the Plataeans can reasonably claim that Sparta, too, is on trial. For if Sparta makes immediate self-interest the test of justice, identifies expedience with right, and dishonors by obliterating the symbol of Greek freedom to placate Thebes, it will commit an offense whose infamy will tarnish its reputation and belie its pose as liberator. Although Sparta eventually turns its back on Plataea, it is sufficiently moved by these arguments to provoke the Theban response despite the latter's initial statement that it would remain silent.[35]

Alone and together, Mytilene and Plataea prepare us for the *stasis* at Corcyra. To begin with there is an intensification and expansion of the war and of brutality. Cleon's harshness intensifies the violence, while Diodotus's principle (shared by the Thebans) of momentary usefulness is

---

[35] I do not want to moralize the issue, almost always a mistake when dealing with Thucydides. Sparta does try to get Plataea to be neutral and to a certain degree recognize the latter's obligation to Athens. But this does not lessen the significance of the deed or the damage it did to Spartan claims. On the significance of Plataea, see Pouncey, *Necessities of War*, pp. 17–19.

without limit.[36] Not only does the Theban speech incorporate the harshness and the principle, it transforms Diodotus's democratic and oligarchic division of the world into an abstract ideological principle that expands the instances when one city is justified in intervening in the domestic politics of another. When the Thebans insist that the enemy is not Athens but Athenianism, they support the idea of attacking a city not for particular deeds done but for their way of life or system of ideas. Such a principle can only extend the war in area and cruelty, as evidenced by the fact that the Plataeans now suffer a fate the Mytileneans averted (after two votes and by a few minutes).[37]

Yet, secondly, the importance of ideology is undermined even as it becomes prominent. Mytilene and Plataea present the two principle antagonists and cultures behaving in a similar way on similar grounds. One could go further: insofar as Sparta accepts Theban demands and arguments, Sparta itself begins to Atticize. That is because the principle of action and idea of history implicit in those arguments are far more Athenian than Spartan. If that is the case, then Sparta's choice, like Diodotus's stratagem, brings immediate success and long-term corruption. Because Sparta was the paradigm of the well-governed polis, that corruption assumes particular significance.

Finally, notice the role of *stasis* at both Mytilene and Plataea. In both cases, foreign enemies are introduced into the city by a dissident faction interested in private power and gain. In the later case, the presence of factions, division, and corruption takes on exemplary proportions.

As I mentioned, Plataea was the place where the final land battle of the Persian wars was fought by a united Greek army in a common cause. As such, the city had come to be a symbol of Hellenic unity, courage, and freedom. Yet this greatly honored ally was later obliterated by the city that had honored it most. The disintegration of Greek unity, and the meaninglessness of living memory Plataea's fall signifies, eventuates in civil war, family bloodshed, and a war of all against all.[38] This deepening division and escalating violence eventually consume speech itself. That loss is prefigured in the tone of Cleon, the disingenuousness of Diodotus,

[36] Both Cogan, *The Human Thing*, pp. 52–62, and White, *When Words Lose Their Meaning*, pp. 75–76, have very good discussions of the devastating impact of such arguments.

[37] Here are the Thebans justifying an earlier unprovoked and impious invasion of Plataea to aid a dissident faction: "If the first men among you in estate and family, wishing to put an end to your alliance with the foreigner [Athens] and to restore you to the common Boeotian country, of their own free will invited us, wherein is the crime? . . . Citizens like yourselves and with more at stake than you, they opened their gates and introduced us into their own city, not as foes but as friends, to prevent the base among you from becoming worse; to give honest men their due; to reform principles without attacking person" (Thuc. 3.65).

[38] See Pouncey's discussion of this disintegration, in *Necessities of War*, pp. 139–44.

the arguments of the Thebans, and the acquiescence of the Spartans. Its cost is made clear in the *stasis* at Corcyra.

With a few exceptions, Thucydides' own views are, like those of the tragedians, embedded in the structure of his work.[39] But there are a few incidents that reveal the whole with particular forcefulness. Such an incident is the civil war at Corcyra. It provides a vividly concentrated image of political corruption and Hellenic dissolution under the pitiless pounding of battle and war. The moral bankruptcy, unleashed passions, and limitless carnage that surface there with singular ferocity disclose the underside of civilization and the eventual outcome of those heroic achievements of mind and deed that give the world human impress. Because Corcyra is the absolute negation of civilization, it also reveals the most about what civilization requires.

The image has a generality even beyond its status as the final play in a trilogy whose first two are Mytilene and Plataea. It is a turning point of the entire war (and *History*) and, as Thucydides tells us, a preview of the brutal excess which later revolutions would refine with perverse inventiveness. He chooses to detail the butchery at Corcyra because, as one of the first to occur, it made such a deep impression. Later ones, he implies, made less of an impression, not because they were less ferocious (in fact they were more so), but because men had become so inured to bloodshed that ferocity became unremarkable. Part of the sickness that convulsed and dissipated the whole Hellenic world was this inability to be shocked and the consequently casual violence that was its accompaniment.

The Corcyran revolution is important not only because it is a turning point in the war but because it helps us understand the *History*'s theoretical power. It does this directly by being the occasion for one of Thucydides's most elaborate and explicit statements about war, civilization, and human nature. The conclusion of that statement—that the sufferings brought upon the cities by *stasis* will recur "as long as human nature remains the same though in severer or milder form, and varying in their symptoms according to circumstances" (3:32)—suggests how and why he thought his work a useful possession for all time. It does so indirectly because what he says about the fate of speech at Corcyra reflects back on his speech and its relationship to that of his compatriots.

The *stasis* at Corcyra began with the return of the prisoners taken by Corinth in sea fights off Epidamnus. Unknown to the Corcyran demos, the condition of the release is that the prisoners turn the city over to Corinth. Unable to do so by persuasion, they turn to intrigue, bringing the

[39] Though I sometimes disagree in detail, the general point is well argued by Hunter R. Rawlings, III, *The Structure of Thucydides' History* (Princeton: Princeton University Press, 1981).

leader of the commons, Peithias, to trial on the charge of enslaving Corcyra to Athens. Made desperate by the failure of their suit, by the success of Peithias's countersuit and the huge fine they must pay, and by the information that Peithias intends to broaden the alliance with Athens, they turn to violence. Armed with daggers, they surprise the Council and kill Peithias and sixty of his supporters, justifying their deed as in the common interest. In the civil war and escalating violence that follows, the commons is ultimately successful. The oligarchs escape total destruction only by seating themselves as suppliants and because the Athenian general intervenes. Ultimately, neither piety nor the Athenians succeed in restraining the commons. Once relieved of their fears by the arrival of a major Athenian fleet, the people proceed to take full revenge.

While the release of the prisoners is the proximate cause of the civil war, the larger cause is the presence of political factions willing to invite an external ally to intervene on its behalf wherever its internal fortunes wane.[40] The willingness of these factions to make the offer, and of the warring cities to accept it, is responsible for the terrible convulsions and many sufferings wrought by *stasis*. "In war, with an alliance always at the command of either faction for the hurt of their adversaries and their own corresponding advantage, opportunities for bringing in the foreigner were never wanting to the revolutionary parties" (3.82) At Corcyra, the simultaneous presence and fluctuating ascendancy of the Athenians and the Spartans and Corinthians add to the Corcyreans' uncertainty about their fate and to their fear. As the war promotes or intensifies civil war, human nature bursts all civilized restraints.

As limits fall and fail, ungovernable passions triumph. Ambition, envy, greed, and the lust for power drive men to a savage and pitiless excess, oblivious to the importunements of justice, honor, mercy, and those "common laws [*koinous . . . nomous*] to which all alike can appeal for salvation should they be overtaken by adversity" (3.84). Everything is inverted and so perverted. Human faculties such as reason and courage are reduced to animal cunning. Established institutions become instruments manipulated for private nefarious ends. Everything is a weapon, everyone an instrument, every act other than it seems, all fair speech a misdirecting ruse hiding violent intent. Nothing is stable or certain; everything is of, by, and for the moment. Disconnected from the legacy of their fathers, unable or unwilling to preserve a realm of freedom for their progeny, certain only of uncertainty and familiar only with unfamiliarity, men are once more creatures of a day. As the moderate and moderation are obliterated, the center cannot hold. The world is out of joint, and men have gone mad. So much for the funeral oration.

---

[40] Cogan, *The Human Thing*, p. 64.

Under such conditions, religion, law, the family, and traditional morality are impotent. Unable to moderate, let alone contain the passion for revenge, they become instead means for their increase. Oaths are undertaken only as a temporary strategy adopted when outmaneuvered or outmanned. Family fares no better. Blood being weaker than party, slogans excuse patricide. The older morality of honor and justice is used to disguise private hatreds as public virtues and so disarm the gullible. With trust and confidence likely to invite attack, domination becomes the goal of all. "To put an end to this," Thucydides writes, "there was neither promise binding enough nor oath fearsome enough; but all parties calculating the hopelessness of a permanent state of things, were more intent upon self-defense than capable of trusting others" (3.83).

The only remaining basis of self-control and solidarity was personal survival and individual advantage. Yet even these gave way before a passion for revenge that risked both. Party was no limit either. Because any offense, however trivial, ancient, or imagined, could be the motive for killing (though such motives were invariably cloaked in the finery of phrases such as "equality" or "moderate aristocracy"), men could not trust even their closest allies. As everyone was a potential enemy, isolation was the only sure guarantee against surprise attack. In the beginning of civil war, men killed their enemies with the assistance of their party. But as the *stasis* intensified, the number of potential enemies increased and the number of possible friends and shared sense of vulnerability decreased, until the only trustworthy friend was oneself and the only safe party was a party of one. Perfect security required absolute sovereignty, but as Hobbes argued (perhaps having learned it from Thucydides), the drive for absolute sovereignty brings absolute insecurity. Moreover, as Thucydides implies and Socrates' critique of Polemarchus makes clear, we are often our own worst enemies, never more than when seeking domination or tyranny.

It is also Plato who seeks to establish the stability of moral and political terms while recognizing the dynamic such words necessarily retain as constitutive of collective life. But it is Thucydides who set the theoretical problem. In peacetime, men have neither the pretext nor desire to act or speak in ways that corrupt their common life. But in war imperious necessities deny men their daily wants, deprive them of their moral sentiments, and so bring their "characters to a level with their fortunes" (3.82). As the conflicts within and between cities escalate, as brutality reaches ever new levels of refinement and excess, and necessities become even more imperious, men lose control of their natures and of events. They strive now not for honor or glory, but to outdo each other in the cunning of their enterprises and the atrocity of their reprisals. It is in such circumstances that "words were forced to change their ordinary meaning and to assume a significance that distorted the extraordinary deeds now undertaken." I quote Thucydides' examples at length:

> Senseless audacity came to be considered the courage of a loyal ally; prudent hesitation specious cowardice; moderation was held to be a cloak for unmanliness; ability to see all sides of a question inaptness to act on any. Frantic violence and animal attacks became the attribute of manliness; caution plotting, a justifiable means of self-defense. The advocate of extreme measures was always trustworthy; his opponent a man to be suspected. To succeed in a plot was to have a shrewd head, to divine a plot still shrewder; but to try to provide against having to do either was to break up your party and to be afraid of your adversaries. (3.82)

As words lose stable meaning, language joins religion, morality, law, and political institutions as casualties of war. Joins is misleading. For language and speech are constitutive of public life, not external to it. Because there is no neutral language from which men and women can speak about their lives as if they were not living them, political corruption and linguistic corruption imply each other. This is not to deny that some ways of speaking are truer or more impartial. It is to assert, with Heidegger, that our concepts have us as much as we have them. As lenses through which we see and structure the world, they are the bonds and bounds that make us whole. We remain communicants and potential friends rather than excommunicants and unavoidable enemies only where there is a community of speech and the speech of a community.[41]

But this is too neat. For one thing, even within a healthy polis men are rivals, as well as friends, involved in complex strategies of persuasion in which the inherent ambiguity of moral terms is integrated in disparate ways. That ambiguity is illustrated by two lines I quoted above:

> *to d'emplēktōs oxu andros moirai prosetethē, asphaleia de to epibouleusasthai apotropēs prophasis eulogos.*

Emplēktōs oxu can mean either temerity or perspicacity; *asphaleia*, caution and timorousness, or security, steadfastness, and assurance; *epibouleusasthai*, reconsideration of a purpose or treachery; *apotropēs*, cow-

---

[41] That is Thucydides' point in the *History* and one of the lessons of Corcyra. Only in a community collectively constituted and maintained can human motives of whatever kind and however self-referential be a rational or coherent basis for thought and action. Here is James Boyd White (*When Words Lose Their Meaning*, p. 76): "The language that makes ambition possible, by giving it form and object, at the same time imposes limits on it; it commits the individual to the culture that can alone give meaning and reality to his desires."

ardly shirking or self-defense; *prophasis*, an alleged excuse or a reason or true cause; *eulogos*, reasonable and sensible, or probable and specious.[42]

For another thing, there is a disquieting affinity between the qualities of mind and action—daring, dynamism, innovation, audacity, immoderation, presentism, and frenetic motion—that characterizes Athens and *stasis*. It is true that *stasis* perverts these traits and that other cities (even Sparta) have some of them some of the time. Still, they are perversions of qualities associated with Athens and which the Athenians embody to a unique degree. This makes it even more significant that the only elaborate analysis of *stasis* the *History* has outside of Corcyra is the description of the oligarchic conspiracy at Athens. Because the point is crucial to the argument of this chapter and the book, let me offer two elaborations, one from tragedy and the other from the *History*.

As I mentioned earlier in this chapter, tragedy takes us beyond the bounds of language. Within the confines of ritual, theater, and stage, its violent action, radical questioning of justice on both the human and divine plane, and its searching exploration of the failure, betrayal, or perversion of public and private morality take us outside the order that is the precondition for tragedy's performance. In the dramatic circle of the orchestra, moral coherence and political health break down. Tragedy stretches the world order to its limits, suspends everyday intelligibility, and deliberately destructures familiar patterns even while affirming the interrelatedness of all parts of the human and divine order through a tightly woven net of symbolic imagery.[43] In the dramas we have studied, strained diction, violent metaphors, perverse speech, and inverted sex roles together force the citizen-audience to face the chaos their mental and material structures had deliberately shut out. But when, as with Euripides' *Bacchae*, the bounds of theater and ritual may not be able to sustain the distance between character and spectators; when the destruction on stage threatens to move out into the audience while they in turn bring their factionalism to the theater;[44] when the "problematizing" of moral and linguistic codes is answered only by a questionable affirmation of the divine and human order, then we have Corcyra.

Thucydides' *History* shows how Athenian daring threatens to dislodge stable meanings. That this should be so at Mytilene, Melos, and with Alcibiades is expected given Thucydides' indictment of post-Periclean

---

[42] See the discussion of these terms and point in Daniel P. Tompkins, "The Problem of Power in Thucydides," *Arion* n.s. 1–2 (1973–1974): 413–15.

[43] See Segal, "Greek Tragedy and Society: A Structuralist Perspective," In Euben, *Greek Tragedy and Political Theory*, pp. 43–75.

[44] If John J. Winkler is right, then even in the best of times the unity of the audience is fragile. See his "The Ephebes' Song: *Tragoidia* and *Polis*," *Representations* 11 (Summer 1985): 26–62.

leadership. That it is so for Themistocles and Pericles is not and indicates the Athenian character of such daring. It was Themistocles who shaped Athens into a sea power. But it is Pericles who identifies Athens with "being nautical." Inasmuch as sea power is uniquely the creation of intelligence, Pericles envisions the empire as the product of the mind "inaccessible to those elements in the world which the mind cannot control."[45] When he calls on his compatriots to conceive of themselves as islanders and act as if that conception were true (*hoti eggutata toutou dianoethentas*, 1.142), he is proposing that they create a conceptual world impervious to the waywardness of reality. (There are limits, of course; he could not ask them to think of themselves as a great landpower.) Such conceptual boldness and power is both constitutive of Athenian greatness and jeopardizes that greatness insofar as it erodes the stable perception of the world essential for even innovative collective action.[46]

It is also constitutive of political theorizing, which suggests both an affinity between Periclean leadership and Thucydidean political theory and a way to talk about Thucydides' theoretical power.

DESPITE THE FACT that Thucydides lavishes great praise on Themistocles and admires the government of the five thousand, the Athenian political leader who emerges as an explicit standard and with whom he has the strongest intellectual affinities is Pericles. One can even say that his work extends and elaborates Periclean foresight and that his theory embodies the virtues of Periclean leadership. In this sense Thucydides' political theory is modeled on Pericles' words and wisdom, though the latter cannot simply be a model for it since one is a speaker in the assembly whereas the other is a writer on events that took place there. Thus Pericles confronts imperatives and constraints Thucydides does not. As an actor in history he experiences events as a mixture of that which is amenable to reason and that which is impervious to it; for a writer of history, however, nothing is really random. This does not mean that Pericles is helpless in the face of chance or that Thucydides never admits his bafflement. What is does mean is that the historian provides an order of intelligibility and consistency greater than anything possible for a political actor, even one as theoretical as Pericles.

Yet the *History* does not simply subsume incidents under a general rule. Instead, like tragedy, it shows us and engenders in us a process of reflection and (self-)discovery through a persistent attention to and a (re-)interpretation of particular incidents and patterns of language. Although Thu-

[45] Adam Parry, "Thucydides' Historical Perspective," *Yale Classical Studies* 22 (1972): 60.

[46] I explore the dialectic between these in my "The Battle of Salamis and the Origins of Political Theory."

cydides is sometimes distant from the self-understandings of his compatriots,[47] he does not so much lead us on a Platonic path upward as invite us to burrow down into the depths of the particular, finding connections that permit us to see more clearly, recognize more fully, and describe more richly.[48] By combining this burrowing with a horizontal drawing of connections in ways that make every horizontal link contribute to the depth of our view of the particular, and every new depth create horizontal links, Thucydides establishes a web of meaning that resists both reduction and reification. At the same time, he provides a sense in which his idea of theory derives from the idea of power that characterized democratic Athens. The Athenians and Thucydides were, of course, aware of vertical power, power over another. But he and they also recognized that their city depended upon a notion of horizontal power that presupposed mutual empowerment, power to do or accomplish, power for some collective end. It is the power engendered by these connections that reappears in Thucydides' theory (or method).

Like tragedy, too, Thucydides is able to present the doubleness of action. I argued in chapter 2 that, as spectators in the theater, the audience was omniscient, even when, as in the *Oedipus Tyrannos*, part of the point was the mysteriousness of the gods and nature. But as actors outside the theater, they were, like the actors they had seen on stage, limited in their knowledge and capabilities. Similarly, Thucydides had, in Lowell Edmunds' words, a remarkable "ability to maintain the strictest standards of historiography and at the same time to represent history from the point of view of the actors." That is why the work is such a "marvelous combination of the intellectually intelligible and the dramatically immediate."[49] In considering how, why, and for whom the *History* is useful, the ways in which it is a possession for all time, and Thucydides' theoretical power, we need to take account of his affinities with Pericles and the differences of his dual perspective as actor and analyst, and of the way the intellectual and dramatic elements yield a whole greater then the parts. First the affinities.

[47] I think Loraux, Edmunds, and Lloyd-Jones right to emphasize the archaic elements in Thucydides' explicit commitments (see nn. 13 and 52). But what the *History* itself does is very unarchaic. By the way he construes Athenian practices, Thucydides not only makes them clearer and more explicit, he breaks the bonds of familiarity and givenness that typically tie citizens to them and to each other. He looses the unreflective moorings of meaning, forcing meaning to appear contingent, relative, and questionable. This is another way of stating the affinity between "Athenianism" and *stasis*.

[48] I have used Nussbaum's discussion of choral lyric in Sophocles for what are definitely my own purposes (see *The Fragility of Goodness: Luck and Ethics in Greek Tragedy and Philosophy* (Cambridge: Cambridge University Press, 1986), p. 69.

[49] Lowell Edmunds, *Chance and Intelligence in Thucydides* (Cambridge, Mass.: Harvard University Press, 1975), p. 147.

Pericles and Thucydides admire and exemplify similar qualities of mind and character. Both analyze power undistracted by adornment, myth, exaggeration, or momentary passion. Each is steadfast in the face of *paralogoi*, refusing to yield to the pressures of extant reality. Pericles holds the same conception of things despite the changing conditions, and so does Thucydides. As Thucydides reveals for his reader the truest occasion of the war unspoken or unknown by the protagonists, Pericles makes manifest to his fellow citizens the unnamed or unrecognized context of their action. The same conceptual boldness present in Pericles' proposal that the Athenians think of themselves as an island is present in Thucydides' vision of the Peloponnesian War as a single war, where his contemporaries saw it as a series of discrete battles or two wars.

The political leader's effort to sustain Athenian unity against the centrifugal forces of democratic culture and war finds resonance in Thucydides' efforts to contain the frantic, unremitting, and far-flung action of the war within the confines of a single story. John Finley describes Thucydides' style as a confrontation between things and ideas so vivid and vital that they nearly burst the integrating concepts that make them a whole. By presenting ideas struggling with each other in human fashion, Thucydides "brings to theory the vitality of action," and, I would add, Pericles brings a theoretical sensibility to action.[50] Similarly, Pericles' attempt to restore Athenian confidence when his compatriots have lost hope, and inspire them with fear when they become unreasonably confident, finds a parallel in Thucydides' juxtaposition of the Archaeology's optimistic presentation of man's progress toward ever-greater accomplishment and mastery with the pessimistic implications of Corcyra where men, having lost control, go mad.

But the implications of Corcyra are more and even worse than that. The problem is not merely the difficulty of learning from the past, but that things get worse when we *do* learn from it. Knowledge of the *stasis* at Corcyra intensified later brutality and refined subsequent excesses. The idea that knowing the recurrence of events will enable us to draw useful inferences about the future is replaced by a more ominous suggestion: "The past will recur, but that recurrence has become a threat not a promise."[51] The foreknowledge that history and the *History* make possible is

---

[50] The quote is from John Finley's *Four Stages*, p. 73. Edmunds (*Chance and Intelligence*, p. 35) argues that Pericles' speeches have a "double nature. On the one hand, they arise from particular occasions and make points bearing on particular, concrete situations; on the other hand, they reflect a transpolitical [what I would call a theoretical] perspective." My elaboration of this point and Edmunds's argument can be found in my "Creatures of a Day: Thought and Action in Thucydides," in *Political Theory and Praxis: New Perspectives*, ed. Terence Ball (Minneapolis: University of Minnesota Press, 1977), pp. 28–56.

[51] Connors, *Thucydides*, p. 104.

not rational prediction and control but the premonition of escalating misery and loss.

Several scholars emphasize Thucydides' pessimism against Periclean rationalism.[52] They have described the *History*'s movement as one from glory to pathos, victory to victimization, the funeral oration to the quarries at Syracuse, foresight and control to illusion and vulnerability to "grand impersonal forces in which the scale of events and the measure of suffering are far beyond the limits of human comprehension and endurance."[53] There are no gods sustaining balance or just retribution, no cosmos of recompense and recovery, as Nicias, for one, foolishly believed there to be. In these terms, Thucydides' theoretical power (or his renunciation of the possibility of such power)[54] consists in presenting a structure of loss only when all there is to lose has been lost.[55] The usefulness of the *History* and its quality for all time has nothing to do with benefiting contemporaries or assisting future statesmen who might alter the world. It is written for men of some later time who, after reading it, will be better able to understand the destruction of their own time. Thus the message is that there is no message beyond there being none; the point of human reason is to show the limits of reason.

I think this view exaggerates Pericles' optimism and Thucydides' pessimism, wrongly poses the question of usefulness, and underestimates Thucydides' claims for his work and so his theoretical power.

At a number of points Pericles demonstrates his awareness of the fragility of historical conditions that sustain human power. He knows well

[52] The most elaborate and ingenious case for Thucydides' pessimism remains that of H. P. Stahl in *Thucydides: Die Stellung des Menschen im geschichtlicken Prozess*, Zemata 40 (Munich: C. H. Beck Verlag, 1966). His argument has been criticized by Pouncey—see, especially *Necessities of War*, pp. 168–69, n. 18—and by Jacqueline de Romilly in her "L'optimisme de Thucydide," *Revue des études grecques* 78 [1965]: 557–75, and "L'utilité de l'histoire selon Thucydide," 39–81. A more recent work that takes account of de Romilly's criticisms and presents a more balanced but still pessimistic Thucydides is Connor's *Thucydides*. Lowell Edmunds, in "Thucydides' Ethics as Reflected in the Description of Stasis," *Harvard Studies in Classical Philosophy* 79 (1975): 73–92, makes a case for Thucydides' pessimism being "archaic," as does Hugh Lloyd Jones, *The Justice of Zeus* (Berkeley and Los Angeles: University of California Press, 1971), pp. 137–41.

[53] Connor, *Thucydides*, p. 104.

[54] Several authors insist Thucydides is not a political theorist. Thus Edmunds ("Thucydides' Ethics," p. 79): "Thucydides was not a political theorist, and he was not interested in political constitutions as such but as reflections of ethical attitudes." Connor ends his book by criticizing those who "are not content with the limits of history as a form of literature and as a mode of thought." Such people will always be dissatisfied with such restraint and "either reject Thucydides; work or seek to impose upon it grander construction" (*Thucydides*, p. 250). It seems to me both arguments beg the question.

[55] Parry, in "Thucydides' Historical Perspective," speaks of this with power and eloquence.

enough how easily men are seduced by success and prone to exaggerate their intelligence, how especially his compatriots are tempted by *pleonexia*, and that destructive forces eventually confound even the greatest minds and collective achievements. Several times, most notably in his final speech, Pericles talks about his city's mortality.[56] What matters to him is less the fact of mortality than what Athens achieves during its life and how it is remembered after its physical demise. Corruption is inevitable, but simply to accept such inevitability is self-fulfilling.[57]

As Periclean optimism should not be exaggerated, neither should Thucydidean pessimism. It is true that one indication of the war's greatness is the great suffering it brings. But the *History*'s lasting impression is more complex and ambivalent. In part, that is because, like Oedipus, the Athenians endured even after the Sicilian disaster. But, in part, that is because for better or worse the vision of the funeral oration retains some of its luminescence even after Mytilene, Melos, and Syracuse. Even for those unimpressed by the oration's patriotism, call to glory and sacrifice, or conception of power, and despite the fact that what follows it immediately (the plague) and subsequently gives us pause, Pericles' eloquence is no more silenced by late voices than the strangled speech of the *Agamemnon* is by the *Eumenides*. This is complicated by the fact that the *History* is itself part of Athenian power and an instance of the qualities Pericles extols. Indeed, the grandeur of his vision intensifies the tragic sense of loss. The eloquence of the speech (which is also Thucydides' eloquence) is itself part a monument that has indeed become a possession for all time. Here is Adam Parry: "Because Athens under Pericles remains an ineffaceable image in the mind the city is truly invincible, and to fix this image is precisely the purpose of Thucydides' account."[58]

Both this task of commemorating great deeds and the disparagement of rivals are traditional bardic aims.[59] Yet Thucydides regards his *History*

[56] *Panta gar pephyke kai elassousthai* (Thuc. 2.64.3). The only recompense for such futility is immortal fame. As a *ktēma es aiei*, Thucydides' work is not subject to the same law of decay, although its status as a possession for all time owes much to the city which does decay (see Edmunds, *Chance and Intelligence*, pp. 205–6).

[57] Jacqueline de Romilly, *Thucydides and the Athenian Empire*, trans. P. Thody (Oxford: Blackwell, 1963), shows how this happens with the Athenian understanding of empire. By demonstrating how the belief that one's action is random is (partly) self-fulfilling. Thucydides suggests why it is never appropriate to passively accept one's fate. I think this is indirect evidence against the idea that he is an intellectual remote from politics.

[58] Parry, "Thucydides' Historical Perspective," p. 61.

[59] Many of his explicit judgments are traditional as well. That is clearest at Corcyra where those traditions are in jeopardy. Thucydides objects to the replacement of traditional valuations by new ones that change the nature of the world as well as the language used to "describe" that world; on this, see Loraux, "Thucydides et la sedition dans les mots." In the *Oresteia*, the validity and efficacy of language is guaranteed by what George B. Walsh calls "magic homeopathic relationships to the things of the world" (*The Varieties of Enchant-*

as new.[60] In what sense is he right to do so? How does that newness substantiate his claim that his work, unlike the self-serving exaggerations of his competitors and uncritical mythologizing of his predecessor, is useful or profitable (*ophelima*) for all time? How, when, and for whom is it useful? Did he believe "that the historian's hindsight could become a statesmen's foresight and that his work would influence the future course of history?"[61]

His work is a possession for all time because of the object it studies and the method used to study it. The object is the unprecedented power and suffering of the Peloponnesian War. The greatness of Athens, together with the scope of ferocity of the conflict, reveals previously obscure truths about politics, morality, violence, and justice. The method of study is a form of analysis that emphasizes ascertainable facts (which include the motives and impulses of actors), rigor, explicit statements of evidence, and rational justification. This is contrary to those who, contemptuous of truth, care only for entertaining their contemporaries with some prize essay (*agōnisma*) adorned by fabulous stories (*mythōdes*) in hopes of receiving immediate applause rather than the recognition and respect of those in the future who wish to be edified. So, even as Thucydides performs the traditional bardic task of memorializing great deeds which will call forth similar deeds in the future,[62] he criticizes the particular memories people have of the past and the idea of memory they have now. Under the impact of war, immediate ambition, and present emotion, memory is beset by distortion or purposely manipulated. And so, one way his *His-*

ment [Chapel Hill: University of North Carolina Press, 1984], p. 80). This means that verbal ambiguity is analogous to the ambivalence of things and that because words possess the nature and structure of things, things are apprehended through words directly. Although Thucydides does not fully subscribe to this view of language, he is close enough to it for us to get a sense of what it meant to him for words to lose their meaning.

[60] Thucydides' methodological structures are less modern than they seem. When he dismisses the mythical and fabulous, he is actually rejecting the extravagant exaggerations chosen by the poets to make their work attractive. What he gets by pruning away the various unattested and improbable accretions is not facts but "mutilated legend." Cornford, *Thucydides Mythistoricus*, p. 133. See also the remarks by Connor in his "Narrative Discourse in Thucydides," p. 7.

[61] The question is asked by Lowell Edmunds (*Chance and Intelligence*, p. 146). His answer is that usefulness is "qualified by its reference to deeds as distinct from speeches, and the possibly unpleasurable factuality of the narration of the deeds; by the expectations of a limited audience; by the nonpractical character of the usefulness; and by the distinction between events of human and of non-human origin" (p. 152).

[62] In this, I disagree with the more austere interpretations of usefulness (partly illustrated by Edmunds in the previous footnote). In part it is a matter of whether you think the *History*'s message is "glory is the only thing" or "the suffering is too much." For all the suffering, I think Thucydides regards glory as an essential aim and achievement of any people who wish to be historical. In these terms Athenian glory is an exemplar rather than an object lesson.

tory is useful is to reveal this fact while offering a new standard of accuracy.[63]

As I suggested before, while that standard owes much to Pericles, it cannot owe everything to him. However much Pericles' speeches offer theoretical comments on power and mortality, he is in the assembly trying to persuade a present audience whereas Thucydides is outside it seeking to persuade a future one. Various political leaders try to succeed in convincing their compatriots to adopt a certain policy; Thucydides shows us how and why they succeeded or failed. They are judged by their audience of fellow citizens. Thucydides judges both them and their audience.[64] A great leader like Pericles or Hermocrates says what the particular occasion demands; Thucydides says what the whole occasion demands. In this regard his speech is the ideal by which all others are measured.

Because he is neither a political leader dependent on the political approval of an assembly nor a singer, tragedian, or poet who must provide fabulous embellishments to win the patronage and applause of his audience, Thucydides can afford to put accuracy above all else. That commitment to truth is one reason why his work will give little pleasure to the reader. It is also why his work is a possession for all time and the basis for his claim to authority.

Truth is unpalatable, however useful it may be, because it interferes with our pleasures and our politics and because the truth, at least the truth of this work, is so unsettling. Like the *Oedipus*, where every riddle solved leaves a larger one unresolved, the experience this text offers us is of trying repeatedly to make sense of its events, first in one way, then another, but never wholly succeeding. By constructing a text that replicates the difficulties for the reader that he faced as an historian describing and making sense of his real world, Thucydides presents for us the problem of trying to reconstitute and comprehend collective experience.[65]

To insist on accuracy and to repudiate an immediate audience is to claim an independence of party or faction. If Thucydides is writing for anonymous readers of future generations, then he is neutral regarding those of his generation. However personal or Athenian his work, however much he may have had ties to the aristocratic class at Athens, there is a sense in which he is absent from his discourse. Or to put it more accurately, he is trying to sustain conditions within the text that makes discourse outside it possible, whether that discourse is among his readers

[63] Again, what Thucydides means by accuracy is a "highly selective inquiry into some aspects of the past" as a demonstration piece (*epideixis*) to show what he can do with the recent past and present. (See Connor's "Narrative Discourse in Thucydides," p. 7.)

[64] See the discussion in MacLeod, "Rhetoric and History," in his *Collected Essays* (Oxford: Clarendon Press, 1983), p. 69.

[65] White, *When Words Lose Their Meaning*, p. 87. Connor's interpretation is similar.

or future actors. In this sense he is trying to repair, in the context of his work, the frayed, moral discourse that shapes the initial debate between Corinth and Corcyra, is barely present at Mytilene and Plataea, and has disappeared by the time of the civil war at Melos.

Thucydides can be so independent because his *History* is a written work with a life of its own and an audience of its own constitution (which is not the same as an audience purposely constructed). As a written "text" it makes permanent a process that is otherwise ephemeral and constitutes a public through the multiplication of readings, changing what is essentially private (the writing of the work) into something public. But this public is, as I have noted, necessarily composed of nameless, individual partners located in disparate cultural contexts. Reading "the" text offers each of them an imaginary experience of cultural reconstitution[66] which might, under certain circumstances, contribute to political reconstitution—which is another way of saying that the community formed between writer and reader retains many of the political attributes no longer possible in times of corruption and civil war. I will come back to this point later.

The claim that Thucydides' *History* provides such a political teaching is denied especially, but not only, by his "pessimistic" interpreters. Most of them would, I think, agree with John R. Grant who quotes W.R.M. Lamb that Thucydides "was himself a man of action who turned his brain and hand to writing," only to reverse the point by claiming that the historian "was himself an intellectual who briefly turned his brain and hand to playing the man of action."[67] Most go on to argue that Thucydides did not write for future statesmen in the belief that they could apply the lessons of the *History* to their own situation, but sought to impart knowledge for its own sake.

There is some truth to this argument, but it is ultimately misleading. It is true that Thucydides does not offer maxims that assure statesmen personal success or success in precluding corruption and *stasis*. It is misleading because by exaggerating Thucydides' pessimism, positing an opposition between the application of knowledge and knowledge for its own sake (which owes more to present academic fashion than Athenian practices), and slighting the importance of historical context for the *History*, it narrows the claims Thucydides makes for his work's usefulness and minimizes its theoretical power.

It is not the case that we can never learn from the past. Some people in

[66] Up to this point I agree with White. I am not sure he would agree with the argument that follows.

[67] "Toward Knowing Thucydides," *Phoenix* 79 (1974): 91. Grant goes on to argue that Thucydides' election as general was due to family connections rather than proven competence.

some situations can, and some cannot. Sometimes those lessons can help our understanding and so how we speak and act in public; sometimes they cannot. Thus, one of the things we can learn from the past is when learning from the past is possible and useful and when it is not. There are certain times and places, such as Athens under Pericles, when human beings can, if not comprehend, predict, and control events, at least control the consequences of events they cannot predict. It may even be that such times are extremely rare. But the fact that even in those times men eventually lost control does not mean they lacked some control before, or that they were wrong or foolish to strive for it, or that we can avoid doing so if we wish to be a historical people. The tragedy, then, is not that the truth is never useful, but that it is sometimes futile.[68]

Thucydides uses his reason to show us why the reasoning of others failed. This does not yield programmatic advice, but it does bring insight. Although it does not mandate any particular decision, it does make manifest the preconditions necessary for political deliberation in general. And, though it does not provide us with rules to be applied, it does give us a form of political knowledge that respects, even recapitulates, the paradoxes and "perspectivism" of political life. Thucydides deprives us of any firm resolution about the usefulness of his work, just as he never resolves the tensions between rationalism and pessimism and the glory of power and the enormity of suffering power brings in its wake. In this, as in other respects, he is imitating the tragedians. It is tragedy that provides an example of political usefulness that is neither narrowly utilitarian nor merely aesthetic. Political and theoretical in nature, tragedy offered its audience of democratic citizens an opportunity to engage in the reflections on the human condition as a context for deliberation in the assembly.

In the end, the opposition between Thucydides, the intellectual, and Thucydides, the activist, begs the question for some of the same reasons that the contrast between the *History*'s teachings as directly applicable knowledge, or knowledge for its own sake, is misleading. For one thing, the opposition obscures the way Thucydides' political theory presents the views of actors and inquirer at once. For another thing, I remain unconvinced that Thucydides ever conceived of the possibility of political knowledge divorced from the exercise of personal ambition and civic responsibility. I am convinced that even in exile he "retained the perceptions and intuitions of one who, from the inside, knows and cares about the complexities of democratic politics"[69] (which is not to say he is en-

[68] That is the concluding phrase of MacLeod's "Reason and Necessity: Thucydides III 9–13, 37–48," in his *Collected Essays*, p. 77.

[69] Carolyn Dewald, "Practical Knowledge and the Historian's Role in Herodotus and Thucydides," in *The Greek Historians: Literature and History*, pp. 56, 62. Dewald con-

199

amored of them). In this regard it may be worth recalling Pericles' dismissal of those who refuse to participate in political life as not unambitious but useless (2.40.2).

But the question then becomes: What happens to such knowledge when one is unable to exercise civic responsibility either in the Assembly or the theater because both have become irremediably corrupt? On what terms is participation possible when the world is Corcyra? Is it not the joint failure of Athenian leaders and demos to stem *stasis* and corruption that encourages the autonomy of a theoretical impulse that has so far been located within the political realm? At a minimum, Thucydides must protect the language of the text from linguistic dismemberment, moral collapse, and political corruption his text portrays.

The *History*'s response is twofold: it offers the reader membership in a community of interpreters, and it retains an implicit idea of political community within the structure of its theory. In these terms, Thucydides' speech contains the speeches of others, thereby creating a whole in which each becomes part of a dialogue and debate with all the others. Thus the work is a unity that sustains the plurality *stasis* destroys in ways the *Bacchae* does not. Within its confines, leaders, cities, motives, impulses, and points of view speak to each other in ways that clarify the nature of action and thought. While it is a unity that excludes many and much (as a comparison with tragedy indicates), it is neither authoritarian nor tyrannical. An example and final point makes this clear.

As W. Robert Connor demonstrates in his analysis of book 8,[70] the political dissolution at Athens is paralleled by a change in the *History*'s narrative style. Torn by factions, the city is no longer a single political unity. It is physically divided between the military forces on Samos, who claim to be the true city, and the oligarchs in Athens, who are themselves split into the more extreme and more moderate factions. Racked by self-serving rivalries for preeminence, individual actors appear with momentary prominence only to disappear into disfavor, obscurity, or death. The literary analogue to this civic disintegration, moral atomism, and loss of control is the decomposition of the units and techniques upon which much of the earlier *History* is built. Now Thucydides is less an omniscient narrator confident in his assessment of motives and strategies than like a fellow inquirer trying to make sense of the decay he sees around him. Yet, even in this meditative mood, it is his voice that makes this disintegration vivid, visible, and intelligible. It is through his still-predominant but not dominating speech that we are helped in our efforts to make sense of

---

trasts the presence of savants, such as Solon in Herodotus, with their absence in Thucydides and concludes that Thucydides had no such figures because he was part of a democratic polity in which everyone was a political actor.

[70] In his *Thucydides*, pp. 214–17.

political, moral, and linguistic corruption. His is the last voice we hear, but it is less that of Cleon, the erstwhile tyrant, than it is of Socrates, the erstwhile philosopher.

I do not mean to exaggerate. The *History* points to, but does not establish, either in its confines or by its existence, a separation between theoretical life and practical life.

"With all his rationalism," Lowell Edmunds writes, "Thucydides is equally on the side of the active life, no matter what its disappointments, and in the active life the prize is not truth, though there may be truth, but immortality."[71]

[71] Lowell Edmunds, *Chance and Intelligence*, pp. 213–14.

SEVEN

Plato's *Apology of Socrates:*
Political Identity and
Political Philosophy

THE *Apology* and *Crito* display and discuss who Socrates is[1] as a citizen of Athens and as one who practices a way of life different from that of his compatriots. In both dialogues he explores and demonstrates what it is that unites him with and distinguishes him from them. They repeatedly misidentify him as a sophist, rhetorician, *physiologos*, or proto-oligarch. For whatever reasons, what he says and does cannot be easily assimilated to the normal paradigms of speech and action available to them. By identifying himself Socrates can make clear what it is that sets him apart in terms of what he shares. The effort is as much for himself as for his fellow Athenians, as much an enterprise in defining Athenian politics as it is a way of life we have come to call philosophic.

Issues about who one is, about origins and exile, membership and dis-membership are familiar themes. So too is a story about a man whose search for knowledge is simultaneously self-discovery. The *Oedipus Tyrannos* as well as the *Apology* depict men who are engaged in a quest that is an education both about the character of what is sought and of the character seeking it. Apollo goads both Socrates and Oedipus into recognizing who they are as mortals and members of particular communities, a Theban king and son of Laius and Jocasta, a philosopher and son of Athens. In addition, dialogue and play are about being a stranger where one most belongs. Finally both play and dialogue force us to ask how much we are in control of the identity we come to have. In chapter 4 I argued that the sphinx's question is not only What is man? but also Can man be defined by men? The answer was that we are partial beings subject to forces we cannot fully control, riddles to ourselves and others but that in part because of tragedy, we are also actors capable of collective understanding and power. What Sophoclean tragedy especially

---

[1] It is also Plato's effort to define Socrates. Even in these early more "historical" dialogues Socrates is a character in a drama written by Plato. On the historicity of the *Apology* and *Crito*, see W.K.C. Guthrie, A *History of Greek Philosophy*, vol. 4 (Cambridge: Cambridge University Press, 1975), chap. 4; and R. Hackforth, *The Composition of Plato's Apology* (Cambridge: Cambridge University Press, 1933).

makes clear is that acknowledgment of partiality is a precondition for understanding and power, or in Socratic terms, that ignorance is the foundation of knowledge.[2]

In chapter 4 I considered Vernant's claim that questions of identity first arose because the Greeks had become aware of a need to choose between the values of an archaic tribal past and the new political-judicial realities of the city-state. Caught between these two points, the new subject had a double consciousness and a feeling of being divided against himself. A somewhat similar statement can be made about Socrates' contemporaries.

But now the "choices" are different. One choice is between a corrupt "classical" past and regeneration of the inadequate prevalent discourses, practices and institutions according to the best ideals of that past as criticized by philosophy. The nature of this choice is made clear in the *Apology*. Not only is Socrates critical of Athenian democracy and its opponents, he specifically criticizes the tragedians (who are unable to render an account of the things they say),[3] the Assembly (in which men cannot speak honestly), the Council (in which Socrates stood alone against illegally punishing the admirals), and the law courts (in which he says he is a stranger only to then mimic the standard defense speeches made there).

A second choice is between citizenship and the soul, a choice made starker if regeneration fails. Such a choice means that for all the parallels between Oedipus and Socrates, the question of identity has come to have a more theoretical and inward dimension. This is not to ignore what I argued earlier—that tragedy was a "theoretical" political institution and "the epistemological form par excellence," charting a path from ignorance to knowledge, deception to revelation, misunderstanding to recognition.[4] It is to indicate that we are now confronting a new axis of the self

---

[2] Socrates explicitly rejects what Sophocles seems to endorse—that the gods allot men fates disproportionate to their actions, a disproportion he emphasizes by describing his *daimon* in pointed contrast to the way Oedipus defines his. Moreover, Crito indicates that Socrates has self-consciously chosen not only his life but the circumstances of his death. (See N. A. Greenberg, "Socrates' Choice in the Crito," *Harvard Studies in Classical Philology* 70 [1965]: 45–82; and Xenophon, *Memorabilia* 4.4.) Finally, though Oedipus does attain self-knowledge it is only at the end and after horrendous deeds and suffering for which he must be exiled. Although Socrates too discovers who he is in the course of his trial (in the largest sense) and undergoes suffering of a kind, he has committed no deed to bring a plague upon the city and rejects exile.

[3] Because the poets are unable to give an account of their views and life, the things they say that are of value must come to them by nature (*phusei*) or divine inspiration (*enthousiazontes*) rather than by wisdom (*sophia*). Like the politicians (and artisans) the poets exaggerate the importance and range of their knowledge and so Socrates leaves their company convinced that he is superior to them in the same respects in which he was to public men (22bc).

[4] "The characters act out and live through the consequences of having clung to a partial

related problematically to household *and* city and that the various paths offered may not, in the end, lead to the same place.

In the *Oresteia* the action takes place on two levels, divine and human, which are integrated (or reintegrated) at the trilogy's end. In the *Oedipus Tyrannos* the protagonist lives a double life, which becomes one only at the end. In the *Bacchae* the multiple visions in and of the play are harshly ordered by Dionysus's concluding commands. In all three instances the human and the divine worlds become one. In the *Apology* (and *Crito*) the double vision is political and philosophic and it is uncertain whether or how these visions can become unified in a way that respects the integrity and necessity of each. I do not think the *Apology, Crito,* or *Republic* answer this question definitively. Indeed the projected estrangement of philosophy and Socrates from politics and Athens makes these dialogues tragic.

James Redfield argues that the Athenians' refusal to accept Socrates was a "catastrophic failure which is the central fact of Athenian history."[5] It is true that by killing a man who seeks to regenerate their now corrupting traditions and institutions the Athenians are eliminating the possibility of moral renewal (or so Plato would have us believe). Recalling Zeitlin, we might call this a "Theban" act insofar as Thebes is incapable of generating new structures or progeny.

But if Redfield means that Athens lost more by rejecting Socrates than philosophy lost by not finding a home in Athens, then he has missed the full extent of the catastrophe. For the *Apology* is a tragedy of philosophy as well as politics or, more exactly, of the failed relationship between them. In the *Oresteia* each side, force and principle, required the reciprocating presence of the other to create a whole that gives meaning and place to both. The absence of such reciprocity means the presence of injustice. Similarly the opposition between Socrates and Athens, mind and action, threatens to leave the city morally impoverished and political philosophy, as described by Socrates in the *Apology*, impossible. In the *Oedipus Tyrannos*, Oedipus is unable to see himself in terms of the abstract answer he gives the sphinx because abstract knowledge obscures particular ignorance. A similar fate awaits philosophy disconnected from politics. Deprived of place and purpose within the city, philosophy will develop nonpolitical aims, nondialogical forms and forums far from the

---

single view of the world and themselves" (Froma Zeitlin, "Playing the Other: Theater, Theatricality, and the Feminine in Greek Drama," *Representations* 11 [Summer 1985]: 72). Although the path for the audience in the theater is more clearly marked than for the actors on stage, what the spectators learn from the chorale ode in Antigone, the misplaced confidence of a Clytaemnestra or Agamemnon, the certainty of an Oedipus, or the rashness of a Pentheus is the Socratic dictum that ignorance is the ground of knowledge.

5 "A Lecture on Plato's Apology," *Journal of General Education* 15 (1965): 107.

PLATO'S APOLOGY OF SOCRATES

agora. Without location, philosophy elaborates the "ontological" home-lessness envisioned by the chorus in *Antigone*, lived by Oedipus, and dramatized in the last scene of the *Bacchae*.

As this implies, the *Apology* and *Crito* are about the identity of Athens and politics as well as of Socrates and philosophy. To read them this way suggests the possibility of interpreting Socratic philosophy as an attempt to reintegrate civic and individual life by reestablishing the preconditions for political deliberation and moral discourse. This involves freeing men from preoccupation with the moment, the blandishments of wealth, the temptation of domination and from *pleonexia*. It also means rescuing justice from its subordination to interest, morality from might, and restoring linguistic coherence. This reintegration is in part continuous with the efforts of Thucydides' Pericles, in part a critique of both Periclean political leadership and Thucydidean political theory.[6]

Socrates' statesmanship is an extension of Pericles' effort to rally his compatriots after the onslaught of the plague. The devastation wrought by what was unforeseen and uncontrollable permanently shattered the dedication and vision presented and present in the funeral oration. Although Thucydides' Pericles is able to quiet the preoccupation with private affliction and rally his fellow citizens to further effort, the unity he instills is instrumental and tenuous. Instead of resting on some positive vision of individual and collective virtue, it relies on fear and self-interest. Confronting Pericles' failure, Socrates seeks to instill such virtue in individual citizens outside the assembly (or theater). That is the only way to practice the true art of politics in the present circumstances[7]—and the only hope for democracy.[8]

An example of this art is the way Socrates turns the accusations leveled against him against his accusers by claiming that he is the one true patriot, the one genuinely pious man, and the one true Athenian. While his accus-

---

[6] That it is both is unsurprising since Socrates is as Athenian as (Knox's) Oedipus. In the *Republic* Socrates becomes more of a character in Plato's drama than a historical figure and so a fourth figure, Plato, enters the equation. But I agree with Jaeger than when Plato wrote the earliest dialogues, "he knew the whole of which it was to be a part. The entelechy of the *Republic* can be quite clearly traced in the early dialogues." "It would be a serious mistake," he concludes, "to believe that, when he wrote these little intellectual dramas, Plato's spiritual range was not broader than their foreground" (*Paideia*, [New York: Oxford University Press, 1939–45], 2:96). George Klosko has recently restated Jaeger's argument in *The Development of Plato's Political Theory* (New York and London: Methuen, 1986), chap. 2.

[7] *Gorgias*, 521e. Socrates mentions one other man who practiced the art of politics: Aristeides the Just.

[8] I. F. Stone, and Neal Wood and Ellen Wood, "Socrates and Democracy: A Reply to Gregory Vlastos," *Political Theory* 14, no. 1 (February 1986): 55-82 do not think Socrates is a democrat, whereas John Wallach, "Socratic Citizenship" *History of Political Theory* 9, no. 3 (1988): 393–413, does not think he has an art of politics.

ers and erstwhile judges expect him to cower before them like a slave, he (like Pericles), is steadfast and insists on acting like a free man, worthy of the courage displayed by their ancestors. Whereas they would insist on uncritical loyalty, he defends a critical patriotism worthy of democratic citizens. It is his accusers, not he, who have forgotten and misunderstood the noblest possibilities embedded in their practices and institutions. In reminding his fellow citizens by precept and example of what they had been, now were, and ought to become, Socrates imitates Thucydides' Pericles in the funeral oration.[9]

Despite these and other continuities and precedents, Socrates (and Plato) regard Pericles and Periclean Athens as deeply flawed. It was Pericles after all who uprooted his fellow citizens from their land, thereby eroding those limits of place and location that inhibit *pleonexia*. And it was Pericles' own lack of virtue, or his failure to teach what virtue he had to his successors, that makes him responsible for the corruption that followed his death.[10] Then there is the funeral oration. The problem with it is not only that its sustaining vision was eroded by plague, but that the substance of that vision was, to Socrates, faulty to begin with. Thus Socrates both chastises his fellow citizens for not living up to their own ideals while subjecting those ideals to critique and reinterpretation in ways that construct an alternative vision of political thought and action. Because Socrates' own life and death are central to that vision, *aretē* becomes detached from the heroic ethic and reassigned to philosophical activity. Then being great becomes being good, courage becomes the willingness to suffer injustice rather than commit it, and the purpose of life is not to conquer Syracuse, avenge one's friends, build an empire, or leave monuments for good or ill, but to conquer tyrannical impulses, harm no one, build a just city, and leave paradigms of right action. In this elaborately moralized heroism, justice is not the interest of the strong or of the weaker either. It is not really an interest at all, except in the sense that what we do to others we also do to ourselves.[11]

If the city is already corrupt under Pericles then Pericles can hardly be

[9] Socrates' efforts to eliminate political corruption are an extension of Thucydides' concerns. One could say that his (or Plato's) philosophy emerges in the *Republic* as a search to discover certain theoretical and practical grounds for "those common laws to which all alike can look for salvation in adversity." This line, which concludes Thucydides' analysis of the *stasis* at Corcyra, anticipates the later Melian admonishment that the Athenians ought "not to destroy our common good [*koinon agathon*], the privilege of being allowed to invoke what is fair and right in times of extreme peril" (3.84, and 5.90).

[10] This is a dangerous argument that was turned against Socrates. It is an ironic one too, given the close affiliations Socrates and Pericles had with Alcibiades.

[11] Thucydides implies this when he juxtaposed the might-makes-right doctrine propounded by the Athenians at Melos with the factionalism demonstrated by the debate over Sicily.

a measure of political leadership. And if Pericles was Thucydides' intellectual predecessor, then Thucydidean political theory cannot be a measure for Socratic political philosophy either. But in what sense is Socrates a measure of political leadership and his philosophy "political" at all?[12] Are there more than casual or tendentious parallels between Socrates' relationship to his circle[13] or fellow citizens and the tragedian's relationship to his audience in the theater or Pericles to the people in the Assembly? Did Socrates understand his vocation as an augmentation of a distinctively critical Athenian tradition that included tragedy, Pericles, and Thucydides? Was he, as I have implied, "appealing from convention and tradition to the principle of reason they reflect and imperfectly embody?"[14]

If Socrates was democratic and political, it was in highly unconventional ways. He shunned official positions, rejected speaking in the Assembly, claimed to be a stranger to the law courts, numbered oligarchs among his friends, and made disparaging remarks about "the many." The question is whether his refusal to observe conventional forms of where and how politics should occur makes him antipolitical and whether his criticisms of Athenian democracy make him antidemocratic.

Certainly Socrates does not accept the dictates of institutional power as a standard of justice and action. But he never suggests that these institutions be abolished or made more oligarchic.[15] More than that, Socrates' conception of who is "political" was, like the rituals associated with trag-edy, more inclusive than other "democratic" institutions. Here is Helene Foley on Euripidean tragedy: "Since all members of the society participate in ritual, if not in political life, through ritual he can raise issues that touch the society as a whole, not simply the narrow political sphere."[16] Here is Gregory Vlastos on Socrates: "Should I say that the conception of that art which Plato ascribes to Socrates is *demo*cratic" in the sense

---

[12] "From its birth the philosophy was to find itself in an ambiguous position. In its inspiration and its development it was related to both the initiations into the mysteries and the disputations of the agora; it wavered between the sense of secrecy peculiar to the cults and the public argument that characterized political activity"; see (Jean-Pierre Vernant, *The Origins of Greek Thought* (Ithaca, N.Y.: Cornell University Press, 1987), p. 59. One can see how Socrates further complicated an already complex situation, and why it was that his accusers were misled in their understanding of what he was doing. (Cf. *Symposium*, 203a–c, where the philosopher is described as being in between what is divine and human. Although he has an intense desire to know the truth, he never acquires such knowledge as a permanent possession.)

[13] One original meaning of polis was a circle formed when an assembly was called.

[14] Gary Frank Reed, "Berlin and the Division of Liberty," *Political Theory* 8, no. 3 (August 1980): 375.

[15] See Vlastos, "The Historical Socrates and Athenian Democracy," *Political Theory* 11, no. 4 (1983): 511–12, and Wallach, "Socratic Citizenship," p. 407.

[16] *Ritual Irony: Poetry and Sacrifice in Euripedes* (Ithaca, N.Y.: Cornell University Press, 1985), p. 256 and passim.

that "it belongs to the demos? No, for that would *under*state its scope; it is for every person, including all those who did not belong to the Athenian demos—aliens no less than citizens, slaves no less than freemen, women no less than men."[17] Because one could never know beforehand who had or could learn the political art, so one could not, *pace* Bloom, assume the rich, powerful, or better "educated" were one's potential interlocutors.

If one must characterize Socratic politics, one might call it democratically aristocratic. The aristocratic theory of government, whatever its shortcomings in practice, insists that self-governance and governance are difficult arts requiring a high order of intelligence, discipline, and character. It assumes that only a few (or a particular class) have the innate capacity of meeting the demands of deliberative life. One who takes democracy seriously does not deny the difficulty but insists that most men and women have deliberative and moral potential and that given the proper education and environment, each man and woman can take their place in the deliberative forum and share the responsibilities of sovereignty.[18] The point of doing so is less the protection of one's interests than the development of one's deliberative and moral character, achieving the dignity of being a ruler of the polity in which one is a member, and sustaining a public realm in which future generations could have this experience of being a free democratic citizen. This ideal helps explain Vlastos's Socrates and Socrates' critical view of democratic practices, why he detaches aristocratic virtues from social class and offers no institutional reforms (since his aim is the moral improvement of those who participate in the institutions).

As I do not think Socrates was or saw himself as antidemocratic, so I do not think that he was or saw himself as antipolitical. He regarded his vocation as of supreme service to the polity, parallel to but even more significant than his military service, because this enemy was more dangerous to collective life. At the very least his confounding of acceptable demarcations between political and nonpolitical, public and private, pushed his fellow citizens to ask what politics is, where it can occur, and who can engage in it. (Of course they would only accept this challenge if they also accepted his diagnosis that their institution's practices and discourses were corrupt.)[19] But he may have been trying to do something more—to

---

[17] Vlastos, "The Historical Socrates," p. 508.

[18] This paragraph is a paraphrase from Joseph Tussman, *Obligation and the Body Politic* (New York: Oxford University Press, 1960), p. 108.

[19] Because this claim is always disputable, Gregory Vlastos is exactly right to question whether the best arguer in Athens who stayed out of policy debates on principle was morally justified in doing so. "When it was moved in the Assembly that genocide was the right penalty for Mytilene, and then again for Scione, and for Melos . . . where was Socrates then? Where was he when the Assembly debated that expedition for Syracuse, whose colossal folly

reconstitute public life in moral terms outside the formal channels of the "state," seeking in his dialogues both the improvement of his fellow citizens and offering philosophical dialogue as a paradigm for how "political" institutions might function. This may not be a theory of politics or even the right paradigm for it, but it is, I think, a "political" position.[20] Jonathan Schell's discussion of Polish Solidarity elaborates the point and clarifies the sense in which Socrates can be said to be political.[21]

Instead of promising all good things in the future and demanding sacrifices now, Solidarity began to do good things immediately and directly, only afterward turning its attention to the state. Its "simple but radical guiding principle was to start doing the things you think should be done and start being what you think society should become." If you believe in freedom of speech, then speak freely. If you love truth, then tell it. If you believe in an open society, act in the open. To reform an adversary (especially when the adversary was the state) might take some time but "in the sphere of one's own actions the just society could be established right away. It followed that evil means could no longer be employed to attain good ends. If the journey and the destination were the same, it made no sense to spoil the conveyance in which one was riding." If one wished to act locally, then what could be more local than oneself? "And if you wished to produce results today then what area of life was more ready to hand, more thoroughly within your grasp, than your own action? And if, accordingly, you made yourself and your own actions your starting point for the reform of society, then how could you permit those actions to be degraded by brutality, deception, or any other disfigurement?" In this way Solidarity generated new and independent centers of power: new because the power was not seized by one group from another but was created where there had been none before; independent because they ignored the state while building up parts of society. What all this suggests is that politics begins wherever people are, and that whenever people come together there can be politics. What it warns against is begging the ques-

---

was to cost Athens more lives and treasures than any of its public actors before or since?" ("Reasons for Dissidence," a review of *Socrates and the State*, by Richard Kraut, *Times Literary Supplement* [August 24, 1984]: 932.)

[20] I am not arguing that it is necessarily a good political position, only that it cannot be dismissed as unpolitical. One could conclude that Socrates' precept that it is better to suffer injustice than commit it is necessarily the ruin of any political society. Perhaps; but Gandhi, Camus, and Martin Luther King, Jr., were not so sure.

[21] It does so long as we remember that the polis was not a totalitarian state (or a state at all for that matter) and so there can be no distinction between state and society. Furthermore, Socrates has no institutional foundation or agenda in the sense that Solidarity had and has. And of course he has a very different attitude toward production, despite his examples drawn from "menial" *technai* and his acknowledgment that artisans do indeed have knowledge.

tion—what is politics?—Socrates raises by confounding the conventional demarcations between activities, spheres, spaces, and functions.[22]

Socratic political philosophy may not only be political in subject matter and concern, it may also regard philosophy and politics as analogous activities. Both Socratic philosophy (as that is discussed and exemplified in the *Apology* and *Crito*) and politics remind us of, and exist because of, our mortality, partiality, and insufficiency. Both emphasize our need for others to compensate for our one-sidedness and incompleteness, which is what philosophical dialogue and political deliberation ideally accomplish. Both aid men in achieving a more inclusive understanding of who they are and what the true significance of their speech and action mean. In each case the presence (in both senses) of others is essential for knowledge and virtue, for knowing about politics and the living of a public life.

Both dialogue and deliberation depend on stable meanings and common discourse, the collapse of which Thucydides chronicles at Corcyra. This subject of how language and culture constitute each other is an implicit concern of virtually all Platonic dialogues and the explicit preoccupation of several. Thus in book 1 of the *Republic* Socrates constitutes a community of interlocutors as he clarifies the meaning of justice. One could even go further and suggest that the constituting of dialogic community reveals something about how political communities are formed, while its "proper" practice provides a standard by which to judge the corruption of deliberations such as those about Mytilene and Syracuse.

Philosophy and politics are analogous in this sense too; both dialogue and deliberation have, as a necessary object, the continuation of their own possibility. Thus every dialogue is about dialogue as well as a substantive issue such as piety, justice, or friendship, just as political debate is about the context of debate as well as about specific decisions (as the Mytilene debate revealed). With both dialogue and deliberation, the question is What shall we do? where remaining a "we" is as essential as the doing.

Finally, because philosophical dialogue and political deliberation presuppose a plurality of voices, they are opposed to tyranny, whether that be the tyranny of order and command as with Creon or the tyranny of mind as with Oedipus. It is essential not to project these qualities on others while denying similar impulses in ourselves, since all of us have tyrannical impulses. It is equally imperative not to damn tyrants out of hand, since tyranny derives as much from our intellectual and moral power as from our intellectual and moral failures. At least that is the view of the

[22] Jonathan Schell, introduction to Adam Michnik's *Letters From Prison and Other Essays*, trans. Maya Latynski (Berkeley and Los Angeles: University of California Press, 1985), pp. xxx, xxxi, and xxxiii.

tragedians, Thucydides and Socrates. Whether it is also Plato's view in the *Republic* is another matter.

THE OPENING LINES of the *Apology* raise the question of who Socrates is and what he is doing in and for Athens.[23] So persuasive have his accusers been that even he has forgotten his own identity. Not only have they created a false impression of him, they have made men suspicious of his speech, and so, like an orator whose motives have been impugned, he must combat the deceptive image perpetuated by his enemies and counter the claim that his doing so is merely another manifestation of the deception.[24] His only hope is convincing them that he speaks the truth, and that he will not, as others do and they expect, suit what he says to the occasion. He will speak here as he does in the *agora* and so people will know that it is the same Socrates they have always known. Besides, it would be unseemly for a man his age to pretend to be what he is not. All he asks is tolerance for his unfamiliarity with the court's ways and permission to speak his "dialect" without prejudice.

The *Apology* is not only about "who" Socrates is and the nature of philosophical activity, it is also about who the Athenians are and the nature of their political activity. Socrates charges that it is not he but they who lack firm identity. Now corrupt, they are unable to adhere to what is best in their own traditions or alter those traditions to realize better the highest aims of collective life as philosophy understands them. Like tragedy Socratic philosophy brings the city to think about the character of its collective goals and the implicit pattern of its actions. It is not that Socrates wants everyone to be philosophers, since he recognizes that the fully examined life is politically unlivable. But he does want them to recognize what is problematic about the practices and decisions of their everyday lives, since the unexamined life is not worth living.

Socrates fosters the examination of collective life not only by what he says but by where he says it. His refusal to speak in the Assembly, like his ridicule of the demeaning litanies of the law courts, is a rebuke that implicitly denies that politics occur in the former or that justice is achievable in the latter. Athenian politics are on trial as much as Socratic philosophy. Moreover, by making the familiar practices seem strange, Socrates lessens the strangeness of his own relocation of political activity and redefinition of justice and philosophy. Indeed, by defamiliarizing accepted practices, Socrates' defense becomes a collective *elenchus*. Finally, in judging his judges and trying his accusers, Socrates creates a potentially uncorrupted

---

[23] On the importance of the *Apology* to Socratic-Platonic political theory, see Eva Brann, "The Offense of Socrates: A Re-reading of Plato's Apology," *Interpretation* 7 (May 1978): 1–21.

[24] In this his situation is analogous to Diodotus's in the Mytilene debate.

public space around himself distinct from the public spaces already corrupted. An example will make this clear.

Socrates claims that he is thoroughly ignorant of court procedures and so must speak in unaccustomed ways. In fact, Socrates demonstrates an intimate knowledge of those procedures.[25] In the first part of the *Apology* (up to 36a), Socrates' statements mimic the classic pattern of the Athenian law court speech. He begins by introducing himself and defining the issues, goes on to narrate the facts of the case, refutes the charges against him, and ends with a peroration in which he appeals to the emotions of the jury and to the gods. Moreover, as was commonplace for an accused, he assures the jurors that he has no skill in speech, that he is outclassed by his adversaries, and that he is a poor man with no experience of public life. But it is not commonplace to call rhetoric lying, to claim one's poverty is holy, and to justify inexperience on the grounds of a higher calling. The way Socrates parodies court procedures and so criticizes Athenian practice by inverting its meaning within traditional forms subverts the pretense that such procedures are a means to justice. It suggests three other things: that Socrates could have gotten off but chose not to; that philosophical activity takes its initial impulse and referent from concrete political practices and institutions; and that he has intimate knowledge of the political traditions he seeks to purge and transform.

To establish his true identity against the false identifications made by his accusers, Socrates begins a defense that defines his way of doing philosophy. The defense (which turns into an offense in both senses) is particularly difficult against the old accusers, whose condemnation shaped the views of his present ones and of his judges. For these older men were many, persistent, unanswered, anonymous, and no longer alive to be cross-examined. Their charge is that Socrates is a wise man who speculates about the heavens and investigates things beneath the earth and that (in part because of this) he can make the worse argument appear the stronger. In effect, they accuse Socrates of an impious disrespect for what is sacred and for the limits of mortality. In this, as in other things, he inverts the proper order of things, confounding the moral arrangements and political conventions of the city.

As with the accusation that he is a clever speaker, Socrates must defend himself against both the explicit charges and the context that gave rise to them. Because the context includes that part of the city's traditions that have shaped contemporary prejudices, this is no mean feat. In a sense he

---

[25] See the discussion on Thomas Meyer, *Plato Apologie* (Stuttgart: W. Kohlhammer Verlag, 1962), chap. 1, section 5; Redfield's essay, "A Lecture"; and Thomas G. West, *Plato's Apology of Socrates* (Ithaca, N.Y.: Cornell University Press, 1979), pp. 74–75.

must make his fellow citizens childlike[26] in order to reach behind and reveal their prejudices to them, at least if that "should be best for you and me" (19a). By linking the question of his guilt to the people's capacity for judgment, that capacity to their prejudices, and their prejudices to the city's formative traditions, Socrates transforms his particular trial into a philosophical examination of the foundations of Athenian culture. That is one reason why he expands the numbers of his accusers and adds to their indictment against him.[27]

Socrates begins his defense by denying that he is either a *physiologos* or a sophist. Although he would not disparage those who are interested and knowledgeable about cosmological matters, he now cares little for them and knows nothing about them. Nor does he educate men in the sense or way the sophists do. He does not teach the excellence of citizens and men to foreigners for a fee because he does not have that knowledge, stays in Athens, and regards the greatest reward for any teaching to be the improvement of one's fellow citizens. As he says: "If I had mastered or possessed knowledge of this art and could teach it, I should be arrogant and condescending. But the truth is, men of Athens, I have no such assurance that I understand these things" (20c). But there must be something Socrates says and does that has made him the object of calumny. The accusations against him may be false but they are not random. Who is he that he is so easily misidentified?

In fact he does have a certain wisdom. But unlike cosmologists that wisdom focuses on human life; unlike the sophists it is human in its limitations. Yet that human wisdom is divinely inspired by the Delphic oracle who answered Chaerephon that no one was wiser than Socrates. Because Socrates knew he was not wise, he was driven to make sense of the oracle by examining those reputed to be wise.[28] He found such men to be ignorant in inverse proportion to their reputation and sense of self-importance. Thus the politician knew nothing about the excellence of man and citizen, though he thought he knew a great deal and was incensed when Socrates tried to show him his ignorance. He next questioned the poets. Though their works did contain wise things, this was a product of inspiration, not knowledge, so they were, like the politicians, ignorant of their

---

[26] On the importance of Socrates as a father in the *Apology* and son in the *Crito*, see Arlene Saxonhouse, "The Family in the Last Days of Socrates" (paper presented at the American Political Science Association Meetings, New Orleans, 1985).

[27] See Leo Strauss's discussion in "On Plato's Apology of Socrates and Crito," in *Essays in Honor of Jacob Klein* (Annapolis, Md.: St. John's College Press, 1976), pp. 155–70.

[28] On Socrates' relation to Apollo, see John Sallis, *Being and Logos: The Way of Platonic Dialogue* (Pittsburgh: Duquesne University Press, 1976), pt. 1; George Anastaplo, "Human Being and Citizen: A Beginning to the Study of Plato's Apology of Socrates," in *Human Being and Citizen: Essays on Virtue, Freedom, and the Common Good* (Chicago: Swallow Press, 1975); and West, *Plato's Apology*.

ignorance. Finally Socrates questioned the artisans, still hoping to find others wiser than himself. Here the story is different. The artisans did indeed know many fine things. But even they believed themselves to be wise beyond their wisdom. Mistaking their particular knowledge for knowledge of the place of that knowledge in the whole of life, they claimed "more than they knew"—in both senses of that phrase.

In the end Socrates comes to understand that his wisdom is precisely his knowledge that he does not know. With this he solves the oracle's riddle and becomes the pious servant and spokesman of the god, revealing to his fellow citizens the limits of human wisdom and the fact that, as mortals, we can never possess the truth. Those who do claim to "possess" it, both in the sense of exclusivity and finality, are, like the sophists, presumptively wise but actually ignorant. Knowledge is not an object that can be finished or completed. In this sense Socratic political philosophy is *praxis* rather than *poiēsis*. To suppose otherwise is to embrace those tyrannical impulses that transform politics into command and obedience and wisdom into abstract knowledge.

For these reasons philosophy requires dialogue rather than the presentation of knowledge in prepackaged forms (such as lectures or books) that deter questioning. Dialogue incorporates our knowledge of ignorance into a collective search for truth and is, as such, a distinctively human enterprise. In dialogue we come across ourselves in the other and the others who condition us as we do them. However critical Socrates is of a position, he clarifies his views and sees himself through his engagement with others. In the end, speaking and acting with others, whether in the polis or in philosophical discourse, provides knowledge undiscoverable and unrecoverable in singularity.

To us this might suggest that "political philosophy" is redundant. It might also suggest that philosophy is the god's gift to Athens and to politics. But this is not what was suggested to most of Socrates' compatriots. For them political philosophy was an oxymoron and Socratic philosophy a plague responsible for right-wing oligarchs, unstable democrats, and general mayhem.

Most Athenians are indignant with Socrates and with philosophy. They resent being refuted and they resent his arrogance. And they are suspicious of the way the sons of the rich follow him around enjoying the discomfort of those he cross-examines. These young men imitate him and so provoke the anger of their victims who, Socrates claims, then blame him for their embarrassment and for corrupting the youth. Indeed, it is this rather than any particular teaching that enrages Socrates' accusers (23d). That explains why their charges merely repeat the cliches said about all philosophers: that they investigate things beneath the earth and in the air, that they make people disbelieve in the city's gods, and that they make the worse argument appear the better or stronger.

Socrates is not optimistic about refuting the cumulative impact of such long-standing, deeply implanted biases, given the short time he has, his outspokenness, and the fact that each of his present accusers seeks revenge on behalf of the groups Socrates has embarrassed.

The indictment of the present accusers is that Socrates corrupts the young and believes in new gods not accepted by the city. (This indictment is different from both that of his first accusers and the first formulation of his present accusers.)[29] Socrates turns to Meletus and asks who improves the young (and by inference who makes them worse). For Meletus the people are made virtuous (and presumably corrupt) by the laws and by living a public life among one's fellow citizens. No "one" teaches them, in the ways we can identify a particular man who teaches horses. Indeed the only specific teacher Meletus identifies is Socrates, and he is a teacher of evil. But if, as everyone seems to agree, the young are already corrupt, it is implausible to think Socrates alone is responsible. Given Meletus's own claim that the laws make men good, it is likely that the laws are also responsible for making men evil. Meletus does not entertain this possibility even though it is the corollary of his charge against Socrates. (His failure to do so is self-serving, for it allows him to avoid self-examination and self-criticism.) If the young are corrupted by what should be improving them, then everything is inverted. The seeming corruptor (Socrates) is the one savior (or true statesman), while the seeming saviors (the laws, traditions, and public life) are the corruptors. (Of course, it is part of the city's corruption that it should not see this.) And if the laws and the many cannot produce virtue in the young, they are unlikely to recognize it in Socrates.

It is even more unlikely that Socrates is intentionally corrupting the young since by so doing he would corrupt himself. Anything that improves the lives of one's fellow citizens improves the conditions of one's life. Anything that detracts from the quality of their lives makes it harder to be a good man and good citizen among them. So if Socrates corrupts the youth, it is inadvertent; that may be cause for remonstrance, but not for litigation.

Socrates then turns to the second charge: that he does not believe in the gods the state believes in but imports new divinities. This charge is incompatible with the charge of atheism, since to believe in gods the state does not is at least to believe in gods. Again Socrates insists that he has been misidentified by being associated with Anaxagoras. But all of his protestations are beside the point. They do not answer what will condemn him

29 See West, *Plato's Apology*, pp. 81–134, for the significance of the shifting accusations.

if condemned: the prejudice and resentment of the multitude, which have destroyed many good and innocent men before him and will do so again. "It is hardly likely that I shall be the last victim" (28b).

Socrates chooses to be a victim. In this he acts not from weakness but from strength. Like Achilles he accepts his fate willingly even though it means death. What matters most is how one lives one's life, not that one lives. And how one ought to live is to care more for the justice of one's acts than for calculations of advantage or safety. When mere survival is the animating principle of life, men act timidly and disgracefully. According to Socrates, Achilles scorned danger and death, fearing more to be a coward than the consequences of avenging his friend. Like Achilles the philosopher has a place, which he must guard whatever the danger. He too has a sacred duty, whether he has chosen his station or had it thrust upon him.

Because it is the god who commands him, it would be impious for him to cease philosophizing. This is so even though it is just this activity that distinguishes him from other men and incurs their wrath. Philosophy does not avoid death either as prospect or subject. Socrates is no more sure that death is evil than he is of any other conclusion. This too is subject to examination. But he does know one thing: "that it is evil and shameful to do an unjust act, and to disobey a superior whether he be a man or god. So I will never do what I know to be evil, and cower in fear from what may, for all I know, really be a blessing" (29b).

For Socrates to renounce philosophy is to be in fact what he appears to be to his accusers—impious and unpatriotic. To do what needs doing for acquittal is to do what would make him guilty. That is why he will follow the god's injunction and philosophize by going among the Athenians saying: "My good man, you are an Athenian, a member of a city which is very great and famous for its wisdom and power. Are you not ashamed to care so much for the making of money and for honor and reputation when you neither take any care for wisdom and truth and the perfection of your soul?" (29d–e). If the person says he does care, Socrates will examine his claim to excellence. If that claim is unfounded, he will admonish him for undervaluing what is most valuable. Socrates will do this to and for everyone he meets, but especially to and for his fellow citizens, since they are more closely related to him.

The piety of Socratic philosophy is also its patriotism, because no greater gift could have befallen Athens than the god's gift of Socrates to them (30d). He spends his life unceasingly on their behalf and in their interest, trying to persuade them to care for excellence in all things public and private. Only if this teaching corrupts the young is Socrates guilty. But if it does not, yet he is nevertheless condemned for teaching it, then the society that condemned him condemns itself. That is one reason why

Socrates insists that if Athens banishes, disenfranchises, or kills him, it will be injuring itself more than him. For by punishing an innocent man whose only crime is to care for justice and excellence above all things, it indicts its own ideals before posterity. Moreover, because he is a gift of the god, his punishment, not his philosophizing, is impious and unpatriotic.

So at best their hatred of him is shortsighted, at worst self-destructive. Where else can they find a god-appointed selfless man who "attaches himself to this city as a gadfly to a horse, which though large and well-bred is sluggish because of its size, so that it needs to be stimulated" (30e–31a). They resent him and his reproaches since, like a drowsy person awakened from a deep sleep, they are indignant at his disturbing them rather than, as they should be, angry with those who encourage their stupor.

As we have seen, the Athenians reject Socrates' patriotism because what he says and does is so unconventional. He does not come forward in the Assembly to advise the city as a whole, but gives advice severally, anywhere he encounters men who will talk with him. He is neither public nor private, or rather he is both, in what he says and where he says it. This refusal to be political in the expected ways has three sources.

One is his divine guide or *daimon*, a voice that he has had since childhood and restrains him. A second is his own sense that "if I had attempted to practice politics (*politika prattein*) I should have perished at once and long ago, without doing any good to you or to myself" (31e). No one can survive politically or physically if he decides to oppose the injustices and illegalities of the multitude. One can fight effectively for justice only as a private citizen (*idiōteuein* as opposed to *dēmosieuein*). Socrates proves his point and his commitment to justice by referring to two incidents well known (and perhaps damaging) to his accusers. He was nearly killed by the democracy when he opposed the trial of the admirals who failed to rescue their men after Arginusae, and by the oligarchs when he refused to implicate himself in the arrest of the innocent Leon of Salamis. Here as elsewhere Socrates shows that he cannot be intimidated by force or fear of death, but only by a fear of doing what is impious and unjust.

The third source is less obvious. I do not think Socrates sought to make philosophical activity identical with political activity, despite the similarities I see between them. For he knew well enough that too much philosophy makes bad politics (just as the absence of philosophy does). If I am right, then Socrates refuses to speak in the Assembly because "success" there might have killed Athens. His choice of where and how to practice philosophy is as much to save the city from philosophy and philosophy from Athens, even though philosophy is potentially the city's savior.

No matter where he has been or what he has done, Socrates has never yielded to unjustice, or knowingly taught injustice to others. Indeed, if by a student one means someone who has private access to a teacher and pays for that privilege, Socrates has no pupils. Nor does he have knowledge in the usual sense or regard. He teaches in public to anyone who will engage him in conversation, no matter what their political persuasion, wealth, or social standing. Because in the narrow sense Socrates is not a teacher of knowledge, he cannot be held responsible for the actions of his putative pupils. But in a broader sense, he is a political educator of the city as a whole. In this sense, he does take responsibility for his "pupils" (his fellow citizens), at least in the sense of showing them what it means to take responsibility for their individual and collective lives. That is precisely what he is doing in the *Apology*. Finally, if he really was corrupting the young, surely some disillusioned student or concerned relative would come forward to corroborate the charge. But none does.

With this Socrates concludes his "defense." It is to the god (as well as the jurors) that he commits his cause and case "to be decided as is best for you and me" (35d).

It may be that the judgment of the god and jurors are different, which is significant for interpreting the trial's outcome. It may also be that there is no decision that is good for both Socrates and his fellow citizens. These uncertainties are due to the kind of case this is and the cause Socrates has undertaken. For Socrates is a philosopher and it is philosophical activity that is on trial, rather than some particular deed, such as not burying the dead after a battle. Any verdict then will be a judgment about whether philosophical activity has place and purpose in the polis.

Up until this point Socrates claims that it does. He has made a case for philosophical activity as pious and patriotic, stressed the benefits philosophy brings to the city while indicating that Athens is the only place he can do philosophy, and insisted that what he does is an elaboration of the traditions of his city rightly understood. His courage now in philosophy's defense is the same as his courage at Potideia, Amphipolis, and Delium. There he bravely defended his city against its foes and is doing no less here, since standing by philosophy is as essential to the moral well-being of his compatriots as standing by his comrades was for their physical well-being. To desert philosophy is to desert the city and he can no more do that than Achilles could desert his dear friend Patroclus.

ATHENS' IDENTITY is defined as much by its "cultural narratives" as by its political institutions. As Socrates' critique of those institutions suggests a direction (though not a program) for political regeneration, so does his amended quotation from Homer's Achilles provide the basis for a critique and reconstitution of a dominant cultural narrative. One could even say that his quotation-misquotation of the greatest Greek hero (except perhaps for Heracles) is analogous to his perfectly imitating a law court speech after saying he is ignorant of legal procedures. Both illustrate how Socrates philosophizes.

For Wilamowitz, Jaeger, and Adam Parry, "Achilles[30] is the central image of the *Apology*."[31] In what sense is this so? And, if it is, why does Socrates "choose" Achilles and which "Achilles" is he choosing? The specific point is clear enough: Socrates wants his fellow citizens to see that he, like Achilles, is more concerned with how one ought to live than with calculations of advantage and mere survival, and that for him to abandon these commitments would be cowardly. But that is a limited if useful reference. It hardly makes Achilles the central image of the dialogue. Here is the relevant passage which I quote at length.[32]

> Perhaps someone will say: Are you not ashamed Socrates of leading a life that is likely now to cause your death? I should answer him with justice and say: "My friend, if you think that a man of any substance and worth ought to calculate the prospects of life and death when he acts, or that he ought to think of anything but whether he is acting justly or unjustly, and as a good or a bad man would act, you are mistaken. According to you, the heroes who died at Troy would be foolish creatures, especially the son of Thetis, who thought nothing of danger when the alternative was disgrace and dishonor. For when he was resolved to slay Hector his goddess-mother addressed him in this fashion: "My son, if you avenge the death of Hector, you will die yourself, for fate awaits you next after him"; when he heard this, he scorned death and danger; he feared much more to live a coward and not to avenge his friend. He said: "Let me punish the evil-doer and afterward die that I may not remain here by the curved ships jeered at, encumbering the earth." Do you suppose that he thought of danger or of death? For this, Athenians, I believe to be the truth. Wherever a man's station is, whether he has chosen it of his own free will or whether he has been placed at it by his commander, there it is his duty to remain and face the danger without thinking of death or of any other thing except disgrace.
> (28b–d)[33]

---

[30] Achilles is never mentioned by name. I am less impressed with that fact than others since the name by which he is called is traditional.

[31] See Jaeger's *Paideia*, 1:262 (Socrates also invokes Heracles at 22b).

[32] I have made a few changes in the translation of F. J. Church, *Euthyphro, Apology, Crito*, Library of Liberal Arts (Indianapolis, Ind.: Bobbs-Merrill, 1983).

[33] As we shall see, Socrates misleadingly attributes to Achilles a concern with "Socratic" justice. But Socrates cannot alter Achilles beyond recognition since that would vitiate the point of invoking him in the first place. One could say that Socrates is "refurbishing" a mythical tradition in ways made familiar by the tragedians.

Most broadly Socrates invokes Achilles as a way of identifying himself with a cultural narrative he is also transforming. He legitimates his stand on behalf of philosophy while redefining what is legitimate and how legitimacy can be established. That is the general aim of the invocation; there also are more specific ones that precede and underlie it.

To begin with, Socrates wants to show that his actions are not as exceptional as they seem and that they seem so only because the Athenians do not take their own cultural legacy seriously. Indeed, he and political philosophy are the true heirs to the heroic tradition whereas his accusers ignore or bastardize it.[34] They expect men to cower and demean themselves before death, whereas he refuses to act slavishly. As with Achilles in book 9 of the *Iliad*, Socrates' adherence to the heroic tradition[35] is a rebuke to those whose noble platitudes mask ignoble actions.[36] And, like Achilles, Socrates chooses his fate. Crito implies that his friend need not have been tried, need not have been convicted, need not have been given such a harsh sentence, and need not have accepted it so passively.[37]

There is another, more general and substantial reason why Socrates invokes Achilles; he understsands his predicament and life as analogous to that of Achilles. Achilles' relationship to the heroic ethic parallels Socrates' relationship to Athens. The former is at one and the same time the supreme embodiment of the heroic ethic and the one figure in the epic

[34] But he is also a rebuke to traditions of warlike virtue that have been built up around Achilles. It is interesting that in the last part of his last speech in the *Apology* Socrates obliquely reintroduces the analogy between himself and Achilles. Only it is now Achilles of the *Odyssey* and the passage where the greatest Greek hero would rather be a serf tilling the soil for another than rule over the dead (11.488–91). As Sallis rightly says (*Being and Logos*, pp. 62–63), Achilles here drops his heroic stance and "calls into question the world of the Homeric hero." (Cf. the *Republic*, 516d, which quotes the same passage of the *Odyssey* now to describe the revulsion the philosopher feels when he descends into the cave of politics.)

[35] In book 1 Achilles defends the heroic ethic against Agamemnon's debasement of it. Though hardly blameless, he rebukes those who fail to adhere to the standards they proclaim. And his compatriots understand him to be doing this. Only later, after his impassioned rejection of Agamemnon's recompense do they find him incomprehensible. There and then Achilles' separation from the heroic ethic becomes something more substantial. As it does, the question What is the point of fighting if reward and recognition can be stripped by unthankful greedy kings? becomes What is the value of a man and most valuable in the world?

[36] My argument owes much to Adam Parry's classic essay, "The Language of Achilles," *Transactions of the American Philological Association* 86 (1956): pp. 1–7. Although Parry has been criticized for overstating his point and turning Achilles into an existential hero, most scholars still accept the general point; for a balanced assessment of the issue, see Seth Schein, *The Mortal Hero* (Berkeley and Los Angeles; University of California Press, 1984).

[37] On this and Socrates' complex relationship to the heroic tradition in the *Crito*, see Greenberg's discussion in "Socrates' Choice."

who comes closest to rejecting the ethic he embodies, while the latter is both the supreme embodiment and severest critic of Athenian tradition.

In the *Iliad*, Achilles' withdrawal from the heroic ethic begins in book 1 but reaches a climax in the embassy scene in book 9 where Phoinix, Ajax, and Odysseus come to offer elaborate recompense if only Achilles will rejoin the battle and save the Greeks from destruction. Although Achilles expresses the warmest sentiments for his old teacher Phoinix and is moved by Ajax's invocation of friendship and loyalty, his response to Odysseus's speech and the gifts is as unexpected as it is overwhelming.[38]

He begins by angrily rejecting the words designed to assuage his anger. As he detests the doorway of death, so he detests "the man, who hides one thing in the depths of his heart, and speaks forth another." He no longer trusts persuasion since he was persuaded to follow Agamemnon to Troy and for glory, yet is now deprived of the latter by the former. He will no longer be cheated by fair phrases, beguiled by rhetoric whose surface meanings mislead, or seduced by appearances that misdirect understanding and commitment. Unlike others he will speak from the depths of his heart, unadorned and undisguised. The offered gifts have become like deceitful speech, yet another false coin and value. As gifts they do not interest him; as gifts from Agamemnon they infuriate him.[39]

If speech is corrupt yet men's deeds are immortalized through song and story, and if gifts manifest heroic achievement but can be stolen (as Agamemnon has Briseis) and so the deeds retroactively diminished, what point is there in fighting for honor and fame? If men hide what is in their hearts, and if assignments for valor are arbitrary, then fate is the same "for the man who holds back, the same if he fights hard." We are all held in "a single honor, the brave and the weaklings." In the end all of us die. There is no winning in battle, no point to striving. The world has become flat and undifferentiated.

Refusing to accept compensation and so conclude the quarrel in the ways prescribed by the culture, Achilles disengages from the healing illusions of his community.[40] Positing an opposition between appearance and reality he calls the reality of heroism into question. His response to Odysseus is full of syntactical harshness, abrupt shifts from smooth hexame-

[38] As D. B. Claus argues, gifts may be a necessary condition of glory but they cannot be a sufficient condition. Otherwise heroic behavior would cease to be seen as something self-imposed and gratuitous, taking place between men who treat each other as equals. "Achilles must be paid but he cannot be bought" ("Aidos in the Language of Achilles," *Transactions of the American Philological Association* 105 [1975]; 13–28).

[39] James M. Redfield, *Nature and Culture in the Iliad: The Tragedy of Hector* (Chicago: University of Chicago Press, 1975), p. 204.

[40] James Boyd White, *When Words Lose Their Meaning* (Chicago: University of Chicago Press, 1984), pp. 48–49.

ters to sharply punctuated exclamations of jabbing anger (9.356–67, 375–77), swift alterations of mood and image, oscillations between elaborate rationality and illogical outbursts, sudden returns to subjects already dismissed, rhetorical questions, and imagined scenes.[41] The confusion and incoherence is symptom and sign of a man seeking an alternative to a world that no longer offers him place or purpose. Trapped by a language and ethos he no longer understands and for which he no longer cares, Achilles has no choice but to prowl "within the closed circle of his rage."[42] Disengaged from the healing illusions of his community, he has no other illusion or community to heal this anger, self-pity, and self-hatred.

Achilles' "alienation" here is more substantial than in book 1.[43] There he is a rebuke to a king who fails to uphold an ethic upon which depended the existence of the army, the expedition, and the *Iliad*. Now he rebukes the ethic itself, or more accurately, he is a voice inside the epic, that allows the voice of Homer and the audience to do so.[44] That the supremely heroic man should doubt the value of heroism; that the character who is thought to best exemplify the ethic is also its severest critic; and that the one who is most inside, central, and at home, is at the same time most outside, marginal, and alien, is a paradox that also marks Sophocles' *Oedipus*, and Socrates' life as portrayed in the *Apology* and *Crito*.

So despite the differences between them, Achilles' relationship to the heroic tradition as interpreted and lived by his fellow Achaeans is similar to Socrates' (and philosophy's) relationship to the Athenian political traditions as interpreted and lived by his fellow citizens. By who they are and what they do, each suggests the precariousness of the tradition that nurtured them. The *Iliad* is a world in flames: Athens is corrupt. In both instances it is unclear whether these traditions were flawed at the outset or have become so.[45]

This shared marginality is suggested by (and derives from) their dual parentage. Achilles' suspension between the worlds of gods and men is a

[41] See Schein's discussion (*Mortal Hero*, p. 105).

[42] The phrase is Redfield's (*Nature and Culture*, p. 15).

[43] Cedric Whitman (in *Homer and the Heroic Tradition* [New York: W. W. Norton, 1965], p. 185) regards Achilles as a "lonely and haunted sojourner among men of inconsequence and half-hearted ideals." Achilles thus emerges as a modern hero who discards the conventions of his society and, facing the meaninglessness of things, proceeds to fashion an identity for himself.

[44] Homer's relation to the resources of the oral tradition—its repository of scenes, diction, concepts, and questions—are (unsurprisingly) analogous to Achilles' relationship to the heroic ethic. See Oliver Taplin, "Homer Comes Homes" *New York Review of Books* 33 (March 13, 1986): 39.

[45] The embassy is not a complete failure. Although Achilles refuses the gifts, he will not leave Troy but will stay until the Trojans have reached the ships. Then he'll rejoin the battle.

legacy of being born of a mortal father and immortal mother. In one sense Socratic philosophy is in a similar position. On the one hand, there is the mortal parent, the city of Athens. In the *Crito* Socrates implies that Athens is father to his vocation as well as the man (though in the *Apology* he speaks of himself as a father or older brother). That is one reason why, in the dialogue with the idealized laws, he is so deferential to the city he criticizes, and one reason why he refuses exile. On the other hand, there is a divine parent, Apollo, whose answer to Chaerephon led Socrates to political philosophy as described and manifest in the *Apology*.

Socrates and Achilles are uniquely "self-conscious" about their predicament. When the ambassadors come upon Achilles he is singing of great deeds even as Homer sings of his, as if Achilles were the character most able to see events in the inclusive terms of the poet.[46] The pattern in which he understands himself is both the song itself and the human condition. That emerges most clearly in the moment of reconciliation between Priam and Achilles in book 24.

In that scene Achilles is reintegrated into the human community, though it is a tenuous, partial, and reluctant reintegration. The scene itself is unbearably painful—distant, even abstract, in its general rumination on the human condition, yet immediately urgent and lucid. Achilles weaves the story of Zeus's two urns into the story of his own life, which becomes the life he shares with Priam and so the story of mortality itself. Reflecting on himself and his fate, he sees his life as an aspect of a universal pattern above that of local circumstance and particular allegiance.

The reconciliation liberates Achilles and restores him. It liberates him because he is finally released from the wrath, self-pity, and self-hatred that has so far prevented him from seeing his tragedy as part of a shared loss. It restores him because Achilles comes once more to demonstrate his generosity and sympathy toward an enemy. He lifts Andromache's husband into Priam's cart, covering his bitterest foe with part of the finery the father has brought as ransom for the son. Now finally Achilles can sleep and eat like other mortals, accepting the physical limitations and boundaries that hem him in as they do all men. The recognition of mor-

---

[46] This implies that "Homer" understood his own deed as analogous to the heroic deeds of Achilles. Analogous but not identical: for though Homer stands with Achilles (or Achilles with Homer) outside the heroic world being consumed in flames, Achilles is still a character in a story as "Homer" is not. About the *Iliad* Alasdair MacIntyre writes: "The poet is not a theorist; he offers no general formulas. His own knowledge is indeed at a more general and abstract level than that even of his most insightful characters. For Achilles in his moment of reconciliation with Priam has no way of representing to himself what Homer is able in his account of Achilles and Priam to represent to others." See *After Virtue* (Notre Dame, Ind.: University of Notre Dame Press, 1981), pp. 120–21. (I am not so sure.)

tality is especially hard to bear for him precisely because he is so close to the immortals.

When Achilles recognizes his common mortality and so himself in his enemies Priam and Hector, he comes to understand his tragedy as universal and shared rather than singular and private.[47] Gazing at the old man, a father deprived of his son, Achilles remembers now not his immortal mother but his mortal father, left desolate, soon to be bereft of his son. He understands now, for this moment, that winning is also losing.

As Achilles and Priam form a community founded on a shared sense of mortality and loss, circumstantial oppositions such as those between Greek and Trojan, friend and enemy, old and young, recede into insignificance, replaced by a more fundamental contrast between men and gods.[48] In this precarious and momentary unity of understanding they provide a vision of human equality that is both a respite from the war and a standard by which heroic culture is judged as life-destroying and self-annihilating.[49]

By this "universal" standard all cultures are inadequate because none can be wholly rooted in the sense of common humanity and fidelity to what is genuine in this moment of reconciliation. In James Boyd White's words, "Man will always forget what he has known, will always kill and always die. Like Achilles and Priam, we are left with a new knowledge, facing the fact that what ought to be will never be."[50] All of us are defined and separated by what is particular and local, by time and place, kinship and obligations, status and gender, membership and point of view. Here is Michael Ignatieff on the same theme. "What is common to us matters much less than what differentiates us, what makes life precious for us is difference not identity. We do not prize equality. We think of ourselves not as human beings first, but as sons and daughters, fathers and mothers,

[47] See the discussion of Achilles' growing sense of common loss in Michael Nagler, *Spontaneity and Tradition: A Study in the Oral Art of Homer* (Berkeley and Los Angeles: University of California Press, 1974), pp. 189–91.

[48] Until this point, Achilles "identifies" with his immortal parent Thetis. Only now does Achilles speak of his mortal father.

[49] As White suggests (*When Words Lose Their Meaning*, pp. 51–58), this moment of quiet amid the turbulence of war is not unprecedented, only more sustained and elaborate. Throughout the *Iliad* there are flashes of gentleness and humanity amid the gruesome detail. But these desires for peace are quickly supplanted by the spirit of battle.

[50] *Ibid.*, p. 54 and *passim*. That may be Homer's view; it need not be ours. It matters of course what is forgotten and whether death is viewed as the culmination of life and the true test of manhood or as life-destroying and a false test of human worth. My implicit argument is that the "heroic" vocation of political theory as that is being defined by Socrates consists in guarding those larger sensibilities that provide the foundations for peace and derive from a common sense of mortality without forgetting the particular people for whom peace matters.

tribesmen and neighbors. It is this dense web of relations and the meanings which they give to life that satisfies the needs which really matter to us."[51]

But there are occasions, like the scene between Priam and Achilles, when men and women can imaginatively disengage from the web of relations to extend their sympathies and sensibilities. Such occasions may even be prescribed by a culture, as rituals of "guest friendship" and "benefactor-suppliant," which, as institutionalized moments of extended sympathy, may have provided a resource and reference point for the reconciliation scene. That such peacetime rituals were reinstated under conditions of utter enmity and by a father kissing the hands of the man who has killed his sons emphasizes the rarity and extraordinariness of the occurrence.

But not its significance or necessity. What I regard as the "theoretical moment" is essential for political and intellectual reasons, in classical Athens as in contemporary America. It is a moment anticipated in tragedy's leading its audience to recognize itself in the other and the other in itself. But it is fully articulated and explicitly defended by Socrates in the *Apology* and *Crito*. As both those dialogues make clear the point is not to permanently dissociate ourselves from the "dense web of relationships" that define us—as we shall see, Socrates fully recognizes his obligations to his sons—but to sustain as memory and disturbance the shared fate epitomized in the reconciliation scene. Only then can one discover the ought to be in the present or fully understand the problems of justice, identity, and membership.[52]

Certainly there are dangers in the moment and in theorizing—dangers of abstraction, of intellectual tyranny and global theories. But as the *Oedipus Tyrannos* suggests there is as much danger in simply rejecting the theoretical impulse and moment as in unequivocally embracing it, especially when confronted by the "sphinx."

There is a coda and one more complication to all this. Socrates actually misquotes the passage from Homer. Achilles says nothing about justice; Socrates attributes it to him (dikēn ... adikounti). Thus there is an asymmetry between their situations. Achilles is part of the tradition Socrates exemplifies and repudiates whereas Socrates is not part of the context for Achilles' actions. Yet by moralizing the heroic ethic, Socrates makes Achilles into a protophilosopher while legitimating his activity as heroic. In doing so he adds to his defense against charges that he corrupts

[51] *The Needs of Strangers* (New York: Viking Press, 1984), p. 29.
[52] The question is not only What is justice? but Who participates in the discussion, who decides on the question, and how one should live justly?

the youth. Ascribing "moral" motives to the greatest of Greek heroes,[53] Socrates retrospectively purges the corrupting vision of heroic action for which Achilles stands. In this he is saving his city from destruction and furthering Greek drama's similar moralizing of mythology.[54]

HIS FELLOW CITIZENS do not see things this way. They find Socrates guilty, though by a surprisingly narrow margin. He had expected the verdict but not the closeness of the vote. His near acquittal gives substance to his claim that he could have convinced them "if there was a law at Athens, as in other cities, that no capital case can be decided in a single day. . . . but it is not easy in so limited a time to exonerate myself of so many prejudices and allegations" (37b).[55] The claim, together with his surprise at the vote's closeness, may indicate that Socrates exaggerated the corruption of his native city. If so, then perhaps he could have spoken in the assembly; perhaps he did not have to die after all.

In any case Socrates is asked to propose a punishment in lieu of the death penalty requested by his accusers. He can only think of one "punishment" suitable for a poor benefactor like himself; free meals in the prytaneum with the Olympic victors. While victors may give men pleasure, Socrates gives them true happiness at his own expense. Neglecting what most men value—wealth, family interests, military commands, public speeches, civic appointments, social clubs, and political factions—Socrates goes to each citizen in order to persuade him "not to think of his narrowly practical advantage until he had taken care for his goodness and wisdom, nor to think of the political or private interests until he had thought of the city as a whole" (36c). For Socrates to propose any other punishment would be to admit that these endeavors are mistaken. He has never yet done wrong voluntarily and is not about to do so to himself now. He would rather accept death whose evil is only conjecture, than propose a certain evil, such as imprisonment, where he could be a slave to successive officials, or a fine, which he could not pay, or exile, which presumes that strangers would be better disposed to what his fellow citizens cannot endure. It would be preposterous for him to spend his final years going from city to city like some sophist, attracting the young men and being expelled for it, either by the young men themselves if he drives

[53] Vengeance too is a kind of morality, though one without real limits (as Achilles' revenge shows). There is a danger of regarding Socratic morality as the only one.
[54] See the discussion of this in Hans-Georg Gadamer, *Dialogue and Dialectic: Eight Hermeneutical Studies on Plato*, trans. and introd. P. Christopher Smith (New Haven: Yale University Press, 1980).
[55] That Athens unlike other nations lacks such a law suggests an impatience typical of its culture (as Thucydides portrays it).

them away or by their fathers if he does not. The final scene of his life would not be tragedy but farce.

The most obvious solution, that Socrates be freed on condition of ceasing philosophical activity, is the most impossible, although he does not expect many to understand why. They are unlikely to believe that *giving up* philosophy rather than its practice is impiety, still less that "no greater good can happen to a man than to discuss human excellence every day" (38a).

They don't: Socrates is condemned to die. True to the pattern of the *Apology*, he turns the judgment on him into an indictment of his judges. By condemning him they have condemned themselves. Those who wish to revile Athens will call him wise and Athens a killer of wisdom. If they had been (uncharacteristically) patient, nature would have done their work for them. As it is, those who have voted against him have shown the world that they prefer the servile pandering of cowardly defendants to arguments made by a free man in his defense. And this in a city proud of its freedom and the freedom of its people.

Their impatience will escalate the estrangement between philosophy and politics. With him dead many more will demand that Athenians give an account of themselves, and they will be younger and harsher than he has been because of what has happened to him. He has held these critics back by his presence, and by the fact that as long as he was allowed to do philosophy, philosophers could hope for a place in the polis. But his death means the young men become more strident in their criticism and the city, in response, will become more indignant at their stridency. In suppressing him and philosophy Athens missed its chance to become as good as it could be. But philosophy too loses. Although it will survive Socrates' death, it cannot be Socratic political philosophy.

Socrates calls those who voted for acquittal his "true judges," and speaks to them in a voice that is friendly, conversational, and reassuring. He is anxious for them to understand that what has happened to him is not the calamity they think it is and may even be a blessing. One indication of the latter is that the divine guide that has always protected him from doing injustice has not interrupted him either before or after the trial. Thus what is thought the greatest of evils may not be so. If, as is commonly believed, death is either the loss of consciousness or the soul's migration to another place, it is a gain. For a sleep so deep no dreams interrupt it is a tranquility even the most powerful would envy. Or if death is a journey to another place where we will find all who have died, a double benefit will accrue. First, men would be freed of the pretended judges here and be delivered to the true judges who "are said to" sit in judgment below. Second, it would be possible to converse with the great poets (such as Homer and Hesiod), with others who have been sentenced unjustly (such as Palamedes and Ajax), and above all to continue practicing philosophy. And because *these* men are immortal, they would certainly not put philosophers to death "if what we are told is true."[56]

His acquitters must face death as he does; with hope, steadfast in the antitragic knowledge that "no evil can happen to a good man either in life or in death" (41d). Because the gods watch out for such men and Socrates is one of them, the gods must be watching out for him now. So it is probably better for him to die and be relieved from troubles and distractions. That seems to be the joint message of the god and *daimon*.

Socrates leaves the question of his guilt to god and the jury. But he leaves the question of the immortality of the soul exclusively to the god. Neither his accusers nor supporters can know what follows death. In this he is consistent with his earlier expression of ignorance on the subject (29a), with the extensions of the Delphic "know thyself" and with the way he distances himself from the myth of immortality by presenting it as a story told by others. Such distancing is all the more notable because it summarizes the themes of the dialogue.

First, it obliquely reaffirms Socrates' patriotism. For the myth reconciles his supporters to the verdict and lessens their sense of loss. Without this they might become part of the factionalism destroying the city. Second, by leaving the final word to the god, Socrates combats the skepticism philosophy is thought to engender, reasserts his piety, and observes the demarcations between heaven and earth he was accused of transgressing. Finally, the uncertainties that surround the myth's presentation preserve the dialogic and political character of philosophical activity.

The myth is offered to Socrates' sympathizers as one of two alternative visions of death. In the first vision death is a loss of consciousness akin to unbroken sleep. If death is indeed tranquil, then "I for one count it as a gain." Yet as we have been told and shown earlier, philosophy seeks to rouse people from sleep. So this view of death is the negation of philosophy.[57]

In the second vision death is a migration of souls in which philosophical activity continues unabated into eternity. Here one might say that an unexamined death is not worth living. Since examining others and oneself in death is to be among men, this view presents Socrates as continuing to live in a community more inclusive than the Athenian community of his life.

Yet immediately following his distant vision of membership in an inclusive timeless community, Socrates mentions his sons and so reaffirms his

[56] The significance of Socrates distancing himself in these passages is discussed by West, *Plato's Apology*, pp. 229–31.

[57] John Burnet, ed., *Plato's Euthyphro, Apology of Socrates, and Crito* (Oxford: 1924) Clarendon Press, p. 244.

mortality and identity as a member of a community situated in time and space. Before, he had refused to use his sons as a ploy to cultivate the sympathy of the jurors since that would have meant demeaning himself, his children, and Athens. Mentioning them now is a way of reconnecting himself with his fellow citizens and turning their attention from death to life. He asks that his sons be treated as he has treated the sons of others; that they "corrupt" his boys as he has supposedly corrupted theirs. In saying this Socrates suggests that he has no more intentionally corrupted the young than he has intentionally corrupted his own children. His concern for Athens as for them has been fatherly throughout.

By bringing up his children, Socrates indicates a care for the city's future. Unlike the sophists who travel from place to place, he understands the rootedness of his life and of philosophy.

THAT UNDERSTANDING and the sense in which he, like Achilles, is simultaneously the supreme embodiment and severest critic of the traditions that have formed him is played out in the dialogue with the laws in the *Crito*.

Most specifically, the dialogue is a response to Crito's confusion over whether Socrates' escape without the consent of the laws would break a just agreement and injure those he least ought to injure. But it also addresses Crito's more general uncertainty about the relevance of philosophic reasoning to political practice. For philosophy seems to demand that Socrates stay in Athens even though remaining means death. As Socrates addresses Crito's concerns (which are also his own), he considers the relationship between philosophy and politics or, more accurately, the relationship between being a member of the Athenian polis and his philosophical practice.

He concludes that the laws of Athens are father to the practice every bit as much as they are to him.[58] When the laws call Socrates their slave and child, they suggest that as infants men are virtual nonpersons and that they become who they are physically, intellectually, emotionally, and morally as a result of the nurture and education received from the city in which they are citizens. This is not a matter of contract but of growing up and into recognizable persons within a specific culture. Thus, when one chooses a vocation, action, or friend, one already is somebody. No one, not even Socrates, is sui generis.[59] Although Socrates gives new content to older Athenian ideals—such as living well, justice, citizenship, friendship, piety, courage, and the unity of intelligence and action—they

[58] "Parents love their children as parts of themselves, while children love their parents as the authors of their being" (Aristotle, *Nichomachean Ethics*, 1161b20).

[59] See the discussion of these points in Hanna Pitkin, *Wittgenstein and Justice* (Berkeley and Los Angeles: University of California Press, 1972), pp. 199, 334.

are Athenian ideals, implicit in what has been said and done before. His critical standards (including what it means to criticize on the basis of standards) are derived from what he criticizes. This fact and Socrates' recognition of it has a number of consequences.

First, it makes criticism appear paradoxical. For if what one chooses to criticize, the fact that one chooses to criticize at all, and the idiom of one's criticism owe much to what one is criticizing (i.e, what has nurtured and educated you), then at least part of what is criticized is simultaneously affirmed. (The paradox works the other ways as well; because Socrates is Athens' son, to condemn him is also a kind of self-condemnation.) Whether one conceives of a tradition as speaking in a single voice, or in many voices, any one of which may become the basis for judgment of another, all political criticism that fails to recognize this paradox repeats the ignorance of Aeschylus's Clytaemnestra who proclaims her murder of her husband an end to violence and a beginning of order while unknowingly perpetuating the cycle of revenge that cursed the House of Atreus. In these terms a claim that a past agreement is unjust can be made intelligible only because of a prior "agreement" about what constitutes an agreement and making a claim.[60]

Second, it imposes on Socrates an obligation to repay his debt to Athens by giving it the best things he can, as it gave him and all citizens the best things it could. Such repayment is only possible among those who share common citizenship and law. And this requires that Socrates assume responsibility for a world he did not make even when he wishes it to be other than it is.

Third, by emphasizing the political source and origin of his philosophic vocation, Socrates becomes part of a tradition of public speech and political leadership that is distinctively Athenian. It is true, as I indicated earlier, that he is highly critical of that tradition and that he refuses to participate in the deliberations of the Assembly. Yet he assumes the mantle of exemplary political action even while relocating the proper arena for such activity. Lacking what only later became a definition of philosophy as a distinctive mode of life opposed to politics, Socrates understood himself as belonging to the tradition of Athenian statesmen-educators from Solon to Pericles.

These are a few of the considerations that lead Socrates to reject the proposal to leave Athens and practice philosophy elsewhere. It is only

---

[60] This argument relates to two charges often leveled at Socrates' views in the *Crito*—that he ignores private rights and the need for an "independent assessment" of the laws' character to justify his commitment to them. But if the very idea of private rights as well as the demand for them is a "product" of the polis, it is not clear what it means to claim a right against Athens. Nor is it clear what an "independent" assessment means or where it would come from.

among his fellow citizens and within the laws they share that philosophy has any prospect of having a voice in the world. Outside them the philosopher would be consigned to futility, flattery, or silence.[61] Thus by running away from Athens Socrates would be disguising his appearance not merely with peasant garments but with pretense. To accept exile would be to give up citizenship and thus philosophy.

It is then as a citizen of Athens that Socrates examines the lives of others. And because all citizens share a common life, the examination of one's own life is also an examination of the life of the city. Only in this way and in this context is it possible for philosophy and politics to be reconciled without compromise, giving philosophy a new subject matter, the polis, and making the highest norms and laws of political action the chief problem of philosophy.[62]

But this is one-sided. For Socrates is not *just* a citizen. Nor does he owe everything to Athens. The polis and laws gave him all the good things they could, but they could not give him everything. (His *daimon* owes nothing to the polis.) Nor are the laws of Athens to which he offers such unconditional obedience simply the laws of contemporary Athens. Rather they are idealizations of an abstract archaic law. It is to this idea of law and of Athens that Socrates offers his obedience. And by making this law holy and the embodiment of wisdom, tradition, and the will of the gods, he implicitly condemns any legal practices that depart from it.

Still, exile is no solution. To the degree that what he has become derives from his being an Athenian, his fleeing would be superfluous, since he will carry part of his native city with him wherever he goes. Given what he owes to Athens, it would be impious to flee in defiance of the laws. Given the philosopher's need for location among fellow citizens, it would be self-defeating for him to leave. In the *Apology* he rejects the punishment of exile on the grounds that he is not so irrational "as not to know that if

---

[61] See Socrates' remarks in the *Republic*, 495c. The theme of silence runs throughout the *Crito*. At the conclusion of the dialogues, Socrates, turning to his "dear friend Crito," yet immune to anything Crito might say, invokes the dervishes of Cybele. In their frenzied passion they can hear only the music of the flutes, as he can hear no words other than those spoken by the laws. Only silence is possible and Crito is left with no choice but to conclude *ouk echō legein* ("I have nothing to say"). John Burnet explains that the Corybantic enthusiasm to which Socrates refers (*hoi corybantiōntes*) has to do with the homeopathic treatment of nervous and hysterical patients by wild pipe and drum music. "The patients were thus excited to the pitch of exhaustion, which was followed by a sleep from which they awoke purged and cured" (*Plato's Euthyphro, Apology of Socrates, and Crito* [Oxford: Clarendon Press, 1924], p. 211). It would take a more detailed treatment of the *Phaedo* to work out the implications of this reference. R. Guardini, in his *The Death of Socrates* (Cleveland and New York: Meridian, 1962), pp. 89–90, interprets this reference differently.

[62] See Max Pohlenz, *Freedom in Greek Life and Thought* (Cordrecht, Holland: D. Reidel Publishing, 1966), p. 57, and Werner Jaeger, *Aristotle* (New York: Oxford University Press, 1962), appendix 2.

you, who are my fellow citizens, could not endure my conversation and my words, but found them too irksome and disagreeable, so that you are now seeking to be rid of them, others will not be willing to endure them. . . . A fine life I should lead if I went away at my time of life, wandering from city to city and always being driven out" (37c–d). For Socrates, being uprooted from Athens is a more certain evil than death.[63]

The archaic quality of the laws directs us back to an older ancestral religion in which exile—expulsion from the tribe—was a punishment worse than death. As we saw with Orestes, Oedipus, and Cadmus, depriving a man of the assistance of his kinsmen, gods, fellow citizens, and ancestors left him homeless, equal to nothing. The outcast, together with his descendants, might even be burdened with a curse until the end of time. Certainly this soul without a tomb or dwelling place was often a malevolent spirit haunting his people forever. Perhaps part of Socrates' fear of exile is the prospect that he and his philosphical descendants will stalk the world as did the malevolent spirits of old.[64]

In one way Socrates is already a political exile and partial stranger among his own people and in his own city. As we saw, he speaks of himself as a foreigner in the law courts and to their manner of speaking. In the *Crito* he withdraws from his friend and fellow citizen into what seems an impenetrable solitude, turning away from Crito to the rarified and reified city of his laws. In this sense Socrates seems to be leaving the circle of commitment, belief, and practice that define common membership.

There is another way to tell this story having to do with the original Greek meaning of "theory."[65] Originally a *theōros* was either an ambassador sent to observe the sacred festivals of a foreign city or an envoy to Apollo's oracle of Delphi. As ambassadors, theorists were spectators (*theatai*) whose distance from the action provided a view partially hidden from those taking part in the spectacle. Whereas participants are bound to the particular, like an actor whose enacting of a part precludes the knowledge of the whole available to the audience, the theorist, like an audience, is able to compare and judge with an impartiality denied the actors. (*Theōreō* literally means both being a member of an audience and comparing or judging.)

[63] "To cut men off from their living center, from the networks with which they naturally belong; or to force them to sit over the rivers of some remote Babylon and to prostitute their creative faculties for the benefit of strangers, is to degrade, dehumanize, and destroy them" (Isaiah Berlin, "Herder and the Enlightenment," in *Aspects of the Eighteenth Century*, ed. Earl R. Wasserman [Baltimore: Johns Hopkins University Press, 1965]).

[64] See the discussion of exile in Fustel De Coulanges, *The Ancient City* (New York: Doubleday, 1956), pp. 17–19.

[65] I have discussed this at length in my essay, "Creatures of a Day: Thought and Action in Thucydides," in *Political Theory and Praxis: New Perspectives*, ed. Terence Ball (Minneapolis: University of Minnesota Press, 1978), pp. 28–56.

As an envoy to the oracle, the theorist was an intermediary between the city and the god, which is one reason why ancient etymology connected *theōros* with *theōs-hora*, to see a god. As an intermediary, the theorist was expected to return with a literal rendering of the priestess's words. He was not a man apart; nor was theorizing a distinctive activity.

There were expansive possibilities latent in this circumscribed conception of theory. As these possibilities were realized, theoretical activity became akin to divine activity. With this, a theorist might now observe the practices of his own city with the same distance he had maintained in his visit to strange lands. This suggests that, as theory became a way of life distinct from citizenship, the theorist might become a partial exile even within his own city. Rather than being an official of his city, he became instead a partial outsider in it. If, as Emile Benveniste has argued,[66] the original meaning of *eleutheria* was being among those who shared your ways and roots, then "choosing" partial exile amongst your own implies an idea of freedom distinct from the idea of membership.

But this is anachronistic and an exaggeration. Socrates does not speak of the city of the soul here as he does in the *Republic*. "Socrates," writes Thomas G. West in the concluding paragraph of his book, "neither flees into a life of the mind that remains oblivious to its political context, nor does he embrace a preference for his fatherland over his own soul. His life's end comprises a profound gesture of obedience to each of the two great authorities over him, but he does not and cannot finally choose one over the other or pay consistent homage to both."[67]

WEST'S CHARACTERIZATION of Socrates echoes Nussbaum's characterization of Greek tragedy and MacIntyre's of Sophocles. For MacIntyre, Sophocles accepts the existence of "an objective moral order, but our perceptions of it are such that we cannot bring moral truths into complete harmony with each other" in any certain hierarchy. To choose one moral truth "does not exempt me from the authority of the claim I choose against."[68] That is what the *Apology* and *Crito* suggest as well.

This theme or tension, expressed and lived by Socrates of the *Apology* and *Crito*, was present from the beginning of tragedy and this book. It was present in the *Oresteia's* imagery of road building and nets, in the "strangeness" of man in the choral ode of *Antigone*, and in Oedipus's exemplification of that strangeness. It was also present in Pentheus's banishment of "the other" which came to dominate and destroy him, and in the dialectic between greatness and suffering in Thucydides. And it is

---

[66] *Indo-European Language and Society* (Coral Gables, Fla.: University of Miami Press, 1973), bk. 3, chap. 3.

[67] West, *Plato's Apology*, p. 232.

[68] The quotes are from *After Virtue*, p. 134.

present, perhaps first of all, in the *Iliad* where war and mortality cry havoc but the center, this time exemplified in the reconciliation scene, still holds.

If I am right to connect the tragic sensibility with Socrates, then we need to remind ourselves of how much that sensibility frames Socratic rationalism,[69] including the rationalism of the *Republic*. And, insofar as the *Republic* is itself a frame for subsequent political theory, that reminder has larger ramifications. Of all the many Socratic paradoxes, this may be the most significant—or if not among the most significant, then among the most ignored.

---

[69] See Kraut's discussion of Socratic pessimism (*Socrates and the State*, p. 208 and passim).

EIGHT

Plato's *Republic*: The Justice
of Tragedy

THE PURPOSE of this book is twofold: to compare three plays and works of political theory around three substantive issues and, in the process, show the ways in which tragedy provided a framework for classical political theory. Given this purpose and the organization of the book outlined in chapter 2, it is time to compare the idea of justice in the *Oresteia* and the *Republic*, which will elaborate the continuities between tragedy and theory. But there is something of a stumbling block to this particular phase of the argument and to the project as a whole—the *Republic*'s harsh criticism if not outright repudiation of tragedy. It is true that Thucydides defined his work against what he regarded as the irresponsibilities of the poets, and that Socrates (in the *Apology*) castigates the poets for their inability to articulate the grounds for whatever knowledge may be present in the words they speak. But the *Republic* is something different and more substantial. If Plato is right about the long-standing feud between poetry and philosophy, then much of what I have said about their relationship (or is implied about it by the book's structure) is, to be generous, misleading. Moreover, if tragedy is a political institution essential to the democratizing of Athens, then Plato's rejection of it implies a redefinition of politics as it was practiced and a repudiation of democracy as that was generally understood.

Given the way I have talked about tragedy and the way the *Republic* is usually read, Plato's assertion seems incontrovertible. In the educational system of the city in speech, Agamemnon's dilemma would not be taught because it could never have happened. No god would force a man to choose between his daughter and avenging injustice. No such moral complexity can be allowed to torment a healthy soul or city. Similarly *Oedipus Tyrannos* should be banned, for its portrait of the gods, for its public consideration of incest and patricide, for its mere suggestion that a fate is undeserved and unchosen, and by its general view of human beings as enigmas beyond the scope of mortal definition and control. The *Bacchae* may be the most offensive play of all given its vivid description of dismemberment and its misrepresentation of Pentheus's literalism as an aspect of tyranny rather than as an aspect of justice. For there is an analogous one-dimensionality to the theory of justice in the *Republic* (one person, one task), the readings of the poets offered by Socrates in it, and the way the young Theban king "reads" Dionysus and his situation. Even worse, Euripides seems to countenance, if not celebrate, Dionysian madness, surely a direct threat to the rule of reason.

Here there can be no tension between roads and nets as in the *Oresteia*; nor any cohabiting of achievement and transgression as in the chorale ode in *Antigone*. What we have instead is a path upward that leaves tragedy as well as the Piraeus (with its radical democrats) far below and behind. Not only them, but Thucydides and perhaps Socrates of the *Apology* as well. It is true that Thucydides had made manifest what was unseen or unspoken through connecting particular decisions, battles, or speeches into a pattern that exemplified the principles of war, power, and empire. But he did not go below the surface to a deeper level of reality as much as redescribe the surface. For his part Socrates of the *Apology* and *Crito* is still wedded to his native city and friend, committed to the idea that the foundation of knowledge is ignorance and to the notion that "political philosophy" is redundant.

But not Plato; at least not Plato of the *Republic* as that is often understood. Here is perhaps the paradigmatic global theory, the strongest claim for knowledge existing independently of and able to control regimes of power. I have pointed to common impulses in Foucault and tragedy. Plato would agree and damn them both.

At a minimum I need to challenge this reading of the *Republic* and the chasm between political philosophy and tragedy it posits. But I do not want to explain away the chasm by yet another tendentious reading of the dialogue. As a way of clarifying my argument and the issues involved, I will present Martha Nussbaum's view that while the dialogues "are a kind of theater . . . they are entirely different from any Greek theater writing we know."[1] The questions for her, as for me, are: How does Plato express a positive debt to this cultural paradigm of political education and ethical teaching? Why and how does he depart from it? For both of us, Plato's debt to theater is not a debt to some arbitrary aesthetic invention but to the social institutions of his culture, which means that his attitude toward tragedy is a way of locating him in the intellectual traditions and political practices that defined Athenian democracy.

Nussbaum begins by asking about the choices Plato had, given the background of existing possibilities for moral instruction available to him. The answer she gives, which is also given by the interlocutors when they consider the core of their new curriculum, is epic and dramatic po-

[1] *The Fragility of Goodness: Luck and Ethics in Greek Tragedy and Philosophy* (Cambridge: Cambridge University Press, 1986), p. 126. Subsequent page references to Nussbaum's book in this section will be given in parentheses in the text.

etry. This answer becomes more plausible when we remember that before Plato there was no distinction between philosophical and literary discussions of human practical problems, or any opposition between texts that seriously pursued truth and others that were primarily entertainment (p. 123).

Like tragedy but unlike earlier Greek philosophy, where the speaker-author claimed to be an initiate, a recipient of wisdom from the gods, or a god on earth, the *Republic* contains more than a single voice. Even its less animated parts present "an active ongoing discussion rather than a list of conclusions or a proclamation of received truths" (p. 126). This open-endedness extends to a dialectical relationship with the reader "who is invited to enter critically and actively into the give-and-take, much as a spectator of tragedy is invited to reflect . . . on the meaning of events for his own system of values" (p. 126) Both reader and spectator are encouraged to work through everything actively in order to see where he or she stands on the judgments or controversies being dramatized or stated. In this way dialogue, like drama, awakens and enlivens the soul, rousing it to rational activity rather than lulling it into drugged passivity. By showing us how and why characters who are not professional philosophers enter into an argument, by showing us what sorts of worldly problems bring people to philosophize in the first place and what contributions philosophy can make to their predicaments, dialogue, like drama, shows us why and when we ourselves should care about political and moral reflection. One can see this in book 1 of the *Republic*. Polemarchus cares about helping his friends and harming his enemies but does not know who his true friends are or what harm is (or whether in harming them he harms himself) and so is just as likely to harm his friends and himself as his enemies and others. For him (as for Thrasymachus, who is equally confused about power) philosophy is the most practical activity of all.

By connecting the different positions on an issue with concretely characterized persons, dialogue, like tragedy, offers many suggestions about the connections between belief and action, between an intellectual position and a way of life. The views of justice offered by Cephalus, Polemarchus, and Thrasymachus emerge from and reflect back on the life they have lived. (Thus it is hardly surprising that Cephalus should think of justice in accounting terms.) Consequently we are led, as readers, to assess our own individual relationship to the dialogue's issues and arguments (including its argument about individual relationships and the connection between intellect and action).

Penultimately, through its depiction of the dialectical process, dialogue can show us moral development and political education taking place. Like the *Oedipus Tyrannos* it can show us the forces that lead to change or increased self-knowledge and the fruits of change in practical life. Seeing such examples is an important part of our learning from a written text. It is a "kind of learning that the inertness and the one-voiced structure of the non-dramatic didactic moral texts deny us" (p. 128).

Finally, "the shared concern of tragic drama and dialogues with debate and responsive interaction can be seen in their common emphasis on elenchos or cross-examination" (p. 129). We can see this most clearly in the *Oedipus Tyrannos* where the king begins confident of his control of the situation only to discover that, like so many interlocutors in the dialogues, he has greatly simplified the actual life he leads, the choices he has made, and the values that have engaged his energies and commitments. The dramatic action consists in Oedipus's painful learning of the deficiencies in his previous learning until he acknowledges his own deep perplexity.

The plurality of voices, sense of intellectual exchange as an activity, the emphasis on individual competence and collective responsiveness, the stress on reflection as emerging from worldly perplexities, the idea of intellect as a preparation for action and of people as capable of moral and political education are all continuous with the nature of Athenian political discourse where (at least in the fifth century) "public debate is everywhere and each citizen is encouraged to be either a participant or at least an actively critical judge." While these practices were subject to manipulation and abuse (as in the Mytilenean and Syracusan debates) "they had at their best the characteristics that Plato seeks" (p. 127).

But for all this, the dialogues are not tragedy and even purged Athenian political discourse is not enough. What we get is "a theater constructed to supplant tragedy as the paradigm for ethical teaching" and political education (p. 120). Not only are the characters in the *Republic* familiar figures who speak in conversational prose, there is no action in the dialogue as there is in drama. Whatever learning takes place is in the mind, not in the action. That learning cannot come from pain and anguish of the kind characters in tragedy suffer. Indeed, the language, argument, and aim of the dialogues is not to move or sway us but to make us ashamed of being moved and swayed by anything other than reasoned argument.[2] Although the dialogues engage our wits and demand that we be intellectually active, they do so by discouraging any arousal of feelings or emotions except to draw us into argument (as in book 1 of the *Republic*).

But tragic *elenchos* depends on the emotions, feelings, and sensuous image,[3] all of which warn us of the dangers inherent in all searches for a

---

[2] Nussbaum thinks the myths in the *Republic* are not emotionally stirring or philosophically central. I disagree, and on that disagreement turn other disagreements.

[3] "Creon learns not by being defeated in an argument, but by feeling the loss of a son and remembering a love that he had not seen or felt truly during the loved one's life. As long as Creon remained on the level of intellect and argument, he remained self-confident, not con-

single form or account of the truth. Drama continually "displays to us the irreducible richness of human values, the complexity and indeterminacy of the lived practical situation" (p. 134). It displays and encourages a process of reflection and self-discovery through persistent attention to and reinterpretation of concrete events, images, and incidents. But Platonic reflection demands that we look elsewhere, that we search for *the* correct account and form of Goodness and Justice. Once grasped, all particulars become instances of universal truths. While drama helps us think about an incident by burrowing down into the depths of particulars, finding images and connections that will permit us to see more truly and describe more richly, Plato insists that we give up "hovering in thought and imagination around the enigmatic complexities of the seen particular." For him we must move from particular to universal, from the perceived world to a simpler, clearer world, from moral dilemmas to ethical objects that are single, natural, and unmixed (p. 69).

In sum, the *Republic* is "theater; but theater purged and purified of theater's characteristic appeal to powerful emotions, a pure crystalline theater of intellect. . . . By writing philosophy as drama, Plato calls on every reader to engage actively in the search for truth. By writing it as anti-tragic drama, he warns the reader that only certain elements of him are appropriate to this search" (pp. 133, 134).

As will become clear, I agree with much of Nussbaum's analysis, and, even where I disagree, it is often simply a matter of perspective. She begins by asking about the resources available to Plato and how his readers would have responded to the hybrid form before them. I also care about those questions, but I have an added purpose—to look at classical political theory from the vantage point of contemporary theory. In those terms the continuities and similarities between tragedy and theory appear more substantial.

Nevertheless, I am uneasy about the opposition she posits between intellect and emotions and her claim that the *Republic* discourages the arousal of emotions and feelings. Nor am I fully convinced that the *Republic* reduces the richness, indeterminacy, and complexity of the practical world in the interest of unmixed forms and certain hierarchy. Finally, I have questions about the purported absence of anger or grief in the *Republic* and her claim that the debate we witness (and enter) is not an outgrowth or a response to tragic events.

By stating what I see as central paradoxes in the *Republic* I will suggest the ways in which the dialogue raises questions both about its own cri-

---

vinced of anything. It took the sudden rush of grief, the tug of loss to make him see an aspect of the world to which he had not done justice" (Nussbaum, *The Fragility of Goodness*, p. 133).

tique of tragic poetry and moves closer to what it explicitly rejects. For instance, what are we to make of the *Republic*'s own poetry? Does it circumnavigate the criticisms it contains? Does it, more positively, offer a way of teaching ethical and political truths? To what extent does the *Republic* present Nussbaum's characterization of its view of tragedy only to undermine it by showing the cost of a flattened, undifferentiated emotional landscape? Or, to take a different example: because Socrates is telling the story of his encounter at Cephalus's house to an unnamed audience, is he not, by speaking in the voices of Cephalus, Polemarchus, Thrasymachus, Glaucon, and Adeimantus, doing precisely what the poets are castigated for doing in the *Republic*? As narrator of a story that he scripts and in which he "plays" many parts, does he not resemble Homer or a playwright? Then there are all those points within the dialogue where Socrates warns us about the incompleteness of the argument, of ways bypassed inadvertently, of shortcuts that have misled us. If we have been premature in the certain conclusions before, do we not need to be uneasy about certain conclusions drawn later? Finally, what are we to make of the dialogue's intensity after the cave parable, where Socrates speaks in anger at the corruption of potential philosophers and the blaming of philosophy for corruption? Is the *Republic* a response to the tragic events depicted in Thucydides, particularly the separation of thought and action?[4] In these terms could we think of it as the third play in a trilogy? The first would be the *History* with its collapse of Periclean leadership into the overactive but thoughtless Alcibiades and the overly thoughtful inactive Nicias. The second would be the *Apology/Crito* where Socrates seeks a bridge to his native city and close friend, even as he pulls back into a self-enclosed world.

Before directly addressing these queries I want to consider, in detail, the *Republic*'s criticisms of poetry. I will begin by showing how the feud between poetry and philosophy is raised immediately, though obliquely, in book 1. Then I will turn to the moral and political critique of poetry in books 2 and 3, followed in the next section by a consideration of the

---

[4] The *Republic* is also about political corruption and so elaborates, responds to, and seeks to alleviate the disintegration of forms, audience, and language depicted in Euripides' *Bacchae* and Thucydides' Corcyra. It was because of such corruption that Plato lost his initial enthusiasm for public life. After seeing how unstable contemporary politics was and having had his hopes dashed by the oligarchic excesses of his friends and the moderate democracy's condemnation of Socrates, he decided that "all existing states are badly governed and the conditions of their laws practically incurable without some miraculous remedy and the assistance of fortune" (*Seventh Epistle*, 324c, 326a–b). The hoped for miracle was the fusion of philosophy with political power. Only philosophers would be capable of discerning the true nature of justice in the city and soul; only politically powerful men could institute it in either. As I suggested in chapter 6, with Plato political corruption becomes psychic corruption. Thus the remedy lies not with his history, but in "therapeutic" philosophy.

philosophic critique of tragic poetry in book 10. Only then, in the fourth section, will I reintroduce the questions just raised as a series of paradoxes that challenge the standard interpretation of the *Republic* upon which the stated animosity between philosophy and poetry rests. In the final section I will compare the *Oresteia* and *Republic* as a way of specifying the ways in which the *Republic* is a tragedy.[5]

VIRTUALLY EVERYTHING Cephalus says is spoken in the voice and on the authority of poets. He refers to an old proverb, tells stories about Themistocles and Hades, paraphrases Sophocles, and quotes Pindar. Thus Socrates' challenge to Cephalus's views is also a challenge to the poets upon whom the old man relies for his view of himself and the world. Because Cephalus relies on traditional wisdom whose import he does not understand, he is unable to give an account of his life. Whatever usefulness poetry may have had in the past, it has become, in this world, useless if not pernicious.

There is a further problem with relying on the poets, or anyone else for that matter. By attributing his views to others as Cephalus does here, he is able to distance himself from them, reducing his responsibility for what he says and deflecting criticism from what he does.[6] I am not suggesting that all Cephalus's views are wrong or harmful. Justice *is* a matter of giving each man and woman his or her due. It does mean that he is unable to distinguish the sense in which they are true and just. Either Cephalus's generalizations misrepresent more complex beliefs or he really

---

[5] Critics have been quick to recognize the poetic elements in the *Republic*. See Iris Murdoch, *The Fire and the Sun: Why Plato Banished the Artists* (Oxford: Clarendon Press, 1977); and Julius A. Elias, *Plato's Defense of Poetry* (Albany, N.Y.; SUNY Press, 1984). They have not been receptive to seeing the *Republic* as a tragedy. Where its dramatic aspects are focused on, the connection is made with comedy. Thus Arlene Saxonhouse points to the importance of animal imagery in the dialogue, which she rightly suggests undercuts the unequivocal "ideality" of the ideal state. She suggests parallels to the *Birds* of Aristophanes and concludes that the comic ugliness of the city is part of an argument intended to show the limits of politics ("Comedy in the Callipolis: Animal Imagery in the *Republic*," *The American Political Science Review* 72, no. 3 [September 1978]: 888–901). In a similar vein Richard Patterson ("The Platonic Art of Comedy and Tragedy," *Philosophy and Literature* 6, nos. 1 and 2 [Fall 1982]: 76–92) argues that because the philosopher alone possesses the knowledge requisite for truly expert composition, he alone will know the nature of the "truly tragic," i.e., the nature of the truly best life for city or individual. And by virtue of this same knowledge he is a master of comedy, "either by creating truly tragic figures who are at the same time popularly comic, or by creating both truly tragic and truly comic figures" (p. 80). For reasons that will become clear, I do not find these arguments wholly persuasive, though I agree there are comic elements in the *Republic*. (It is interesting, though hardly conclusive, that book 10 refers to tragedy six times and comedy twice without particular citations and in the same paragraph.)

[6] Here, as elsewhere in book 1, there is an anticipation of book 10 where the critique of poetry is linked to a myth that insists on our individual responsibility for the lives we lead.

241

holds views that deny complexity. In either case he needs to learn what he really thinks and who he truly is.

Because he has not thought about his life and statements, Cephalus is vulnerable to sophistic criticism. Because his wisdom is traditional, he is irrelevant to the dialogue that follows. Given his view of justice, which he learned from the poets (or which he dignifies with convenient poetic citations), he is, for all his amiability, dangerous. Having renounced eros (with Sophocles' authority), he is philosophically impotent. It is at least interesting that Cephalus, the character who relies most on poets, is also the only character we meet who is excluded (or excludes himself) from the subsequent dialogue.

Cephalus is vulnerable because the authority for his statements and life is part of a rapidly eroding and increasingly corrupt culture. Thus his piety (he prefers finishing a sacrifice to philosophical discussion) is susceptible to sophistic attack and manipulation as Socrates shows by offering a typical sophistic counterexample. So too is poetry that teaches traditional wisdom.

Cephalus and traditional wisdom are also irrelevant. That is suggested by the separation of generations. While the old man attends to the religion of hearth and home, his son, Polemarchus, is down in the Piraeus watching a new, more spectacular religion imported from Thrace. Sons have already left their fathers. That is hardly Socrates' fault, although the fragmentation such generational discontinuity represents is part of the political corruption he must combat.

Cephalus is dangerous because his definition of justice derives from his preoccupation with money. In the *Republic* each definition of justice is the issue of a life, which it in turn justifies. Each definition is also an implicit claim for the superiority of that life, proposing that the traits of character embodied in it should be the most admired and powerful. In this sense every conception of justice is a claim to rule and power, and injustice is a claim to more power or respect than is warranted.

In Cephalus's case the definition of justice becomes the balancing of ledger books, which is why Socrates chooses an equation that identifies sons and money. Cephalus cares for material things, as opposed to glory or philosophy. Perhaps that is why he provides the material conditions for the dialogue (it is his house), and why, like the lower class in the *Republic* of which he would be a member, he is not a participant in the dialogue.

While that is one reason why Cephalus does not remain part of the dialogue, it is surely not the only one. With the authority of Sophocles to support him, Cephalus has renounced eros. That renunciation has given him a sense of focus and stability he apparently lacked before. Now immune to the distractions of youth and those passions that, by disturbing, disrupting, and distorting judgment, produce weakness and inconsistency in action, Cephalus is no longer subject to the desires of the body or the dangers of disorder. He is also closed off to the world of tragedy.

Sensuality, passion, and sexuality all connect us to the world of risk and mutability. The activities associated with bodily desire not only exemplify such mutability in their own internal structure; they also lead us and bind us to the world of perishable objects and fragile relationships, to the risk of loss and the danger of conflict. To renounce these attachments as Cephalus does is, from tragedy's point of view, to live an impoverished and one-sided life.[7] If Cephalus's renunciations are vindicated—and there is more than a little similarity between his renunciations and those of philosophy—then tragedy is indeed banished from the *Republic*.

But if philosophy is a passionate undertaking, if eros impels us, as tragedy did, to make part of ourselves what is foreign and other, to reach out and embrace a knowledge and beauty beyond anything unerotic men or women can experience, then the *Republic* does not sanction the unerotic life Cephalus now chooses. That life may well be appropriate for a man whose life is near completion, which is one reason why Cephalus cannot remain with Socrates to found the city in speech.

But perhaps Cephalus leaves not because he is confused by Socrates' counterexample, but because he is amused by it. Perhaps he has attained a serenity in which such disputations seemed child's play. However imperfect it may be, he has a piety that insulates him from the corruption around him, though as a father he is also responsible for it. Moreover, it is Socrates who first mentions the poets (328e) and so invites the kinds of responses that follow. Part of his doing so no doubt derives from the fact that this is the way to talk to men like Cephalus. But in part it implies what is obvious even amid his harshest criticisms: that Socrates fully appreciates the power of poetry. Whether he can admit it in his republic as Plato does in his is another matter.

But it is at least worth noting that the myth of Er, which follows the critique of poetry in book 10 and ends the dialogue, elaborates the story of rewards and punishments first mentioned by Cephalus. Although he is physically absent from the dialogue, there is a sense in which his presence frames it.

There is one final reason why Cephalus is excluded (and excludes himself) from the dialogue. Socratic philosophy's principle task is to guide those fiercely erotic drives that issue in tyranny and *pleonexia*. Insofar as Cephalus is without such drives, he is no longer in need of the most important ministration of philosophy. Unlike the other interlocutors, he no longer believes that the most desirable life is that of doing whatever one

---

[7] Nussbaum, *The Fragility of Goodness*, pp. 7–8 and chap. 2.

wants whenever one wants to do it. If his disinterest in power precludes him from the dialogue, it also makes his presence unnecessary.

When Polemarchus interrupts to affirm that justice is indeed speaking the truth and giving back what one has taken, (he says) he is quoting the poet Simonides. Thus Socrates' subsequent interrogation of Polemarchus is an interrogation, once again, of the way poetry is understood and used.[8] That is suggested not only by the treatment of Simonides but of Homer as well, who it turns out has fathered a poetic tradition from which Polemarchus has learned that the just man is useful only in war and that justice is the art of stealing.

Polemarchus is unable to give a consistent account or interpretation of the lines he quotes or the life he leads. Like his father he has never thought about what he takes to be obvious. This leaves him even more vulnerable than his father to confusion and manipulation, for he lacks both the traditional piety that (barely) contains the tyrannical impulses and the particular circumstances of old age which dissipate their strength.

Eventually Polemarchus "decides" on the traditional definition of justice as helping friends and harming enemies. But as I suggested, he does not know how to distinguish real friends from seeming ones, does not know what truly harms or helps someone, and is ignorant of how harming another brings harm to oneself. As a result, he is as likely to act in ways that contravene his intentions as he is to act consistently with them. Unless he can distinguish between appearance and reality, between what seems to be and what is truly so, Polemarchus will live a logically and existentially contradictory life.[9] Because philosophy, not poetry, allows one to make these distinctions, it is the most practical activity of all. If one wants to be a "good" friend and warrior as Polemarchus does, one cannot rely on Simonides or any other poet. For poets leave one confused about what matters most. Either they do not know what justice is, or they once did but could not teach it to others, or their teachings are now irrel-

[8] Hans-Georg Gadamer argues that Plato's critique is directed at what poetry had become and that his moralizing of the poetic tradition was an extension of that tradition so extreme that it necessitated the banishment of poetry; see his "Plato and the Poets," in *Dialogue and Dialectic: Eight Hermeneutical Studies on Plato*, trans. and introd. P. Christopher Smith, (New Haven: Yale University Press, 1980). William Chase Greene, "Plato's View of Poetry," *Harvard Studies in Classical Philology* 29 (1918): 83–84) argues that Plato is thinking about "the sort of plays that were being exhibited in his own day, in which strange and debased types of character were shown in morbid or questionable situations, and in which at the same time every device that the stage could devise was being used to make the presentation seem lifelike."

[9] Metaphysics and ontology (and so the philosophical critique of poetry) are already present in the repeatedly stated oppositions between what appears to be and what is really so, between seeming and being. So too is the critique of tragedy present insofar as tragedy is responsible for Polemarchus's constant shifting of views.

evant and pernicious, however useful they may have been in some earlier age or some other place. If Cephalus and Polemarchus are any indication, poetry is merely a storehouse for trite one-liners devoid of any informing ethos.

While Cephalus's concerns frame the dialogue as his home provides the material setting for it, it is his son Polemarchus who initially brings the interlocutors together and thus makes the dialogue possible. It is he who orders his slave to insist that Socrates and Glaucon wait for him and who introduces the themes and oppositions that will dominate the subsequent discussion: mastery, strength, power or excellence (*kreittous*), persuasion (*peisōmen, peisai*) and listening (*akouontas*). His "playful threat"[10] to force others to do his bidding and his teasing refusal to listen to any disagreement raises a series of questions about this dialogue on justice and about dialogue in general.

For one thing, Polemarchus introduces the contrast between the power of numbers and the power of reasoning. At first the contrast between coercing someone and persuading or convincing them seems clear. We persuade someone by giving them reasons, making arguments, building a case. But unless we can say what people know about the situation about which the case is being made and how cultural norms work to sustain patterns of deference and inequality, the contrast is overly abstract and the difference between coercion and persuasion unclear. However subject to abuse the ideas of false consciousness or manufactured consent may be, no discussion of justice or truth can ignore them. At least that is implied by Plato's moral and ontological critique of poetry.

For another thing, the contrast between the power of numbers and the power of reason raises the issue of power in general. In what does the power of reason lie and how is it different from political or economic power? Can you (is it possible and legitimate to) "force" someone to confront the truth in order to liberate them from ignorance and confusion? Does the end justify the means (and if not, what can)? Is poetry a form of coercion because it lies and philosophy never coercive because it seeks or tells the truth? (Of course it matters which it does.) If I am right that Polemarchus's (mocking) threats help constitute the community of discourse, does this mean that all such communities rely on such threats (whether explicit or implicit) including the community of interlocutors Socrates is constituting? Is he merely a slyer Thrasymachus because he has the sense to know but not say aloud that every community of speech and action is constituted by the ruling power or element? Is the noble lie in particular or the *Republic* in general a "gentle coercion" that blocks

[10] The phrase is Paul Shorey's from his translation of the *Republic* in the Loeb edition (Cambridge, Mass.: Harvard University Press, 1963), p. 4, footnote e.

that interrogation of true beginnings that would leave men skeptical toward their constituting mythologies? Does Plato agree with Hobbes that no political society can truly confront its origins and remain a community?

Finally, how seriously are we to take Polemarchus's "How could you persuade us if we do not listen?" as a warning about the dialogue, ideas of justice, and critique of poetry? Why *do* people listen, or, alternatively, why do they sometimes go to extraordinary lengths, as Oedipus does, to remain deaf and blind? Why do we seem to have such stakes in our ignorance? And what is poetry's role in maintaining the deafness, blindness, and ignorance?

Part of our stake is maintaining a familiar world, especially when that world is losing its hold and coherence. As Polemarchus's shifting definitions suggest, words have lost their meaning, leaving their users speaking and living inconsistently. Like actors or rhapsodes whose playing of many parts divides them—in contrast to justice which demands a wholeness of function, purpose, and being—Polemarchus's vacillations leave him multiple and divided. His conception of justice (like that of his fathers') is at once too universal and rigid and too particular and changeable.

Unlike Cephalus and Polemarchus, Thrasymachus cares nothing for poetry or the traditional wisdom it maintains. He quotes no poets, although he does reveal the vulnerability of those who do and, by his mere presence, the inability of poetry to achieve the most important task of political education: containment of the constantly pressing tyrannical impulses that plague even the best of men. If the two previous interlocutors were vulnerable to Socratic counterexamples, they would be hopelessly mismatched against sophistic realism.

Thrasymachus insists on confronting the real world unobstructed by fanciful moralism, traditional pieties, or philosophical disputation. He regards himself as emancipated from past authorities and able to see the world whole. He sees through disguise and rhetorical facades and is unmoved by conventional cadences of deference or civility. He has no need either to listen to other voices, except for strategic reasons, or to engage in arguments not on his grounds and in his own terms. Unlike Cephalus and Polemarchus, he is perfectly willing to accept the selfish implications their positions imply but which they are unwilling to recognize due to poetic pieties and traditional inhibitions. Justice, happiness, and goodness involve the power to do whatever one wants, whenever one wants to do it. In the dialogue and in the world Thrasymachus is the potential tyrant.[11] If it were not for Socrates, he would dominate both spheres. Here the contest between force and persuasion takes on added dimension.

[11] The political questions of the *Republic*, what people need (as distinct from what they

But realists are unrealistic. Thrasymachus defines justice as the advantage of the stronger, regards the aim of power as the domination of others, and seeks happiness in the total satiation of random desires. Yet he does not know what is to his advantage and what power is, or what are the preconditions for successful action. Nor does he realize that publicizing his views would destroy any political community he might rule, and that being a slave to one's desires makes one confused, paralyzed, and impotent. Like Polemarchus, Thrasymachus is ignorant about what he regards as the most practical matters, and so philosophy, which reveals that ignorance is more practical than the realism that ridicules it. In fact, the knowledge Thrasymachus's ruler requires to avoid mistakes also requires a radical reconceptualization of what ruling and justice entail.[12] With full knowledge of the art of ruling comes the knowledge that all arts aim to improve, not to exploit, the materials they work on.

In many ways Thrasymachus is the most important interlocutor in book 1 and perhaps in the entire dialogue. As I indicated, he says what others are afraid to say, and his presence, as well as his arguments, reveal the vulnerability of traditional morality to the attractions of tyranny. (That is shown most clearly in the case of Glaucon and Adeimantus whose passionate restatement of Thrasymachus's position is made up of equal parts moral revulsion and fascination.) Moreover, it is Thrasymachus who introduced the theme of power and rule, which, coming when and where it does, links the critique of poetry to that theme. If the poets and tragedians were indeed the political educators of Greece and were, as such, regarded as statesmen, then the question of power includes the question about the power of poetry and tragedy. It is at least interesting that Socrates's principal adversaries in book 1 are poets and tyrants.

Thrasymachus is important for one other reason. I have so far alluded to, but not pursued, the possibility of parallels between the structure of book 1 and the ideal state. As a man concerned with money and possessions Cephalus would be a member of the lowest class. Although essential in supplying the material needs of others (as he does in the dialogue and in the *kallipolis*), he is excluded from the dialogue and from ruling, which would demand his giving up private possessions. Polemarchus, the second interlocutor, is a man whose views and manner mark him as an auxiliary.

---

desire), what is their own and what is rightly shared with others, etc., are also questions about dialogue.

[12] Whether Socrates silences Thrasymachus or "convinces" him through "legitimate" argument is an important question but not the whole point. Critics who find logical flaws in Socrates' argument, or who provide Thrasymachus with the responses he should have made to avoid Socrates' criticism are engaged in a useful but limited activity. Socrates is trying to draw out Thrasymachus's life as well as his arguments, and the fallacies he falls into are an ironic commentary on that life. The danger of this argument is that it exonerates Socrates from any conceivable error.

He is potentially a well-bred dog, fierce to his enemies and kind to his friends, useful when guided by philosophy, dangerous when left on his own. If this symmetry between the sequence of interlocutors in book 1 and the hierarchy of the ideal city were to continue, we would expect the philosopher to be the next interlocutor. But instead of a philosopher we get the erstwhile tyrant Thrasymachus. There are at least two reasons for this asymmetry. The most obvious one is that the philosopher, Socrates, has been present all along. But there is a less obvious but more provocative reason, one familiar from chapter 2's discussion of Creon: an affinity between "philosophy" and tyranny.

On the face of it positing such an affinity seems perverse since one of philosophy's principal objects in the *Republic* is the curbing of those tyrannical desires present in all and dominant in a few. More specifically, one of the charges brought against poetry is that it is helpless to combat and even stimulates such desires. What then are the affinities between tyranny and "philosophy"?

There is, first of all, the drive for order and consistency, which is impatient with the tacit, often contradictory and allusive aspects of traditional wisdom. There is, secondly, as part of that drive, a tendency to insist on an unambiguous hierarchy of talents and goods, a *technē* of *technē* (a political art which knows the values of all other arts) available to the few. There is, thirdly, the ferocity and passion of tyrants, whose perverse eros typifies a great nature corrupted by poor education.[13] It seems that the passion for more is not so different from the passion to know—that, as the choral ode indicates, the impulse to create contains within it the impulse to destroy.[14] There may even be, as Nietzsche suggested, an unspoken conspiracy between absolute goodness and absolute evil, the one seeming to love others too much and itself too little, but in reality loving itself as the world, the other seeming to love only itself but perhaps being the truer lover after all. But for my purposes the affinity

[13] At 491e Socrates argues that only a strong vigorous nature can ever accomplish anything of substance and that the worst men, tyrants, are the potentially best men ruined by bad education. Earlier (at 462a–e) he talks about how love of one's own carried to perfection, which is what the tyrant does, destroys the city by making it many as opposed to one and calls eros a tyrant (see also 573b, 587a–b).

[14] The analysis of corruption in book 8 "uncovers the nexus between ideality and actuality under the form of a historical report. The lesson to be gathered from this report is that the worst constitution is intelligible only with reference to the best from which it is a degraded descendent. It owes whatever vitality it possesses to the lingering remnants of the eternal mode. Even that evil *Eros* who frantically drives the declining city into final self-deception is the heinous caricature of the divine guide toward wisdom. Lust, lurid and insatiable, mimics the boundless striving of Love." See Helmut Kuhn, "The True Tragedy: On the Relationship between Greek Tragedy and Plato, II," *Harvard Studies in Classical Philology* 53 (1942): 46.

that counts and encompasses the others is the fact that tyrants and "philosophers" reject the world tragedy depicts and presupposes.[15]

Thrasymachus defines justice as domination and attempts to dominate the dialogue. He is as impatient with its inconclusiveness as he is with its substance. His passion is not simply a desire for more but, like Agamemnon and Creon, a rage at the vulnerability and passivity that thwarts human power. In tragedy characters often reject, avoid, or seek to dissolve the contingent and complex aspects of their political and moral lives. And we can see why; simplifying and harmonizing our lives seems to free us from the guilt and remorse imposed by practical choices in a political and moral universe that escapes definition and control. To accept the existence of enigmas and riddles, of loss inside gain, and suffering or pollution as the concommitant of greatness—to accept, that is, a tragic view of "the" human condition—is impossibly painful for ambitious rational beings.[16]

Implicit in Thrasymachus's desire for absolute sovereignty is an epistemological passion (which Socrates elicits) for absolute knowledge. "Philosophers"[17] too are tempted by a rage for certainty and control, by a passion to silence voices inside and outside the self in the name of peace and order, by contempt for riddles and divided obligations that intercept firm hierarchies.

The question is whether these traits common to philosophy and tyranny are offered only to be undermined, or whether they disclose an aspect of philosophy that necessarily accompanies whatever benefits philosophy may bring (like the *pharmakos* in chapter 4). Perhaps this is the kind of philosophy Socrates predicted would occur after his death. In these terms "Plato" is being true, not to Socrates' spirit, but to his prediction and to my argument that Socrates' death meant the death of Socratic political philosophy.

In book 1 each interlocutor defines justice in a way intended to advance his own place, power, and prestige within the dialogue and in the world outside it. Each definition contains something that is true but the truth is distorted. Like the artisans of the *Apology*, the participants here generalize the knowledge and competence they have beyond the scope of its application and so exaggerate their wisdom. Ignorant of the limits of their definitions and life, they seek more than their due and so act unjustly. Because each is a part thinking of itself as a whole, they require leadership

[15] Before Herodotus "tyranny" was not an equivocally pejorative word. Even after him some Athenians regarded tyranny with favor. See chapter 4, n. 30. (It was the tyrant Pisistratus who did much to establish tragedy as an essential part of public life.)

[16] Nussbaum, *The Fragility of Goodness*, pp. 25, 45, 50.

[17] I put "philosophers" in quotes because what philosophy "is" is the subject of the *Republic* and I do not want to beg the question (see Part IV below).

and restraint lest the inevitable conflict between their claims issues in civil war.

Like a just ruler Socrates does not dismiss them and their claims. The truth in what they say must be brought to light and what is legitimate about the lives they lead must be acknowledged. But for them to realize the truth and legitimacy of their particularity they must be made to see and think less particularly. Only when they envision themselves from a more inclusive perspective will they understand what they are doing to themselves and others, to their souls and to their city. That requires revealing the inconsistencies that prevent them from living purposeful, virtuous, and happy lives. The consequent disorientation—Socratic *elenchos*—is a necessary (though not sufficient) condition for bringing men and women to think about the whole and their place in it. Parochialism is our comfort and our constraint.

The first book of the *Republic* makes it clear to the interlocutors and readers alike that Socrates is the only one who knows the place of each claim, the value of each art or trait, and the respect due each quality in cities and souls. He alone knows where each part fits to make a whole. Whereas each man or woman may have a *technē*, the philosopher has the *technē* of *technē*. But his claim, unlike those of the others, is not grasping for more. Precisely because the philosopher has that *technē*, he does not claim his "due" as other men understand it. Whereas they seek wealth, power, honor, or glory, he does not, at least not as they see or seek them. His care is for knowledge and wisdom, for the whole and what is shared and common.

Surely this kind of philosophy is not tyrannical. In fact, Socrates' constituting a community of interlocutors so that they can become various voices in a conversation seems a legitimate exercise of authority, more like Solon than Thrasymachus. Moreover, whatever hierarchy exists reminds one of a teacher with his students rather than of Creon with his subjects. Although there are inequalities between Socrates and the other interlocutors (and differences between them as well), there is more reciprocity and democracy here than there is in the ideal state that results from their conversation. At least in book 1 "Socrates" is continuous with the Socrates of the *Apology* and *Crito*.

But what are we to make of the fact that the community of interlocutors appears to be so different from the community that community will construct in speech? What is the significance for interpreting the *Republic* as a whole and its banishment of tragedy, in particular of the contradiction between the conclusions about philosophy the dialogue comes to and the kind of philosophy we see in the dialogue? Is it true that Socrates would have been banished or killed in the "ideal" state as he was by the less than ideal state of Athens?

BOOK I is primarily concerned with what poetry had become and how it was being used. But for Plato this raises a prior question: What was it about poetry and tragedy that allowed it to be used in this way? If present fault is the result of past deficiency, then poetry is as responsible for its present abuse just as Pericles was responsible for the Athenians under his charge who brought charges against him.[18] Now the question is, In what ways are poetry and tragedy essentially rather than incidentally corrupt and corrupting?

Plato's censure of poetry in books 2 and 3 is inspired by Glaucon's and Adeimantus's disconcertingly passionate restatement of Thrasymachus's argument about justice. It is they who find poetic authority for that argument and thereby connect poetry and tyranny. Even our great moral teachers, they suggest, agree with the admittedly immoral Thrasymachus that justice may be called good but it is actually drudgery, whereas injustice is sweet, easy, and the road to happiness. Because justice is shameful only by opinion and law (or embraced by men too old or cowardly to do it successfully), the best thing is to appear just and so reap the rewards bestowed on those who are conventionally moral (or at least avoid the punishments meted out to the immoral), while actually being unjust, and so gaining the happiness of illicit wealth and power. What matters in the world is seeming, not truth. The best man is the clever liar who shields his true character and aims behind facades and pretenses. But what Adeimantus wants to know is what justice or injustice does to the soul regardless of whether it is noticed by gods or men. As far as he knows, "no one has ever adequately stated in poetry or prose a conclusive argument that [injustice] is the greatest of evils a soul can contain, and justice the greatest good" (*dikaiosynē de megiston agathon*, 367a).

In response to this challenge Socrates suggests that they proceed analogically, looking first for justice in the state before looking for it in the soul. That will make their task easier in the same way that reading something nearer is easier than reading the same thing far away. (Also the city is the more familiar tangible object than the soul.) To find justice in the city, he proposes that they construct one in speech. In the course of that creation they will also see when and why poetry was invented. So while the interlocutors are directly answering the questions about the just city and soul, they are indirectly considering the claims of the poet-tragedians to be teachers of justice.

Poets tolerate, if they do not celebrate, reputation and seeming at the expense of truth and reality. Because what matters to them is whether you "appear" rather than "are" just, they honor appearances. In this they

---

[18] See the *Gorgias*, 515a–516d, where Socrates makes (perhaps purposely) a thoroughly perverse argument which ignores the historical constraints under which political actors live.

are like Cephalus, who does not know what is owed to whom under what circumstances; like Polemarchus, who does not know who his friends are; and like Thrasymachus, who craves power but does not know what it is.

The ignorance of poets is matched by their perversity. Instead of honoring actions that enhance courage, moderation, and wisdom, they depict gods and heroes as cowardly, intemperate, and foolish. Instead of glorifying goodness, they sing of sons who punish fathers, or gods who war with each other, of mothers binding sons and fathers casting out children, and of impious heroes and violated oaths. And all this is represented to children who are then expected to live good and just lives. Is it any wonder that cities are filled with *stasis* or that Polemarchus defines justice as helping friends and harming enemies?

Furthermore, poetry is shallowly optimistic and subversively pessimistic.[19] On the one hand, it presents the gods as if they can be bribed, as if the right offerings and rituals can rectify a life of gross injustice. The assumption is that men can control and are the measure of the gods rather than the other way around (365c–d). The implication is that there is no point in living a truly good life or even a seeming one, until just before the end when recompense falls due. Is it any wonder that Cephalus regards justice as a matter of repayment?

The poets, however, also present the gods as indifferent to human deeds and needs. In this mood they suppose a man helpless to change a fate that is beyond his control and arbitrarily assigned. The gods allot misfortune and evil randomly to good and bad men alike. Because there is no necessary connection between merit and reward, there is no reason to be meritorious. In the first view men control their fate through corruption of the gods; in the second they are puppets of gods who rule capriciously. In the first view men can escape responsibility for their deeds by giving gifts; in the second they avoid responsibility by blaming forces beyond their control.

The problem is not merely that men pervert the gods (and thus themselves) but that those perversions are contradictory and so lead to a further perversion. Different poets say different things about the same issues, the same poet says different things at different times, and so the gods appear in contradictory guises and are portrayed as themselves changeable. (Recall the *Bacchae* in this regard.) "Do you suppose," Socrates asks, "the god is a bewitcher capable of purposefully deceiving us by revealing himself at different times in different forms, at one time changing himself and passing from his own form into many transformations, at another time deceiving us and making us think such things about him?" (380d). Instead of a standard by which to judge action and men in the

---

[19] See Kuhn, "The True Tragedy," pp. 40–41.

world, the gods are portrayed as participating in the flux and particularity of that world. The need is for someone or some criterion by which just men and actions can be accurately and effectively portrayed. And that requires both knowledge of what is noble and a capacity to embody that knowledge in tales that compel imitation without coercion and attract without flattery. That is the challenge and opportunity for philosophical poetry.

Although such poetry describes the *Republic* as a whole, including the tale of education in the ideal state which is the subject of books 2 and 3, Socrates here rejects the idea of philosophical poetry, cautioning Adeimantus that they are not poets now but founders of a city (*ouk esmen poiētai egō te kai su en tōi paronti, all' oikistai poleōs*, 379a). As such they are to provide models for stories (*eidenai . . . mythologein*) but not compose them in detail. Later in book 3 Socrates suggests a more fundamental reason for rejecting the fusion of philosophy and poetry: they do not yet know what philosophy entails and so what justice "is" (392c). Any full assessment of poetry including the prospects for philosophical poetry must wait for the analysis of the Forms, which is why Socrates' reconsideration of poetry in book 10 is in epistemological and ontological terms. Still, we do have some sense of what a philosophically informed poetry would be like.

Certainly it would show men that they, not the gods, are responsible for their fate and that those gods never cause evil (though they may well punish men for their own good). Surely such poetry would itself provide appropriate exemplars to shape the souls of (especially) the young. This means that poets cannot decide on the content, style, or purpose of their poetry but must subordinate these to moral ends determined by philosophers.[20] Because we become what we imitate, poets will be compelled on pain of punishment to "embody in their poems the image of good character or else be forbidden to write poetry among us" (*tēn tou agathou eikona ēthous empoiein tois poiēmasin ē mē par' hēmin poiein*, 401b). Whoever helps us see and sense the world necessarily affects our vision of it and our orientation in it. Whoever molds our language shapes our thought, our feelings, and so our character. Whoever moves us to passion moves us to action. Whoever touches our soul changes who and what we love. The striking image or the memorable phrase engraves itself on the mind and in the heart.[21]

[20] Philosophical poetry would be attached to truth even when, like a physician who must carefully prescribe an appropriately limited dosage lest the cure kill, it temporarily withholds the truth from those it might harm. For example, given the plasticity of the young and their need for righteous models and mentors, it would be dangerous to tell them Homeric stories about the gods fighting each other even if it were true.

[21] "Whoever helps us see a world . . . necessarily affects our vision of and orientation in

Because we become what and who we imitate (395d), all models must tune the soul to justice, which is exactly what imitative poets, such as the tragedians, cannot do. As opposed to narrative poetry in which the speaker remains distinct and distant from the actors whose deeds he recounts, imitative poetry requires the actor or speaker to take on many roles. But if justice is fitting a man's nature to his art, thereby avoiding the inner and civic conflict that arises when men do more or other than they are suited to do, then imitative poets are unjust in themselves, in what they require actors to do, and by the example they set for others. Because those who write or enact tragedy imitate all things and everyone, they are never whole but are instead "alienated" from their true selves and nature, divided in parts like a city in the throws of civil war, hidden behind disguises and shifting aspects. Such men are clearly unfit teachers of the guardians and so must be excluded from the ideal state. If by some miraculous chance a clever man (*sophias*) capable of assuming an infinite variety of shapes and imitating all sorts of things were to come to the ideal city intending to peddle his wares we would, Socrates says,

> kneel down and worship him [*proskunoimen*] as a sacred man [*hieron*], wondrous [*thaumaston*] and pleasing [*hēdun*] but we should say to him that there is no such man among us in the city, nor is it lawful for such a man to arise here and send him away to another city, after pouring myrrh over his head and crowning him with wool. We ourselves would, for the sake of our souls, use a more austere and less pleasing poet and storyteller, one who would imitate the style of the good man and would tell his stories according to the patterns prescribed at the beginning [*lexin mimoito kai ta legomena legoi en ekeinois tois tupois*]. (398a–b)

It is worth emphasizing how far this argument—that imitative poetry lowers our character as it fragments it—is from the aim of tragedy and Socratic dialogue as described in the *Apology*. In chapter 2 I argued that tragedy enabled its citizen-audience to achieve an impartiality impossible amid the pressures of debate and the urgency of decision. Putting oneself in place of another, coming to see things from their point of view, extends our moral horizon and makes us more open-minded and flexible.[22] This

---

the world. Whoever shapes our language shapes our thought. Whoever molds our feelings molds our character. Whoever moves us to passion moves us to action. There can be no uninformative, uneducational poetry. The striking image, the memorable phrase, the well-wrought metaphor inevitably engrace themselves on the mind; the beautiful, impressive utterance leaves an indelible imprinting that becomes part of the permanent cognitive, as well as ethical configuration of the soul." See Laszlo Versenyi, "Plato and Poetry: The Academicians' Dilemma," *AN* 16 (1977): 135.

[22] See the discussion in Julia Annas, *An Introduction to Plato's Republic* (New York: Oxford University Press), pp. 95–101.

characteristic of tragedy is clearest in the *Oresteia*: in Orestes' view of his act as opposed to the view of their similar acts taken by his mother and father; by Athena's greeting to Orestes and the Furies; by the insufficiencies of Apollo and the Furies; and by the transformation of the latter into Eumenides. The same concern for impartiality is present in the *Apology* and in the *Republic* itself, insofar as the latter is a dialogue. What is also present there but not in tragedy or the *Apology* is the prospect of objectivity, of a science of knowledge and the absolute attainment of truth and knowledge of the Good (511c). It is the prospect of such knowledge which makes tragedy and dialogue seem inadequate. But if such a prospect is unrealizable or uncertain, if the doubts and hesitancies Socrates expresses are more than ploys, if the dialogue's turning back on itself and its layers of irony force open what is explicitly being closed, if the discussion of higher dialectic and the Idea of the Good take place in the creation of a state whose status as an ideal and prospects for realization are equivocal at best—if all this is true, then the critique of poetry's insufficiencies becomes problematic.[23]

IN MOST RESPECTS the censure of poetry in book 10 draws out the implications of arguments introduced in books 1-3. Numerous passages and points in the earlier books anticipate the ontological and epistemological critique of the later. There is Cephalus's and Polemarchus's inability to distinguish between what appears to be and what is, which, together with their adherence to poetically inspired positions that are overly abstract and overly particular, leaves them confused in their thought and life. Then there is the way they hide behind the poet as the poets hide behind their characters, everyone avoiding responsibility in a world of disguise and pretense. Again, the early focus on the dangers and deficiencies of imitative poetry prepares for book 10's critique of imitation as a whole and its singling out of tragedy. In addition, the portrait of imitative poets and actors as lacking firm psychic identity and political form anticipates the later criticism of the tragedians as flatterers appealing to the irrational tyrannical part of the soul. Finally, there are places in the early critique of poetry where Socrates pointedly breaks off the discussion on the grounds that it has gone as far as it can given the present understanding.

In each case the break includes a promissory note. Thus Socrates insists against Adeimantus's impulse actually to write the stories to be told the guardians, saying that the interlocutors are not poets "now," and he cuts short the critique of poetry's content until they know what justice is. Now they know. The question is whether that knowledge substantially changes

[23] Greene, "Plato's View of Poetry," p. 48.

what can be seen and said about poetry, and whether, armed with this knowledge, they can now be philosophical poets themselves. That prospect seems even more remote than before because the philosophical critique of poetry made possible by the middle books of the *Republic* is deeper and wider than the earlier one: deeper because the earlier political and moral interrogation is given ontological and epistemological foundation; wider because the issue is no longer how poetry should be reformed but whether it should be permitted at all. If the prospects for philosophical poetry are dim, the prospects for philosophical tragedy are virtually nil, since what is to be forbidden is not merely the use of poetry in the education of the guardians but the attendance of the people at dramatic performances.

Book 10 begins with Socrates reaffirming the soundness of the groups' previous decision to banish imitative poetry. (In fact, that is not quite what they did; a good man imitating an even better one was allowed.) He can be sure now because he has presented the theory of the Forms, established the tripartite division of the soul, and shown that the tyrant, rather than being the happiest of men, is actually a madman in the grasp of monstrous desires that in better men are confined to the privacy of dreams and fantasies (571c–d). Rather than being free and powerful the tyrant is driven, compulsive, and wretched since the part of him that urges the whole man toward his true well-being has shriveled into nothing. Having established the nature of Reality, Socrates can show how far the poets, especially the tragic poets, are from it. Having established the tripartite structure of the soul, he can show how tragedy appeals to the lowest irrational part of the psyche. Having portrayed the tyrant, he can show exactly what the psychic and political costs are of stimulating perverted eros.

Given the divided line, we can see that poets inhabit the lowest realm, that of imagination (*eikasia*); given the allegory of the cave, we see that they are like the prisoners who face the back wall and see only the shadows cast by the fire. Socrates likens the poet to a painter whose representation of the image of an object in reality leaves him three times removed from that reality. Whereas the artisan imitates the Idea, the painter imitates the imitation, just as the imitative poet, even in the best of circumstances, imitates not a good man but a good man imitating a good man. Thus imitation is not just the assumption of a character or a role, but a mere reflection (in both senses) of it twice removed, and so a double distortion. Like the painter who portrays all sorts of objects he does not use, does not make, and so does not understand, the poet is ignorant about the moral and ontological status of the many lives and actions he portrays or enacts. Both suppose they are depicting nature when they obscure it;

both offer revelations that are "really" distortions; both cast lights that shunt men into a shadowy realm of confusion and madness.

Tragic poets do not cultivate our critical faculties, capacity for judgment, civic virtues, abilities to apprehend the unity behind seeming multiplicity, or our discernment of measure beyond the pull of immediate sensual pleasure. Instead they appeal to the irrational part of the soul. By drawing off and distorting the motive to probe and seducing the eros that should draw us to philosophy, they make the appetites master of reason.[24] Rather than offering paradigms of consistently moral action in a grounded world, such poets portray and imitate men's strife, inconsistencies, moral lapses, and moments of cowardice in the fleeting unsubstantial world of external appearances. Thus they leave us, as they have left Thrasymachus,[25] powerless in the face of events and others.

Homer's failure to leave any great deeds behind as a memorial to his knowledge, power, or virtue is evidence of this. If Socrates were to ask this "first tragic poet" about the most important matters of which he attempts to speak, he could legitimately ask him: "Dear Homer, if you are not third from the truth about virtue, a craftsman of a phantom . . . but are also second and able to recognize what sorts of practices make human beings better or worse in private and in public," tell us which of the cities was better governed thanks to you? What city gives you the credit for having proved a good lawgiver and benefited it? What war was fought better because of your advice? What useful objects did you invent? What private individuals did you educate in virtue? We have Pythagoreans but where are the Homerites? (599e–600c).

If the criterion of knowing something is being able to have a direct effect on the practices, arts, and actions of life, then poetry's failure to sustain any connection between what is universal and particular is a philosophical and a political deficiency.[26] It is philosophically deficient because it presents what are in fact particular manifestations of a larger pattern or order as isolated occurrences. It is politically deficient because of a parallel inability to forestall the disintegration of the community into isolated individuals. The question is whether there is a form of philosophical poetry, say the *Republic* itself, that, because it is second rather than third from the truth, can prevent the epistemological and political corruption Thucydides adumbrates in his discussion of Corcyra.

In these terms philosophy is, once again, proved to be more practical than poetry. Despite the *Republic*'s ascent to the abstract teachings of the middle books, and despite the claims of poets to be knowledgeable about

[24] Iris Murdoch, *The Fire and the Sun*, p. 45.

[25] This suggests that he too is, in this regard at least, influenced by the poets.

[26] Because we regard both philosophy and poetry as impractical, the perversity of the claim is lost on us.

all aspects of the everyday world, it is philosophy that draws us to the world and tragedy that draws us from it. Our resources of feeling, lucid empathy, disciplined sentiment, and ordered apprehension are not boundless. Because they are not, those who bestow on fictional joys or imagined sufferings intense emotions, energies of recollection, and powers of recognition are dissipating those dynamics of consciousness that are vital for the right conduct of a public life. When the cry in the street is less real than the scream in tragedy and we facilely enter into the comforting grandeur of some imagined scene or world, then we are in danger of diminishing if not devouring our resources for just perception and responsibility. Where aesthetic enactments replace political ones, when passions like words lose their meaning, as men and women become thoughtless in the sense Socrates warned about, then we get those "butchers and clerks of totalitarian rule who in their personal private lives respond with cultured delight and genuine sentiments to the claims of fiction and the arts. We know now that a man can torture in the afternoon and be moved to truthful tears by Schubert at night."[27] Plato did not know Hitler. But he did know Thrasymachus.

The problem is not only that imitative (tragic) poetry parades inappropriate moral exemplars across a stage in front of overly impressionable people, or that it is three steps removed from reality, or that it deflects our energies from what is closest to us and most in need of our attention. The problem is also that all representations of reality offer a limited perspective, which is unrecognized as such for two reasons. First, most people suppose the theater to be a place where the exercise of reason and the rule of reality is unnecessary. With its audience so disarmed, tragedy can take advantage of the conflict in the souls of basically decent but insufficiently educated people.[28] Second, even the fullest representation of a noble deed or the life of a supremely good man (Socrates for instance) would provide at most a partial, fragmentary perspective. While it may lay hold of a small part of each thing, any particular imitation does not know its partial character and so, like the artisan in the *Apology* and the interlocutors in book 1, it unjustly claims more for itself than it deserves.

Even if tragedy could in principle portray the supremely good men, it

[27] The quote and the previous paragraph's paraphrase is from George Steiner, "Language under Surveillance: The Writer and the State," in *New York Times Book Review*, January 12, 1986, p. 1. In an article, "What TV Drama is Teaching Our Children," *New York Times*, August 23, 1987, pp. 23–24, Herbert London suggests that they are being taught to be the kind of men and women Glaucon and Adeimantus hold up as representing what "the many" believe but will not say (in the beginning of book 2).

[28] That is the argument of Elizabeth Belifiore in her "Plato's Greatest Accusation against Poetry," *Canadian Journal of Philosophy*, suppl. vol. 9 (1970): 39–62. She also argues that Plato is less concerned that an audience will mistake images for originals than that they will mistake the merely pleasing for the truly beautiful and the painful for the truly evil.

cannot do so in practice, for such men are boring to a mass of spectators who only approve what titilates them: Agamemnon sacrificing his child, Agave dismembering Pentheus, Oedipus killing his father and sleeping with his mother. Tragedians do not educate the intelligence of their fellow citizens, they flatter their vices. Rather than rendering a systematic, rational account of their skills and the world, they exist to distract and confuse the ignorant.

This is not only the case now; it is necessarily the case. The very context of performance, with its mass of spectators gathered in boisterous agitation dominated by a herd mentality but possessing the power to judge, is a corrupt setting for a search for knowledge or the teaching of civic virtue (492c). In fact, it feeds those tyrannical delusions that destroy cities. Worst of all and most perversely, it corrupts those men and women whose extraordinary natures make them fit for philosophy but who, when seduced by tragic poets, turn into vicious tyrants. The quarrel between poetry and philosophy is nothing less than a contest for the souls of the best and so a contest for us all.

Still, Plato does leave the door open, or rather ajar. Evidently the quarrel is not irreconcilable. Hymns to the gods and the celebration of good men are to be permitted.[29] And poetry's supporters will be allowed to *argue* that it is beneficial as well as pleasurable. It would be best if they could make persuasive arguments since excluding poetry does violence to what we are and care for. But if the poets refuse to reform and their supporters remain unable to make an adequate case for them, they must be banished and chants sung to drown out their siren's song.

WHAT WE MAKE of the *Republic*'s criticism of tragic poetry depends, of course, on how we interpret the dialogue as a whole. The usual interpretation of the *Republic* regards the ideal state as consisting of three classes ruled by philosopher-kings whose apperception of the Good legitimates their rule and delegitimates the political and moral claims of others. Because philosophers know the truth, they, not the tragedians, are the proper political educators of the city. Ideally the ideal state would be "realized" in institutional form or in the organization of the soul (which is, after all, the point of departure in book 2). If this is too much, then at the very least the ideal must be established as the norm that guides our lives as individuals and citizens. In either case poetic speech is deceptive and distracting, an enemy rather than an ally.

I think this is a plausible reading of the *Republic*. Certainly there is

[29] "And so when we meet those who praise Homer as the educator of Hellas we should embrace them as men who know no better but must ourselves reject such men and admit to the city only hymns to the gods or the celebration of good men" (607a).

evidence for it and so truth in it. But there is also evidence that speaks against it and the truths it asserts. That evidence surfaces in a series of paradoxes (or contradictions) that "problematize" the standard interpretation's view of philosophy, of politics, and their relationship to tragedy.

To begin with, there is the curious fact that Socrates shows special animus toward imitative poetry even though the *Republic* is a narrative in which he imitates the character as he recounts the arguments of others (and as Plato imitates the voices of others including Socrates). It is Socrates playing Thrasymachus who defends justice as the advantage of the stronger and who, as Glaucon and Adeimantus, puts the case for amoralism so vigorously. Thus the argument made in the *Republic* rejects the "form" in which the argument is made.

This is no minor paradox. For Socrates' multifacetedness contravenes his basic principle of justice,[30] that each person do the one task they are best fitted to do by nature and not do those they are unfit to do. It is because of its blatant disregard for this principle that democracy is so abhorrent. Yet here is Socrates playing many roles.

More than that, there is something paradoxical about Socrates' literal reading of the poetry he quotes. For one thing, on many occasions what he quotes in order to censor alerts us to precisely those personal ties—to husbands, wives, children, loved friends—he is about to banish.[31] What we see (and are subject to) are readings whose literalism reminds us of Pentheus, the young tyrant king of Thebes whose rigidity led to his dismemberment. Such stark literalism not only stands in stark contrast to the multidimensional analysis the *Republic* itself demands, it makes us aware of Socrates' simplification and the losses it entails. One way Socrates eliminates the very possibility of those complex moral choices tragedy dramatizes is by detaching himself and us from particular affections and commitments. But when such detachment depends on literal readings of unequivocal crudeness, the whole process turns around, and the *Republic* makes us conscious of the loss its simplifications seem to commend. This awareness of what is pushed aside and below is precisely what tragedy encouraged.

This paradox is allied to another; the *Republic* criticizes poetry and tragedy, yet it is a poetic and tragic work. So the question is: Where is the *Republic* in the republic?[32] What are we to make of those haunting myths

---

[30] As Arlene W. Saxonhouse argues in her "The Politics of Interpretation: Poetry in the Republic," paper given at the Conference on Methodological Approaches to Plato and His Dialogues, Virginia Polytechnic Institute and State University, Blacksburg, Va., April 21–24, 1988.

[31] *Ibid.*

[32] There is an analogy here to Plato's comments about writing. By placing Socrates' criticisms of writing in his own writing, Plato invites, if not forces us to ask ourselves about the

and stories that "enchant [Plato's] readers and draw them toward his visionary's grasp of life and reality?"[33] Is the dialogue a chant sung to keep the interlocutors and us from being tempted by poetry and tragedy (608a) or a new form of philosophical poetry that meets the criticisms leveled at poetry in the *Republic* or a way of absorbing while transforming myth, image, and allegory in the way individual cities were absorbed by the Athenian empire.

Myth, allegory, images, and metaphors are essential elements of Socratic *paideia*. Rather than being subservient to reasoned argument, they often frame it, certainly supplement it, sometimes lead it, and on occasion interrogate reason's limits in philosophical and political education.[34] In the *Republic* the education of the guardians (where the critique of poetry is first developed) is said to be a myth (*Ithi oun, hōsper en mythōi mythologountes te kai scholēn agontes logōi paideuōmen tous andras*, 376e). Similarly, although images have the lowest standing in the divided line, the line itself is referred to as an image (*eikona*) as is the cave allegory. In the allegory Socrates describes the revulsion the philosopher will feel when he must descend once more into the shadow world of everyday politics with a quote from the Odyssey where the embittered Achilles insists that he would rather be the slave of a landless man and be alive than be the ruler of all the souls in Hades. That same line was previously cited

---

extent to which his own literary innovations have managed to escape his own strictures. (Nussbaum makes this point in *The Fragility of Goodness*, p. 126.)

[33] Thomas Gould, "Plato's Hostility to Art," *Arion* 3 (1964): 7.

[34] See the discussion of these points in Stephen Salkever, "Tragedy and the Education of the *Demos*," in *Greek Tragedy and Political Theory*, ed. Euben (Berkeley and Los Angeles: University of California Press, 1986), pp. 274–303. In the *Phaedrus* (244b) and *Ion* (533e), the fact that poets are unable to give an account of what they do and say does not preclude their having an honorable and divine madness, which inspires their poetic gifts. The *Phaedrus* also places the artist with the philosopher as closest to truth, while relegating the imitative poet to the sixth step from it, which is still, in opposition to the *Republic*, one step higher than artisans. Just to complicate matters further, the *Timaeus* compares the Demiurge to a painter and sculptor whereas the *Symposium* includes Homer and Hesiod (but not Aeschylus and Sophocles) along with Solon and Lycurgus as men who have "given the world many noble works and been the parents of virtue of every kind" (209e). Finally, in the *Laws*, the Athenian Stranger compares their creation of a city to a tragedy. If any tragedian should come to their city expecting to put on performances before the populace, they would say to these rivals and opponents: "we also are tragic poets to the best of our ability, and our tragedy is the fairest and noblest [*kallistēs . . . aristou*] for our whole polity is an imitation of the fairest and noblest life, which is truly, we affirm, the truest tragedy" (817a–e). I do not make more of these passages because there are problems with quoting individual passages from other dialogues as corroborating or complicating evidence. There is first of all the issue of Plato's "development" (about which see George Klosko, *The Development of Plato's Political Theory* [New York and London: Methuen, 1986]. Secondly, if one takes the dramatic context as part of the "argument," then excerpting particular passages is a dangerous enterprise without an elaborate surrounding context.

(386c) as the sort of thing no sane society would allow to be taught.[35] Again, Socrates responds to Adeimantus's challenge to prove philosophers are not personally vicious and politically useless with images (487e, 488a) and likens their whole project to a painting. Finally, book 10, which begins with a critique of poetry, ends with an example of it.

The fact that book 10 begins with a critique of Homeric poetry and ends with an example of Socratic poetry suggests that the *Republic* is a form of philosophical poetry intended to reconstitute the tradition of tragic poetry initiated by Homer. Speaking to Glaucon, Socrates proposes that, should they confront any who love Homer as the educator of Hellas and who pattern their lives according to his strictures, they must love them "as being and doing the best they can be," conceding that Homer is "the most poetic of poets and the first tragedian." But they must not admit any poetry into their city other than hymns to the gods and the celebration of good men. Should they admit any other sort of poetry, they will be ruled by pleasure and pain rather than the law or argument (607a–c). The *Republic* praises the gods and right actions, and presents in the person of Socrates a man of exemplary virtue. Thus the *Republic* is what it seeks and commends, a philosophical poetry that resolves the ancient quarrel between philosophy and poetry.

This is too neat and begs the question. Even if the *Republic* is poetic and dramatic and Plato a philosopher-poet, it does not follow that the dialogue is a tragedy. Indeed the Myth of Er suggests the contrary. In that story the gods are not responsible for human destinies, which are freely chosen by human beings before birth. If any man chooses foolishly—if, for instance, he prefers tyranny to philosophy—that is his decision and the dire consequences that attend that decision are fully merited. In the long run justice will pay and the just man will be watched over by the gods, honored by his fellows, hold important offices in his city, and be able to choose a wife from whatever family he pleases.

If men freely choose their destinies, and the consequences that attend such choices are always warranted by the character and deeds of the chooser; if there are no dark shadows or irrational and mysterious forces to confound our intelligence and chosen paths; if, as Nussbaum argues, the object of poetry (as considered in the *Republic*) is to still rather than to invigorate our passions in the interest of living sane lives, then how can the *Republic* be a tragedy? These questions bring me to a third paradox, having to do with the ideas of philosophy and politics in the dialogue.

There is a discrepancy, if not contradiction, between the kind of philosophy practiced by Socrates in his conversation with the other characters in the dialogue and the conclusions they come to about philosophy.

---

[35] See the discussion of this point in Gould, "Plato's Hostility to Art."

The first "Socratic" way is continuous with the *Apology*, which means that Socrates remains a gadfly, questioning the interlocutors about the unexamined premises of their thought and life. The point is not to define justice once and for all, but to show us how to think about it. Thus philosophy remains a search for wisdom, not a claim to possess it. Because ignorance is still the foundation of knowledge, even (or especially) those who know most must recognize their partiality and thus their need for others, whether that be in political deliberation or philosophical conversation. Although there may well be those who, by education, temperament, and character are able to raise themselves above the parochialism that inflects the lives of others, they remain one among these others. Although capable of sublime moments of apperception in which they discern the figure of permanent form, philosophers too must live with the imperatives of everyday life. Philosophy and dialogue become for them a way of recollecting, recovering, and sustaining those luminous intimations of the Good which, in the best of circumstances, keep the city and soul from the moral confusion, political degeneration, and intellectual corruption. The forms are Real, but interpretations of them (as of the *Republic*) are necessarily various and even conflicting. Like the sailor's horizon that recedes before even the most vigorous advance, the Forms remain beyond our firm and certain grasp. The measure is there, and we can know it is there, but we cannot know it whole, unallayed, permanently. That is one reason why, as I suggested, philosophers too need others, as citizens and as interlocutors. In the best of circumstances these others make us more complete by assisting us on that path toward true knowledge, a path that never ends and ends too soon.

Because there is no final answer to the question what is justice? there can be no permanent elite who have the right to rule because they know it. Thus no human being can be to another as a shepherd is to sheep (which is, of course, not to argue that "Socrates" is here an egalitarian except in the important sense that all men's needs must be met equally). In these terms the ideal state and the philosopher king become less an answer to the question What is Justice? than a particular response to the specific challenge posed by Glaucon and Adeimantus. The ideal state and philosopher-king may answer *their* questions but other questions asked by other men might lead to a different set of conclusions.

The more conventional "Platonic" reading of the dialogue regards philosophy as the possession of knowledge, not simply the search for it. Through proper education, with the right initial temperament, and under the appropriate circumstances, certain men and women can ascend from the cave of everyday life and achieve not merely the impartiality that comes from seeing the world from more than one point of view, but objectivity, seeing the world whole from a single vantage point outside it.

Because philosophers can know the Good, they can prescribe a just society on earth (though the actual realization of it is certainly difficult). Those who know are properly our rulers and teachers. Seeing the Forms, they are founders of the ideal polis and the polis of the soul. In both cases they are vehicles for realizing a divine blueprint.

The "Platonic" *Republic* has been praised as an improvement over Socratic political philosophy as stated and practiced in the *Apology* and castigated as a radical departure from that philosophy. The praise is based on the belief that Plato came to realize that the search for wisdom as stimulated and constrained by the knowledge of ignorance is politically disruptive and intellectually inadequate. Men and women cannot live by questioning alone, but need answers, if not *an* answer, lest they know, or think they know, that everything is possible. Socratic questioning implicitly accepts the idea that man is the measure and thus contributes to the corruption it would end. There must be some unquestioned measure derived from nature or Being that exists independently of any historical configuration of power. The acceptance of this imperative led Plato to elaborate political questions, first into moral ones (as Socrates did), then into epistemological, metaphysical, and ontological ones. If Thucydides disinterred politics from cosmology and Socrates largely accepted that autonomy even while criticizing its amoralism, Plato reinserted politics into a cosmological framework and so gave the Socratic moral critique the grounding it required while necessarily transforming its place in, and attitude toward, public life.

The pejorative assessment argues that Plato succumbed to the tyrannical impulses of philosophy for order, consistency, and closure. By redefining political philosophy, he confused politics and philosophy, action with argument, and *praxis* and *poiēsis* in a way that both Thucydides and Socrates avoided. Regarding men and women as inanimate materials analogous to the wood or leather a craftsman shapes into an object according to his idea, Plato is a totalitarian and antipolitical. Seen in this light, the *Republic* is more diatribe than dialogue, and the interlocutors are less characters with independent points of view than convenient appendages who disagree on cue and agree all too often. Their passivity and inferiority lend plausibility to the authoritarian political analogies of the *Republic*.

The conclusion of this indictment is that Socrates would have been banished if not killed in the ideal state Plato has him construct. One might say that Plato comes to agree with Socrates' accusers and kills Socrates' intellectual being as the Athenians did his physical being. Once Socratic political philosophy is vanquished, we get not gadflies but philosopher-kings, not questioners, but rulers who manipulate myths, poetry, and the language of fraternity in order to establish a regime whose principle raison d'être is making the world safe for philosophy.

The two ways of doing philosophy have corresponding ideal "states." One is the community of interlocutors whose material conditions are provided for by Cephalus, who are "forced" together by Polemarchus, and who are transformed into a moral community by Socrates.[36] The other community consists of three classes: the lowest who are preoccupied with the material matters, the auxiliaries who are kind to friends and fierce to enemies, and philosopher-kings who rule them both in the interests of all. Both cities—the city the interlocutors create with Socrates' leadership and the community they create by creating that city—are based on the need men have of each other. Both cities are communities of partners and friends who compensate for the insufficiency that afflicts all human beings. In both, the active presence of others embodies the principle of justice as performing the part for which one is best fitted. Yet the nature of friendship and partnership is different in each as are the way men participate in the respective cities and how the principle of justice is manifest. In the one, mutuality and reciprocity take place in a conversation about which the interlocutors share some common understanding and in which there is relative equality.

Here, as in the theater, individuals form themselves into a community of response through shared participation in a collective endeavor. In this community justice is manifest in the process of dialogue itself and by Socrates' respect for the character and arguments of the interlocutors. Particular characters and standpoints are not treated as mere exemplifications of general rules (which is not to deny that Glaucon and Adeimantus are types as well as individual characters). Nor is the perceived world simply a preface to the perception of another world whose greater lucidity and coherence transform the political world, by comparison, into a cave. Rather than rushing from the realm of opinion and multiplicity to a simple, more ordered one, there is a "hovering in thought and imagination around the enigmatic complexities of the seen particular."[37]

In the other city, what mutuality and reciprocity there are take place

---

[36] When (369c–d) Socrates suggests building the city in speech, he says it "will be brought into being by our needs," meaning both the needs men have in general and the needs of the interlocutors who are also constituting their own city as they constitute the other. There are in fact a number of ideal states, each of which appeals to one part of us (or to us part of the time). Thus the initial "natural" state appeals to those of us seeking a simplicity of life unattainable in the complex lives we do in fact lead. The following inflated city appeals to those of us attracted by "consumerism." One could go on in similar fashion discussing the attractions of each refinement and restatement of "the" ideal city.

[37] Nussbaum, *The Fragility of Goodness*, p. 69. One of those enigmas is Socrates himself. That is one important reason why the second ideal state remains tied to particularity even as its content becomes more universal.

within a structure of qualitative inequalities represented by the authoritarian analogies that dominate the dialogue. In this city philosophers participate not in the collegial enterprise of dialogue but as single participants in transcendent ideas. This striving to purify their soul in order to grasp ethical objects equally pure contrasts with the "impurities" of the interlocutors and the human and divine conflicts of tragedy.

What is the overall import of these paradoxes, especially this final one about philosophy and the ideal state(s) on our understanding of the *Republic* as a whole and the animus between philosophy and tragedy in particular?

It certainly complicates the questions of whether "the" ideal state can be realized, what its status is as utopian ideal (or as an anti-utopia intended to undermine idealism), how "it" can be realized, and where it can be realized.[38] It also complicates any discussion of the relationship between politics and philosophy, since the *Republic* does not yield a single description of either nor, consequently, of the relationship between them. To suppose it does misses what I take to be the import of Plato's warning about the limits of writing philosophy (which he puts in his written philosophy) and underestimates the significance of the dialogue's turning back on itself—its obvious contradictions, discrepancies within posited analogies (between justice in the city and soul), its calling attention to its own incompleteness, and so the problematic status of its surface consistency. And it dismisses the way the *Republic* warns both against succumbing to the tyrannical closure that reason seeks in ignorance of its own limitations and the romanticizing of the dialogue which rejects closure on principle. To insist that the *Republic* is utopian or anti-utopian, conservative or radical, an epic theory designed to transform belief and action or a repudiation of such transformative aspirations, an idealist blueprint for a good society or a critique of idealism is to posit simplified polarities that beg the questions Plato is trying to raise and cauterize the dialectic he is trying to establish. Or, to put it another way, the *Republic* is a dialogue about what "it" is and what philosophy can and ought to be. To ignore this and opt for one polarity at the expense of the other (or to accept them as controlling binaries) is to equate a part with the whole, exactly the error committed by the interlocutors in book 1 and by Apollo in the *Oresteia*.

I do not think the *Republic* fully endorses or wholly repudiates either city or mode of philosophy. Rather each sets limits and interrogates the other, much as the opposed forces in the *Oresteia* do. Such interrogation

[38] The community of interlocutors (rather than the city in speech or the city of the soul) has remained a salient ideal. Something like it underlies the ideals of Gadamer and Habermas (which is why Socratic dialogue has come under attack by "postmodernists" such as Lyotard).

means that "Plato" entertains the possibility that Socratic political philosophy is itself part of the problem—that Socrates' accusers were intuitively right even if they could not make the argument on proper epistemological and ontological grounds. In these terms philosophy may have to be tyrannical, although it will be the gentle tyranny of beautiful stories told by philosopher-poets based on knowledge of the Good. If the *Republic* contains an immanent critique of even this gentle tyranny which philosophy is driven to by Socrates' failure, then the *Republic* is as much about the limits and corruption of philosophy as it is about the limits and corruption of politics. And that means we should no more privilege "the" philosophical understanding of philosophy's relation to politics than we should the political understanding of the same relationship. To do so is to simplify the dialectical nature of the *Republic* and reduce the multiple vantage points it provides for understanding itself as a work of political philosophy.

Socrates wins and loses in the *Republic*. He wins because the interrogation of each form of philosophy and of politics by its alternative is an essentially Socratic enterprise. In this sense the *Republic*'s antinomies (between utopianism and anti-utopianism, the individual and the city, divine and human justice, philosophy and politics) do not issue in some third term or higher synthesis. Instead they create a dialogue in which the subject is not only a particular issue (such as justice) but how the common discourse dialogue presupposes is constituted, what it excludes in that constitution, and how it can remain permeable to what it necessarily marginalizes.

Socrates loses because Plato accepts Socratic questioning but pushes it beyond Socrates with un-Socratic results. By questioning Socratic questioning, "Plato" forces us to consider the possibility that questioning is part of the political problem and inadequate as a form of political philosophy. If it is, then we need to consider the possibility that we can indeed know things with certainty; that the authoritarian state may be a real and necessary political ideal; and that consistency, order, rule, coherence, and closure are essential for the living of a human life and the doing of political philosophy. From this standpoint the fully examined life is unlivable except by Socrates and is too much to ask of anyone else.

Agamemnon had to choose first between Troy and Iphegenia and then between remembering his obligation to what he chose against and obliterating the memory as he did his child. Political philosophers may have to choose between "Socrates" and "Plato"[39] while remembering the ob-

---

[39] I do not mean that this is the only choice or that we can unhermeneutically identify the choices with Socrates and Plato (which is why I put quotations around their name). With proper recasting we could see the contest between "Socrates" and "Plato" in terms of Foucault's discussion of global theorizing and genealogy.

CHAPTER 8

ligation to what they choose against. To silence either voice is to simplify
the complex and contradictory impulses in political philosophy and eliminate the vulnerability such complexity recognizes and sustains. For political philosophers, self-knowledge depends on an honest effort to do justice to all the impulses of their vocation, to see and feel its many-sidedness
and so be wise about its wisdom. Or to put it in the language of chapter
6, "Socrates" and "Plato" represent two contrasting forms of theoretical
power, neither of which can be ignored even when circumstances, such as
the radical corruption of the city, seem to recommend one (the "Platonic") at the expense of the other ("Socratic") form. The idea that theorists may be forced to choose one good at the expense of an equally
compelling good, which remains compelling even after it has been chosen
against, is, to repeat, the way MacIntyre and Nussbaum characterize
tragic dilemmas. Because we regard political theory as an academic enterprise no different than any other, such a choice lacks the urgency and
tragic dimension it had for a man like Plato who stands firmly if uneasily
within a tradition of tragic poetry.

But unlike tragedy, political theory does not regard either the hope or
attempt to resolve moral and political conflict in some transcendent unity
as aberrant. The paradoxical aspect of theory (which tragedy lacks) lies
in this simultaneous commitment to radical transformation of existing
institutions and a suspicion of the tyrannical impulses that accompany
such transformations. Indeed, when the preconditions for tragedy no
longer obtain, when for instance the audience is sufficiently factionalized
that the genealogical impulse in tragedy has no structure or center to play
against, then political philosophy may be the only recourse.

All this could be true and Nussbaum still be right. The existence of
paradoxes, contradictions, and complexity in the *Republic* seem to be no
more than intellectual puzzles which, while they engage our mind, hardly
develop our sensuous knowledge of the world. The issue then is not
whether the *Republic* makes us think—no one has denied that—but how
it makes us think, what it takes thinking to be, and whether it respects,
allows for or encourages the passional knowledge that comes from the
heart as it touches the soul.[40]

I think it does, although it is a passion chastened by a sense of loss.
That sense is present in all the tragedies we have considered, but it is most
acute in the *Oresteia*, precisely because its final vision of joyful celebration—in which previously disparate parts and warring parties consecrate

[40] I suppose the passionate debates over what the *Republic* means could be taken as evidence that it does indeed engage the emotions of academics whose culture is deeply suspicious of tragic emotions.

a unity that enhances their distinctive contributions to a shared life—contrasts so sharply with the experience of the audience and our own.

I am aware, of course, that Aeschylus "is not concerned to offer an argued analysis of the concept of justice of the kind presented in the *Republic*"[41] and that it is an overstatement to characterize the trilogy as a work of political theory (though not as having its theoretical aspects). Nevertheless, there are common themes and certain structural parallels between the drama and the dialogue that justify the comparison and direct us to the sense of loss that helps us see the ways in which the *Republic* is the last Greek tragedy.

THE *Oresteia* and the *Republic* are works about justice. In fact, they both depict justice coming into being: Aeschylus in the *Eumenides* with the creation of the Areopagus at Athens, Plato in the city of speakers and in the city in speech.[42] Both then are concerned with the foundation of justice and the need to define, refound, and nourish it.

In addition, the *Republic* and *Oresteia* have similar conceptions of justice. As we saw in chapter 3, Aeschylean justice has four aspects: reconciliation of diversity; reciprocal sharing of authority and mutuality of decision; recognition, in the sense of acknowledging the legitimacy of another, taking others into account, giving their voice and presence real consideration; and judgment, the capacity to see an action, person or event from other points of view and thereby accept the human condition of plurality. A just city is one where diversity is acknowledged and the inevitable conflicts that arise from its presence are muted without violation.

The *Republic* too regards justice as a matter of reconciliation, reciprocity, recognition, and judgment, particularly in the city of interlocutors. Especially, but not only in that ideal state, education seeks to reconcile previously warring forces, characters, and parties. Both modes of education aim at establishing reciprocity between antagonistic principles, forces, and characters in a way that enhances their respective prerogatives and augments an efficacy unattainable in singularity or opposition. Moreover dialogue, like drama, insists on recognizing the distinct demands of

[41] R. I. Winton and Peter Garnsey, "Political Theory," in *The Legacy of Greece: A New Appraisal*, ed. M. I. Finely (New York: Oxford University Press, 1981), p. 38.

[42] Aeschylus shows the foundation as the joint venture of gods and men in a way Plato does not. But if we think of Plato's theology as metaphysics, then the Forms play a role comparable to that of the gods, and the relationship between them and the sensible world is analogous to that between gods and men in tragedy. In each case action remains part of an order that escapes complete comprehension and control. Despite the Myth of Er and the *Republic*'s rationalism, the world remains as allusive and elusive as it had been for Sophocles.

others and acknowledging their legitimate contributions to the whole. All must be taken into account by a community that accepts what men can offer and provides them with what they need. Because Socrates recognizes what their needs are and that their deepest need is for each other, he leads them in a dialogue that is both a discussion of justice and the creation of a just community. He, like Athena, brings potentially warring factions together and shares his authority with others while doing so. His example, like hers, teaches the audience in the dialogue and the readers of it how to think about justice and how to lead a just life.

As we saw in chapter 3, from another point of view it is not Athena who teaches, but Aeschylus himself. What she does in the play he does through it. This involves instructing men and women in civic virtue through explicit content and dramatic form. Something similar goes on in the *Republic*. From one point of view it is not Socrates who teaches but Plato inspired by Socrates. And he does so by relying on dialectic between explicit content and dramatic form, though here the explicit argument plays off against the implicit teaching instead of having structure reiterate content as in the *Oresteia*. Justice requires reciprocity between content and form, which is another way of saying it requires an active complementarity between opposed understandings of philosophy, of politics, of the relations between them, and of the *Republic* itself.

Cast in terms of the *Oresteia* the tensions between "Platonic" philosophy and "Platonic" politics in the *Republic* can be elaborated by recalling the examples of just relations discussed in chapter 3. For Aeschylus justice entails that men and women be a limit on and complement to each other such that each becomes a condition for the other's integrity. Unbalanced by the "feminine" commitment to home and place, the masculine drive for excellence and recognition becomes a willful using of the world (including women) as if all in it were inanimate obstacles. Uprooted from the restraining hold of family and city, heroes are driven beyond what they see or know to passions that trample down the altars of the gods and sacrifice the regenerative forces of life. However liberating the heroic ethic may be, however necessary it is for escaping the confining female preoccupation with hearth and home, that ethic and those men destroy what initially led them to conflict.

A similar dialectic operates between the two conceptions of philosophy and politics in the *Republic*. The temptation of "Platonic" philosophy is an abstract universalism and passion for objectivity indifferent to the particularities of time, place, and person.[43] Such philosophy does not locate

---

[43] This dialectic resembles the dilemma I spoke about in chapter 7 where I contrasted the moment of universality attained in the reconciliation between Priam and Achilles with local attachments which, though essential to the living of a human life, move men and women away from the recognition of their common mortality.

itself in the world it projects and imposes on others in the name of regeneration. Rather it stands aloof and outside, looking in and down. However much this conception of philosophy may liberate us from the passions of the moment and confining attachments to the world, however inspiring its ideal of knowledge may be, it too is destructive of house and city. On the other hand, "Socratic" philosophy as depicted and described in the *Apology, Crito,* and the subtext of the *Republic* is too particular and local.[44]

The *Republic* also contains a tension between what is old, traditional, and inherited and what is new, innovative, and chosen. The problem is introduced in the relationship between Polemarchus and Cephalus and elaborated in the tension between traditional wisdom as embodied in poetry and the new skepticism that manipulates it. In this battle political philosophy, like Orestes, is trapped by its continued need of an inheritance that gives it life but which, because of its corruption, also promises death. The new cannot simply extend or replicate what is old; neither can it discard it. The innovative and chosen must be built on the still living foundations of tradition. That is what Athena teaches Orestes and the Athenians in the play and Aeschylus teaches his fellow citizens watching it. It also describes the *Republic*'s relation to the older poetic and dramatic tradition it criticizes and refounds.

Finally, as I argued in chapter 3, the structure of the *Oresteia* seconded its substantive teaching, such that the form of tragedy exemplified the justice the play explicitly commends. This can be seen in the way reconciliation, reciprocity, recognition, and judgment operate within the tensions between intelligence and passion, political discourse and poetry, and wisdom and suffering. Here again each requires the other as an enhancing limit. The *Republic* presents similar tensions and a similar need for reciprocity.

In discussing the affinity between philosophy and tyranny I suggested that passion and eros have the same double capacity they presented in the *Oresteia*: a capacity for renewal and violence, making known and obliterating, empowering and consuming. In both the drama and the dialogue, passion is the foundation of reason and the reason why knowledge has to contain the disruptiveness of passion. In both there is a juxtaposition of lucid speech, argument, and analysis with poetry, myth, and images of startling intensity.

Some commentators regard the presence of the latter as an indication of the inadequacies of the interlocutors. Others see the inadequacy as lying in reason itself. It is true that the interlocutors have characters that

---

[44] It is interesting that Socrates is called effeminate but that we know of no such charge leveled against Plato.

limit what can be said to them, when, and how. It is also true that reason has a tyrannical aspect to it. But the need for poetry, imagery, and evocative stories has less to do with the inadequacy of reason than with reason's limits[45] and with Plato's appreciation that only when language appeals to all parts of the soul can reason be maintained in the sphere proper to it. The limits of reason are suggested by the *Republic*'s recourse to parables and images when approaching the ultimate foundation and justification of the entire argument and enterprise. Reasoning and dialectic can bring one toward the Good but the nature of the Good cannot be presented in terms of dialectic and reason even if it justifies them. To put it in terms of the *Oresteia*: philosophy must be as silent about its foundations as Aeschylus's Athens is about its foundation. At the core, which is simultaneously the highest and the basis, there is, despite dialogue, silence.

Finally, there is the reciprocity between wisdom and suffering. In Aeschylus, the passions men and women have and the trials they experience because of them are the most powerful teachers of political wisdom and the firmest support for political justice. Without them, learning, knowledge, and righteousness would lack depth, hold, and point. Yet the education advocated in the *Republic* seems designed to shield its students from such suffering in the name of justice. In a play like the *Oedipus Tyrannos*, the suffering of the characters and audience is caused not so much by a specific calamity as by a perplexity at the apparent disproportion of the moral order. However, the *Republic* seems to deny such disproportion, a "startling negation of tragic potentiality" which may "have appeared to his contemporaries as the distinguishing feature of Plato's philosophy."[46] In tragedy suffering is not an alternative path to knowledge that philosophy can provide equally well or better by other means. Nor is it an instrument for generating such knowledge. It is, rather, a different sort of practical wisdom altogether. Yet Plato seems to deny the existence of such wisdom. When he does recognize its existence, he either delegitimizes it or subordinates it to the rule of reason.

Lastly, as I have argued, not only does suffering bring wisdom in tragedy, but the wisdom tragedy offers brings suffering, a recognition that even the most awesome human accomplishments (such as the establishment of justice and the polis) are threatened by the very passions and forces whose unity constitutes the accomplishment and whose presence is necessary for its continued vitality. This is made clear in the action of the trilogy and by the discrepancy between its final celebration of an idealized

[45] This is the argument of Julius Elias in *Plato's Defense of Poetry*, esp. chap. 2.
[46] Helmut Kuhn, "The True Tragedy: On the Relationship between Greek Tragedy and Plato, I," *Harvard Studies in Classical Philology* 52 (1941): 1–40.

Athens in which men have solace for their sorrows and the contemporary city, which resembled Argos of the *Agamemnon* as much as Athens in the *Eumenides*. This double juxtaposition emphasizes the precarious nature of whatever has been gained and the constant proximity of loss. It is precisely this sense of loss that connects the *Oresteia* with the *Republic*, tragedy with political theory. The wisdom of the *Republic*, as I understand it, brings a suffering for its readers that reopens the work to many of the passions and dilemmas it had previously exorcised or excised.

Loss is manifest in the contrast between the community of interlocutors led by Socrates and the world these historical characters actually inhabited. The *Republic* presents this dialogic community as a possible paradigm for political life even outside the confines of Cephalus's house and a book. In such a community there would be no social constraints or inequalities of power to distort the exchange of views and formation of consensus.[47] But, as Plato's contemporaries would have known (the dramatic date of the *Republic* is fifty years prior to its composition), most of the principal characters were killed. Polemarchus and Niceratus were brutally murdered for their fortunes by an oligarchic faction led by Plato's relatives, while Socrates was executed by the restored democracy. The men who are friends in the *Republic* will soon be killing one another for power and property outside it.[48] Under such circumstances the community of philosophical dialogue constituted and led by Socrates is hardly a promising paradigm for political life. At best it is a model Plato offers only to take away, or, more accurately, its realization in the world is no more likely than that of the vision of a fully just city with which the *Oresteia* concludes.

The sense of loss is compounded by the enormous hope for reason and its ultimate failure. Few works can match the *Republic*'s vision of ideality or its dramatizing of human longings for perfection and permanence. With a singular intensity Plato invites us to understand human experience in a comprehensive context of Being and time, to undertake an ascent to a promontory from which we can understand our own particularity with full universality. Looking down on the world complete, we can, godlike, be theorists of our own society[49] and spectators of our own actions, at once playwright, actor, and judge. With such knowledge and power the mind can transform public life and command human destiny.

---

[47] This is one way, but hardly the only way, in which Habermas's ideal of undistorted communication is drawn from Plato; see especially *The Theory of Communicative Action*, vol. 1 (Boston: Beacon Press, 1984).

[48] Nussbaum, *The Fragility of Goodness*, pp. 136–37.

[49] Because a theorist was originally one who traveled abroad to look upon the practices of other peoples, to be a theorist of one's own society is to look upon one's own practices as if one were a stranger.

As I suggested, this is something new. Tragedy did not so much offer solutions as give depth and complexity to problems. The same is true of Thucydides, though he (in the Archaeology) and Pericles (in the funeral oration) suggest that by changing our collective self-understanding we can change the world. Even Socrates of the *Apology*, though he sought to bring his fellow citizens back (and forward) to what was best in their tradition, never lost sight of human partiality. All of them regarded human folly, greed, and insufficiency as a given. But not Plato in the *Republic*. Here there seem to be solutions. Here men seem in control of their fate and character, at last self-sufficient and invulnerable. No longer must men choose between daughters and glory, be fated to unknowingly transgress nature, or seek tyranny in defense of their power.

As is obvious from the previous pages, I regard this as one-dimensional. Both the "success" and the "failure" of the ideal state evoke a profound sense of privation. Plato shows us the loss entailed by the ambition to transcend the merely human and the loss of failing to succeed in the attempt. Either path risks ignoring something that is necessary to thought and action: the special beauty of a human life invigorated by passion and alive to complexity and mutability, or the sublime order of permanent form. If the ideal state "succeeds," men and women will sever their connection with their bodily sensuous natures. If it fails, they may be ruled by them, and are certainly fated to live as the strange creatures described by the choral ode in *Antigone*. And though the other ideal state (the community of interlocutors) mediates between these alternatives, that only shifts the sense of loss. It does not alleviate it.

At the end of the play Oedipus in defeat rises to a stature unattainable in triumph. It is not simply that he accepts the fate that has been his all along, or that his exquisite tenderness toward his daughters reminds us of the opening and so the consistency of the man through it all, though these are important enough. It is rather that now suppliant and master, victim and actor, he embodies the fate of us all. Similarly, the *Republic*'s "failure" as a rationalist manifesto gives it a stature of richness and generative capacities that is nearly unique. The way it stimulates questions about the issues it raises and about itself are a testament to its rationalist aspirations and the intellectual and passional interrogation of those aspirations. Few works confront the possibility that their fondest hopes may be exaggerated or even pernicious, raise a paean to reason only to answer with a chorus about reason's insufficiency, or assert the capacity and necessity of mind to interpret, shape, and control experience while recognizing the tyranny implicit in the hope.

Few works, that is, outside of Greek tragedy. It is tragedy after all that dramatizes life and action as riddles with inexhaustible meanings that resist even the most audacious political and intellectual constructs. Like the

Oresteia, Oedipus Tyrannos, and *Bacchae,* the *Republic* points to and beyond its reduction of complexity so that its readers, like the spectators of tragedy, come to see both the necessity and the fact of reduction. As in tragedy generally, but Sophocles' play in particular, the *Republic* gives a dual message. As a form that makes formlessness and mystery intelligible, it is and provides for others a sense of intellectual mastery. As spectators or as readers we are provided with a sense of the whole denied any actor on the stage or any interlocutor in the dialogue. But because both drama and dialogue demonstrate the impenetrability of reality, they remind their audience that they too are also actors in the world (even if only theoretical actors) and are, therefore, bound to commit errors comparable with those they have witnessed. As mortals the mastery that is our glory is often misdirected and always partial.

Insofar as the *Republic* engenders a sense of loss, it brings to its readers a wisdom invigorated by suffering and a respect for suffering as a way of knowing coeval with that of intellect. It is true that we find no explosive rages in the *Republic* (except perhaps by Thrasymachus). Nor is there any flow of tears or sign of the intense emotions tragedy displayed and (supposedly) stimulated. But there are emotions in the conversation among interlocutors and in the dialogue with the interlocutor-readers "outside" it. The passions are certainly not the passions of an Agamemnon or an Oedipus or a Pentheus, but are rather like the disciplined intensity of the *Oresteia* and *Oedipus Tyrannos* and *Bacchae* as a whole.

If I am right, the *Republic* can be understood as a tragedy that self-consciously competes with those of Aeschylus, Sophocles, and Euripides, and Plato can be understood as an heir to the tragedian's vocation of civic educator. But given the corruption Euripides[50] and Thucydides depict, that inheritance and vocation require a new conception of what tragedy can be, where it can be "performed," and who its projected audience might be.

Certainly Platonic tragedy is not a political institution and so cannot educate a democratic citizenry as the playwrights could. But this does not preclude such education from occurring in the dialogue between the *Republic* and its readers-interlocutors. Plato may even have supposed that only such dialogue, by providing guidance for judging what is most worth doing, could contain the triumph of undifferentiated passion and so res-

---

[50] In chapter 5 I suggested that, insofar as the world of the *Bacchae* was the world of contemporary Athens, tragedy could no longer be the educative institution it had been and that, as a result, both audience and drama had to be reconstituted. In some respects this is what the *Republic* is trying to do. My point parallels Gadamer's (see n. 8), where he argues that Plato carried the moralizing of the tragedians so far that he rejected tragedy itself as immoral.

cue democracy from itself; that only if reason is unconsumed by interest can men (and perhaps women) deliberate together in the assembly.

But we cannot know for sure because, as with Thucydides, the *Republic* establishes a community with its readers distinct from the historical community whose corruption is the occasion for theoretical reflection. It is to this community of unlimited, anonymous, necessarily individual partners, located in an unspecified time, place, and culture, that Plato offers himself as a teacher, providing an experience of cultural reconstitution against the dismemberment of discourse and practices surrounding him. In one sense this community could be considered a third ideal "state" and way of doing philosophy, although it has affinities with the community of interlocutors and perhaps with the audience's experience of tragedy.

The *Republic* invites us to join the dialogue even as it educates us to its conception of an ideal reader. Thus it instructs us how to read our way into becoming a member of an audience it cannot define (as a tragedian could), but one "who understands each shift of tone, who shares the judgments the text invites him or her to make, and who feels the sentiments proper to the circumstances."[51] In this way we become a character in the world created by "the" text insofar as the text calls on us to function out of what we know and to realize some of our possibilities for perceptions and response, for making judgments and taking positions. To read the *Republic* is to become different from what one was. But the question is, different how?

It is like being a character in a Greek tragedy, confronted with having to choose between "Socrates" and "Plato." This is especially so if we look at writing and reading as strategy, as an action made upon a reader more than as a container from which a reader extracts a message.[52] In these terms something is always happening when we read, every linguistic experience is affecting and pressuring, pulling us along or up short, making promises that are honored or disappointed, offering conclusions that turn out to be premises.

I end this chapter (and prepare for the next) with a quote from Stanley Fish whose language recalls the themes of this book and whose argument captures much of what I have said about the *Republic*.

[51] The quote and subsequent notion of an ideal reader comes from James Boyd White, *When Words Lose Their Meaning* (Chicago: University of Chicago Press, 1984), pp. 15–16.

[52] Stanley Fish, "Literature in the Reader," in *Self-Consuming Artifacts: The Experience of Seventeenth-Century Literature* (Berkeley and Los Angeles: University of California Press, 1972), pp. 79–112.

Rather than following an argument along a well-lighted path . . . he is now looking for one. The natural impulse in a situation like this, either in life or in literature, is to go forward in the hope that what has been obscured will again become clear; but in this case going forward only intensifies the reader's sense of disorientation. The prose is continually opening, but then closing, on the possibility of verification in one direction or another. There are two vocabularies . . . one holds out the promise of clarification . . . while the other continually defaults on that promise. . . . And the reader is passed back and forth between them.[53]

[53] *Ibid.*, p. 385.

PART IV
CONCLUSION

NINE

The Road Home: Pynchon's
The Crying of Lot 49

WHY DOES Thomas Pynchon name his central character Oedipa,[1] thereby inviting comparisons between her quest in America and Oedipus's in Sophocles' play? In what way is the name a clue to the novel's meaning? Although one cannot overlook the name, it is dangerous to make too much of it given a novel that is full of clues that mislead or rather lead down unanticipated paths toward undefined destinations. There is no key that unlocks the enigmatic structure of the book (which is, of course, one thing it shares with Sophocles' play), and Oedipa's explicit doubts that her view of the world is anything more than a projection is a warning for any interpreter of the work. That warning is elaborated in the book's concentration on entropy, a concentration that, like Socrates' *daimon*, proscribes but does not prescribe certain interpretative strategies. If, as I shall argue, Pynchon means to teach us how to keep a text alive, and if such life demands resistance to closure, systematization, and homogeneity, to single readings and roads, and to flattened landscapes and mind-numbing routine, then we had better be alert lest we become part of the problem. This is a particular danger for academicians for whom the textbook is often the paradigmatic packaging of knowledge and the vehicle of instruction. One could say that *The Crying of Lot 49* is an antitext.

Textbooks not only give us information; they give us information about what counts as information.[2] By presenting the world as easily comprehensible and directly available, textbooks *make* sense in the same way we make (i.e., manufacture) sense of whatever may exist outside us. "By making easy sense it tells us that sense can be easily made and that we are capable of easily making it."[3] "Making" things in this sense kills

---

[1] In "The Enigma Variations of Thomas Pynchon," James Dean Young argues that Oedipa is only ironically an Oedipus figure because she does not answer the riddle of *Lot 49* (*Critique* 10, no. 1 [1967]: p. 72). That depends on what one thinks the riddle to be and whether one thinks Oedipus "solved" the riddle of *Oedipus Tyrannos*.

[2] The information presented in chapters move progressively toward the end, while at the conclusion of each chapter we are often provided with the questions appropriate for what we have just read. Thus the text's world is completely insulated and insular.

[3] Stanley Fish, *Self-Consuming Artifacts: The Experience of Seventeenth-Century Literature* (Berkeley and Los Angeles: University of California Press, 1972), p. 390.

both the intellectual and the natural landscape. We must be sure we do not kill his novel in the process of interpreting it.

Thus we are inundated with clues and made self-conscious about our designs on the novel. Besides the connection with Sophocles' play, there are other names and characters who invite comparisons. If this were a book on Pynchon it would be essential to consider the novel as a work of American literature (in the tradition of Whitman, Melville, Veblen, Bourne, and Henry Adams), as a theological meditation, and as an assessment of modern technocracy. Even though this book is not about Pynchon, we still have to recognize the connections between his classical allusions and these alternative narratives, particularly because this is his way of bringing separate worlds together.

Oedipa's first name may remind us of Sophocles' Oedipus, but her second name "Maas" means "more" in Spanish, "loophole" in Dutch, and alludes to "mass" as in physics, in a religious service, and modern "mass" society, thereby connecting science, religion and politics. Then there is the title, "Crying": the crier in a New England town[4] proclaiming all is well; crying as weeping for the loss of America, for wasted human and natural resources, the flowing of tears Sophocles thought essential to wisdom;[5] crying as the auctioning off of stamps, the selling of America. Lot: the story in the Bible, used-car lots, lots as plots for tract homes, one's lot or fate. Forty-nine which joins transcendence and mundanity, God with mammon, speaking in tongues miraculously understood, the moment of "undistorted communication," community, unity, Dionysus; but also the forty-niners, the gold rush, greed, the founding of the San Francisco with its night full of possible clues, a conspiracy, or drugs.

Finally if we compare the opening scene of the play with that of the novel, the invitation to understand one in terms of the other seems to be merely the first of what will be many (often bad) jokes. The play opens in front of the king's palace with an assembly of children and citizens led by a priest sitting as suppliants before Oedipus "whom all men call great" (as he tells us). There is a plague in Thebes, a blight that blanches life from all living things while growing "rich in groaning lamentation." They have come to him to be saved as he saved them from the sphinx before. And Oedipus has no doubt that he can answer their prayers.

Here, by way of contrast, is the opening sentence of *The Crying of Lot 49*.

[4] Pynchon's ancestors go back to Puritan New England where they did not always conform to religious orthodoxy.

[5] See Nussbaum's discussion of Antigone in *The Fragility of Goodness: Luck and Ethics in Greek Tragedy and Philosophy* (Cambridge: Cambridge University Press, 1986), chap. 3.

One summer afternoon Mrs. Oedipa Maas came home from a Tupperware party whose hostess had put perhaps too much kirsch in the fondue to find that she, Oedipa, had been named executor, or she supposed executrix, of the estate of one Pierce Inverarity, a California real estate mogul who had once lost two million dollars in his spare time but still had assets numerous and tangled enough to make the job of sorting it all out more than honorary.[6]

Oedipa holds no official position of power. No suppliants kneel before her or ask that she save them and their city. She is an ordinary person living a banal existence, passive, as one day merges imperceptibly into the next. She has saved no one, done nothing noteworthy, and has many doubts that she can carry out a task that seems far less arduous than solving the sphinx's riddle. At no point does she feel master of her fate.

Moreover, she is a woman, a point emphasized by her wondering if she is an executrix rather than executor. She thinks of herself as Rapunzel, confined to her tower which imprisons yet also insulates her from what she supposes to be the void outside or below. She had waited for some man to release her from the tower and save her from the void, to take her away in a romantic voyage of forgetfulness, or help her avoid some impending task that might somehow come to her such as making a tapestry of the world. But no man could save her. In Mexico City with Pierce she had seen a painting where a number of "frail girls with heart-shaped faces, huge eyes, spun-gold hair, prisoners in the top room of a circular tower, embroidering a kind of tapestry which spilled out the slit windows and into a void, seeking hopelessly to fill the void: for all the other buildings and creatures, all the waves, ships and forests of the earth were contained in this tapestry, and the tapestry was the world." Facing the painting and the act of creation its allusions to Genesis provokes, Oedipa cried. "She could carry the sadness of the moment with her that way forever, see the world refracted through those tears, those specific tears, as if indices as yet unfound varied in important ways from cry to cry" (p. 10).

Oedipa is not only an ordinary person and a woman; she also never mentions her parents (though the novel is about regeneration). But Oedipus is remembered for what he did to his parents. Pynchon not only ignores this aspect of the Oedipus story; he explicitly distances himself from it. "As things developed, she was to have all manner of revelations. Hardly about Pierce Inverarity or herself; but about what remained yet had somehow, before this, stayed away" (pp. 9–10).

Yet there are enough echoes of the play even in the novel's earliest pages to make the differences between them thought-provoking rather

[6] *The Crying of Lot 49* (New York: Bantam Books, 1967), p. 1. Subsequent page references are given in parenthesis in text.

than vitiate the comparison as a whole. For one thing, in executing a will Oedipa will "pierce untruth," the plastic surface to whose enormous human cost she had become numbed or indifferent. The surface was like Fangosso Lagoons, Pierce's man-made lake with its plush recreational facilities washing calmly over the bones of those killed in war purposely left below as tourist attractions; or like writing itself, with its dependency on ink, which comes from the charcoal of dead bones, as if writing itself is parasitic on death. For another thing, there is a similarity between Oedipa's fears and those of the chorus in the play as they watch Jocasta and Oedipus come closer to rejecting the god as well as his oracle. Her fear of the void is theirs; what if there is no world, only the tower of our minds, an ivory tower, from which we can only project a world? Are plays and novels tapestries woven to fill the void? What if philosophy is not, as Socrates supposed, a search for truth, but avoiding the void, a furtive flight from nihilism, an acknowledgment that we are by our condition isolates, strangers to ourselves, others and the world at once? Then Oedipa's crying would echo that of the chorus in *Antigone*, "My mind is split at this awful sight."

Even the Rapunzel story has affinities to that of Sophocles' Oedipus: parents desperate for a child and a prince who leaps from the tower into thorns which "pierce" his eyes. The question is whether, like Rapunzel's tears which brought sight back to the blind prince, Oedipa's tears will cure the blindness of whoever it is that cannot see, or whether she will fail, or like the *pharmakos* will do both, solving the riddle of the "sphinx" only to bring on a plague.

As the first sentence of the novel indicates, Oedipa, like Oedipus, begins by solving a problem having to do with a dead man. In both cases the death is related to a plague: Thebes is decimated, its land and people are dying; Pierce, the real estate mogul and preeminent industrial capitalist, has laid waste to the land, leaving America plagued with sprawling, garish, sterile landscapes. Zeitlin argues that Thebes is permanently plagued, that no cure is possible; having no means of establishing a viable system of relations and differences, it oscillates between the extremes of rigid inclusions and exclusions on the one hand and radical confusions on the other, and as a result the city is unable to "generate new structures and new progeny." The issue is whether Oedipa or anyone else can save America from becoming Thebes.

Initially Oedipus and Oedipa are somewhat removed from the problem since the dead men seem remote from them. But they soon discover how deeply implicated they are in the solution to the problem, even how much they are both the problem and possible solution. As their search becomes a search for meaning and identity in the context of confronting mortality, the reasons for Pynchon choosing "Oedipa" as his main character become less obscure. But why, then, does he choose an ordinary woman who never mentions her parents and name her Oedipa? Perhaps to make a point, or rather three points, about heroism, about gender, and about the novel as genre.

By dramatizing Oedipa's growing heroism, Pynchon shows how in our time ordinary men and women come to think with such tenacity and act with such courage. As a heroine Oedipa retains traditionally "feminine" traits while exemplifying those regarded as "masculine," as if to demonstrate why the comfortable polarities of gender (or class or ethnicity) will not do.[7] Oedipa is spoken of (or speaks of herself) as having female cunning and as being pregnant (though it may be hysterical) and becomes alternatively Mother, Madonna, nurturer, and Virgin. Yet she is also a hard-nosed detective, an intelligence operative, analytic and courageous. Combining both "masculine" and "feminine," she is herself a miracle, the coming together of two worlds in what may be a paradigmatic, energizing androgyny.[8]

Pynchon's pointed exclusion of any mention of Oedipa's parents may be his way of retrieving the story of Oedipus from the dominance of psychoanalysis, from our national mania for self-absorption, and from the privatization of the novel form, in order to restore the publicness the story had in Greek tragedy by virtue of drama's institutional position. Or perhaps the omission of Oedipa's parents from the story is an oblique commentary on the radical discontinuities of generations in America where children kill their parents not through physical assault but through disinterest.

The echoes of the play in the novel's opening scenes become louder and so my comparison less idiosyncratic as the novel goes on. Both *The Crying of Lot 49* and the *Oedipus Tyrannos* center on the issue of identity

---

[7] I have argued that Euripides is engaged in a similar effort. It may or may not be significant that Teiresias was a woman before "he" was a man.

[8] If we recall Zeitlin's argument of plots in Greek tragedy and recognize how central plots and plotting are in the novel, we may be able to see another reason why Pynchon's principle character is a woman. The plots of tragedy were, as Aristotle puts it (*Poetics*, 1455b), a combination of "binding" and "unbinding"; an "interweaving" that describes what Zeitlin calls "the fabric, the texture of the play." The tragic world works its ruinous effects through modes of "entrapment and entanglement." There "the metaphoric patterns of binding and unbinding continually operate in a reciprocal tension as signs of constraint and necessity, on the one hand, and of dissolution and death on the other, defining the parameters between which characters are caught in the "double bind." Zeitlin links plots and plotting to female characters who "frequently control the plot and the activity of plotting and manipulate the duplicities and illusions of the tragic world." This special access to powers beyond men's control is linked to women's exclusion from the central area of masculine public life. See "Playing the Other: Theater, Theatricality, and the Feminine in Greek Drama," *Representations* 11 (Summer 1985): 74–75.

and both explore that issue through a consideration of three themes: unity and diversity, fate and will, and "literature" as a culture form.

AS I ARGUED in chapter 4, our identity is revealed by what we say and do and by the character and fate that is distinctively ours. When we identify someone we point to those things that set them apart from others. But, as this implies, others must be present for distinctiveness to be possible. Thus identity is a matter of standing with as well as standing apart, of sharing a world as well as being different within it. What then distinguishes Oedipa? And to what community does she belong? On one level she is a member of the community of characters in the novel. Thus "who" she is is defined in terms of her relationship with them. On another level she is a member of a community which includes the reader. Here the community is America and the question is one about the status of identity and membership in a modern or postmodern society.

If identity is a matter of differentiation within a community, then loss of identity is the collapse of a community in which men and women can distinguish themselves (in both senses) or, conversely, the obliteration of differences and so the end of a *political* community. Sameness or homogeneity erases distinctions between people, leaving them part of an undifferentiated mass, passive victims of others or adjuncts of nature. Such a prospect impels Oedipus to insist that his fate is his alone, even though it means accepting responsibility for the most appalling transgressions. It impels Oedipa to enter a locked room with men in black who may be fallen angels or redeemers rather than accept a world of endless tract homes, every day being like every other day, where every lot, plot, fate, destiny is the same.

Exile or isolation leaves us bereft of those whose power empowers us, facing the prospect of an unremembered and unmourned death. That is part of the reason why Orestes risked all to reclaim his inheritance, why Socrates refused exile, and why the punishment of exile Oedipus unknowingly calls down upon himself is so horrendous. It is also why Oedipa searches out the legacy of America at such cost to her peace of mind. Something must be done, but she cannot do it alone. Something must be found, but if "it" exists, it will be among the cultural debris cast off by the winners, whose triumph now reveals the defeat within their victory. America has too much unity and too little: too much because the unity is a uniformity in which we act the same but not together; too little because we remain exiles even while replicating each other. We are, like Inamorati Anonymous, a community of isolates. "How," Oedipa asks, "had it happened here with the chance so good for diversity?" (p. 136).

The *Oedipus Tyrannos* is about incest as the limiting case of unity, and exile as the limiting case of diversity. A man who commits incest, Oedipus is too much a unit, too much one, unnaturally singular, repetitive, homogeneous. So too is Thebes, which turns back in upon itself without issue. But Oedipus is also an exile, from Corinth, from Thebes and in the end from human concourse. When he boasts that he is a self-made man, he gives voice to his so far unvoiced sense of being an outsider, without sure identity, discontinuous (he thinks) with those and the land around him.

Sophocles implies that incest and exile, too much unity and too much diversity, are not opposites but are, literally, two sides of the same coin. He also suggests, what the audience believed, that incest and patricide are acts that obliterate the distinction between man and beast, inside and outside, the wild and civilization. What Oedipus lacks (and Thebes as well) is some middle term, an Aristotelian polis that mediates between our divinity and animality, making us whole in a community constituted by diversity.

Pynchon's novel is also about incest and exile, unity and diversity. Oedipa's husband, Mucho, finds his job as a used-car salesman unbearable because of the way "each owner, each shadow, filed in only to exchange a dented, malfunctioning version of himself for another, just a futureless, automotive projection of somebody else's life. As if it were the most natural thing. To Mucho it was horrible. Endless, convoluted incest" (p. 5). Incest is repetition, the sameness of undersides rusted by the elements, the half-hidden violence that wrecks lives lived on the promise of progress and largess, promises broken by endless trade-ins, staying in place, being bought by buying. For "them," for the outsiders or internal exiles, for the "Negro, Mexican, cracker" fenders are bound to be "repainted in a shade just off enough to depress the value." They are the "wrong" color, or "framed" wrongly. Like the rest of us, but more so, they are being used by the machines they are using, living lives "wasted" in both the literal and pharmaceutical senses, investing themselves in objects that are never truly theirs, and in work that lacks significance. Looking at the residue of their lives, Mucho has "no way of telling what things had been truly refused . . . and what simply (perhaps tragically) had been lost" (p. 4). In the passage that follows, the used-car lot with its signs of wasted lives is linked to war and the killing of others, a killing that kills the killers over and over again. "You comfort them when they wake pouring sweat or crying out in the language of bad dreams, yes you hold them, they calm down, one day they lose it; she knew that. But when was Mucho going to forget?" (pp. 6–7). He does forget by seeking solace for his pain in the amiable oblivion of drugs supplied by an ex-Nazi physician carrying out an "experiment" (pp. 104–5).

In the beginning Mucho recognizes that every system is incestuous, drugged against what is outside, other and anomalous. Routine does not numb him as it does others to the wasted lives and suffering progress and exclusion entail. Alone in his recognition, in his sense of the tragedy of America, Mucho's sight is too much to bear. As Oedipa comes to see, he "chooses" blindness, becoming a closed system himself—narcissistic, solipsistic, an internal exile (in both sense), trapped by a world he now embraces.

As a closed system he is a world unto himself, oblivious to all voices except those in his head.[9] Narcissistic, he is self-absorbed, hearing only the words of others that echo his own, seeing only those parts of others that reflect him. Like Narcissus he has created a world in his own image and it kills him. Solipsistic, like virtually every other man in Oedipa's life, Mucho makes the self foundational, no longer aware that what he "privileges" may be as constructed, as lacking in "real" grounding, as the world the self rejects or replaces. Like the other characters in the novel, he is an exile in his own land, wandering aimlessly, without home or connection, utterly alienated from any legacy that might be life-affirming.

The disappointment, pain and ambiguity the characters feel and encounter push them to find solace in final resolution, single readings, and certainty of meaning—in drugs, running away with teenage girls, madness, suicide, or paranoia. What they cannot stand is the tragic world of Greek drama and so the significance of "Oedipa." They move away from her as she becomes more like a Greek heroine. It is her hope in the regenerative possibilities of a community of the dispossessed, a community she could join, that gives her strength to go on. It is the absence of any such hope that deprives others of the resilience necessary to face their mortality.

Television rather than Greek tragedy, Pynchon suggests, is our institution of political education. But unlike tragedy, television is essentially a passive medium. Rather than energizing our passions and mind, it enervates them. Rarely does television deal with moral complexity, profound suffering, or people changed by the trials of their lives. Rarer still does it bring before the public and interrogate the unacknowledged cultural accommodations, polarities, or hierarchies that bound cultural life. Television is like plastic, providing a smooth surface on which all is made simple, happy, and entertaining. More than that, it is a narcotic, as numbing as alcohol and drugs,[10] creating the homogenized culture[11] that dissoci-

---

[9] Because Pynchon invites us to think of a novelist in the same way, it is dangerous to simply dismiss Mucho (or any other response to "the" world, which may only be in our heads anyway).

[10] In the second sentence of the novel Pynchon connects television to being drunk and to God as if to suggest that television has become a debased form of religion, truly an opiate of the masses.

[11] Later Oedipa goes to visit Mr. Thoth, hoping he can help her with her obsession to

ates us.[12] All of us see the same programs, but we see them in private and as privatized individuals.

Pynchon poses the issue of incest and exile, unity and diversity in terms of the problem of entropy. In thermodynamics entropy is the degree to which a given quantity of energy is available for doing useful work. Energy can be extracted only when a system contains molecules of differing temperatures. Where there is sameness, uniformity, homogeneity, total order—where, as in the *Agamemnon*, characters are interchangeable—the system runs down. In information theory entropy is the loss of information. The lower the randomness and noise and the greater the unexpected message, the more information becomes available. But there are limits to how unexpected the message can be and remain a message. If a message is too discontinuous with a previously established context—if, that is, it is outside of or even on the fringes of the system—it may not be heard as a message at all but as random noise. Similarly, if there are too many messages, if information is communicated faster than it can be absorbed, the circuits will overload and we become oblivious to all communication. Under such a constant bombardment, the only sane response may be paranoia, which is at least one way of sifting the needless number of signs. The perfect image of entropy is Oedipa's can of hair spray caroming off the wall when she accidentally knocks it over. "The can, hissing malignantly, bounced off the toilet and whizzed by Metzger's right ear, missing by maybe a quarter of an inch. Metzger hit the deck and cowered with Oedipa as the can continued its high-speed caroming; from the other room came a slow, deep crescendo of naval bombardment, machine-gun, howitzer and small-arms fire, screams of chopped-off prayers of dying infantry" (pp. 22–23).[13] Our modes of communicating are killing us. Inundated by messages we cannot understand, we are like the can of hair spray, frenetic, until in exhaustion we just lie on bathroom floors, having destroyed the ozone layer or whatever life support system is handy. Even the novel is not exempt because ink comes from the bones of dead soldiers.

In thermodynamics, as in information theory, the danger is redundancy or sameness *and* cacophony or utter difference, a rage to order that is part

---

bring "something of herself" to the scatter of business interests that had survived Pierce's death. It is a part of an effort to provide order and "create a constellation" that she visits the man whose namesake was the mythical inventor of letters and numbers and the Egyptian god of magic and wisdom. She finds him in front of a television watching cartoons.

[12] The parallel between information and identity is significant here and throughout.

[13] The sounds come from an old television movie in which Metzger as a child plays a leading role. The connection between television and war is complicated by the fact that the reels are reversed, suggesting a conflation of time analogous to that in the *Oedipus Tyrannos*.

of escalating disorder and a reactive disorder that leaves the order it would overturn more firmly entrenched. The challenge is to have unprogrammed messages that are intelligible, systems that are not incestuous, narcissistic projections of meaning oblivious to contrary meaning. The task, to repeat, is finding a medium or middle term that does not attempt to dominate or terminate the other terms in some grand dialectic. "We" need to reject binary systems of p and not p, and to discover a way for worlds to connect in a manner that generates information and energy. For Pynchon either America finds a way of recognizing the other without the assimilation or it is doomed. In the tradition of American writers and in a language that recalls Aeschylus, he seeks to promote "elements of eccentricity in the sounds that make up America while searching for a design that does injustice to none."[14]

But how is this possible given the multitude of voices now anxious to be heard and the fact that although every system numbs us to the waste outside, we cannot live without systems? Oedipa's situation suggests one possibility: though systems may numb us, they do not blind us. Even in her Tupperware and Muzak world she has intimations of what could be, but has so far stayed away.[15] For all their exclusiveness, systems are not impervious or impermeable; at least our system is not—yet. There is always the chance that something unexpected, some chance event (which may or may not be chance) like executing a will, can draw us out of ourselves toward a recognition of possibilities present but unseen. Perhaps there are reminders and traces of an America which, if recognized, could help us stave off the momentum toward self-destruction. Yet for all our hygienic exclusions, our banishing of the physically diseased, eccentric, mad, and old to hospitals, homes, and clinics; for all the hair dyes and transplants, face lifts and "tummy tucks," our imitation of the young or our running away with them, we can never run fast enough. There is always something left over that does not fit the theory, some intimation of what in the world and ourselves is left out.

An earlier lost America of inventors and entrepreneurs is lamented by Stanley Koteks, an engineer Oedipa "accidentally" meets while wandering, also lost, in the Yoyodyne plant, an Aero-Space factory which is San Narciso's principal industry. Koteks bitterly resents his brainwashing in

[14] Richard Poirier, *The Performing Self* (New York: Oxford University Press, 1971), p. 4.
[15] Here is David Grossman (in *The Yellow Wind*, trans. Haim Watzman [New York: Farrar Strauss and Giroux, 1988], p. 9), listening to an old Palestinian woman talking about her past: "Everything happens elsewhere. Not now. In another place. In a splendid past or a longed-for future. The thing most present here is absence. Somehow one senses that people here have turned themselves voluntarily into doubles of the real people who once were, in another place. Into people who hold in their hands only one real asset: the ability to wait." As a Jew Grossman can understand that very well indeed.

school where he came to believe the "Myth of the American Inventor," one man per invention. But when he and his friends grew up "they found they had to sign over all their rights to a monster like Yoyodyne; got stuck on some 'project' or 'task force' or 'team' and started being ground into anonymity. Nobody wanted them to invent—only perform their little role in a design ritual, already set down for them in some procedures handbook" (p. 64). "We" have lost both a common sense of shared mortality *and* any distinctive destiny, both an appreciation that we all must face death in the end *and* that we possess individual destinies. We are neither people with particular fates nor people who recognize themselves in others, as does Achilles when he sees himself and his father in Priam, an old man come to ransom a dead son.

Something like this dual obliteration is present in our cities. Like San Narciso, they are leveled into characterless uniformity, jumbled waste landscapes without center or shaping purpose to direct their random development (or perhaps they are forced to develop in certain directions by "them"). San Narciso is called "grotesque" in Montaigne's sense of the word, a monstrosity pieced together of the most diverse members without distinct form in which order and proportion are left to chance.[16] Cities appear as weird assemblages of "auto lots, escrow services, drive-ins, small office buildings and factories . . . beige prefabs, cinderblock office machine distributors, sealant makers, bottled gas works, fastener factories, warehouses, and whatever" (p. 14). Later, near the end which is no ending, Oedipa realizes that San Narciso was merely an "incident among our climatic records of dreams and what dreams became among our accumulated daylight, a moment's squall-line or tornado's touchdown among the higher, more continental solemnities—storm systems of group suffering and need, prevailing winds of affluence." Here there was no true continuity, for the city "had no boundaries. No one knew yet how to draw them. She had dedicated herself weeks ago to making sense of what Inverarity had left behind, never suspecting that the legacy was America" (p. 134).

In America there are no boundaries, only mazes. No one knows how to draw them, though they are indeed drawn, whether randomly or conspiratorially into binary systems of mutual exclusion or permissive inclusion that deflates all differences and distinction. Here no one seems sure of the border between fact and fiction, animate and inanimate, the projected and the perceived.

For Pynchon entropy is a political and a literary problem, a matter of

[16] The point is taken from Peter L. Cooper, *Signs and Symbols: Thomas Pynchon and the Contemporary World* (Berkeley and Los Angeles: University of California Press, 1983), p. 55.

acting as well as reading, which explains why reading the book is like living in Oedipa's America. As readers and potential actors, we are challenged to make sense of events without reducing them to a single temperature and to accept plural meaning as a condition of life rather than as pathology. Oedipa is overwhelmed by clues that may or may not solve a mystery, which may or may not be her projection onto the world; we are inundated by Pynchon's erudition, which may or may not lead us to the heart of the novel. As she cannot tell what is fact and what is fiction and cannot see the end of her quest, we are swamped by details that may be true or false, or which do not add up or add up differently each time. It is as if history were a set of fictional representations while fiction contained important truths. Paul DeMan has insisted on precisely this point—that all philosophical and historical texts are significantly fictional and that all fictional texts have a philosophical dimension. For him texts reveal the impossibility of ever stating the "facts" as they "really" are. Every one contains not just a view of the world, but the view that its view cannot be a fully accurate representation of the world. All texts read deconstructively, including deconstructive texts, warn their readers not to take them literally, not to assume that their world is the world.

Pynchon elaborates, dramatizes and disagrees with DeMan's argument. He elaborates it by indicating why rejecting the fact-fiction opposition (as well as other polarities) is a necessary condition for keeping any novel alive. That is why he goes to such intimidatingly inventive lengths to keep us off balance, to prevent his book from being used or wasted, accommodated, re-fused, finished (off), ended. He dramatizes it by making the novel turn on the question of what Tristero is, whether it exists, and what grounds we could have to decide one way or the other. He differs from DeMan by leaving open the possibility that texts do refer to or represent "the world," that deconstruction (as it is now called) is a symptom of what may be a disease and may, in America (but perhaps not in France), be part of the problem. For Oedipus, Oedipa, and Pynchon the search for truth and meaning is fraught with danger and full of destructive temptations. Yet not undertaking the search would be, for all three, a betrayal. In this Pynchon is different from other contemporary novelists like Barth and Nabokov. He does not abandon the search for sportive contrivances that revel in their own compensating possibilities. He agrees that we embroider plots to fill the epistemological gap between ourselves and the unknowable, but he does not suggest, at least in this novel, that we design purely self-reflective fictions where the only norm is aesthetic bliss or intellectual playfulness.[17]

Greek tragedy also resisted narrative closure. For one thing, it main-

[17] Ibid., pp. 27, 44.

tained the tensions between lyric and epic, poetry and dialogue, and mythical heroes and a chorus who represented the contemporary audience created by the overthrow of such heroes. For another thing, every action was seen from a god's point of view, which was also the audience's, and from the more partial view of the characters, which was also that of the audience, now actors in the Assembly rather than spectators in the theater. Then too, tragedy simultaneously analyzed (i.e., broke down and apart) the cultural constructions that made its own existence possible and reaffirmed their necessity. It was because of this plurality and as an aspect of it that tragedy demands that we speak and listen poetically as well as discursively, that we read (or hear or see) the lines and between them, that we defer to prophets and prophecy as well as assert our intellectual mastery. Similarly, the novel encompasses without homogenizing sensibilities and disciplines that are (for us but not for the Greeks) conventionally opposed to each other: transcendence and mundanity, computers and lyric poetry, the order of mathematics and violent hallucinations (in the metaphor DTs). Oedipa deciphers hieroglyphics and can weep for wasted lives. She is a hard-nosed detective trying to solve a mystery, yet has the different courage to accept the risks of vulnerability Nussbaum finds definitive of Greek tragedy. She accepts the values of the academy, its concern with evidence, verification, sources, and correct research strategies, but learns most from a moment where she ignores them all and embraces an old man.

She has just finished a night of wandering in San Francisco. She feels defeated by the deliberate malignant repetition of post horns, each one an intrusion into this world of another world, each a sign of an underground that had chosen not to communicate by U.S. Mail (or male). "It was not an act of treason, nor possibly even of defiance. But it was a calculated withdrawal, from the life of the Republic, from its machinery. Whatever else was being denied them out of hate, indifference to the power of their vote, loopholes, simple ignorance, this withdrawal was their own, unpublicized, private" (p. 92). Then she comes upon the old man, huddled, shaking with "grief she couldn't hear," on the stairs of a flophouse, and asks him, "Can I help?" He gives her an old letter to mail to a wife he has left long ago to be put in the W.A.S.T.E. can under the freeway that kills and obliterates the memory of death. Oedipa imagines his room, his life, his ruin.

> Cammed each night out of that safe furrow the bulk of this city's waking each sunrise again set virtuously to plowing, what rich soils had he turned, what concentric plants uncovered? What voices overheard, finders of luminescent gods glimpsed among the wallpaper's stained foliage, candlestubs lit to rotate in the air over him, prefig-

uring the cigarette he or a friend must fall asleep someday smoking, thus to end among the flaming, secret salts held all those years by the insatiable stuffing of a mattress that could keep vestiges of every nightmare sweat, helpless overflowing bladder, viciously, tearfully consummated wet dream, like the memory bank to a computer of the lost? She was overcome all at once by a need to touch him, as if she could not believe in him, or would not remember him, without it. (p. 92)[18]

Oedipa climbs the remaining stairs to hold him and his tears, reluctant to let him go, as if he were her own child.

This gesture of love and moment of empathy is all the more miraculous and moving for its terrifying uniqueness. Here, and for the only time, Oedipa reaches out and touches someone, an old man-child, the past and future of America, much like Oedipus reaches to touch his two daughters, his unnatural past and their cursed future. In this moment of vulnerability she really does learn something, becomes energized and feels pregnant, though she is not sure she can help him or the nation. Weeping she comes to see.

There are then at least two experiences the novel brings to us or that we bring to the reading of it. One is like Oedipa coming to Genghis Cohen's apartment-office with its "long succession or train of doorways, room after room receding in the general direction of Santa Monica, all soaked in rain-light" (p. 68). We can only understand novels, incidents, characters, events, words, if they are framed, situated, contextualized, placed in a discourse, a legacy of meaning. Yet frames are themselves framed, situations are situational, contexts need contextualization, legacies of meaning themselves require meaning. What we see, or what we think we see, is that our boundaries and categories are projections of meanings, transgressions against the world's complexity, against others, and perhaps against parts of ourselves.

But that is not the only experience: there is the moment with the old man. Here is a different kind of knowing where questions of meaning are parenthesized and we are touched in ways that move us beyond closed systems, paranoia, solipsism. When our imagination pushes through our contrivances, we find areas of irreducible, heartbreakingly simple, often inarticulate, human need.[19] Perhaps all our constructions as well as our

---

[18] Earlier (p. 69) Oedipa wonders if "she too might not be left with only compiled memories of clues, announcements, intimations, but never the central truth itself, which must somehow each time be too bright for her memory to hold, which must always blaze out, destroying its own message irreversibly.

[19] See Poirier, *The Performing Self*, p. 22, and his "The importance of Thomas Pynchon" in *Mindful Pleasures: Essays on Thomas Pynchon*, ed. George Levine and David Leverenz (Boston: Little, Brown, 1976), pp. 15–29.

suspicion of our constructions have nearly obliterated our capacity to love and touch another. Perhaps Rousseau is right: society has so transformed our nature that we can no longer feel even the most basic human compassion. But there are moments: the reconciliation scene in the *Iliad*, Oedipus's loving hand to his daughters, the concluding vision of a just city in the *Oresteia*, Oedipa and the lonely old man.

OEDIPUS does come to understand his fate and the role he has played in it. But he does so only at the end when he proclaims himself and Apollo joint authors of his deeds. Until then he has walked in ignorance of who he was, what he was doing, and to whom he was doing it. If this ignorance is unique to him, then we may pity him but take comfort from the fact that we are different. Of course, he thought *he* was different, and so our comfort may be misplaced. If it is misplaced, must we then conclude that no man or woman can know their fate in advance and that there are "outside" forces that shape our beliefs and actions in ways we do not understand until afterward, when it is usually too late? If these "forces" are aspects of our character, can they be known by others even if they are beyond our grasp? Is the *Bacchae* right in pointing to the ways in which what seems outside and other is often inside, animating our passions and our interests even as we deny their legitimacy or presence?

Sophocles seems to be saying that we cannot control our fate because we cannot know ourselves and that we cannot know ourselves because it is the condition of mortals to be "historical" creatures, partial in the double sense of incomplete and one-sided. In these terms the question of fate is an epistemological and a political one: epistemological because it involves questions of what we can know, about ourselves as individuals, as sons and daughters, as citizens and as mortals; political because it involves the question of whether and how we can empower each other to modify if not to control our fate.

As I suggested in chapter 2, there is a tension between what the characters learn on stage and what the audience in the theater learns, particularly if Zeitlin is right about Thebes as the other place. The audience may well take Oedipus's fate as a warning, but it need not replicate his folly precisely because they, but not he, have attended the tragedy. If drama is a mode of political education, then presumably tragedies arm us to withstand or to appreciate better the tragic dimensions of a world those not similarly educated misunderstand. So a member of the audience might be reminded of two things: that as mortal beings men and women are inevitably partial, subject to forces they do not recognize, acted upon rather than actors; and that there are ways, tragedy being one of them, to become more impartial, initiators rather than reactors, able, as Pericles urged, to conceive of themselves as island-dwellers and then act as if they were one.

No matter how we interpret Sophocles on these matters, the language of "fate," "destiny," and one's "lot" in life seem hopelessly archaic. It is a basic tenet of American culture that we make ourselves and our "fate," or that, at the very least, everyone could if they were provided with equal opportunity. With the proper will, drive, and opportunity we can, as individuals or a nation, fashion ourselves as we fashion our persons. Whatever obstacles we confront are either evanescent or will yield to all sorts of aids—psychoanalysis, computer hardware, technical know-how, scientific method, laissez-faire or central planning, mathematical modeling or policy analysis. Those who are skeptical or resist such progress and prospects are, especially if they invoke ideas of fate and destiny, regarded as romantic reactionaries (Ellul and Adams come to mind), "pessimists" (Adorno), or generally voices of "doom and gloom."

Such optimism has not, of course, gone unchallenged. Talcott Parsons's Weber has become a prophet of the iron cage. Marx, once the prophet of revolutionary emancipation, freedom, true consciousness, and human history, is now read as himself overwhelmed by the riddle of a capitalism that was man-made yet mysterious; that operated by rational methods yet issued in irrational unpredictable results; and that, though generated for the most mundane purposes of producing goods and services, continually veered out of control or broke down.[20] Marx's theory confronts a crisis of production just as capitalism does. Having to integrate new concepts, empirical insights, and illustrations in a necessarily expanding structure means that his theory came close to losing its center and parameters. Although Foucault might be more sympathetic to this Marx than the "old" one, his critique of total theory, of liberation and of the theory of ideology with its assumptions of true consciousness is directed at Marx.[21] *The Crying of Lot 49* anticipates this new Marx and Foucault. But Pynchon looks less to Marx (or Weber) than he does to Sophocles and to the idea of fate central to the *Oedipus Tyrannos*. In doing so he makes that ancient notion available to us in a way that energizes our understanding of freedom and limits. One could say that by bringing the classical and contemporary worlds together, Pynchon is creating a miracle of the kind Oedipa strives for in the novel.

[20] Sheldon Wolin, "On Reading Marx Politically," in *Nomos* 26, ed. J. Roland Pennock and John Chapman (New York: New York University Press, 1983).

[21] But Foucault has emphasized how much these criticisms of Marx are within a Marxian politics and how useful Marx is once we are no longer Marxists. On the relationship between Foucault and Marx, see Barry Smart, *Foucault, Marxism and Critique* (London: Routledge Kegan Paul, 1983); and Mark Poster, *Foucault, Marxism and History* (Cambridge: Polity Press, 1985).

Pynchon's concern with fate is evidenced by "lot" in the title, by the images of tract homes and used-car lots through which he represents uniformity and waste respectively, and by a general preoccupation with intelligibility and mastery. The question is whether Oedipa can master the world in the novel and we the world of it. Every attempt on her part at making sense of events and every attempt on our part to make sense of the novel fails, at least if success is defined in terms of mastery. Oedipa is unsure of when and how much she is an initiator, coconspirator, or victim of actions and events. Similarly we are unsure how much our interpretation of the novel is our plot against it or its plot against us. In either case we are "tantalized" by the possibility and desirability of order only to have the nourishment continually recede before our grasp, as Oedipa sees Genghis Cohen in his apartment-office "framed in a long succession or train of doorways, room after room receding" (p. 68).

In the novel's final paragraph (which begins with "Its time to start") the auctioneer is likened to a puppet-master[22] and by implication Oedipa to a puppet. If what she is confronting is indeed an elaborate conspiracy organized by Pierce, then someone else is indeed pulling the strings. But even then Oedipa is free in the sense Oedipus is; she seizes her fate and confronts her mortality as others in the novel do not. They flee the darkened room, which both ends the novel and ends (solves, completes) nothing, into whatever evasion they fancy at the moment. Oedipa is no puppet, but she is subject to an ungovernable tragic ignorance. The passage from Arrowsmith I quoted in chapter 4 seems more appropriate to Oedipa than to Oedipus. "We do not know who we are or who fathered [or mothered] us but go, blinded by life and hope toward a wisdom bitter as the gates of hell. The cost of action is suffering and heroism is the anguished acceptance of our own identities forged in action and pain in a world we never made."

This is an exaggeration when applied to the original audience watching the play, not only because Thebes is the other place, but because the presence of the gods, the existence of an inclusive order (however enigmatic) of the polis as a unity of differences, mitigates the waywardness of action and communication. But it is not clear whether the America in the novel is another place or whether the presence of the gods is anything more than

---

[22] "The men inside the room wore black mohair and had pale, cruel faces. They watched her come in, trying each to conceal his thoughts. Loren Passerine, on his podium, hovered like a puppet-master, his eyes bright, his smile practiced and relentless. . . . She heard a lock snap shut; the sound echoed a moment. Passerine spread his arms in a gesture that seemed to belong to the priesthood of some remote culture" (pp. 137–38). Earlier (p. 94) in the scene with the old man, Oedipa is given a letter to mail with the familiar eight-cent airmail stamp with a jet flying by the Capitol dome, except that on the dome "stood a tiny figure in deep black, with its arm outstretched."

paranoia or whether order is simply projected onto the world as a defense and assault against "it." Nor do we live in anything approaching a Greek polis.

What if anything can we do here and now to reverse entropy and re-found a community of individuals? And who in America is the "we"? Clearly issues of gender, ethnicity, and class are issues for Pynchon as they were not for the Greek tragedians.[23] Oedipus's search for self-knowledge and identity was part of the city's collective endeavor to attain self-knowledge and identity through the medium of tragedy. Does Pynchon think something analogous is possible through the novel?

WRITING ABOUT PYNCHON, one critic insists that "no contemporary writer has achieved such fame and such anonymity at the same time, and arguably no other contemporary writer has done so much to create—or bring to birth—a new kind of reader who must do 'quite half the labor.' "[24] Why has Pynchon gone to such lengths to remain anonymous and how is this connected to his midwifery in bringing a new kind of reader to birth? What is new about that reader and what sort of labor is now required of him or her?

We have a few clues in the novels' preoccupation with entropy and narcotics. For Pynchon the problem of unity and diversity is a literary as well as a political one. To be bombarded by information is to be paralyzed as readers and actors. But to be given information in a thoroughly system-atic way, to have details and events subsumed under a single interpretation—what Foucault calls "the meta-historical deployment of ideal significations and indefinite teleologies"[25]—is to kill the "text" and the "reader." So the "literary" problem of keeping the text and reader alive is analogous to the political one of keeping the culture and citizenry alive. The analogy is forced on us by the parallels between the act of reading *The Crying of Lot 49* and living in America.

There is another clue, or perhaps it is simply the first clue differently stated. The novel is critical of escapism, which reading a novel often is. So the challenge is to prevent reading from becoming yet another drug or feeding our narcissistic appetites. Let me put the point in terms of the *Bacchae*. Speaking of that play, Segal remarks that the "text, like Diony-

[23] I have suggested that they were sometimes raised with considerable power as in Euripides' *Bacchae*. But at no point is it suggested that women or barbarians or slaves (except in exceptional circumstances) fully share in political power.
[24] Tony Tanner, "Pynchon and the Death of the Author," in *Thomas Pynchon* (London: Methuen, 1982), p. 12.
[25] "Nietzsche, Genealogy, History," in *Language, Counter-Memory, Practice; Selected Essays and Interviews*, ed. and introd. Donald F. Bouchard (Ithaca, N.Y.: Cornell University Press, 1977), p. 150.

sus, provides a relief, a drug (pharmakon), from the pain of life; like Dionysus, it also provides an intensification, an almost unbearable condensation, of the pain of life."[26] Pynchon tries, I think, to keep the novel from becoming an aesthetic form that negates the formlessness of the world Oedipa confronts, while at the same time refusing to indulge the centrifugal forces of that world—entropy, inexplicable suffering, chaos—to the point that we simply give up reading or acting.

Pynchon teaches us how to read differently so we can think and act differently[27] and is, in this regard, a political educator. It is a democratic or participatory mode of education, in the sense that he encourages the reader to become actively, critically, and self-consciously coauthor of the novel's meaning as against the division between a tyrannical author and a passive reader. One might think of the novel as a founding document, a constitution or framework that must be renewed and reconstituted by each generation lest the legacy lapse into routine and the citizenry into apathy. Certainly there is evidence that Pynchon thinks of his text this way. Not only is Pierce called a founder of San Narciso and San Narciso said to be America; there is one particular passage where a character seems to make the point to the reader as much as to Oedipa.

She has just seen Wharfinger's *Courier's Tragedy* and comes backstage to question its director, Randolph Driblette about the play's reference to Trystero. To her persistent (academic-sounding) inquiries about the definitive version of the play Driblette responds: "You can put together clues, develop a thesis, or several, about why characters reacted to the Trystero possibility the way they did, why the assassins came on, why the black costumes. You could waste your life that way and never touch the truth. Wharfinger supplied words and a yarn, I gave them life, that's it" (p. 56).

Pynchon is giving us the words (the outline or framework) and a yarn (a story but also strands woven into tapestries) to which the reader-citizen must give life even as those words teach him or her how to return the favor. In this way the novel tries to encourage in its readers the vitality and vigor Nussbaum argues tragedy encouraged (though also presupposed) in its spectators.

But why bother? Why not withdraw from America and reading the book? Why not ignore the state and politics, live like a recluse in northern

---

[26] I am not suggesting there is anything programmatic about the novel. Nothing could be further from the truth. Rather, like Greek tragedy, Pynchon shows us a pattern of action and cultural movement obscured by the urgency of everyday life and our taken-for-granted cultural accommodations.

[27] It does not matter so much whether this picture of reading is true so much as whether it is believed to be true. The question is what difference it makes if we believe one rather than the other.

California, refusing literary prizes and official recognition? It is only an option if we ignore Winthrop Tremaine and his ready-to-wear SS uniforms for the fall-return-to-school-season and Oedipa's response to him: "You're chicken, she told herself, snapping on her seat belt. This is America, you live in it, you let it happen" (p. 112). "We" cannot withdraw but need instead to reread our past and read our present more attentively for emergent possibilities, residues of lost opportunities, values, fossils, and traces, the things Driblette says "Wharfinger didn't lie about." And we need to read different things, to see cultural artifacts as hieroglyphs: bathroom walls, circuits, used cars, mattresses, recreational communities, railroad tracks, phone lines, horns and posthorns, stamps, and freeways.

There is another reason why opting out is not really an option. It is a reason that also points to another way Pynchon encourages a self-critical literary and political activism and to how the question of one's lot or fate is, as Zeitlin suggests, implicated in the very idea of a narrative.

I argued in chapter 4 that the *Oedipus Tyrannos* calls attention to its own context of performance and to itself as spectacle in ways that make the citizen audience self-conscious of themselves as spectators. *The Crying of Lot 49* does something similar by making us uncomfortably self-conscious about its devices of construction and our devices of interpretation. Doing so, it suggests that there is no escape from plots and plotting so long as human beings attempt to make sense of their lives.

The book is full of the language of plots, conspiracies, and paranoia. That has at least three results: we come to see the novel as a plot against us, we become aware of our plotting against it, and we are made suspicious of all plots by all authors and authorities.

The Crying of Lot 49 goes to elaborate lengths to make us suspicious of its own plottings. Indeed, we stand to it as Oedipa does to Tristero. She is unsure whether she is confronting a genuine conspiracy by the community of the dispossessed who are real people really communicating outside the state-sanctioned systems of communication; or whether it is a simulated conspiracy made up of genuine clues plotted for her bewilderment by Pierce (who may or may not be Pynchon) or whether it is all just her craziness, her hallucinations, a world she constructs and peoples as real people disappear and she is left isolated and exiled in her own land. As readers we have similar uncertainties. We do not know where Pynchon is leading us or if he is always misleading us, or if the point is not to let ourselves be led at all. Nor do we know for certain whether San Narciso really is America or if it is all Pynchon's paranoid projection of America. Finally, we are not sure what to make of the novel's elaborate (often self-mocking) overplotting, which alternatively exhausts, frustrates, and bores us while warning us of the unseen plottings that coopt and conspire against us.

Even writing may be a plot against fellowship and a certain way of experiencing the world (Mr. Thoth is the namesake of the Egyptian god who brought writing to King Thamus). Reading the written word changes one's habit of mind. It fosters an analytic management of knowledge and an analytic conception of knowledge. The sequential, propositional character of the written word means that reading requires our literally following a line of thought that requires in turn "considerable powers of classifying, inference making and reasoning." It also means that we uncover lies, confusions, and overgeneralizations, detect abuses of logic and common sense, weigh ideas, compare and contrast assertions, and connect one generalization to another. "To accomplish this, one must achieve a certain distance from the words themselves which is, in fact, encouraged by the isolated and impersonal text."[28] In this sense writing and reading are isolating acts. It is an isolation that must be overcome if we are not all to wind up members of Inamorati Anonymous.[29]

The point is not merely that plots and novels are conspiracies against the reader, but that readers form plots and conspiracies against the novel. "We" have as many designs on the text as it has on us. "We" use it to fill a void as much as it uses its plot to the same end—thus our need for plots, conspiracies of meaning, for seeing each element as a clue to consistent intentions, rational results, and unseen pattern. Like Oedipa with the *Courier's Revenge*, we use our considerable research skills to uncover "authoritative" texts. Once we do—once we explain, categorize, organize, sort, schematize, and pacify it, after we lecture on it and write about it—it becomes the deadest of all things: a textbook.

The novel aims to energize our resistance to plots. It forces us to recognize our own complicity in and need for them, and realize who and what are left out when we become part of one. In this Pynchon is like Foucault, if William Connolly is right in arguing that the latter's linguistic escalation is intended to evoke "the experience of constructedness while deconstructing standards which deny or delegitimize that experience. . . .

---

[28] This and the previous quote come from Neil Postman's *Amusing Ourselves to Death: Public Discourse in the Age of Show Business* (New York: Viking, Penguin, 1985), pp. 51, 13. Postman relies on Walter Ong's *Orality and Literacy* (New York: Methuen, 1982) but does not seem to know Eric Havelock's *Preface to Plato* (Cambridge, Mass.: Harvard University Press, 1963). These claims about oral and written culture (as about the presentness of speech and distance of writing) are controversial subjects. My point is simply that by invoking Thoth, together with other references to writing, Pynchon raises the issue.

[29] In *The Book of Laughter and Forgetting*, trans. Michael Henry Heim (New York: Penguin, 1981), Kundera talks about "graphomania," the obsession with writing books. It is, he says, "a mass epidemic" whenever society develops to the point that people can devote their energies to useless activities, whenever there is an advanced state of social atomization with its resultant feelings of isolation, and whenever there is a radical absence of significant social change (p. 92).

He loosens the hold of 'our' discourse and arguments by displacing metaphors which carry them, and we become more alert to the finely honed 'discursive practices' in which our knowledge is 'contained.' "[30] As part of this resistance Pynchon echoes Nussbaum and MacIntyre's emphasis on the need to honor what we choose against and on the danger of discarding those parts of the moral world and ourselves that the need for decisions forecloses.

But life and freedom, such as they are, cannot be random. The absence of system, as well as the dominance of system, lead to entropy. The plotless drifters who live for the moment while rejecting relations to the past or thought of the future, who lack the capacity for love and who respond with reactive violence to their exclusion, tend to join in the very betrayals and deanimations within the culture that have driven them outside. The political and literary question remains: Is there some middle term, some structure that is not a conspiracy, a discourse that remains self-interrogatory, some tension between diversity and unity that is energizing? The question brings us back to Oedipa and to Tristero.

If there is any hope in the novel, it rests with Oedipa.[31] She is the only one who does not give up the quest or the questioning, the only one who stays alive without answers. She is, or appears to be, the middle term, the sensitive, the refounder of the republic or someone to keep the ball bouncing. She is the detective who discovers the murdering and tries to (but fears she cannot) help; a woman who is pregnant with meaning and perhaps America (though her pregnancy may be hysterical); a madonna who is also an intelligence operative examining conspiracies with "female" cunning; a courageous "actress" who weeps. As I noted, this variety of roles and guises suggests a confounding of traditionally male and female activities and voices. Here perhaps is the miraculous connection of two worlds. Oedipa doesn't fit. She is neither inside nor outside the dominant Tupperware/Muzak/U. S. Postal conspiracy/system/plot. As a white middle-class woman, she is in between, a bridge, the translator.[32]

If Oedipa has any hope of saving America, it depends on her relationship to Tristero. But we do not know whether or in what sense Tristero exists. It may be a suppressed otherness, an "alienation" that is part of

[30] "On Richard Rorty: Two Views," *Raritan* (Summer 1983): 134.

[31] Oedipus was a pollutor as well as a savior of Thebes and there is a hint that Oedipa is too. If she is pregnant, and *if* Pierce is the father, the offspring may be a descending angel or perhaps the son of a god or of God.

[32] Woman as translator, as concerned with integration and relationships rather than with power (as with Oedipus), is a very typical image (as Carol Gilligan suggests in her *In a Different Voice* [Cambridge, Mass.: Harvard University Press, 1982]) and a politically problematic one (for reasons suggested by Kathy Fergueson in *The Feminist Case against Bureaucracy* [Philadelphia: Temple University Press, 1984]).

our ontological homelessness. Or it may be a homelessness particular to industrial capitalism. Or it may be Pierce's revenge on her (and Pynchon's on us), his way of living on, of being in control. Or it may be nothing at all, a figment of her imagination, a projection. If Tristero does not exist (in whatever form), then the clues point to nothing. If she is or suspects herself of projecting meaning and value out of her need onto a world that is wholly alien and communicates nothing, then the worst fears of Sophocles' chorus are realized.[33]

Let us follow Oedipa who, to maintain her sanity, assumes that Tristero is a collection of outsiders representing a possible infusion of energy. If they are a genuine society of communicants in which real information is exchanged and real diversity sustained, then the waste of the system contains cultural traces that make rebirth possible and Oedipa is the founding mother who can save America from the established mail-male system. This is the hope Pynchon holds out to us.

But it is hardly an unqualified hope. There are many clues to make us uneasy about Tristero as savior. The letter sent through the alternative mail system that Oedipa reads is thoroughly banal: "Dear Mike, how are you? Just thought I'd drop you a note. How's your book coming? Guess that's all for now" (p. 35). Then there is the name Tristero, from trist which means sadness in French, but malignity in Italian (and, as the English tryst, is a clandestine meeting of lovers). Then there is the fact that Tristero apparently includes Nazis and Mafiosi as well as the poor and disenfranchised, revolutionaries of the right as well as the left. Moreover, their avenging violence suggests the possibility that these outsiders will seize the state only to create another equally pernicious outside; that they will have their own normalizing agenda obscured by the banner of liberation; and that they too will rewrite history, not perhaps in the heavy-handed way of the Peter Pinquid Society, but in a way that imposes their own functionalizing logic on the past and "illegitimate" discourses.[34]

Pynchon's refusal to romanticize the plotless drifting outsiders who may nevertheless be our saviors is most striking in the scene with the old man. In the midst of the most poignant lyricism in the novel, at the very point where Oedipa has finally made contact with another and America, in the flophouse where she sees the full extent of loss and of the void she glimpsed in the tapestry, she offers the man-child money in front of an-

---

[33] "If she has projected meaning and value onto her world merely because she wants her world to have meaning and value, she is hallucinating, and worse, the world is wholly alien. . . . It communicates nothing. As she sees it, if her 'project,' the Tristero, does not exist, the codes break down. The signs point to nothing at all" (Molly Hite, *Ideas of Order in the Novels of Thomas Pynchon* [Columbus: Ohio State University Press, 1983], p. 77).

[34] See the discussion of this point in William M. Plater, *The Grim Phoenix: Reconstructing Thomas Pynchon* (Bloomington: Indiana University Press, 1978), 48–49.

other "resident." This old man, who but a moment ago was cradled in her arms, turns to her and on her: " 'Bitch,' said the sailor, 'Why didn't you wait till he was gone.' "

In *The Crying of Lot 49* a Greek tragedy provides a point of reference and energy for understanding contemporary American culture.[35] That has been a rationale behind, and the argument of, this book. I have tried to show how the study of Greek tragedy and classical political theory read in its terms can invigorate our political and theoretical sensibilities. As Pynchon warns, such outside energy is possible only if we do not assimilate tragedy and theory to the present system or make it totally other. Binary systems, theoretical polarities, and "historical" divisions between ancient and modern, or modern and postmodern, not only simplify, they enervate.

Greek tragedy and classical political theory lose their life when consigned to academic disciplines that treat them with such reverence that all profanity and darkness is banished or reified as "The Origins of Western Civilization." If nothing else the *Oedipus Tyrannos* and *The Crying of Lot 49* teach us that single readings mean entropy and death.

The irony of treating Greek tragedy with reverence is that the tragedians themselves did not treat their own culture's reifications with comparable reverence. As I have argued, Hephastus's sons, whether tragedians or theorists, warn against the achievements they constitute and may in the end regard as essential. One can see this tension in Thycydides' portrait of political and intellectual power, in Socrates' view of his and philosophy's relation to Athens and politics, and in the dialogue between "Socrates" and "Plato" in the *Republic*. Especially there we see how essential form and theory are to keep us from being immobilized or seduced by sheer multiplicity, trivial excitations, and inconsequential choices. But we also see how form and theory flatten and reduce the world, stopping the flow of tears, subjugating or marginalizing parts of the self or others or history. If I am right then classical political theory engaged in a movement of reduction it knew to be such.

This paradoxical aspect of political theory can be seen as an elaboration and exemplification of the "strangeness" implied in the double meaning of *deinos*. That double meaning (as with that of *pharmarkos*) derives from the "fact" that mortals alone among living creatures are beasts and gods at once. As such they lack a fixed place and identity and so oscillate between divinity and bestiality, which unexpectedly turn back

---

[35] To reiterate: an understanding, not *the* understanding. Emphasis on the novel's religious symbolism, for instance, would yield a somewhat different novel and a somewhat different America.

on or into each other. This condition was mediated by the polis which Aristotle presents as a middle term. Standing between beasts and gods, it is a human realm in which, because two worlds connect and energize each other, "men" become whole.[36]

This is, of course, far too humanist and normative for Foucault. Although he refers to class struggle, uses phrases such as "disciplinary society" and "carceral archipelago," and terms such as domination, subjugation, and subjection, he insists that no normative framework is presupposed by or follows from such usage.[37] Nor is he willing to speculate on what institutions or practices might follow from or build upon his critique. Such foundationalism is essentialist and totalizing, most insidiously so when couched in the humanist discourse of emancipation, liberty, rights, and freedom, all of which now function to mystify, and normalize.[38]

But I wonder if such reticence and refusal is enough either for Foucault or for "us." For instance, I am not sure he can give us reasons[39] for taking the side of prisoners or for resisting even at the local level.[40] And I wonder whether, without distinctions between legitimate and illegitimate power,[41] we can distinguish totalitarian from democratic

[36] Saying this does not solve the problem because the Greeks were perfectly comfortable with the idea that some men and all women were not properly part of that realm.

[37] See Nancy Fraser, "Foucault on Modern Power: Empirical Insights and Normative Confusions," *Praxis International* 1, no. 3 (1981): 272–87, esp. 282.

[38] That is why Foucault's critique of humanism is primarily rhetorical rather than theoretical, why his principal (though not only) strategy is inciting subjugated aspects of the self, "evoking a response in readers which disturbs the artificial unity engendered through subjectification." Thus he reveals the metaphorical character of descriptive discourse and explodes the calming obviousness of conventional rhetoric substituting "interrogate" for "question," "surveillance" for "observation." Through such a strategy, the warlike character of modern discourse and society is substituted for the lulling cadences of rights and legitimacy. Such rhetorical shifts and escalation may be "designed to speak to the subdued experience of disciplinary control, and *if* the self implicated in the discursive practices so characterized receives these messages, unorganized dimensions of the self may be awakened" and the bearers of subjugated knowledges may be incited to oppose more actively established forms of control. The point and quotes are from William E. Connolly, *Politics and Ambiguity* (Madison: University of Wisconsin Press, 1987), chap. 8, esp. pp. 124–25.

[39] I am not sure either whether Foucault thinks it is possible to give reasons of this sort or whether the very demand for them does not presuppose the humanism he criticizes.

[40] Sometimes Foucault's idea of resistance seems more like resistance in an electrical current, automatically present and reactive rather than chosen and shaping.

[41] If we look for the ground of Foucault's passion and the moral force his arguments have for us, they lie, I think, in his tacit reliance on the connotations of words like domination and subjection he presumes to isolate from their cultural context and in his equally tacit adherence to the ideals of autonomy, reciprocity, mutual recognition, and dignity. "Can we," Nancy Fraser asks, "sum up our objections . . . by saying that panoptical practices and the like produce an offensive economy of bodies and pleasures or by saying that they fail to respect the rights which express our sense of how persons ought to be treated?" Isn't Fou-

regimes.[42] Finally, I am not sure genealogy is sufficient or whether as Nietzsche insisted "all living things require an atmosphere around them, a mysterious vapor; if they are deprived of this envelope, if a religion, an art, a genius is condemned to revolve as a star without an atmosphere, we should no longer be surprised if they quickly wither and grow hard and unfruitful."[43]

It seems to me that Foucault is not sufficiently attentive to the benefits of socially engendered harmonies and the need to make qualitative distinctions between political regimes on the basis of how these harmonies are established and maintained, who benefits from them, and who participates in their reaffirmation and reconstruction.[44] Aristotle may be right when he argues that all regimes constitute and are defined by a hierarchy of characters, values and contributions, and that no society can remain a community at all unless there is some fundamental agreement on what

cault's real objection to the modern power regime that it objectifies people, negating the autonomy they deserve; that "it is premised upon hierarchical and asymmetrical relations" which negate "the reciprocity and mutuality we value in human relations?" Isn't the idea of justice the informing background of his thought and still more his actions? If Fraser is right then Foucault implicitly relies on those humanist principles he excoriates much as Marx does on enlightenment moral principles unintelligible within a materialist ontology. (See her "Foucault's Body-Language: A Post-Humanist Political Rhetoric?" *Salmagundi* 61 [Fall 1983]: 56, and "Foucault on Modern Power," p. 284.)

[42] "I think that it is not simply the idea of better and more equitable forms of justice that underlies the people's hatred of the judicial system . . . but—aside from this and before anything else—the singular perception that power is always exercised at the expense of the people. The antijudicial struggle is a struggle against power and I don't think that it is a struggle against injustice" (Foucault, "Intellectuals and Power," in *Language, Counter-Memory, Practice: Selected Essays and Interviews*, ed. and introd. Donald F. Bouchard [Ithaca, N.Y.: Cornell University Press, 1977], p. 211). Foucault begins by suggesting a subordinate but still significant place for justice but ends by relegating justice to the realm of the epiphenomenal. I am less concerned with this ambivalence, his narrow juridicial idea of justice, or whether struggles for power in regimes do in fact invoke ideas of justice, than with suggesting, with Fraser, that the power of his arguments rests on a set of moral convictions that may not be wholly intelligible within his "system."

[43] "On the Uses and Disadvantages of History for Life," in *Untimely Meditations*, ed. N. J. Hollingdale (Cambridge: Routledge and Kegan Paul, 1983), p. 97.

[44] Unless Foucault can tell us more about some of the major political and social issues of the day, the prospects for democratic participation, and nonbureaucratic, nonauthoritarian politics generally; about the ecological crises and nuclear war; about scientism and the domination of technique; about the general debasement of public rhetoric and life; about sexism, racism, homophobia, imperialism, disarmament, mass culture, the family, and poverty, the adequacy of his analysis remains in doubt. (The list is drawn from Fraser, "Foucault's Body-Language.") My criticisms are echoed by Charles Taylor, "Foucault on Freedom and Truth," *Political Theory* 12 (May 1984): 152–83, and Michael Walzer, "The Politics of Michael Foucault," *Dissent* 30 (Fall 1983): 481–90. But see both Paul Bové's "The Foucault Phenomenon: The Problematics of Style," foreword to *Foucault*, by Gilles Deleuze (Minneapolis: University of Minnesota Press, 1988), and his *Intellectuals and Power* (New York: Columbia University Press, 1986).

actions are most worth doing, what people are most worth imitating, and what achievements deserve the greatest recognition. Such agreement is not opposed to diversity but makes it possible; it is a necessary (though hardly sufficient) condition for plurality—that is, the recognition of and capacity to hear other points of view. If Aristotle is right, then Foucault's critique of normalization is only part of the story.[45] Apparently construction is as necessary as deconstruction; nourishment as essential as critique; visions of greatness as crucial as awareness of the suffering such greatness leaves below and behind; ideals of justice, the good life, and political freedom as central as an understanding of the injustice, evil, and oppression such ideals generate. We cannot help but be road builders and boundary makers, bonded and bound by the divisions we draw, the stories we tell, and the theories we employ to guide us through terrain that would otherwise paralyze us. It is true that every "we" implies a they, that every affirmation rest on denials, that closure and enclosures posit an outside and limits even as they create closeness. Foucault is surely right to demand that we confront, in some practical way, the exclusions that seem "essential" to our being a people yet endanger us as a democratic people. He pushes us to ask whether there are times analogous to the Festival of Dionysus and places analogous to the theater in Athens where a modern society could recognize, even honor those traits, actions, and people not "normally" present in their thoughts and lives? If, when roads divide, we can only take one path and the one not taken makes all the difference,[46] how shall we greet those who have taken other roads or our own departures from the beaten path?[47]

Pynchon dramatizes Foucault's concerns and the significance of what lies outside those concerns. In this he not only imitates Greek tragedy and political theory read in its terms, but establishes an alarm system for contemporary political theory. Such theories need to be alert to their own reductions, respectful of ties of place, time, and people, yet assist people

[45] When Foucault suggests that all regimes of power are productive in the sense that each creates molds and sustains a distinctive set of cultural practices and that no positive form of life can subsist without power, he seems to share Aristotle's view. (On this see Fraser, "Foucault on Modern Power," p. 285.)

[46] The line and the title of the book are taken from Robert Frost's poem "The Road Not Taken," in his *Selected Poems* (New York: Holt, Rinehart and Winston, 1966), pp. 71–72. I chose my title from his for reasons elaborated in chapter 2. But I also have two less obvious reasons: one is that Frost's reception (or rather initial dismissal) as a "true" poet illustrates Foucault's point about discursive formations; the other is my agreement with Edward Said's critique of "functionalist criticism" in his essay "Roads Taken and Not Taken," in *The World, the Text and the Critics* (Cambridge, Mass.: Harvard University Press, 1983), chap. 7.

[47] Although this is not the place to make the case, there is much to be said for the Greek idea of guest-friendship as an exemplar.

to see the limits of those ties and be attentive to voices other than their own which they neither assimilate nor romanticize.[48] Because theories need to avoid becoming homologous and so constitutive of the polities they study, they need to retain some critical distance from political practice even as they see their own theoretical activities in terms of democratic practices. More specifically, political theory like Greek tragedy may need to engage as much with popular culture as "elite" culture, be as cognizant of bathroom walls, old mattresses, telephone lines, and spray cans as it is of Sophocles, Plato, and Foucault. It may need to help disclose traces from otherwise maligned traditions and practices in order to at least keep the ball bouncing, move things an inch, while seeking more substantial renewal, watching always for Winthrop Tremaine with his ready-to-wear SS uniforms. Such political theory would take entropy and mortality, isolation and incest, Oedipus and Oedipa as its significant "subjects."

I have indicated the ways in which the form, content, and performance context of Greek tragedy anticipated the need and contours of such a theory. I have also indicated the ways classical political theory filled in those contours while changing its shape. We are the executors and executrixes of that legacy and inheritance.

In saying that, I do not mean this is our only legacy or that I have given anything like a definitive statement of it. I do want to suggest that the legacy as I have outlined it can disclose to us the routine betrayals and spiritual poverty of our official delivery systems, help us negotiate the labyrinthian complexities of our public and private lives, alert us to the guerrilla warfare Kundera notes, and remind us that the road we have taken is not the only one, but that, for better or worse, it is the one we are on.

---

[48] After the events of May 1968 Sartre announced that he was now an *intellectuel gauchiste* rather than an *intellectuel de gauche*, which for him meant that the intellectual must write with and through the masses, putting his technical knowledge at their disposal rather than standing apart as a critic. Deleuze and Foucault make similar comments in "Intellectuals and Power," in *Language, Counter-Memory, Practice*, pp. 205–17.

Achilles, 222, 223; and critique of heroic ethic, 222; reintegration of, 223; and Socrates compared, 216, 219; Socrates' transformation of, 220

Ackelsberg, M. A., 11

Action, irony of, in Aeschylus, 86

Adorno, T. W., 143, 296

Aeschylus, as political educator, 91. See also *Oresteia*

Agamemnon: and problem of necessity, 72; and tragic choice, 69

agōn, in *Oedipus Tyrannos*, 108

algos, 13

Anastaplo, G., 213

Anaxagoras, and Socrates, 215

Annas, J., 254

anonymity: in America, 290; in Pynchon's novel, 298

Antigone, 40, 41, 49, 236; and choral ode, 34–37; and *Oedipus Tyrannos*, 102–3

antiquity, and modernity, 6

Apollo, 27, 34, 78, 80, 102, 112, 118, 125; ambiguity of, 78–79, 80; as goad to Socrates and Oedipus, 202; and Oedipus, 126; and Socrates compared, 216

Apology, 94; and the *Bacchae*, 203; and corruption in Thucydides, 210; and *Iliad*, 220–21, 222, 225; and *Oedipus Tyrannos* compared, 126–27, 202, 203, 222, 225; and *Oresteia*, 203, 233; and the *Republic*, 233, 234; as tragedy of philosophy, 204

Arendt, H., 6, 7, 10; and modern individualism, 9

Areopagus, 83

Aristotle, 6, 10, 147; on tragedy, 35

Arrowsmith, W., 44, 55, 72, 106, 152

atē, 173

Athena, 77, 86, 88, 91; in *Oresteia*, 80–83

Athenians, 32, 76, 131

Athens, 7, 15, 190; and Pericles' Funeral Oration, 195; as roadbuilders, 131; as Socrates' mortal parent, 223

Bacchae, the: and *Antigone*, 152; and *Eumenides* compared, 130; and *Iliad*, 159; interpreted historically, 134; as inversion of *Oresteia*, 130–31, 133, 134; and *Oedipus Tyrannos*, 131, 133, 138; and the *Republic*, 161, 163; theatricality in, 154

Bacon, H., 72, 81

Barthes, R., 21, 59

Benveniste, E., 97

Betensky, A., 93

Bonino, J. M., 11

Bookchin, M., 11

boundaries, 291; violation of in *Oedipus Tyrannos*, 98

Bové, P., 4, 27, 306

Brann, E., 211

Burkert, W., 75

Burnet, J., 231

Cameron, A., 104

Castellani, V., 149

Cephalus, 241ff

character, 253; and fate, 125. See also *daimōn*

choice, 233, 267, 276

chorus, 117; concern for tragedy in *Oedipus Tyrannos*, 118

Cleon, 178–82; and Diodotus, 180

Cochrane, C. N., 173

Cogan, M., 181

community, 224, 245; of interlocutors, 265; of interpreters, 200; in Pynchon, 286

conflict, generational in *Oresteia*, 68, 75, 76

Connolly, W., 26, 56, 301

Connor, W. R., 171, 179, 182, 193, 197, 200

Constant, B., 6

Cook, A., 51, 74, 173

Corcyra, 135–36; revolution and tragedy, 177; and theoretical power, 174; violence at, 185

Cornford, F. M., 172, 173, 180, 196

corruption, 189, 201; linguistic, 170; in Thucydides, 168–69; of young by Socrates, 215
criticism, 230
Crying of Lot 49: and Aeschylus, 290; and *Agamemnon*, 289; and the *Bacchae*, 295, 298; and *Oedipus Tyrannos* compared, 281–86, 290, 298, 300; and the *Oresteia*, 295; and the *Republic*, 304

Dahl, R., 47
daimōn, 217, 228; and character of Oedipus, 125
deinos, 93, 152; in *Oedipus Tyrannos*, 124
Deleuze, G., 4
De Man, P., 292
democracy, 3, 199, 276; and Athenian empire, 180
Derrida, J., 4, 16
Diamond, I., 11
dikastēs, 82
dikēphoros, 82
Diodotus, 180ff
Dionysus, 145, 146, 152, 163; as god of forgetting, 158; as liberator of women, 155
discourse, 137
dismemberment, 144; Euripides and Thucydides compared, 168; of language, 45; of Pentheus and Thebes, 43. See also *sparagmos*
Dodds, E. R., 52, 81; on the *Bacchae*, 163
drama, 239; in Athens, 50; as ritual dismemberment, 138
drasō, 85
Durkheim, E., 6, 7, 8

earthquake, scene in the *Bacchae*, 149
Edmunds, L., 173
elenchus, 211, 250
Ellul, J., 16
empowerment, 18
enlightenment, 60
entropy, 61, 281, 289; as literary problem, 292; as political problem, 291; as sameness and isolation, 98; in thermodynamics, 289
ephebate, 144
Epidamnus, 174, 176
episkēptō, 122
epistemology, 137

erōs, 242
estrangement, 227
exile, 98, 286, 287; in Pynchon's America, 291

Farenga, V., 99
Ferguson, K., 92
Finley, J. H., 68, 171
Finley, M. I., 135
Fish, S. E., 94, 276, 281
Flamang, J. A., 11
Foley, H., 28, 48, 155, 156
foreknowledge, 193
Foucault, M., 14, 18, 19, 20–30, 60; and Greek tragedy, 24, 25, 26, 27, 102; and classical political theory, 31; and otherness, 29; and Pynchon compared, 296, 307, 308; and rejection of dramatic narrative, 25; and Strauss and Arendt compared, 24
Fraser, N., 4, 21, 29, 305
Frost, R., 307

Gadamer, H. G., 16, 123, 226
gender, in Aeschylus, 92ff
genealogy, 23ff
Giroux, H. A., 11
Goldhill, S., 4, 27
Gould, T., 105
Graham, M., 14
Grant, J. R., 198
graphein, in Thucydides, 174
Greenberg, N. A., 203
Grube, G.M.A., 149
Guardini, R., 231
Guthrie, W.K.C., 202

Habermas, J., 7, 273
Hackforth, R., 202
Havelock, E. A., 52
Heidegger, M., 189
Heraclitus, 123
Herington, J., 33
heroic ethic, 71, 73, 75; Socratic critique of, 206, 225, 226
heroism, of Oedipa, 285
hēsuchia, 141
hierarchy, 250
historians, 174
Hite, M., 303

Holmes, S. T., 4–9, 15, 19, 46; and Pynchon, 297
homelessness, 303
Homeric poetry, 262
human condition, 85
humanism, 4, 21, 23

ideal reader, in the *Republic*, 276
ideal state, 247
identity, 39, 40, 41, 42, 46; in *Apology*, 202, 203, 211, 218; in the *Bacchae*, 139, 145; in *Oedipus Tyrannos*, 96, 100, 101, 107, 108; in Pynchon, 285
Ignatieff, M., 4, 14, 18, 96, 101; and Greek tragedy, 46, 60; and language of past, 11, 12
Iliad, embassy scene, 221. *See also* Achilles
incest, 128; in *Oedipus Tyrannos*, 99; in Pynchon, 287, 289
injustice, 77
intellectuals, 23
isonomia, 48

Jaeger, W., 205
Jones, J., 76
journey, as metaphor, 32
justice: in *Oresteia*, 39, 67, 81, 83, 84; in the *Republic*, 241, 247, 249, 251, 269, 270, 271; the *Republic* and *Oresteia* compared, 269–75; of Socrates, 217; as unity of difference, 84
just polis, 85

Kagan, D., 31
kallipolis, 247
katestrammai, 74
katharsis, as healing, 153
keleuthopoioi, of Athenians, 32
Kirk, G. S., 148
Kitto, H.D.F., 68, 178
Klosko, G., 205
knowledge, 54
Knox, B., 41, 106
koinōnian, 9
Kundera, M., 48, 303

Lamb, W.R.M., 198
Lang, M., 178
laws, in *Crito*, 229
Lesky, A., 70
Lloyd-Jones, H., 77

Locke, J., 3, 7
Loraux, N., 137, 173

machēs, 74
MacIntyre, A., 50
MacLeod, C. W., 67, 173
Marx, K., 3, 5, 6–8, 296
Meier, C., 52, 56
member, as male sex organ in the *Bacchae*, 132
membership: in the *Bacchae*, 43, 130; and *Oedipus Tyrannos*, compared, 131; in ecstatic community, 44; and identity, 131
metatragedy, in the *Bacchae*, 138
methodism, criticism of, 94, 95
Michnik, A., and Polish Solidarity, 11
Mill, J. S., 8
Miller, J., 15
misogyny, and Aeschylus, 91–93
modernity, 12–18
moral bivalence, in *Oresteia*, 79
More, T., utopianism of, 14
Murdoch, I., 257
Mytilene, debate over, 178ff

narcissism, in Pynchon, 288
net, image of, 33, 102, 233
Nichols, J., 6
Nietzsche, F., 5, 13, 49, 60, 248
nikasthai, 74
Norwood, G., 143
nostalgia, 13–14. *See also* Ignatieff
nostos, 13
Nussbaum, M., 36, 38, 70, 94, 99; on tragedy, 236–40, 243, 268; and tragic vulnerability, 293

Oedipa, 62, 281ff
Oedipus, 105, 122, 125; and Athens, 106; etymology, 103–4; and Oedipa, 282–84; and paradox, 102; as quasi-divine, 109, 110; self blinding, 124; and Socrates, 126; and Sphinx, 113
Oedipus Tyrannos: unity and diversity in, 54–56; and *Oresteia* compared, 103, 287; theatricality in, 107, 108–9
oikos, 68
ōmophagia, 151
oracle, 118; and skepticism, 120

Oresteia, 39, 68, 266; as trial of Athens, 91; and the *Republic* compared, 39, 67; 269–75
Orestes, view of justice, 82

paideia, 261
panopticon, 19
paradox: in Greek tragedy and political theory, 34; of justice, 260; between philosophy and politics, 262
paranoia, in America, 61, 298
parodos, 69
Parsons, T., 296
passion, 89
Pateman, C., 93
paternalism, 110, 229
patriotism, Socratic, 217
Paul, Angus R., 17
Peloponnesian War, unprecedented nature of, 190
Pentheus, 143, 151, 160; etymology of, 148; and Oedipus compared, 148; ripped to pieces, 132
Pericles, 197; affinities with Thucydides, 192; and Cleon, 178; and conceptual power, 191; as political and theoretical actor, 191; and Socrates, 205
persuasion, 245
philosophy, 36; as distinctively Athenian, 230; as praxis, 214; as technē of technē, 250; two types in the *Republic*, 266; and tyranny, 36–38, 225, 246–50
phronēsis, 136
Pitkin, H., 10
plague, at Athens, 14
plastos, 116
Plater, W., 303
Plato: as civic educator, 270; critique of tragedy, 235; dramatic aspects of, 58; on tyranny, 211; utopianism of, 14, 266
pleonexia, 173, 243
plethos, 141
plots, 300
Podlecki, A. J., 82
poetry, 251, 252; and divided line, 256; imitative vs. narrative, 254; informed by philosophy, 253; ontological criticism of, 255; and reality, 258
poets: and gods, 252; as ignorant, 252; opposed by Plato and Thucydides, 45; and Plato, 46

Pohlenz, M., 231
Pokorny, J., 50
Polanyi, K., 8
Polemarchus, 244ff
polis, in Aeschylus, 84
Polish Solidarity, 11, 209
Port Huron Statement, 15
Poster, M., 24
Postman, N., 301
power: and Cephalus, 244; and Foucault, 22; and knowledge, 22; as network of relations, 22; numbers vs. reasons, 245; theoretical and political, 172; in Thucydides, 172; vertical and horizontal compared, 192
praxis, 9
problem-solving, in Pynchon and Sophocles, 107–9, 284
progress, as transgression, 71
proteleia, 71
public, vs. private in *Oresteia*, 56
Pynchon, 59–63; as genealogist, 60; as political educator, 299; and the *Republic*, 63; and uniformity of our cities, 291

Quine, W. V., 28

Raaflaub, K., 52
Rabinowitz, N. S., 32, 87
Rajchman, J., 25
realism, of Thrasymachus, 246
reason, 272, 273; and tyranny, 272
reciprocity, as justice, 75
reconciliation, 88, 223, 295
Redfield, J., 204
Reinhardt, K., 68
Republic, the: 273, 275; and *Apology*, 236, 271; and Homeric poetry, 262; as last Greek tragedy, 269; and *Oedipus Tyrannos*, 235, 237, 238, 272, 275; and *Oresteia* compared, 269–75; as philosophical poetry, 253, 257; and "Platonic" interpretation, 264; as poetic and tragic book, 260; politics in, 266; as rationalist manifesto, 274; and "Socratic" interpretation, 263; as theater, 239; as tragedy recast, 275
reunion, of gods on *Oresteia*, 89
riddles, *Oedipus Tyrannos* and *Lot 49* compared, 283
ritual, Dionysian, 155

Rivier, A., 143
roads, 13, 35; in Pynchon, 307; as transgressions, 35, 233
Roberts, D. H., 78
Romilly, J. de, 173
Rorty, R., 28
Rousseau, J., 9

Said, E., 58
Said, S., 70
Salkever, S., 155
Sallis, J., 213
Saxonhouse, A., 78, 111, 213
Schein, S. I., 220
Schell, J., 11, 209
Schwartz, J., 105
Segal, C., 4, 35, 55
sexuality, and Pentheus, 144
sexual politics, in *Oresteia*, 91–93
sight, in *Oedipus Tyrannos*, 44, 101
Simmel, G., 6, 7, 8
skepticism, 54, 107
Snell, B., 101
Socrates, 203, 206, 212, 232; and criticism of tragedy, 127; and democracy, 207; and examination of collective life, 211; and Pericles, 205; as *physiologos*, 213; punishment of, 226; rationalism of, 234; as teacher, 218
Solidarity, 209. *See also* Polish Solidarity
sophia, 136
sophos, in the *Bacchae*, 54, 161
sparagmos, 132. *See also* dismemberment
speech, 87, 88, 183
Sphinx, and Oedipus, 113
Stahl, H. P., 194
stasis, 44, 184; in the *History*, 167ff
Strauss, L., 6, 213
suffering, 90, 159, 303
system, 29, 287, 290, 291

Taplin, O., 78
Taylor, C., 4
technai, 30
Teiresias, 108, 114, 115; as rationalist in the *Bacchae*, 142
television, and Greek tragedy compared, 288
theama, 109
theatai, 50
theatrōn, 50

Thebans, and historical revisionism, 183
Thebes, as "other" place, 99, 133. *See also* Zeitlin
theoretical moment, 225
theoretical power, 186, 268
theorizing, inherent dangers of, 225
theōros, etymology of, 232
theory: as critical activity, 233; dramatic and tragic nature, 58; paradox of, 268; as response to disorder, 38; in the *Republic*, 236
Thomson, G., 77
Thrasymachus, as tyrant, 246
Thucydides: as actor and analyst, 192; affinities with Euripides, 173; and dramatic aspects, 58; independence from party or faction, 198; and Themistocles, 191; and tragedy, 173
Thucydides' *History*, 46, 58, 62; and *Agamemnon*, 195; and the *Bacchae*, 171; and *Lot 49*, 62; and *Oedipus Tyrannos*, 167, 170, 171, 192
Tocqueville, A., 5, 9; and politics in America, 7
totalitarianism, in the *Republic*, 264
tragedian, 56, 259; Platonic critique of, 250ff; as teachers of justice, 251; and theory, 30
tragedy, 4, 49, 51, 56, 94, 162, 234; and collectivization of heroic ethic, 51; and Corcyran revolt, 190; and critique of reductionism, 37; and democracy, 46, 52, 55, 56; as genealogical, 30; and theory, 56, 57; and use of past, 53
Tussman, J., 127, 208
tyche, 121
tyranny, 36–38; of Athens, 179; attractions of, 247; in *Oedipus Tyrannos*, 118; of philosophy, 246–50; and political theory, 127; in the *Republic*, 225, 267

Vernant, J. P., 4, 35, 51
Vickers, B., 92
Vidal-Naquet, P., 4
Vlastos, G., 207

Walzer, M., 4, 47
Wasserman, F. M., 178
Weber, M., 6, 7, 8, 296
West, T., 215
White, J. B., 175, 185, 187, 197

Whitman, C., 25

Winkler, J. J., 51, 190

Winnington-Ingram, R. P., 70, 74, 143, 182

wisdom, 213, 214, 242

Wolin, 94, 296

xenos, 80

Young, J. D., 281

Zeitlin, F., 4, 35, 57, 67, 78, 135